Irish Government Today

2nd Edition

Sean Dooney

and

John O'Toole

GILL & MACMILLAN

Gill & Macmillan Ltd
Hume Avenue, Park West
Dublin 12
with associated companies throughout the world
www.gillmacmillan.ie

First edition of this book published in 1992
0 7171 2669 2
Index compiled by Helen Litton
Print origination by
Carrigboy Typesetting Services, County Cork
Printed by ColourBooks Ltd, Dublin

The paper used in this book is made from the wood pulp of managed forests. For every tree felled, at least one tree is planted, thereby renewing natural resources.

A catalogue record is available for this book from the British Library.

7 6

CONTENTS

PREFACE

To put it succinctly, the task of the government is to run the country. The public service plays a central role alongside ministers in that task. This book provides comprehensive information, prepared by writers who know the system intimately from within, on the institutions of government, the central departments, the local authorities, state-sponsored bodies and health boards.

It describes the operation of government in practice and includes a great deal of information not hitherto published about cabinet procedures, the appointment and responsibilities of ministers, private offices, political advisers, the election and work of TDs, the whips' offices, the work of the Dáil and the changes on the way, what civil servants do, and so on. It outlines the provisions of the Constitution and discusses the functions of the President.

There is a description of the informal and formal means by which people may seek, and get, redress from the actions of public bodies, which gives valuable insights into the 'representations' system and the use of parliamentary questions. The influence of EU membership on the work of government and the public service is examined, and the book concludes by exploring a number of current issues including management practices and techniques as well as public service reform.

This is a thoroughly revised and updated edition of the text which reflects the extensive changes in the Irish system of government, particularly in recent years, in areas such as:

- strategic management;
- parliamentary procedures;
- the management of EU business;
- freedom of information; and
- developments in information technology.

A new chapter on the legal officers of the state is also included.

The book is aimed primarily at first- and second-year students in a number of faculties, especially those studying politics, public administration and management, law, commerce, social science, journalism, marketing and business studies. It will, of course, be of interest and use to a wide variety of other readers, such as public servants and those considering a career in the public service; trade union officials, politicians, journalists and other commentators on public affairs; persons in agriculture, business and the professions who have dealings with the civil and public service; and those working in international organisations who want reliable and up-to-date information on government in Ireland.

Irish Government Today is written by two experienced practitioners who draw widely on their knowledge of how the system actually works and on their experience as part-time lecturers on the degree courses at the Institute of Public Administration. Arising from the conventions relating to civil servants writing about government, it is considered appropriate to indicate that Chapters 1, 2, 6, 7, 8, 9 and 11 were written by Sean Dooney and Chapters 4, 5, 10, 12 and 13 by John O'Toole. Chapter 3 was written jointly. Any views expressed by the authors are personal and do not reflect the views of any organisation.

Because of the constraints on size and price, the authors are aware that the book is not totally comprehensive and cannot provide all the answers to questions on the various subjects in the table of contents.

To avoid the continual use of awkward constructions such as 'his/her' or 'her/his', the words 'he', 'his' and 'him' are used throughout the book for both sexes whenever the sex of the person in question is of no consequence for the discussion.

ACKNOWLEDGMENTS

The authors gratefully acknowledge the immense amount of encouragement, advice and information they got from many of their friends and colleagues in the public service who, in accord with the best traditions of the service, wish to remain anonymous. Mary Prendergast, Librarian in the Institute of Public Administration, and her deputy, Renuka Page, were, as always, patient and pleasant in providing books, articles and references, often at short notice and at busy times. In particular, the authors want to express their thanks to the editor, Angela Rohan, but for whose skill the book could not have been published.

Above all, we appreciate the tolerance and support of Clodagh and Patricia, who so agreeably accorded 'the book' the priority which we thought it warranted.

SEAN DOONEY
JOHN O'TOOLE
January 1998

1

THE GOVERNMENT AND THE TAOISEACH

The Government: Structure and Scope

The Constitution acknowledges that all powers of government derive, under God, from the people, whose right it is to designate the rulers of the state; that the state is to be governed in accordance with the provisions of the Constitution; that the executive power of the state is exercised by or on the authority of the government; and that the government is responsible to the Dáil. The government consists of not less than seven and not more than fifteen members. It is frequently referred to as the cabinet, though this term does not appear in the Constitution. The members are selected by the Taoiseach (or, in the case of a coalition, by agreement between the leaders of the parties involved in government) and appointed by the President. No specific qualifications, beyond membership of the Oireachtas, are prescribed for membership of the government, but it is generally accepted that in the selection of ministers, considerations of general ability, suitability for particular portfolios, personal popularity, service to or standing in the party and geographical location are matters taken into account. The Taoiseach may request a minister to resign, and if he refuses to do so, the President, on the advice of the Taoiseach, must terminate his appointment.

The government meets and acts as a collective authority and is collectively responsible for the departments of state. The Constitution contains no specification regarding the number of departments (this depends largely on the preferences of individual Taoisigh), and if there are more than fifteen at any time, individual ministers are assigned responsibility for more than one department. The Taoiseach and the Tánaiste, as well as the Minister for Finance, must be members of the Dáil; the other members of the government must be members of the Dáil or the Seanad, but not more than two may be members of the latter body. (Since the foundation of the state there have, in fact, been only three appointments of senators; Joseph Connolly in 1928, Seán Moylan in 1957 and James Dooge in 1981.) Every member of the government has the right to attend and be heard in each House of the Oireachtas. On the dissolution of the Dáil, ministers continue to carry on their duties and hold office until their successors are appointed.

In addition to its general provision that the government is the chief executive organ of the state, the Constitution contains express provisions relating to the powers, duties and functions of the government in certain matters. For example, in relation to the public finances, presentation of the estimates to the Dáil by the Minister for Finance follows detailed consultation with his colleagues, and it is the government itself which has the final control over the form and amounts of the estimates, as well as the responsibility for them. The Dáil may not authorise the spending of money for any purpose unless such spending has first been authorised by the government and recommended to the Dáil by the Taoiseach.

The distribution of business between the government departments and the designation of members of the government to be the ministers in charge of particular departments are matters governed by law. The law is contained in the various Ministers and Secretaries Acts, the earliest of which was passed in 1924 and the most recent in 1995. The 1924 act designated the eleven departments then set up and indicated the work allocated to each. It provided that the minister in charge of each department would be a *corporation sole*, i.e. that he could sue and be sued as a corporate entity rather than as an individual. Subsequent acts provide for the setting up of new departments and for outlining their work. Under the Public Service Management Act 1997, managerial responsibility for the department is assigned to the secretary general (as secretaries were retitled in the act), while the minister remains responsible for the administration of the department.

The Work of the Government

In addition to the Ministers and Secretaries Acts, there are various acts which confer functions and powers on the government. For example, the government appoints the Civil Service and the Local Appointments Commissioners, the chairmen of some state-sponsored bodies, senior officers of the Garda Síochána and the Provost of Trinity College, Dublin; and it decides on applications by barristers to become members of the inner bar and to be designated senior counsel. As the chief executive organ of the state, the government also has a considerable amount of work to do besides that which is specifically conferred on it either by the Constitution or by statute. This work includes such diverse duties as considering applications for increases in air fares, allocating emergency aid to groups affected by natural disaster, appointing army officers, approving cultural agreements with countries abroad, refurbishing government buildings and considering visits to Ireland by foreign heads of state.

A major task, which impinges on every citizen, is the consideration of the advice and recommendations of the officials in the Department of Finance

Government Buildings

and the Office of the Revenue Commissioners relating to the total tax revenue for the year ahead. Within this total, the government decides on the changes to be made in the rates and scope of individual taxes and also on the introduction of new taxes or the abolition of existing ones.

Factors which the government takes into account include the estimated expenditure on what are called goods and services for the year ahead, the level of Exchequer borrowing and the desirability of reducing this, the estimates of tax revenue based on existing rates, the effects on the economy and the individual sectors thereof of increasing or decreasing individual rates, the need for equity between the various groups in the community, EU requirements in regard to reduction in rates of value added tax and of excise duties, and political commitments made by the parties in government before an election or as part of a post-election government programme in regard to taxation matters. Such matters are considered by the government over a number of meetings, and the final decisions are announced by the Minister for Finance in his budget speech.

The government is the centre of the administrative system in Ireland. In a sense it is the board of directors which formulates policies, promotes legislation and directs the operations of the various departments of state. Farrell (1988: 42) describes the cabinet as a 'closed group . . . bound together by shared experience . . . indisputably in charge of the executive organs of the state and usually able to push through its own legislative programme'.

The role of government was elaborated by the Public Services Organisation Review Group in its report published in 1969 (the Devlin Report):

> In addition to the basic functions of defence of the nation against outside aggression and maintenance of law and order, the role of government now embraces the provision of adequate health, education and welfare services. It also embraces the provision of environmental services and assistance of cultural activities. Government must exercise some regulatory function in regard to individual enterprise and ensure that the rights of the individual are exercised with due regard to the general good. It encourages economic activity in the private sector, and there are certain activities which it has undertaken itself.
>
> The government has two main tasks. First, it has to run the country, under the Constitution in accordance with the rules laid down by the Oireachtas and with the resources granted by, and accounted for to, the Oireachtas each year. Secondly, it deals in the Oireachtas with changes affecting the community . . . Through its legislative programme (including financial measures) the government exercises its main influence over the future development of the country; thereby it influences the economy and the structure of society. Acting collectively, the ministers decide what is needed and how it should be achieved; their decisions depend on the quality of the information available to them and on their assessment of the requirements. They will, of course, become aware of these requirements in several ways – through their political machine, through the press and through the representations of the interests concerned – but, primarily, they will need to know the emerging needs of the community through the public service which operates existing programmes.

Legislation

Proposals by ministers which call for new or amending legislation must always be submitted to the government. If approval is given, the papers are sent to the Attorney General's office, where a bill is drafted by the parliamentary draftsman. The bill (at this stage known as a 'white print') is submitted to the government to approve of the text and to authorise the minister concerned to present it to the Dáil (or Seanad) and have it circulated to members.

Before the government brings forward any legislation, it may publish a green paper (a document setting out its proposals and inviting suggestions thereon) or a white paper (a statement of decisions taken). Any such papers are prepared in the promoting department.

Bills (other than those dealing with budgetary matters or estimates) are usually, when published, accompanied by an explanatory statement outlining the existing law and how the new bill proposes to change it.

Other Business

The government agenda also includes matters which ministers consider it advisable to bring to their colleagues' notice. The Minister for Foreign Affairs, for example, will communicate information on political developments abroad and their consequences; or the Minister for Justice on criminal matters. Among the many items regularly laid before the government for scrutiny are the annual reports and accounts of state-sponsored bodies before their presentation to the Oireachtas.

Farrell (1988: 76) commented:

> The available evidence . . . suggests a considerable degree of overload in the Irish cabinet system. The complex, the controversial and the insoluble compete with the current, the commonplace and the critical for scarce time and attention on the government agenda. The internal problems of Northern Ireland, the latest transport strike, the painful disciplines of controlling public expenditure, the dismissal of a postman, the effects of technical developments in the EC policies, the appointment of a Supreme Court judge, the timing of a by-election, the detailed discussion of major legislation and a myriad of other things crowd out considerations of longer-term strategic planning.

There are also what are loosely termed 'twelve o'clock' or informal items. The phrase derives from an arrangement whereby the government sets aside time for consideration of matters not on the formal agenda which a minister wishes to raise informally and which may be dealt with quickly, for example any matters of current topical interest. Ministers also use this procedure to consult their colleagues informally as to the attitude they should take in relation to matters which come to them for decision on a day-to-day basis in the management of their departments but which might not be regarded as suitable for submission to government in the normal manner. Ministers may also wish to signal in advance problems which have arisen in their respective areas and in relation to which they may be submitting formal proposals at a later date. Matters thus mentioned might include strikes or pay disputes, petrol prices, proposals for visits abroad on St Patrick's Day, meetings with deputations or the attitude to be taken on a private member's bill. Business initiated in this way is rarely the subject of formal government decision, but any informal decisions are conveyed by the government secretariat to the relevant ministerial offices, usually by telephone.

Government Meetings

The government normally meets weekly, on Tuesday, for about two and a half hours in Government Buildings, Upper Merrion Street, Dublin. Attendance is confined to the members of the government, the Government Chief Whip (see below), the Attorney General and the Secretary to the Government. On occasion, however, other persons such as ministers of state or civil servants may be called in to assist in the discussion of specific matters. There is no quorum for meetings. The government secretariat co-ordinates all the proposed business and prepares the agenda for each meeting. While meetings are in progress ministers and officials can avail of a fully equipped communication room which provides facilities for obtaining any up-to-date or additional information which they may need.

Because of the volume of business with which the government has to deal, the agenda for its meetings is always heavy. Sometimes there may be up to thirty items for consideration. In the light of this and to enable the members of the government to assimilate material quickly and thoroughly, a detailed procedure is laid down for the submission by departments of issues for decision. This procedure is set out in a booklet entitled *Government Procedure Instructions*, prepared in the Department of the Taoiseach.

Every item of business must be the subject of a memorandum from the minister concerned. Its format is rigidly prescribed. The first paragraph should outline what is being requested of the government. This may be the authority to initiate legislation, or to establish, modify or abolish some programme, or perhaps to bring forward for consideration an entirely new policy option; it may be to note developments in some areas of national importance, or to make a statutory instrument. Then comes the background information, and, in cases requiring substantive action, an account of the problem, the solution being put forward and the arguments for and against. The costs and staffing implications are then indicated, as well as the views of other ministers concerned, together with any counterviews of the promoting minister. The rule is that memoranda should be as brief as possible and not discursive, and that detailed material be supplied in appendices. The aim is that, ordinarily, memoranda should not exceed ten pages, and, where they do, they should be accompanied by a brief self-contained summary of the proposals, with the arguments for and against.

Thirty copies of each memorandum are sent by the private secretary of the promoting minister to the Secretary to the Government. These must reach the latter not less than three days before the meetings at which they are to be considered. At the same time, a copy is sent to the offices of the ministers consulted during the drafting.

On occasion, a minister may wish to have a matter considered at a particular government meeting but it may not be possible to have the memorandum finalised in time to meet the specified deadline. In such circumstances a certificate of urgency is signed by a senior official stating why the matter is urgent and why the memorandum could not be ready by the prescribed time. The reasons must be good if they are to result in such an item being accepted, ultimately by the Taoiseach, as urgent. If a minister is unable to attend a government meeting, his private secretary is obliged to inform the government secretariat as soon as possible and to state whether any other minister is to be briefed to deal with any item on the agenda which is of relevance to the absent minister's department.

Where there is disagreement on the merits of a proposal, the minister concerned is asked to consider its modification. Where ministers disagree, the matter may be referred to a subcommittee of the government to resolve. If disagreement persists, it may be necessary to have a decision reached by vote. No record of any such vote is kept other than its outcome. Cabinet proceedings are strictly confidential, and the principle of collective responsibility applies to decisions taken. The issue of cabinet confidentiality has been under debate in recent years, i.e. whether it is necessary or desirable in the public interest that ministers should continue to be free to air their views at cabinet without the risk of these being made public on some subsequent occasion. In this connection, an amendment to the Constitution was enacted in 1997 providing that the confidentiality of discussions at government should be preserved except where the High Court rules that disclosure should be made either (a) in the administration of justice or (b) on foot of an application by a tribunal of inquiry.

Immediately after meetings, the Secretary to the Government transmits the decisions relating to particular departments to the private secretaries of the ministers concerned so that they may be acted on departmentally. It is the responsibility of individual ministers to ensure that such decisions are implemented at the earliest practicable date. In this connection, the government secretariat prepares at regular intervals a schedule of outstanding decisions, indicating the current position in each case. This schedule enables the Taoiseach to monitor progress and to raise with his colleagues any major deviations from targets.

As explained above, cabinet minutes record only the decisions taken. In 1976 the then Taoiseach, Liam Cosgrave, instituted a policy of releasing, for inspection by the public, cabinet minutes and supporting records which were more than thirty years old. With the passing of the Archives Act 1985, there is now a statutory obligation to make such minutes available for public inspection in the National Archives, the new body which has replaced the State Paper Office and Public Record Office. (A copy of the minutes of the meeting held on 13 December 1966 is reproduced in Appendix 1.)

Incorporeal Meetings

Apart from the formal meetings, there are, on occasion, what are termed incorporeal meetings. These meetings relate to the conduct of unforeseen business which is so urgent as to require a decision before the next ordinary government meeting. It is business of a type that does not require substantive discussion and is extremely unlikely to provoke disagreement. An incorporeal meeting could be held, for example, if it were necessary to clear some routine report with a publication deadline, or if it were necessary to approve the urgent departure from the country of the President to attend, say, a funeral abroad, or to finalise a decision on a matter discussed earlier.

The procedure in such cases is that the minister concerned prepares a brief note on the matter at issue which is circulated by the government secretariat to all ministers available, together with a notification that an incorporeal meeting will be held to discuss the matter at a specified time. In practice, what then happens is that the Secretary to the Government telephones all the ministers available at that time to get their agreement to what is proposed. The meeting is formally recorded as having taken place under the chairmanship of the Taoiseach, Tánaiste or most senior government member available.

Collective Responsibility

Collective cabinet responsibility is a fundamental principle underlying the operation of Irish government. It results in all ministers being obliged to support government actions and policies regardless of their personal opinion or private feelings. Thus the cabinet is collectively responsible for public policy, and the policy programmes of individual ministers must complement it. Once a cabinet decision is taken, it reflects the decision of all the ministers, and a minister who is fundamentally opposed to the decision should, in theory, resign.

In practice, a minister will, on occasion, be fundamentally opposed but may not wish to make his opposition public. Nevertheless, if he is unable to accept a decision, wishes to distance himself in public from a decision or feels he must explain his point of view in public, then the question of resignation must be seriously considered. Occasions have arisen when ministers have expressed fundamental opposition in public and have not resigned. James Gibbons, Minister for Agriculture, made public his opposition to the Family Planning Bill 1979, but did not resign. Nor did the then Taoiseach, Liam Cosgrave, or his Minister for Education, Richard Burke, resign after voting against the Control of Importation, Sale and Manufacture of Contraceptives Bill 1974, introduced in the Dáil by the Minister for Justice in the cabinet of which they were all members. On the other hand, Frank Cluskey, Minister for Trade, Commerce and Tourism, did resign in December 1983 when he found himself opposed to government proposals in regard to the Dublin Gas Company. Considerable efforts are made to achieve consensus. Seán Lemass, a former Taoiseach, said it is ‘the job of the Taoiseach to keep a team of ministers who are all individuals with their own personal characteristics working in harmony and ultimately emerging with agreement upon every matter put before them' (interview in the *Irish Press*, 3–4 February 1960).

In 1972 the Review Body on Higher Remuneration in the Public Sector, in its consideration of the role and functions of various office holders, including the Taoiseach and other members of the government, commented:

> We regard as of paramount importance the collective responsibility of ministers, as members of the government, for the business of the government, i.e. the formulation of national policy and its execution subject to the approval of the Oireachtas. No greater or more complex task and no more important task for the well-being of the people faces any other body or group in the country.

Ministers' Obligations

Should an occasion arise where a minister or his family has an interest in a matter before the government for decision, there is an obligation on him to bring this to notice before the matter comes up for discussion. Unless the government decides otherwise, the minister concerned may not take part in the discussion or vote on the issue, or seek to influence the attitude of his colleagues.

In so far as business interests or membership of other organisations is concerned, the basic rule is that a minister should not engage in any activity that could reasonably be regarded as interfering or being incompatible with the proper discharge of the duties of his office.

Ministers may not hold company directorships carrying remuneration. Even if remuneration is not paid, it is regarded as undesirable that a minister should hold a directorship. A resigning director may, however, enter an agreement with a company under which the company would agree his reappointment as director on the termination of public office. Similarly, ministers are not permitted to carry on a professional practice while holding office, but there is no objection to making arrangements for the maintenance of a practice during the period of tenure of office.

It was long regarded as undesirable that ministers should retain membership of subordinate public bodies, such as county councils or health boards, while in government. Nevertheless, this was a practice tolerated by successive governments. The Local Government Act 1991 now provides that ministers and ministers of state are excluded from election to or membership of local authorities.

Members of the government proposing visits or receiving invitations to travel which involve government-to-government contacts or public attendance abroad, as distinct from attendance at meetings of bodies such as the EU or the OECD, are obliged to consult the Minister for Foreign Affairs and the Taoiseach. They must have the approval of the latter before entering into commitments. Ministers who intend to visit Northern Ireland must advise the Minister for Foreign Affairs. In the case of private travel abroad by ministers, it is normal practice that Irish diplomatic missions and the authorities of the countries concerned are advised of the minister's travel plans.

The Ethics in Public Office Act 1995 provides for the disclosure of interests by holders of certain public offices, including ministers and members of the Houses of the Oireachtas. It also deals with gifts to holders of public office and it established a Public Offices Commission and a Select Committee on Members' Interests in each House of the Oireachtas. The fundamental principle is that an office holder should not accept an offer of gifts, hospitality or services where this would, or might appear to, place him under an obligation. The Commission has issued guidelines to office holders. Broadly, these require that office holders should disclose certain gifts and that they should surrender valuable gifts to the state where these are given by virtue of office. There are guidelines also for gifts which can not readily be surrendered to the state, such as property, below-cost loans, free services and so on. In sum, the guidelines provide information on the steps office holders need to take in order to comply with the requirements of the act.

The Taoiseach: Office, Duties and Powers

The Taoiseach is appointed head of the government, or prime minister, by the President on the nomination of the Dáil. He may resign at any time by tendering his resignation to the President. If the Taoiseach resigns, the other ministers are deemed to have resigned also.

In addition to being head of the government, and apart from the responsibilities which that role entails, the Taoiseach has, in himself, certain constitutional and statutory powers and duties. He may, in effect, compel any minister to resign for any reason which to him seems sufficient. He nominates the Attorney General for appointment by the President, and the ministers of state for appointment by the government. He appoints eleven members of the Seanad. He also appoints the Clerks (chief officers) and Clerks Assistant of the Dáil and Seanad, as well as the Superintendent and Captain of the Guard in the Houses of the Oireachtas, after consultation with the chairmen of the Houses and the Minister for Finance. The Taoiseach initiates the process for the selection by interview board of candidates for the office of Director of Public Prosecutions and proposes the candidate selected to the government for appointment. He is required to keep the President informed on matters of domestic and international policy and he is, besides, an ex officio member of the Council of State. He presents the bills passed by the Dáil and Seanad to the President for his signature into law. In the event of both Houses passing resolutions for the removal of the Comptroller and Auditor General, or of a judge, it would be the duty of the Taoiseach to notify the President.

On the advice of the Taoiseach, Dáil Éireann is summoned and dissolved by the President, but the President may, at his absolute discretion, refuse a dissolution to a Taoiseach who has ceased to retain the support of a majority in the Dáil. In fact no President has yet refused a dissolution. Thus in Ireland the practice differs from that in several European countries where the head of state frequently calls upon another member of the parliament to form a government in such a situation.

The Taoiseach must resign upon ceasing to retain the support of a majority in the Dáil, unless the President dissolves the Dáil on his advice and he secures the support of a majority in the new Dáil. A unique situation arising from these provisions occurred in 1989. The twenty-sixth Dáil, on convening after the general election in June, failed to elect the (outgoing) Taoiseach, Charles Haughey. Relying on the constitutional provision just cited, the opposition parties pressed the view that the Taoiseach should resign. The Taoiseach did not accept the opposition view, on the basis of advice received by him from the Attorney General, and proposed instead that the Dáil adjourn to enable consultations between the parties with a view to forming a government. He acceded, however, to the political pressure and resigned, with his ministers. They remained in office, in an acting capacity, pending the outcome of the inter-party negotiations, which eventually led to Mr Haughey becoming Taoiseach of a coalition government. These events evoked considerable discussion on the interpretation of the provision in the Constitution.

Leadership: Style and Influence

In relation to the Taoiseach's position as head of the government, he has been described by a former Secretary to the Government as 'captain of the team'.

> In this capacity, he is the central co-ordinating figure, who takes an interest in the work of all departments, the figure to whom ministers naturally turn for advice and guidance when faced with problems involving large questions of policy or otherwise of special difficulty, whose leadership is essential to the successful working of the government as a collective authority, collectively responsible to Dáil Éireann, but acting through members each of whom is charged with specific departmental tasks. He may often have to inform himself in considerable detail of particular matters with which other members of the government are primarily concerned. He may have to make public statements on such matters, as well as on general matters of broad policy, internal and external (Ó Muimhneacháin 1969).

The Taoiseach presides over all government meetings and has considerable influence in relation to the business transacted. In the first place, the agenda is prepared under his direction. If there are items of business which he wants taken at a particular meeting, this can usually be arranged. Secondly, in his capacity as chairman he can structure the discussion and so determine the manner in which the various items on the agenda, as well as other matters which ministers may wish to raise, are dealt with. Thirdly, and perhaps most importantly, the Taoiseach may put forward a proposal to government himself by way of memorandum or otherwise on any item of major policy. The length of meetings is influenced by the personal style of the Taoiseach.

Ultimately, the Taoiseach carries the responsibility for the achievement or lack of achievement of the government. It is sometimes said that the office of Taoiseach is what the holder wishes to make of it. His authority has been described as 'a function not merely of the office but of the multiplicity of roles thrust upon him – simultaneously chief executive, government chairman, party leader, national spokesman, principal legislator, electoral champion and media focus' (Farrell 1988: 44). In formulating public policy on all major issues, the Taoiseach plays a leading part in bringing together various strands of opinion around the cabinet table and in achieving consensus on the lines of major policy to be adopted. The Review Body on Higher Remuneration in the Public Sector has commented on the implications of the Taoiseach's overall authority:

> He has a special responsibility and a particularly onerous one. Apart from his constitutional position and responsibilities . . . he is in growing degree personally identified with – and regarded by the public as answerable for – the totality of government policy. He must concern himself with all departments of state, in particular on all major matters. He must co-ordinate the efforts of his colleagues in the development and implementation of national policy. The achievement or lack of achievement of the government is laid primarily at his door.

Chubb (1982: 201) sees the pre-eminence of the Taoiseach among his colleagues as stemming from four facts. First, he is usually the party leader. Second, elections often take the form of gladiatorial contests between two designated party leaders, thus emphasising the personal leadership of the victor, and television and modern campaign practices have increased the propensity to focus on the leader. Third, except in the case of coalition governments, he chooses his colleagues. Fourth, by the nature of his position, he has a special responsibility to take the lead or speak when an authoritative intervention is needed.

The role of the Taoiseach has altered from being first among equals under the 1922 Constitution to one of effective authority under the 1937 Constitution. W.T. Cosgrave, President of the Executive Council from 1922 to 1932, reflecting the older approach, said that it was not open to the head of the government to ask for and to compel the resignation of a minister (*Dáil Debates*, 14 June 1937, cols. 347–8). Under the 1937 Constitution successive Taoisigh have moved ministers from department to department or dismissed them. The power of the Taoiseach to rid himself of members of his government by requiring their resignation enables him to hold considerable dominance over his ministerial colleagues. Many commentators today speculate on a transition from cabinet to prime ministerial government.

Jack Lynch dismissed Charles Haughey and Neil Blaney in 1970 on the occasion of what was known as the 'arms crisis'. In 1986 the government, on the recommendation of Garret FitzGerald, dismissed four ministers of state, Joseph Bermingham, Donal Creed, Michael Darcy and Edward Collins, the last for alleged conflict of interest and the others for differences over government policy. In 1990 Mr Haughey dismissed his Tánaiste and Minister for Defence, Brian Lenihan, because of conflicting statements made by Mr Lenihan about the making of telephone calls to the office of the President on the occasion of the defeat of the government in a Dáil vote in 1982. In November 1991 Mr Haughey dismissed the Ministers for Finance and for the Environment, Albert Reynolds and Pádraig Flynn, for publicly expressing lack of confidence in him as leader of the Fianna Fáil party. In 1995 John Bruton effectively dismissed Hugh Coveney, Minister for Defence, for a breach of the ethical standards appropriate to members of the government. In fact Mr Coveney tendered his resignation. He was subsequently appointed a minister of state. In 1996 Mr Bruton effectively dismissed Michael Lowry, Minister for Transport, Energy and Communications, for conduct unbecoming to a minister. Again, in fact, Mr Lowry resigned.

In sum, it is difficult to define the office of the Taoiseach. It can only be described in terms of the use to which it is put by different individuals of varying personalities who face different problems and deal with different colleagues. A Taoiseach may, to quote Farrell again, see himself as either a chairman or a chief, encouraging, co-ordinating and monitoring the work of other ministers, or exercising a very positive leadership role and virtually dictating policy for the cabinet as a whole.

Department of the Taoiseach: Functions

The Department of the Taoiseach provides the assistance which the Taoiseach as head of the government and as a minister needs. It also provides the services which the government, acting as a collective authority, needs. It has a total staff of about 180 and is headed by a secretary general, as is every other department. The government has a separate secretary. These officials are on the same level. The responsibilities of the department include:

(1) the organisation, co-ordination, preparation and processing of government business in the Dáil and Seanad;
(2) the formulation of policy and overseeing of the implementation of settled policy in respect of matters of major national import in which the Taoiseach needs to involve himself from time to time, for example international and Northern Ireland affairs;
(3) the preparation of replies to parliamentary questions addressed to the Taoiseach;
(4) the maintenance of liaison with the office of the President;
(5) major state protocol;
(6) the processing of correspondence addressed to the Taoiseach;
(7) government press relations and the government information services;
(8) the provision of the secretariat to the government and to government committees;
(9) the administration of specific functions of government discharged from time to time under the aegis of the Taoiseach, for example the work of the Central Statistics Office and that of the Local Appointments Commission.

In recent years the Taoiseach has been increasingly active in the foreign relations of the state, mainly as a result of Ireland's membership of the EU. The focal point in the European context is the European Council, which normally meets twice a year. Many of the major issues in the EU now come to the Council for discussion, for guidance and for decisions. While the Department of Foreign Affairs has overall responsibility for the co-ordination of European Community affairs, and while the Department of the Taoiseach relies heavily on the departments primarily concerned to keep it informed about important and sensitive issues in this and other international areas, each Taoiseach since Ireland's accession has found it desirable to maintain within his own department an advisory unit sensitive to his personal approach and preoccupations.

Department of the Taoiseach and Dáil Business

Government Chief Whip

Every Taoiseach assigns a minister of state to his department to act as Chief Whip of the government party. His task relates essentially to (1) the progression of government business which is placed before the Dáil for discussion and determination, and (2) the attendance of deputies from the government side. The Chief Whip maintains close liaison with the whip of any other party in government and also with the whips of the opposition parties.

Before each Dáil session, through circulars addressed to all ministers, the Government Chief Whip finds out what legislation (or other business) their departments expect to place before the Dáil in the coming session and its state of preparation. During Dáil sessions he prepares weekly reports for the Taoiseach on the progress of legislation in the pipeline.

The officials in the Chief Whip's office keep in touch with ministers' private secretaries about business which ministers might wish to have dealt with in the week ahead, for example approval of a supplementary estimate or the introduction of a bill which has become urgent. Arising from these contacts, and having regard to the items which may be already on the order paper (agenda) of the Dáil – there being nearly always a backlog of items awaiting discussion – the Chief Whip prepares an agenda and a timetable for each sitting day of the following week. By convention, this is discussed with the opposition whips each Wednesday. While the business to be dealt with is primarily a matter for the government, the opposition may on occasion seek to have time allocated by the government to discuss a matter which they consider to be of particular current importance. In such an event the Government Chief Whip will consult the minister responsible; sometimes it may be necessary to consult the Taoiseach or even the government. On these occasions the length of the debate as well as the length of the contributions to be made by the minister responsible, the opposition spokesman and other deputies are normally determined by precedent. The relationship between the whips of all parties is one of friendly trust. No minutes of whips' meetings are kept; a whip's word is his bond.

When agreement has been reached on the business for the week ahead, the Government Chief Whip sends to each deputy on the government side a notice which informs him of the times during which the Dáil will meet in that week, of the business to be transacted, of the times at which the various items will be taken and when voting is most likely to take place. The notice indicates the varying degrees of importance attached to the business and to deputies' attendance. Deputies are advised to be in the House at all times. This weekly notice is commonly called the whip. If a deputy cannot be present, there is an obligation on him to notify his whip and explain his absence.

On each day when the Dáil is in session the Taoiseach announces the business for the day. Each item on the order paper (already circulated) is numbered, and the Taoiseach's announcement indicates the order of their discussion. Sometimes the order of business is disputed by the opposition parties, for example when it does not provide for discussion of some business considered urgent by them, when it provides for the taking of all stages of a bill on that day, or when no explanation is given as to why items are to be discussed in a particular order.

Deputies wishing to contribute to a debate normally notify their party whip. In general, they determine the nature and length of their contributions themselves, that is to say no effort is made to prevent overlapping. This, of course, leads to considerable repetition.

The rule under which government deputies may not be absent save with the permission of the whip is necessary to ensure the carrying of any measure put forward by the government in the event of its being challenged to a vote by the opposition. If a member is unavoidably absent or (in the case of a minister) because of government business elsewhere, the government whip approaches the whip of the main opposition party for a pairing; he requests that in the event of a vote one opposition deputy abstains from voting for each government deputy absent. The practices in this regard are largely governed by convention. Informal arrangements between deputies of opposing parties are frowned upon by the whips on both sides; all pairing arrangements are expected to be made through the whips' offices.

Parliamentary Questions to the Taoiseach

A period of three-quarters of an hour is set aside every Tuesday and Wednesday for Dáil questions to the Taoiseach. In practice, the Taoiseach answers questions most weeks.

In general, the issues on which the Taoiseach answers questions are those relating directly to government policy and to the activities of his department, such as:

- Northern Ireland;
- the Strategic Management Initiative;
- Partnership 2000;
- the President;
- the European Council;
- the Government Information Services;
- the National Economic and Social Council.

He also answers questions about statements made by him in the course of speeches outside the Dáil. Questions relating to the other matters for which he has responsibility, such as the Central Statistics Office, are generally answered by the Minister of State at his department.

Parliamentary questions are not allowable about the discussions which take place at meetings of the government; nor are questions about government subcommittees, on the grounds that the work of such committees is a direct extension of the work of the government itself. In addition, questions may not be asked about matters for which the Taoiseach is not responsible to the Dáil, such as:

- legal advice given to him by the Attorney General;
- bodies which are independent of the government; or
- meetings with private individuals.

Some deputies prefer to address their questions to the Taoiseach if the subject is even remotely relevant to his department; some do so because of a misunderstanding on their part. In the vast majority of such cases the question is transferred to the appropriate minister. This is a practice which frequently arouses the ire of the opposition, who accuse the Taoiseach of seeking to avoid responsibilities which they regard as proper to him. Examples of questions transferred are those asked about Sellafield (transferred to the Minister for Transport, Energy and Communications), EMU (Finance) and the Local Employment Service (Enterprise and Employment).

Department of the Taoiseach: Other Areas of Responsibility

Northern Ireland

The Taoiseach may assign another department to himself in addition to his own (for example, the Department of the Gaeltacht in 1987 and 1989). In addition, successive Taoisigh have reserved to themselves responsibility for Northern Ireland affairs. It is the Taoiseach who makes significant policy statements in this area and who answers parliamentary questions. It is the practice for the Taoiseach and the British Prime Minister to avail themselves of meetings of the European Council to discuss in the margins thereof matters of common concern.

However, in so far as Northern Ireland policy affects relations with the British government, such policy is also the concern of the Minister for Foreign Affairs. That minister is the permanent Irish ministerial representative to the Anglo-Irish Conference. The Department of Foreign Affairs has primary responsibility for the day-to-day operation of the Agreement and of Anglo-Irish relations generally.

Liaison with the President

The constitutional requirement that the Taoiseach keep the President informed on domestic and international policy is fulfilled by visits by the Taoiseach to Áras an Uachtaráin, or otherwise as suits both parties. There is regular contact between both offices at senior official level.

Apart from the constitutional requirement, there are a number of matters on which consultation between the Department of the Taoiseach and the office of the President is necessary. These include the arrangements to be made for visits abroad by the President, including the drawing up of programmes and the preparation of speeches; the provision of advice on invitations received by the President to extend his patronage to events or to attend functions; messages to and from other heads of state; and matters relating directly to the work of other departments, including the presentation of credentials by incoming ambassadors, the signing of commissions for officers of the defence forces and the appointment of judges.

Protocol

On the occasion of visits to Ireland by heads of state, prime ministers or other persons in high office (such as the President of the European Commission), the protocol arrangements are made in consultation with the Department of Foreign Affairs. Major state protocol is the responsibility of the Department of the Taoiseach, for example the ceremonial surrounding the inauguration of the President, the national day of commemoration and state funerals.

Correspondence

As might be expected, a large volume of representations, correspondence and requests for meetings is received by the Taoiseach. Almost all of the correspondence is about issues for which the Taoiseach has no direct responsibility. The procedure generally adopted in dealing with such correspondence is that material for reply thereto is sought from the department concerned, if not already available in the Department of the Taoiseach. The reply itself is signed by the Taoiseach, by his private secretary or by one of his departmental officials. Alternatively, the correspondence is merely acknowledged and referred to the department responsible for direct reply. Replies to constituents are always signed by the Taoiseach himself.

Requests by individuals or groups for meetings are normally directed to the appropriate minister. In general, the Taoiseach personally meets only those groups which are representative of what are loosely termed the social partners (representatives of employers, unions, churches, etc.) in connection with issues of major national policy.

Government Press and Information Services

The Government Information Services (GIS) are headed by the Government Press Secretary, who advises the Taoiseach and ministers on their dealings with the media and briefs political and specialist correspondents on the background to current political issues and government decisions. He does not attend government meetings, but is briefed after each meeting by a minister designated to do so. He normally accompanies the Taoiseach on official visits abroad and, in collaboration with the Irish ambassadorial staff in the country concerned, briefs the media from the Irish point of view.

The GIS supply news and official documents to press, radio and television and provide them with information and facilities, arrange press conferences for ministers, brief correspondents on the background to official statements and interpret public feeling to departments. They advise on the co-ordination of departmental publicity and information and collaborate with the Department of Foreign Affairs in relation to the dissemination of information about Ireland abroad. Government Press Secretaries in recent years remain in office only for the duration of a government's term of office. The GIS include a number of press officers, permanent civil servants, who deal with general media queries.

REFERENCES

Chubb, Basil, *The Government and Politics of Ireland*, 2nd ed. (London: Longman, 1982)

Department of the Taoiseach, Statement of Strategy, 1997

Farrell, Brian, *Chairman or Chief?: The Role of the Taoiseach in Irish Government* (Dublin: Gill & Macmillan, 1971)

Farrell, Brian, 'The Irish Cabinet System' in Jean Blondel and Ferdinand Müller Rommel (eds.), *Cabinets in Western Europe* (London: Macmillan, 1988)

Government of Ireland, *Report of the Public Services Organisation Review Group, 1966–69* [Devlin Report] (Dublin: Stationery Office, 1969)

Government of Ireland, *Report of the Review Body on Higher Remuneration in the Public Sector* (Dublin: Stationery Office, 1972)

Ó Muimhneacháin, Muiris, *The Functions of the Department of the Taoiseach*, 2nd ed. (Dublin: Institute of Public Administration, 1969)

APPENDIX 1

G.C. 12/4
13 Dec. 1966

MEETING OF THE CABINET
HELD IN THE COUNCIL CHAMBER
TUESDAY, 13 DECEMBER 1966 – 11 a.m. to 1 p.m.

MINISTERS PRESENT:

1. Taoiseach	Mr Lynch
2. Minister for Transport and Power and Minister for Posts and Telegraphs	Mr Childers
3. Minister for Agriculture and Fisheries	Mr Blaney
4. Minister for Local Government	Mr Boland
5. Minister for Lands and Minister for the Gaeltacht	Mr Moran
6. Minister for Defence	Mr Hilliard
7. Minister for Labour	Dr Hillery
8. Minister for Finance	Mr Haughey
9. Minister for Justice	Mr Lenihan
10. Minister for Social Welfare	Mr Brennan
11. Minister for Education	Mr O'Malley
12. Minister for Industry and Commerce	Mr Colley
13. Minister for Health	Mr Flanagan

MINISTERS ABSENT:

Tánaiste and Minister for External Affairs	Mr Aiken

ALSO IN ATTENDANCE:

Parliamentary Secretary to the Taoiseach	Mr Carty
Secretary to the Government	Dr Nolan

S.2330 F 1. MARITIME JURISDICTION (AMENDMENT) ACT, 1964 (SPECIFIED STATES) ORDER, 1965: Amendment

Following consideration of a memorandum dated 8 December, 1966, submitted by the Minister for External Affairs relative to the amendment of the Maritime Jurisdiction (Amendment) Act, 1964 (Specified States) Order, 1965, the Minister was authorised to arrange for the preparation of an Order, for execution by the Government, on the basis of the heads thereof accompanying the memorandum.

S.13593 2. MINISTER FOR AGRICULTURE: Report, 1964–65

On the submission of the Minister for Agriculture and Fisheries, a document entitled

An Roinn Talmhaíochta: Annual Report of the
Minister for Agriculture, 1964–65,

was presented prior to its being presented to each House of the Oireachtas.

S.17530E 3. NATIONAL INDUSTRIAL ECONOMIC COUNCIL: Report on Distribution, October, 1966

On the submission of the Taoiseach, a document entitled

National Industrial Economic Council: Report on Distribution,

dated 21 October, 1966, was presented with a view to having it laid before each House of the Oireachtas with a statement in the terms of the enclosure to the memorandum dated 9 December, 1966, submitted by the Taoiseach on the matter.

S.17768 4. CIVIL SERVICE: Special leave

Following consideration of a memorandum dated 8 December, 1966, submitted by the Minister for Finance,

(1) it was agreed that, subject to the application to her case of the conditions normally governing such special leave,

Catherine Carmel Colclough,

an Engineering Draughtsman in the Office of Public Works, should be granted special leave, without pay, from the Civil Service for a period not exceeding two years, to enable her to engage in social work in Venezuela for Viatores Christi; and

(2) the Minister for Finance was authorised to grant special leave, in future, in appropriate cases,

(a) with pay, subject to the recoupment of salary plus the usual contribution for pension liability, or
(b) without pay,

for services overseas under the auspices of missionary or charitable organisations, subject to the following conditions:–

(i) that the Minister in charge of the Department in which the officer is serving recommends the grant of the special leave and is prepared to release the officer,
(ii) that the total period of special leave granted to the officer will not exceed five years, including extensions and regardless of the number of organisations served, except in cases where special circumstances obtain, when the Minister for Finance will have discretion to sanction a longer period, and
(iii) that the grant of special leave will be subject to the conditions normally governing the grant of special leave.

S.16230 G 5. CYPRUS: Irish contingent with United Nations' Peace-keeping Force

Following consideration of a memorandum dated 9 December, 1966, submitted by the Minister for External Affairs relative to the Irish contingent serving with the United Nations' Peace-keeping Force in Cyprus,

(1) it was agreed to maintain the contingent at its present strength for a further period of six months beyond 26 December, 1966, on the same terms and conditions as at present, on receipt of a formal request from the Secretary-General and an assurance from him of full recoupment of the extra and extraordinary expenditure on the contingent in respect of that period;

(2) it was agreed that, if the Secretary-General does not furnish the assurance referred to at (1), the members of the contingent at present serving in Cyprus should be authorised to remain with the Force beyond 26 December until they can be repatriated in an orderly manner and, in any event, not later than 18 January, 1967, and that, if necessary, a small rear party should remain in Cyprus to handle the repatriation of equipment and stores; and

(3) if the Secretary-General furnishes the assurance referred to at (1), the Minister for Defence was authorised to make preparations for the selection, training and equipping of a unit of the Permanent Defence Force of approximately 500 all ranks, provided that sufficient volunteers are forthcoming, to replace the 7th Infantry Group, on the same terms and conditions as at present, when its tour of duty expires on 27 March, 1967.

S.17252 6. POSTAGE-STAMPS: Special issues in 1967

Following consideration of a memorandum dated 29 November, 1966, submitted by the Minister for Posts and Telegraphs, it was decided that special postage-stamps should be issued in 1967 in connection with

(a) the Conference of European Postal and Telecommunications Administrations,
(b) the centenary of the Fenian Rising,
(c) the tercentenary of the birth of Dean Swift,
(d) the centenary of the Canadian Confederation and
(e) International Tourist Year.

The meeting adjourned at 1 p.m.

SEÁN Ó LOINSIGH
16/xii/66

2

MINISTERS AND THEIR DEPARTMENTS

Selection and Appointment

Ministers do not attain their positions by accident. A mixture of personal ambition and public service reinforce each other in a TD's desire to be a minister. As membership of the Dáil is increasingly becoming a full-time career, more and more TDs are likely to aspire to ministerial status. To this end a TD must make considerable efforts to be well thought of in his party, in the Dáil, by the media and, above all, by his party leader. As already mentioned, it is the Taoiseach who at his absolute discretion, subject to the provisions of the Constitution, nominates ministers for appointment by the President (except in the circumstances where an inter-party arrangement to form a government has had to be worked out).

No formal selection criteria are prescribed, and Taoisigh do not indicate why they appoint a particular person to be a minister. At the same time, various 'qualifications' may be identified. These include such considerations as seniority, loyalty, popularity and length of service within the party. Ability to perform properly all of the tasks expected of a member of the government is not always seen as an overriding consideration, though occasionally a newly elected deputy has been appointed a minister on first election to the Dáil (for example, Niamh Bhreathnach in 1992 and previously Noel Browne, Kevin Boland, Martin O'Donoghue and Alan Dukes).

Whether or not it is desirable that a minister should have detailed expert knowledge of his portfolio is a widely debated question, i.e. whether it is desirable that the Minister for Health should himself be a medical doctor, or the Minister for Education a teacher. On the one hand, there are those who argue that it is entirely logical that this should be the case. On the other hand, many say that the minister has sufficient advisers both within and without his department to provide him with all the expert information he needs. They say that what is required in a minister is that he be reasonably objective and be able to make decisions based on an intelligent appraisal of the advice proffered to him, in the light of his government's policy and of any other relevant political considerations.

On a more personal level, the Taoiseach is likely to take into account a prospective choice's compatibility both with himself as leader and with the rest of his ministerial team. On the other hand, he may possibly consider the inclusion in his cabinet of someone who might provide a focus for party disaffection if left on the backbenches. This was said to be the case when Liam Cosgrave appointed Garret FitzGerald to Foreign Affairs in 1973, and when Jack Lynch appointed Charles Haughey to Health in 1977; also when Mr Haughey appointed Desmond O'Malley to Trade, Commerce and Tourism in March 1982, and when Dr FitzGerald appointed Austin Deasy to Agriculture in December 1982.

Although constitutionally the selection of his ministers is a matter for the Taoiseach himself, there can be little doubt that he discusses the subject with his closest advisers in the party. Not in doubt either is that he informs those selected before he makes his formal announcement in the Dáil on his return from Áras an Uachtaráin following his own appointment by the President. At that stage he also announces the assignment of departments. A debate on the nominations for membership of the government follows, to which only the main spokespersons of the political parties contribute. When the Dáil approves of the names, it adjourns for a few hours to enable the new ministers also to go to Áras an Uachtaráin and receive their seals of office from the President. The first meeting of the new government, lasting for fifteen or twenty minutes, takes place in the Áras and then there are photographs and a drink with the President.

Disposition of Portfolios; Interdepartmental Relations

The Taoiseach decides what the departmental structure of the government is going to be and assigns ministers to particular departments. The order in which ministers' names are presented to the Dáil for its approval is determined by the Taoiseach and becomes the order of precedence. Although the hierarchical principle has no basis in the Constitution, it is generally perceived by the electorate that some departments are of more importance than others. Some reasons for the perception would be the size of the department and its budget, its accepted importance in the life of the nation, its day-to-day impact on the ordinary citizen. It is obvious that the ministers in charge of the Departments of Finance and Foreign Affairs have a higher political profile than, say, the Ministers for Defence or the Marine.

If a minister is absent for a period of time, or is ill, his ministerial responsibilities are usually assigned to another minister, or indeed to the Taoiseach, during his absence. (The Finance and Justice portfolios are those generally assigned to the Taoiseach.)

In recent years there have been several changes in the titles and in the functions assigned to the various departments. Changes of personnel, i.e. cabinet reshuffles, are rare, but do occasionally occur. Such changes may be made in order to improve the technical or administrative efficiency of a government, to signal a new priority or to change an existing priority, to give the impression of dynamism and reform or to alter the balance of power within a government.

Every minister, in addition to being a minister responsible to the Dáil, has two commitments. The first is as an individual heading a department; and the second is as a member of the government collectively responsible for what other ministers do. Because of the second of these, there is a need to resolve conflicts between individual ministers to the satisfaction of ministers collectively. Issues where individual departments and ministers do not see eye to eye arise all the time as the programmes of individual departments get entangled with one another. For example, in the international negotiations on the General Agreement on Tariffs and Trade, the Departments of Foreign Affairs, Agriculture and Food, and Industry and Commerce may not always adopt the same line (the last two departments tend to see a continuing need to protect the interests of farming and industry, while the Department of Foreign Affairs is liable to take a broader view and see particular issues as part of global problems). Differences arise frequently between the Department of Finance and other departments in relation to various financial matters; for example, a dispute between the Department of Finance and the Department of Industry and Commerce regarding the sale of Irish Steel Ltd was widely reported in the press in February and March 1990. There is no fixed procedure for dealing with such issues other than a spirit of give and take between officials in the first place and between ministers eventually. The ultimate arbiter is, of course, the government. However, the Taoiseach and ministers themselves do not take kindly to government business being clogged with issues that could (and should) be settled between the departments involved.

Taking up Office

The new minister, on his first full day in office, is conducted by the secretary general of his department to the office in the department vacated by his predecessor. All documentary material has been removed from that office – emphasising that the new incumbent is starting from scratch. One of the minister's first tasks is, therefore, to discuss with the secretary general the question of the staffing of his private office, who his private secretary is to be and how many support staff he needs. The private secretary is generally in the grade of higher executive officer. This is the highest grade which ministers are, under Department of Finance regulations, permitted to have.

Only the Taoiseach may have a higher grade; his private secretary is an assistant principal. It is not unusual for a new minister to appoint the private secretary of his predecessor, thus displaying his confidence in the apolitical nature of the civil service. More often, however, he appoints a new officer to the post and in such cases he is guided by the secretary general in conjunction with the personnel section of the department. That section provides the names of four or five persons whom it considers suitable for the post, and those are normally interviewed by the minister before he makes his selection. The other staff assigned are usually those who have worked in the private office up to the date on which the previous minister left office.

On his first day in the office the new minister normally meets his senior officers – the assistant secretaries and the technical officers of equivalent rank, and perhaps principals and others as well. At this meeting the minister may outline his plans, priorities and aspirations for his period in office and seek the co-operation of all present in advancing these.

He then turns to his incoming correspondence, much of it from various pressure and interest groups seeking early meetings. His acknowledgments generally plead for time to familiarise himself with his portfolio and promise action as soon as possible.

In his early days in office the minister spends much of his time with the secretary general of his department, upon whom he realises he must depend greatly. He seeks briefing on the major issues facing the department and on the timescale for action on these. He will discuss, in particular, the matters relating to his department which were highlighted in the government's pre-election programme and will endeavour to implement them as a matter of priority. He seeks information on the various groups with which the department deals (Dooney (1989) describes thirty-seven bodies which play a substantial part in the work of the Department of Agriculture and Food and lists 138 others which play a lesser part). He learns of the sensitive areas of the work and, in particular, of those where he may find himself engaged in public controversy. He finds out what legislation is pending and the background to this, as well as the attitude of the opposition parties and outside individuals or groups who are concerned. He inquires about the progress of any state-sponsored bodies under his aegis, the relationships between his department and them, and the appointments to the boards thereof which fall to be made during his period of office. He learns of the meetings abroad which he will have to attend, whether of the EU or of other international bodies or for the promotion of his department's work otherwise. He asks what money is available to carry out his plans. Above all, he is advised of any impending crisis and how best this might be dealt with.

Internal Department Work

A minister's route to office is always more political than administrative. He is not some kind of superior civil servant. In many cases, the responsibility which a minister assumes on taking office is one he is facing for the first time. The organisation and management of their departments is an aspect of their work for which ministers have not been trained and for which they may have little experience. As it is one in which the officials have long experience, ministers are generally happy to leave the day-to-day running of the department to the secretary general. As a general rule, ministers do not see their job as motivating their officials, improving the organisation of the department or monitoring the performance of routine tasks. Nora Owen, Minister for Justice, was criticised by the opposition parties in 1996 and 1997 for allegedly not taking sufficient interest in the organisation of her department. 'The skills needed to compete with other egoists in a parliamentary party are not the same as those required to provide executive leadership in a large bureaucratic organisation' (Rose 1987: 81). For his part, the secretary general is happy to accept the responsibility, since not alone is he familiar with the ethos of the department and its needs, but he also knows the staff and their needs and is thus in a position to prevent any of the upheavals which might otherwise arise on changes of minister.

There is, however, one function where the minister must personally approve. That is the promotion of staff. As indicated in Chapter 6, the minister is the employer of all of the staff in his department; it follows that he is responsible for their promotion. In practice, however, ministers do not interfere in the actual promotion arrangements made by the Department of Finance for intra- or interdepartmental promotions but accept the recommendations in this respect submitted for approval by the secretary general. Nor, by convention, do ministers intervene in staff matters, unless they are absolutely forced to do so. They see no profit for themselves in interfering and are thus very willing for such matters to be dealt with by the personnel unit and the secretary general.

The main task of a minister is to ensure that his department advances the national interest and, in particular, the interest of that sector of the community or of national life for which it was established. Success in this calls for the correct policies and for the effective implementation of these. Policies are, in the main, outlined in the pre-election programme. If the minister has ideas for a new policy, he simply sets out in broad terms what his wishes are and then leaves it to his officials to indicate what might be done. A former economic adviser to the British government noted that the tasks of the civil servant properly include 'beating the woolly vague impractical ideas that exist on any issue into some set of workable alternatives. Only then can a minister make any real choice' (Opie 1968: 73).

Ministers and Civil Servants

In the course of their collaboration care is taken by both the minister and the departmental secretary general to avoid any issues of a purely party political nature. In particular, neither touches on, even by implication, the personality or performance of the previous minister. For his part, the secretary general maintains the traditional attitude of the civil service: that it is there to serve successive ministers with equal commitment and loyalty. Likewise, the minister is conscious of the unwritten rules of the political club to which he belongs, one of which is that members do not criticise each other in front of officials. The official who might seek to ingratiate himself with his minister by passing a critical comment on the minister's predecessor can be assured of an icy response or none at all.

At the same time, neither minister nor civil servants allow themselves to forget the obligation of officials to involve themselves in, and be committed to, the policies and political preferences of the government of the day. Civil servants' tasks include support for ministers in promoting the interests of the government against those of the opposition. For example, in writing speeches for the Dáil, in preparing replies and accompanying notes for parliamentary questions and in assembling briefs for other occasions, civil servants present their minister's case in the best light possible without reference to the positive aspects of the opposition case. At all times the aim is not so much to denigrate the opposition as to enable the minister's light to shine as brightly as possible. This applies equally when the opposition is the former minister. Thus, in addition to technical or expert advice that is intellectually rigorous and does not avoid inconvenient questions, ministers get support of a positive nature. The roles of the minister and of his civil servants are complementary. The minister is the link between the department and the representative aspects of government and politics, and the deference that it is customary to pay to his office is, in a certain sense, a deference to the democratic process itself.

Civil servants like to see their minister display certain attributes. They want him to project what they regard, in almost a proprietary way, as their department in the best possible light, as a dynamic organisation with a competent and enthusiastic staff concerned at all times with the national interest. They want him to advance or defend, as occasion demands, the department at cabinet meetings, in the Dáil and elsewhere. This aspect of the relationship has been succinctly and humorously described by a former British minister:

> The overriding duty of a departmental minister, in the eyes of his mandarins, however, is to defend and, where possible, to advance the territory of the kraal to which he happens to be assigned. For British civil servants are territorial animals, and nothing arouses such passion around the [Whitehall] village as trespass . . . for while departments expect their ministers to fight the good fight

> for departmental interests and departmental territory, to be seen off by a neighbouring predator is regarded as a badge of shame for which a minister will not lightly be forgiven by his mandarins; the whims of 10 Downing Street are accepted as blows of fate (Bruce-Gardyne 1986: 62).

Civil servants greatly value decisiveness in their minister in dealing with the department's work, including knowing what he wants. Above all, when they put forward proposals to the minister for decision they want to have decisions taken. Indecisiveness in a minister is the characteristic which most frustrates them. Official proposals are never lightly put forward. They are always the outcome of intensive and extensive examination of the subject at issue and are presented in such a way as to lend themselves to decision-taking. Civil servants do not generally mind what the nature of the decision is. What does upset them, though fully recognising the minister's prerogative and responsibilities, is the non-return of the papers because the minister is unable or unwilling to make up his mind. They do not want to be continually approaching the private secretary to place the papers on the top of the minister's pile and otherwise to nudge him towards a decision. Equally upsetting are changes of mind on the part of the minister. It goes without saying that courtesy and appreciation are always valued by officials, especially a minister's willingness to back them when they are under attack by the media, pressure groups or others.

Different ministers have different practices in dealing with their officials. Some discuss the work only with the secretary general, the assistant secretaries and the heads of the technical branches. Some prefer to go deeper into the hierarchy and discuss issues with the officials actually dealing with them. The more restrictive style of consultation is undoubtedly more convenient for ministers, but it has two disadvantages. The first is that it cuts them off from those who are closest to the ground, so to speak. The second is the disadvantage noted in the Devlin Report and commented upon frequently by civil servants themselves. This is the forcing of unnecessary detail on senior officers at the expense of time which could be more usefully devoted to organisation, planning and more policy-oriented initiatives. Hence matters which in a well-run business organisation would be dealt with at middle or lower level are in a government department dealt with at the top.

Discussions with his officials take up part of every day that a minister spends in his office. Even if he does not have matters which he wants to discuss with them, they will have matters which they want to discuss with him, so as to get a guideline or a decision, and will have apprised his private secretary accordingly. Nevertheless, the vast majority of officials, especially in larger departments, never meet their minister; indeed, a large number of them may never see him except on television.

Files

The work of officials is carried out on a file, the first page of which may be a note from the minister or from his private secretary or the secretary general of the department saying that 'The minister wishes to have . . . examined.' The civil servants concerned take the matter on from there. In due course the file containing all the details of the examination, including accounts of the discussions carried out with concerned parties, is presented to the minister. He is not expected to read all of these details, but they are there for him if he wishes to do so. The last page of the file contains a very brief summary of what has gone before and a recommendation to the minister as to what action seems desirable. In the normal course the recommendation is that of the secretary general, who may or may not concur in the recommendation made by the officials who have carried out the examination. For example, a Minister for Agriculture and Food under pressure from small farmers wanting to increase the size of their holdings or from landless people wishing to enter farming might ask his officials to examine how such people could be facilitated in achieving their aims. Policies might include controls on the sale of land, or the provision of low-interest loans or grants. Any social and economic advantages of the course proposed would be pointed out, as would any likely objections from all possible quarters. When the matter has been examined the minister must decide whether or not to accept the recommendations arising from the examination, either fully or in part.

Ministers have different ways of dealing with files. Some read the file from cover to cover. This, however, is rare, since time does not normally permit such attention to detail. Most ministers read the final page only and draw up a mental or written list of questions (usually the former) to ask the secretary general. Others may not read any of the papers but may invite the secretary general to tell them what they contain. Some ministers are more disposed to discussion than to reading. One way or the other, the minister arrives at some decision – even if it is a decision to put the file away among his papers for further consideration at a later date. When a positive decision is taken – and such a decision may be not to proceed further – this is communicated. Again, ministers differ in their manner of communication. Rarely does a minister write at length on a file. More generally, he merely writes 'I agree' or 'Go ahead' over his initials, or will communicate his wishes orally to his private secretary or to the secretary general of the department, who will then briefly note the minister's decision on the file. The file is returned through the assistant secretary to the official directly involved, who then arranges for whatever action is required, e.g. the putting in train of new legislation, the drafting of a scheme or the writing of a letter. The minister does not normally bother himself with the details of the implementation of his decision, though this depends on the importance of the issue. If there is need for a publicity campaign, the minister will wish to be very much involved.

A wide variety of other files is also submitted to a minister. These include files on which his wishes are sought, on whom he wants to have appointed to a particular board or committee, or on whether he will attend a certain function or meet some deputation. It is not unusual that a recommendation is made to him in each of these situations. They include also files where his signature is required on statutory instruments or on warrants of appointment.

All files and all requests by officials to see the minister are channelled through the private secretary. The latter uses his discretion in presenting the files and requests, choosing the most opportune moment for doing so. On those occasions when it is vitally necessary to have some matter cleared quickly, the private secretary can usually find a way to help his departmental colleagues, using his own experience of when and how it is best to get his minister's consent.

Meetings, Communications and Public Relations

Meeting people is an essential part of a minister's daily work. The meetings he attends range from formal assemblies such as Dáil sessions and cabinet meetings to private interviews with individuals or small groups in his own office. The minister and his staff must make special preparations for each type of meeting. For many of these occasions he is provided with a brief which (in the case of meetings conducted by the minister himself) explains the background and purpose of the visit and suggests what action might be appropriate. In addition, the minister has contact with a much wider circle of people by means of correspondence; he also devotes considerable care to maintaining a high profile and projecting his image in the most favourable light among the public in general.

Dáil

Ministers must attend the Dáil for all business relating to their own departments. By convention, they also attend for the announcement of each day's business. They normally assemble for these occasions in the office of the Government Chief Whip in Leinster House and enter the chamber in file behind the Taoiseach, usually occupying the same seats each time. When presenting their own legislation ministers are accompanied in the chamber by the officials who have prepared it. Thorough briefing is provided, and ministers ensure that they are familiar with its every detail. The same level of briefing is not required when a minister is replying to a motion, whether one being debated in private members' time or on the adjournment of the Dáil, since on these occasions he delivers a prepared speech and the opposition have little opportunity to raise detailed questions of an ad hoc nature.

Government Meetings

Ministers are expected to attend all government meetings. The agenda always contains one or more items that have been placed there at ministers' requests, seeking authority to proceed with some piece of legislation, to introduce some new programme or merely to bring to the notice of the government some matter such as the accounts of a state-sponsored body.

At meetings a minister argues forcibly for measures that he wants to introduce and must be in a position to counter arguments put forward by other ministers, particularly by the Minister for Finance, who is always fully briefed on every proposal. Ministers are often judged on their success in achieving what they seek at government meetings, where, however good their briefing, they must also exhibit considerable personal skills.

A second role which a minister has at government meetings is to contribute to the collective deliberations and decisions of the cabinet as a whole on matters which are intrinsically important or sensitive. His officials do not, because they are not so equipped, advise on matters which do not concern their own department, and for such briefing the minister relies greatly on the counsel provided by his political adviser. The skills required by a minister in cabinet include succinctness and persuasiveness as well as analytic ability and a general understanding of issues not obviously interconnected. Also helpful is 'political weight' and a past record of good judgment.

Party Meetings

All the political parties hold weekly meetings of TDs, senators and members of the European Parliament in Leinster House when the Dáil is in session. Meetings of the party in office are attended by ministers, who advise the backbenchers of legislation and other projects under consideration in their departments. The ministers, for their part, receive grassroots views on how the public is reacting to the government's policies and on the issues which are of most immediate public concern. From these grassroots reactions the ministers quickly gauge how they themselves are performing.

Government Backbenchers

Government backbenchers may meet a minister individually or as a group. Individual interviews are much more frequent, because government parties have few backbench committees. The minister is not accompanied by officials when meeting backbenchers.

Ministers take particular care to be helpful to their backbenchers and many deputations are met at their request. Any information which is likely to be helpful to them in their constituencies is made available, and if a minister is going to visit a constituency, the first to know about the visit, and be invited to take part, are his local backbench colleagues.

Constituents

The needs of his constituents are very high on a minister's list of priorities, because ministers are keenly aware that without their constituents they would not be in office in the first place. In practice, however, constituents' needs do not generally take up much of a minister's personal time while in his office, since they are comprehensively dealt with by the staff in his private office.

Constituents do, however, take up a considerable amount of time at weekends. It is not unusual for a minister to spend Friday evening, all of Saturday and even part of Sunday in meeting his constituents. The latter, for their part, expect this attention. At these meetings, or 'clinics' as they are called, the minister listens, notes and promises to do all he can about the problems presented to him. It is then for the staff of his private office to follow up.

Deputations

In the case of deputations, which are usually seeking some specific action or favour, the minister is presented with a detailed brief informing him of all he should know about them, what further information he should seek from them and how far he can accommodate their demands. Ministers generally have considerable skill in using their briefs at the actual meetings and in being able to send groups away impressed with their reception. Should unanticipated matters arise in the course of a meeting on which the minister does not consider himself adequately briefed, he turns to the officials accompanying him for elaboration. Ministers are invariably accompanied by officials on these occasions. This is an arrangement which clearly suits the minister, but it is one which also suits the officials, since it keeps them in the picture. It has been cynically observed that the civil servants are there to ensure that the minister does not give anything away; civil servants might not altogether disagree with this, but are more likely to say they are there to ensure a productive outcome.

Members of the opposition parties normally visit a minister's office only as part of a joint deputation on some constituency issue. This applies even to former ministers or current shadow ministers.

Courtesy Visits

In the case of visitors who have no specific business and whose visits are more in the nature of a courtesy call (e.g. foreign dignitaries or ambassadors or the heads of international organisations), the minister's brief contains information about the caller personally, the current state of relations between his organisation and the department and suggestions as to matters which the minister might raise with him. Officials do not generally attend on these occasions.

Journeys Abroad

These journeys fall into four broad categories: to attend meetings of international bodies; to promote the image of Ireland abroad and to encourage investment both in Ireland and in Irish exports; to study particular developments that might be relevant to planned initiatives at home; and to support members of the defence forces engaged on foreign duty.

Meetings in the first category include those of the EU, mainly held in Brussels and Luxembourg, and of bodies such as the World Health Organization, the International Labour Organization, the World Trade Organization, the United Nations and the Organization for European Co-operation and Development. The meetings of the Council of Ministers of the EU are the most numerous and regular. The ministers most in demand are those for Foreign Affairs, Agriculture and Food, and Finance, who have generally at least one meeting a month. Meetings demanding the attendance of other ministers are held less frequently and at irregular intervals. The minister attending is provided with a brief on each item on the agenda and also with a speaking note (a short speech) on those items in which Ireland has a specific interest. Before each Council meeting the minister and his officials generally discuss the brief with Ireland's Permanent Representative to the EU and his staff to ensure that they have the latest information on the subject at issue, including the stances likely to be adopted by the other member states, and that agreement is reached on the line to be taken at the Council.

Attendance at Council meetings generally involves bilateral contacts with other ministers or with members of the European Commission itself. These meetings, held on the margins of the Council meetings, are also attended by the officials.

In addition to the formal Council meetings, it is sometimes necessary for a minister or even a group of ministers to go specially to Brussels to make representations on behalf of Ireland or to explain more fully its position in certain cases, for example in the case of Ireland's application for structural funds.

Meetings to promote investment at home or marketing abroad are generally arranged by the state-sponsored bodies concerned, such as the IDA Ireland

(Industrial Development Agency), An Bord Bia (the Food Board) or Bord Fáilte (the Irish Tourist Board), or by the co-operative An Bord Bainne (the Milk Board). Potential investors or purchasers are invited to meet the visiting minister, while appearances on local television and at other social functions are also arranged. The detailed programme is put in place by the state-sponsored body concerned, some of whose officials accompany the minister, as does always one from his department. Sometimes the party is accompanied by exporters and by journalists.

Visits by the Minister for Defence to the forces on duty abroad under the auspices of the United Nations are largely for reasons of morale but also to see at first hand the situation in which they operate and to acquire information which may be of use in advising on government policy. On such occasions the minister is accompanied by the Chief of Staff and by one of his departmental officials.

Another regular occasion of visits abroad is the celebration, by parades, concerts and other social occasions, of St Patrick's Day, particularly in the USA and Australia. Irish ministers are often the central figures in such celebrations.

Correspondence

All letters addressed to the minister are processed in the first instance by his private secretary, who reserves by far the greater proportion to be dealt with by himself and the department's staff. The minister sees very little of the routine correspondence and is entirely dependent on the private secretary as to what he should see.

The private secretary is also responsible for determining which replies should be signed by the minister himself, and he carefully scrutinises each of these. The general guidelines are that ministers sign letters to other ministers, to government backbenchers, senators and local councillors, to previous ministers of any party, to shadow ministers, to people who are considered 'important' and, perhaps most frequent of all, to the minister's own constituents.

Public Relations

A development particularly noticeable in recent years is the constant and increasing search for publicity by ministers of all governments. All ministers are now very concerned with their public image and take considerable care to ensure that their activities are projected to the public as frequently and as favourably as possible. This projection is effected in a number of ways.

Nearly every department has an information section headed by a press or information officer, with whom the minister is in constant touch. This section is the point of contact for journalists and others seeking information about the department's activities. Civil servants do not speak to the press themselves, but are expected to supply promptly all requested material through the information section.

A significant part of the work of an information section is the issue of press releases about departmental developments through the Government Information Services (GIS) to the daily and provincial newspapers, to the radio and television stations and to relevant journals. These may be announcements about projects being introduced or being discontinued; exhortations to the public about health or safety measures; statements about moneys procured by the minister from the EU, or about his attendance at meetings at home or abroad.

The addresses given by ministers on purely party political occasions are not circulated by the GIS, even though they touch on the work of the minister's department. Instead they are circulated as appropriate by the minister's private office, with the phrase 'as requested' as a heading instead of the usual heading used by the GIS.

The same degree of propriety is exercised in regard to material sought by ministers for use either by themselves or by other ministers at national party conferences or during general election campaigns. This is a delicate area, and one in which each side appreciates the sensibilities of the other. It is generally dealt with by tactful requests on the part of the minister's private office and by the provision of purely factual information on the part of the civil service. The minister or his special adviser injects the desired political slant into the material provided. On major political occasions, however, such as regional party conferences or by-election conventions, the Government Press Secretary usually gives copies of the speeches to the political correspondents.

Ministers prepare carefully for their appearances on television and radio programmes or at press conferences. In recent years the preparation includes coaching by public relations and media consultants. It is sometimes rather cynically observed that ministers are inclined to decide in advance exactly what information they wish to impart in such interviews, and that they make sure they do so regardless of the questions that are actually put to them.

Most ministers and their information officers seek to establish a close relationship with the specialist journalists covering the work areas of their departments and, indeed, with journalists generally. Journalist contacts are used to get publicity for ministers' legislative and policy plans, for their stance in cabinet, for their victories over colleagues, or to publicise cuts by the Department of Finance affecting their projects. This publicity is achieved through phone calls from the minister himself, through interviews and press releases, through entertainment and through invitations to accompany the minister on his official visits and other public appearances.

Ministers of State

Ministers of state are commonly referred to as junior ministers. They are not members of the government and have no right of attendance at government meetings. They may attend when invited, to present information on subjects with which they are particularly familiar. Their responsibilities are assigned to them either by special orders (known as delegation of functions orders) made by the government and vesting ministerial powers in named ministers of state, or by specific delegation by the minister in charge of the department.

It is the minister of state who initiates legislation in the areas of his responsibility, but he may not himself submit any proposals to government. Such proposals must first be approved by the minister in charge. If the minister does not approve of them, the proposals do not emerge publicly and must be abandoned by the minister of state. If they are approved by the minister and reach government, the minister of state may, depending on the attitude of the minister as noted above, present them there. In such a situation it is normally the minister of state who presents them to the Oireachtas subsequently and pilots them through the various stages there. Parliamentary questions in his area of work are also taken by the minister of state.

In general, the work of a minister of state is largely the same as that of a minister – in relation to his Dáil and constituency work, meeting deputations and attending to the needs of backbenchers and party members. In all of this work he has available to him the services of officials, including a private office almost identical in staffing and structure to that of the minister.

A minister of state carries out his responsibilities under the watchful eye of his superior, who does not want to be upstaged and who wishes to be kept informed on everything that is going on. Indeed, it is not unusual to have a certain rivalry between minister and minister of state in the carrying out of the work of the department. Generally, a minister retains all of the high-profile work, such as that relating to the EU and the announcement of new projects likely to be well received publicly.

The role and status of a minister of state, therefore, to some extent depend on the attitude of the senior minister. Those to whom little of the department's work has been delegated must console themselves by devoting their time to their constituencies. Nevertheless, frustration occasionally leads them to approach the Taoiseach. Depending on the personality of the member of the government concerned, the complaint can sometimes be redressed. If it cannot, the Taoiseach can usually find a means of utilising the services of the minister of state by assigning him some work of benefit to the party, such as reviving party organisation in a constituency where it is flagging. In departments where rivalry exists between minister and minister of state, the officials, by a judicious exercise of their traditional discretion, not to say caution, are generally able to maintain the balance to the satisfaction of all concerned.

The Minister's Private Office

Guidelines as to the staffing of ministers' offices have been laid down by the Minister for Finance. The guidelines refer to the private and to the constituency offices, though in practice no such separate offices are discernible. The staff in the private office, headed by the private secretary, carry out whatever tasks the minister requires, making no distinction between departmental and constituency tasks. The guidelines provide that the number of staff in a private office should not exceed ten, that there should be not more than six in a constituency office, and that there should be not more than one personal secretary, one personal assistant and one special adviser per minister, i.e. a potential total of nineteen. Either the personal assistant or the personal adviser may be actually located in the minister's constituency office. The tables in Appendix 2 show the numbers of staff in ministers' offices on 13 March 1997 as given in reply to parliamentary questions on that date. It is unlikely that these numbers changed materially under the government which took up office in June 1997. Up to the 1970s the number averaged about four.

The purpose of the private office is threefold: to provide a secretariat for the minister, to co-ordinate his activities and to act as a liaison between him and his department. The office communicates ministerial instructions to the sections of the department and also acts as a filter between them and the minister. The private secretary must be prepared to work long and irregular hours. These arise particularly when the Dáil is in session. Ministers may be required to be in Leinster House until the Dáil adjourns and often some time after that. These late hours are a favourite time for backbenchers to seek out a minister. They are often accompanied by outsiders whom they want to introduce to the minister. The private secretary usually meets such persons in the first instance, advises them of the minister's availability and notes their requirements for passing on, if necessary, to the department on the following day.

A major part of a private secretary's job is to get to know how his minister thinks so that he may confidently advise the departmental officials what view the minister would take in a particular situation or so that he may take decisions himself in the absence of the minister.

He must know which letters should be seen by the minister personally and which he may himself sign on the minister's behalf, which telephone calls should or should not be put through, and what firm appointments can be made. Thus a new private secretary or a private secretary who gets a new minister requires some months before he is at ease in this aspect of his job.

The private secretary must normally deal with all of the correspondence addressed to the minister. A large proportion of this relates to constituency matters, from the minister's own constituents and from other ministers and backbenchers about their constituents' affairs. The balance is not of such an overtly political nature and deals, indirectly or directly, with the subject matter of the minister's portfolio, making suggestions, drawing attention to developments and extending invitations. Nearly all of the correspondence is sent elsewhere for reply – to the heads of the various divisions. The replies fall into different categories. Some are for signature by the minister himself (a minister's signature always appears on letters to constituents), some by the private secretary, and some (mainly those with no political element) by the officials as part of the normal departmental correspondence. The private secretary usually signs the letters to politicians not belonging to the government party and also such other letters as in his judgment the minister would be content to have him sign.

A certain amount of confidential or sensitive material is also received in a minister's office. This may relate to national security, political, financial or other such matters. This correspondence does not leave the minister's office. Examples are the reports from the Anglo-Irish secretariat received in the Departments of Foreign Affairs and Justice or those from diplomatic missions received in the former, and the budgetary and financial data received in the Department of Finance.

A diary of all the minister's engagements for each week is circulated to the offices of the minister of state and the secretary general. Liaison is maintained with the Dáil staff, with the government secretariat, and with the Government Chief Whip's office in regard to the minister's attendance at government meetings and in the Dáil and Seanad. The private secretary is also responsible for ensuring that his minister has a firm 'pairing' arrangement if his official functions prevent him from being available for a critical vote in the Dáil. He also ensures that the minister has all the necessary papers for meetings of the government; that he has, in good time, the replies to his oral parliamentary questions; that he has, also in good time, copies of the speeches to be made on the various occasions; that he has the briefs for meetings well in advance; and generally that he is provided with whatever service he requires. If there is slippage, the minister complains to the secretary general of the department, who then 'reminds' the entire staff of what is expected of them, through the issue of an appropriate notice over his own name.

The private secretary presides over a busy suite of offices with the most up-to-date equipment, including secure telephones, controlled by the Garda Síochána, with frequent changing of codes. The secretary's office is immediately adjacent to that of the minister, and the two are in constant liaison. The degree of formality between the minister and his private secretary varies greatly, and it is not unusual for those ministers with a less formal disposition to find time to chat with the staff in their office. All the staff in the private office develop a special loyalty to the minister of the day, different in some indefinable way from their loyalty to the department.

Special Advisers

The practice of appointing special advisers to ministers dates back to the inter-party government of 1954–7, when two appointments were made. The next appointment was not made until 1970, when Dr Martin O'Donoghue (on the staff of Trinity College, Dublin) became personal adviser to the Taoiseach, Jack Lynch. The governments which took office in 1973 and 1977 had four and six advisers respectively. Since the early 1980s almost every minister has an adviser (variously designated as special, political, economic, social or policy adviser). The Taoiseach usually has more than one.

Advisers are not normally civil servants. The selection is made by the minister himself, but the appointment must be approved by the Taoiseach. The job is not advertised. Ministers appoint someone who is personally known to them, generally a party supporter in whom they have complete trust, with qualifications and contacts which the minister considers useful, and who will be totally committed to advancing the minister's policies and career. The qualifications need not be those of an expert. Advisers frequently accompany a minister from one portfolio to another.

In considering the role of advisers of this nature, it is necessary to bear in mind that while civil servants are conscious of political realities generally in furnishing advice to ministers and in recommending courses of action, they see their role as that of serving successive ministers and not as one of taking overtly political matters into account in framing policies, even if they were competent to do so. It is necessary to remember also that officials' experience is such as to enable them to provide information and advice only on the subject matter of the minister's portfolio and not on the wider issues with which, as a politician and as a member of the government, a minister must concern himself.

The adviser, on the other hand, regards his employer as a politician, as a deputy, as a member of the government and as a person. Thus the service which he provides for a minister is essentially different from that provided by officials. It includes the following elements:

(1) Discussing with the minister the political and electoral implications of the advice coming from the civil service, including its likely reception by the media, especially in the case of delicate measures such as the withdrawal of a benefit or the imposition of a charge, for example a fee for a fishing licence.

(2) Discussing organisational changes suggested by the secretary general of the department, or changes which the minister himself is thinking of proposing, for example in regard to the location of staff away from headquarters.

(3) Examining matters in breadth as well as in depth by consulting outside sources and taking soundings on (1) and (2), and drawing attention to aspects which the civil servants may not have referred to.
(4) Researching matters for discussion at government meetings and providing briefing for his own minister so that he can, if he wishes, take part in the discussion and put a point of view. As implied earlier, this is a service which the minister's own officials cannot provide.
(5) Dealing with constituency matters in a broader framework than the normal constituency correspondence handled by the private secretary demands. This entails keeping in touch with government, local authority or other public service developments in the constituency and with commercial and business interests there.
(6) Examining formal speeches and informal addresses from a presentational point of view, having regard to the minister's personality and style of delivery, and thus turning information from within the department into politically usable material.
(7) Writing speeches of a specifically political nature for the minister.
(8) Acting as a replication of the minister in many respects, as an extension of his political personality, as an extra pair of eyes and ears, doing for him what the minister would do for himself if he had the time.

Advisers have access to departmental files and may see all submissions to the minister.

The arrangement bears some, though only a very limited, resemblance to the so-called 'cabinet' system which obtains in many European countries and in the EU. Under that system a minister (or a member of the European Commission) has a group of eight to ten people, known as a 'cabinet', whose work is broadly that described above, though on a more elaborate scale. There have been casual references from time to time to the establishment of a 'cabinet' system in Ireland, but the matter has not been considered in any detail. Its introduction would necessitate radical changes affecting the patterns, traditions and values of Ireland's political culture to an extent which would probably be unacceptable.

The current system of advisers has found general favour. In support, three broad arguments have been advanced. The first is that it prepares ministers for discussions at government level on areas outside their departments' responsibilities, thus enabling them to make a constructive contribution to the collective decision-making process of any government. The second is that it supplies specialised advice to ministers on certain policy areas, providing a different perspective (and thus a valuable alternative) to the expert advice available within the department. The third is that it gives advice on the political implications of policy or other measures, including the maintenance of a high public profile, thus enabling the civil service to keep out of party politics. Ministers and advisers often say that officials can be hidebound by their narrow specialist approach to issues and that they do not sense, and are not interested in, the political angle.

In general, civil servants live happily with advisers, especially now that their appointments terminate with the minister's leaving office. (Up to 1981 those advisers who wished to remain were often appointed established civil servants 'in the public interest', as provided for in the Civil Service Commissioners Act 1956. Needless to say, this practice did not find favour with existing civil servants, since it interfered with promotion arrangements.) Strains can arise, however, as when advisers reword letters, speeches or replies to parliamentary questions prepared by officials to make them overtly political or to include material discarded as unsuitable by the civil servants, or when advisers intrude into routine departmental work or departmental contacts, creating confusion as to who actually speaks for the minister. Nevertheless, a spirit of altruism generally prevails. Civil servants recognise that ministers and advisers tend to live for the present, whereas departments take the long-term view and have seen ministers come and go; they recognise the minister's prerogative in making such appointments and understand their political desirability. The advisers, for their part, though impatient at the outset at what they sometimes refer to scathingly as 'bureaucracy', come in time to see at least some of its advantages. Both sides know the rules of the game, and each is conscious of the need to keep off the other's territory.

Programme Managers

A new development introduced by the 1993–4 Fianna Fáil/Labour government was the appointment of programme managers. Some of these were civil servants and some were appointed from outside the service. The practice was continued by the succeeding Fine Gael/Labour/Democratic Left government but was discontinued by the Fianna Fáil/Progressive Democrat government which took office in 1997, save for the Taoiseach and the Tánaiste.

In reply to a parliamentary question on 29 March 1993 the Minister for Finance stated:

> The role and function of the new managers is quite distinct from that of departmental secretaries general and senior line managers. Senior civil servants will continue to have responsibility for the development of policy proposals, the overall management of schemes and programmes and have charge of their departments generally. The programme managers, on the other hand, have been assigned the specific function of providing administrative support to

> ministers in progressing the Partnership Programme for Government in the next few years. The posts are designed to assist ministers in managing and co-ordinating the achievement of the objectives of the government's programme.

The managers met formally each week, when they monitored the implementation of legislative and other commitments in the programme for government. They also met bilaterally, where they sought solutions to interdepartmental disagreements and so saved ministers' time.

REFERENCES

Bruce-Gardyne, Jock, *Inside the Whitehall Village* (London: Sidgwick & Jackson, 1986)

Dooney, Sean, *Irish Agriculture: An Organisational Profile* (Dublin: Institute of Public Administration, 1989)

Opie, Roger, 'The Making of Economic Policy' in Hugh Thomas (ed.), *Crisis in the Civil Service* (London: Anthony Blond, 1968)

Rose, Richard, *Ministers and Ministries* (Oxford: Clarendon Press, 1987)

APPENDIX 2

Staff Employed in Ministers' Offices

The figures below were supplied by ministers in response to parliamentary questions in March 1997.

HEO:	Higher Executive Officer	**CO:**	Clerical Officer
EO:	Executive Officer	**CA:**	Clerical Assistant
SO:	Staff Officer		

1. Taoiseach

Private and Constituency Office (20)
Private Secretary
1 HEO
1 EO
6 COs
4 CAs
Programme Manager
2 Special Advisers
2 Personal Assistants
2 Personal Secretaries

Minister of State (1)

Private and Constituency Office (12)
Private Secretary
1 EO
2 SOs
2 CAs
Special Adviser
Personal Assistant
Personal Secretary
Part-time Researcher[1]
2 Civilian Drivers

[1] Engaged on consultancy basis at the rate of £94 per diem.

Minister of State (2)

Private and Constituency Office (8)
Private Secretary
1 CO
1 CA
Special Adviser
Personal Assistant (EO)
Personal Secretary
2 Civilian Drivers

Minister of State (3)

Private and Constituency Office (9)
Private Secretary
1 SO
1 CO
3 CAs
Special Adviser
Personal Assistant
Personal Secretary

2. Agriculture, Food and Forestry

Minister's Office

Civil Servants:
1 HEO
2 EOs
4 COs
2 CAs
2 CA/Typists

Non-Civil Servants:
1 Programme Manager
1 Special Adviser
1 Personal Assistant
1 Personal Secretary

Minister of State's Office

Civil Servants:
1 HEO
2 EOs
2 COs
3 CAs
1 CA/Typist

Non-Civil Servants:
1 Special Adviser
2 Civilian Drivers
1 Personal Assistant
1 Personal Secretary

3. Arts, Culture and the Gaeltacht

Minister's Private Office

Established Officers
2 Executive Officers (including my Private Secretary)
2 Clerical Officers
4 Clerical Assistants

Non-Established Officers
1 Programme Manager
1 Special Adviser

Minister's Constituency Office

There are three established officers and three non-established officers working in my Constituency Office as follows:

Established Officers
1 Executive Officer
1 Clerical Officer
1 Clerical Assistant

Non-Established Officers
1 Personal Assistant
1 Personal Secretary
1 Temporary Clerical Assistant (on Irish language duties)

Office of the Minister of State

1 Executive Officer
1 Clerical Assistant

4. Defence

Civil Service Staff
Higher Executive Officer
Staff Officer
Clerical Officer
Clerical Assistant

Contract Staff
Programme Manager
Special Adviser
Personal Secretary
Personal Adviser

The contract staff salary costs are shared jointly between Defence and Marine Votes reflecting my dual ministerial role.

There are three civil service staff attached to the Office of the Minister of State as follows:

Higher Executive Officer
Clerical Officer
Clerical Assistant

There are no contract staff employed by the Minister of State.

5. Education

Minister's Office

12 1/2 civil servants (wholetime equivalent posts)
1 Higher Executive Officer
2 Executive Officers
1 Staff Officer
4 Clerical Officers
1 1/2 Clerical Assistants
3 Clerical Assistant/Typists

5 non-civil servants
1 Programme Manager
1 Special Adviser
1 Press Officer
1 Personal Assistant
1 Personal Secretary

Minister of State (1)

6 civil servants
1 Higher Executive Officer
1 Executive Officer
1 Staff Officer
1 Clerical Officer
2 Clerical Assistant/Typists

3 non-civil servants
1 Special Adviser
1 Personal Secretary
1 Personal Assistant

Minister of State (2)

3 civil servants
1 Higher Executive Officer
1 Executive Officer
1 Clerical Assistant

6. Enterprise and Employment

CIVIL SERVANTS

Grade	*Number*
Higher Executive Officer	1
Executive Officer	3
Clerical Officer	4
Clerical Assistant	6

TEMPORARY UNESTABLISHED STAFF

Title	*Number*
Programme Manager	1
Special Adviser	1
Personal Assistant	1

Minister of State (1)

CIVIL SERVANTS

Grade	*Number*
Higher Executive Officer	1
Staff Officer	1
Clerical Officer	2
Clerical Assistant	2

TEMPORARY UNESTABLISHED STAFF

Title	*Number*
Programme Manager	1
Special Adviser	1
Personal Secretary	1

Minister of State (2)

CIVIL SERVANTS

Grade	*Number*
Higher Executive Officer	1
Clerical Officer	2
Clerical Assistant	2

TEMPORARY UNESTABLISHED STAFF

Title	*Number*
Special Adviser	1
Personal Assistant	1
Personal Secretary	1
Civilian Driver	2

7. Environment

Permanent Civil Servants		Others	
Number	*Grade*	*Number*	*Title*
	Minister		
1	Higher Executive Officer – Private Secretary	1	Programme Manager
		1	Special Adviser
3	Executive Officers	1	Personal Assistant
2	Staff Officers	1	Personal Secretary
5	Clerical Assistants		
	Minister of State (1)		
1	Higher Executive Officer – Private Secretary	1	Special Adviser
		1	Personal Assistant
2	Executive Officers	2	Personal Secretaries*
4	Clerical Assistants	2	Civilian Drivers
	Minister of State (2)		
1	Executive Officer – Private Secretary		
1	Clerical Officer		

* Two part-time staff filling one post.

8. Equality and Law Reform

There are nine established civil servants employed in the general Ministerial Office and the Constituency Office. These comprise

- 1 Assistant Principal
- 1 Higher Executive Officer
- 2 Executive Officers
- 2 Clerical Officers
- 3 Clerical Assistant Typists.

There are four temporary unestablished civil servants employed in these offices, comprising

- 1 Programme Manager
- 2 Special Advisers
- 1 Personal Assistant.

9. Finance

The following is a list of staff, by grade, who work exclusively in my private and constituency offices and those of the Ministers of State at my Department. While all the staff listed below are civil servants, a number are non-established contract staff.

Minister

Grade

- 1 Higher Executive Officer (Private Secretary)
- 2 Executive Officers
- 1 Staff Officer
- 4 Clerical Officers
- 3 Clerical Assistants (including two job-sharers)
- 1 Programme Manager
- 1 Special Adviser
- 1 Personal Assistant
- 1 Personal Secretary

Minister of State (1)

Grade

1	Higher Executive Officer (Private Secretary)	1	Special Adviser
3	Clerical Officers	1	Personal Assistant
1	Clerical Assistant Typist	1	Personal Secretary
		2	Civilian Drivers

Minister of State (2)

Grade

1 Administrative Officer (Private Secretary)
1 Higher Executive Officer (Private Secretary)
1 Personal Secretary
1 Clerical Assistant
1 Special Adviser
2 Civilian Drivers

10. Health

Minister's Office

Civil Service Posts

Main Office	1	Higher Executive Officer (Private Secretary)
	1	Executive Officer
	1	Staff Officer
	1	Clerical Officer
	1	Clerical Assistant
	1	Clerical Assistant/Typist
Constituency Office	1	Executive Officer
	2	Clerical Assistants
	2	Clerical Assistant/Typists
Non-Civil Service Posts	1	Programme Manager
	1	Special Adviser
	1	Personal Assistant
	1	Constituency Adviser

Minister of State's Office (1)

Civil Service Posts

Integrated Main Office and Constituency Office	1	Higher Executive Officer (Private Secretary)
	2	Executive Officers
	1	Clerical Officer
	1	Clerical Assistant
	2	Clerical Assistant/Typists

Non-Civil Service Posts	1 Special Adviser
	1 Personal Assistant
	1 Personal Secretary
	1 Driver

Minister of State's Office (2)

Civil Service Posts

Main Office	1 Administrative Officer (Private Secretary)
	2 Executive Officers
	1 Clerical Assistant/Typist
Constituency Office	1 Clerical Officer
	1 Clerical Assistant/Typist
Non-Civil Service Posts	1 Special Adviser
	1 Personal Assistant
	1 Personal Secretary
	1 Driver

11. Justice

Office	Number and Grade of Staff
Minister's General Office	2 Executive Officers
	1 Clerical Assistant
	1 Personal Secretary
	1 Personal Assistant
Minister's Private Office	1 Programme Manager
	1 Higher Executive Officer
	1 Executive Officer
	1 Staff Officer (assigned to Executive Officer duties)
	2 Clerical Officers
	4 Clerical Assistants
Minister of State's Private Office (1)	1 Higher Executive Officer
	1 Clerical Assistant
Minister of State's General Office (1)	1 Personal Secretary
	1 Clerical Officer
	1 Clerical Assistant
Minister of State's Office (2)	1 Higher Executive Officer
	1 Clerical Assistant

12. Marine

I have four staff employed in my Office on contract and whose salaries are shared equally with the Department of Defence, reflecting my dual ministerial responsibilities. The positions held by these staff are:

Programme Manager,
Special Adviser,
Personal Secretary and Personal Assistant. (The Personal Secretary and Personal Assistant are based in the Department of Defence.)

In addition, I have a

Private Secretary (Higher Executive Officer) who is a Civil Servant.

There are eight staff engaged in the Minister of State's Office. Apart from the

Minister of State's Private Secretary (Higher Executive Officer) and
1 Clerical Assistant Typist, who are Civil Servants,

the following are employed on a non-established contract basis:

1 Special Adviser;
1 Personal Secretary;
1 Personal Assistant,
1 Clerical Assistant Typist and
2 Civilian Drivers.

I do not have a constituency office in the Department of the Marine, as all related matters are dealt with by my office in the Department of Defence. The Minister of State's constituency office is staffed by his

Personal Secretary,
Personal Assistant and
1 Clerical Assistant Typist.

13. Social Welfare

There are seventeen staff in my ministerial offices. Fourteen of these are established civil servants. These include

1 Programme Manager,
1 Private Secretary,
3 Executive Officers,
7 Clerical Officers and
2 Clerical Assistant/Typists.

Three are unestablished staff employed on a contract basis:

1 Special Adviser,
1 Personal Assistant and
1 Personal Secretary.

In order to support my role as a Party leader in government, a small research unit was established to provide me with advice and analysis on policy issues which arise on the general Government agenda outside my Departmental responsibilities. This unit is staffed by four unestablished staff employed on a contract basis:

1 Senior Research Assistant,
1 Research Assistant,
1 Part-time Research Assistant and
1 Administrative Assistant.

Minister of State

There are thirteen staff assigned to the private and constituency offices. Nine of these are established civil servants. These include

1 Private Secretary,
2 Staff Officers,
3 Clerical Officers and
3 Clerical Assistant/Typists.

Four are unestablished staff employed on a contract basis:

1 Personal Assistant,
1 Personal Secretary and
2 Civilian Drivers.

14. Tánaiste and Minister for Foreign Affairs

1 First Secretary
2 Higher Executive Officers
1 Executive Officer
4 Clerical Officers
2 Clerical Assistants
2 Personal Assistants (at AP and HEO grades)
1 Programme Manager
2 Special Advisers
2 Personal Secretaries

Minister of State (1)

1 Higher Executive Officer
1 Executive Officer
1 Clerical Officer
1 Clerical Assistant
1 Special Adviser
1 Personal Assistant
1 Civilian Driver

Minister of State (2)

1 Higher Executive Officer
2 Clerical Officers
1 Clerical Assistant

15. Tourism and Trade

Minister

In my private and constituency offices there is

1 Higher Executive Officer,
2 Executive Officers and
4 Clerical Assistants.

I have also

1 Programme Manager,
1 Personal Assistant,
1 Personal Secretary and
1 Special Adviser.

Minister of State

1 Higher Executive Officer and
3 Clerical Assistants of whom 2 are job-sharing.

Also

1 Personal Assistant,
1 Personal Secretary,
1 Special Adviser and
2 Drivers.

16. Transport, Energy & Communications

Minister

Number	*Grade/title*	*Constituency office/ private office*	*Employment status*
1	Political Adviser	Private	Non-civil servant
1	Partnership Programme Manager	Private	Non-civil servant
1	Personal Secretary	Constituency	Non-civil servant
1	Private Secretary	Private	Civil servant
2	Executive Officer	Private	Civil servant
1	Staff Officer	Constituency	Civil servant
2	Clerical Officer	Constituency	Civil servant
3	Clerical Officer	Private	Civil servant
3	Clerical Assistant/ Typist	Both	Civil servant
TOTAL 15			

Minister of State

Number	*Grade/title*	*Constituency office/ private office*	*Employment status*
1	Special Adviser	Both	Non-civil servant
1	Personal Secretary	Constituency	Non-civil servant
1	Personal Assistant	Constituency	Non-civil servant
1	Private Secretary	Private	Civil servant
1	Executive Officer	Private	Civil servant
2	Clerical Officer	Constituency	Civil servant
1	Clerical Assistant	Private	Civil servant
2	Clerical Assistant/ Typist	Both	Civil servant
TOTAL 10			

3

THE DÁIL AND THE SEANAD

The Constitution provides that the national parliament be known as the Oireachtas and it consists of the President and two Houses, namely Dáil Éireann and Seanad Éireann. The Oireachtas has the sole power of making laws, but any law repugnant to the Constitution may be annulled by the Supreme Court. It may not declare acts to be infringements of the law which were not so at the time of their commission. The Dáil and the Seanad must hold at least one session each year, and sittings must be public. In an emergency, however, either House may decide, with the agreement of two-thirds of the members present, to sit in private. Each House elects its own chairman, designated Ceann Comhairle in the case of the Dáil and Cathaoirleach in the case of the Seanad, and deputy chairman (Leas-Ceann Comhairle and Leas-Cathaoirleach) and determines its own rules and standing orders. Each House also determines its own quorum – twenty for the Dáil and twelve for the Seanad. Members have the privilege of immunity from arrest in going to and coming from either House, and are not answerable to any court or authority other than the House itself for any remark make within either House. No person may be at the same time a member of both Houses.

The Dáil

Membership

Membership of the Dáil is open to citizens over the age of twenty-one. Members of the judiciary, civil service, defence forces and the Garda Síochána are ineligible, as are persons undergoing prison sentences and undischarged bankrupts.

The total number of deputies is fixed by law, though the Constitution specifies that this number may not be less than one for every 30,000 of the population or more than one for 20,000. The twenty-eighth Dáil has 166 members.

Deputies represent constituencies also fixed by law, and the constituencies must be revised at least every twelve years in the light of population changes. The Constitution provides that the ratio between the numbers to be elected

Dáil Éireann

for each constituency and the population of each constituency is to be as far as practicable the same throughout the country. In practice, constituencies are revised on the publication of the results of each census of population (normally every fifth year). The practice is for the government to set up an independent commission, presided over by a judge of the High Court, to recommend a revised scheme of constituencies which may or may not be accepted by the Dáil when submitted to it.

The Ceann Comhairle of the previous Dáil is returned automatically as a member.

Elections and Convening

Members are elected under a system of proportional representation (PR) by means of a single transferable vote, and no constituency may have fewer than three members. (An extract from a government publication describing the system is given in Appendix 3.)

The Constitution provides that no Dáil may continue for more than seven years and that a shorter period may be fixed by law. Such shorter period has, in fact, been fixed and is five years. The Minister for the Environment determines the date of the poll when the President has dissolved the Dáil. A general election must take place not later than thirty days after a dissolution, and the new Dáil must meet within thirty days of polling day. (An example of the PR system in operation in a representative constituency is given in the official return reproduced in Appendix 4.)

When the votes have been counted at a general election, the person responsible for the conduct of the election in each constituency (who is called the returning officer and is normally the county registrar) notifies the Clerk of the Dáil of those who have been elected. The Clerk then notifies each member to attend at Leinster House to sign the Roll of Members, in his presence. A member is not entitled to take his seat nor to be paid any allowance until he has signed the Roll.

The first business at the first meeting of the Dáil after the election is the reading by the Clerk of the proclamations of dissolution and convening, and then the names and constituencies of all the members elected. The Clerk acts as chairman until the Ceann Comhairle is elected.

Procedures

The Ceann Comhairle

The duties of the Ceann Comhairle are set out in elaborate detail in the standing orders of the Dáil. Broadly speaking, these are to preside over the sittings, to keep order, to call members to speak, to put questions to a vote if called for at the end of the debate, to enforce the rules of the debate, and generally to exercise supervision over the conduct of business. The Ceann Comhairle appoints a number of deputies who may preside when neither he nor the Leas-Ceann Comhairle is able to do so. These are called panel chairmen; they receive no extra remuneration.

The Ceann Comhairle, or the presiding chairman, has no vote except where there is equality of voting. He has then a casting vote, which he must exercise. The basis on which the casting vote is given is the usual one, namely maintenance of the status quo, thus providing an opportunity for review of the question at issue. In effect, this involves the Ceann Comhairle voting with the government of the day.

Standing Orders and Conventions

In the conduct of the day-to-day business the Ceann Comhairle relies greatly on the standing orders. These provide for the conduct of proceedings, the passage of bills, the rules of debate, the rules of financial procedures, the preservation of order, and the operation of committees. The Ceann Comhairle's rulings on the interpretation and application of these orders may not be questioned in the House, though members may bring complaints to the attention of the Committee on Procedure and Privileges (see p. 70). To ensure consistency in interpretation, a book containing rulings of the chair, i.e. a book of precedents, is kept, showing all rulings made by chairmen since the foundation of the state.

A member who behaves in a disorderly fashion may be suspended on a motion by the Ceann Comhairle. The duration of the suspension is determined by the frequency of the offence.

The standing orders are supplemented by conventions and practices. Many of these relate to the behaviour of members. For example, when the Ceann Comhairle rises to speak, any member then speaking must sit down; members must bow to the chair when passing to or from their seats in the chamber; they must address the chair; they are called on to speak at the discretion of the Ceann Comhairle; it is the practice that members are called upon in turn by party, with a preference for ministers and for leaders of the opposition parties. In general, members may speak once only in debate, though interventions not exceeding thirty seconds may be permitted in certain circumstances by the Ceann Comhairle. Words which may be deemed offensive or disorderly may not be used; imputations of improper motives and personal reflections on members are regarded as disorderly. Members who persist in irrelevance or repetition may be ordered by the chair to stop speaking, though ruling deputies out of order is extremely rare. Other conventions are that matters sub judice may be discussed in certain circumstances only, and that a member making a maiden speech is heard without interruption.

Debates

The Dáil has three sessions a year, from early October to Christmas, from about the third week in January to Easter and from after Easter to about the end of June. It meets on Tuesday at 2.30 p.m. and on Wednesday and Thursday at 10.30 a.m.

By convention, a minister or minister of state (not necessarily the minister whose business is being discussed) is present in the chamber throughout each debate. He is accompanied by officials whose task it is to assist him with matters that arise during the debate and to take notes of points raised by speakers for the use of the minister in the course of his reply. The disposition of members and officials is shown in the diagram opposite. The press gallery is situated behind the Ceann Comhairle, and the public galleries are behind the members. The business under discussion is shown on the indicator board in the chamber by reference to the number of the item on the order paper, and on closed-circuit television in all the principal areas of Leinster House, with the name of the member speaking, and in the case of a bill, the stage it has reached.

At the end of each day's sitting, members may bring forward matters which they wish to have discussed, by way of a five-minute speech. Four matters may be discussed under this arrangement and in each case a minister has five minutes to reply. The matters selected must, of course, relate to public affairs connected with government departments or to matters of administration for which a minister is responsible.

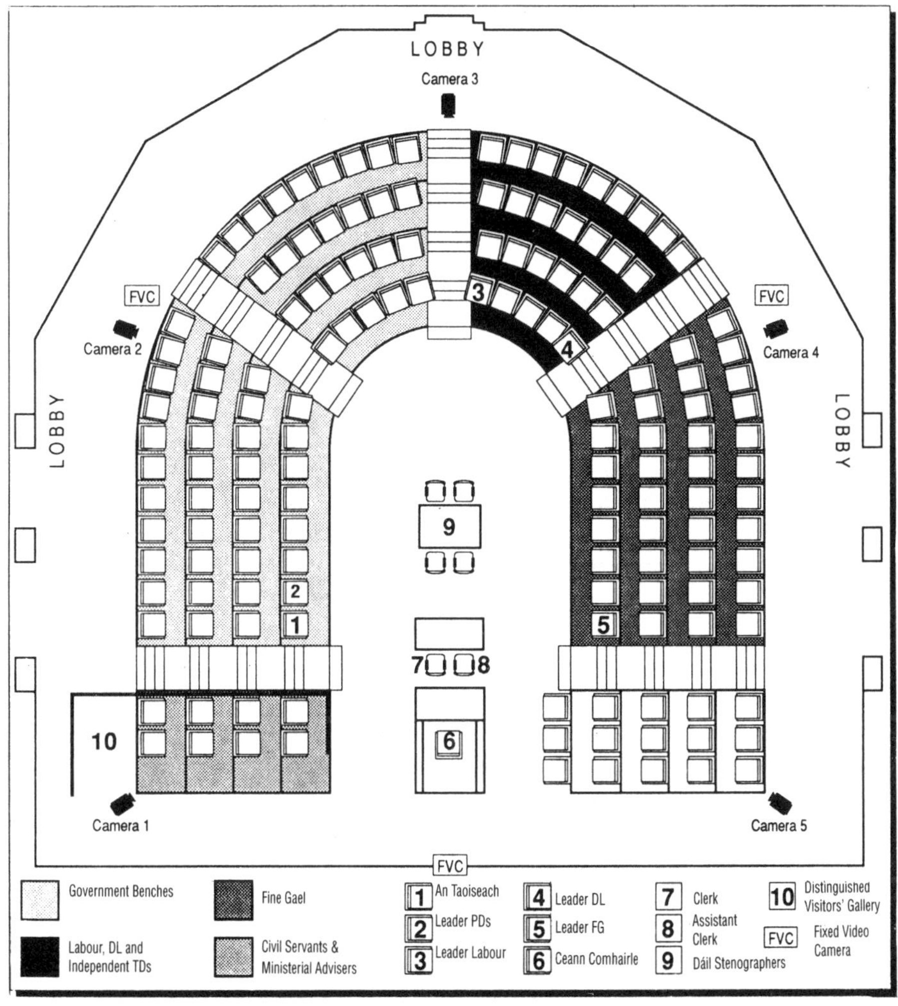

The Dáil Chamber
(June 1997)

When a vote is to take place, electric bells are rung for not less than four minutes in Leinster House and also in the offices of those ministers in the immediate vicinity, e.g. in Merrion Street and Kildare Street. The doors to the chamber are locked after a further four minutes and only those actually present may vote. Having gone up the steps facing camera 3, those voting for the government turn left and those opposing turn right into what are usually referred to as the Tá and Níl lobbies. Tellers are appointed by the government side and by the opposition, two for each, and they count the numbers entering each lobby. The result of the vote is brought to the Ceann Comhairle by the tellers for the lobby in which there was a higher vote. The Ceann Comhairle formally announces the result and then proceeds to the next business.

An official report of the debates of each House is published under the supervision of the Ceann Comhairle. These are periodically revised, collated, indexed, bound and published in volumes and are on sale at the Government Publications Sales Office. Minutes of the daily proceedings of each House are made by the Clerk. These include times of sittings, business transacted and related matters. Signed by the Ceann Comhairle, they are the permanent official record of the work of the Dáil and are referred to as the *journal of proceedings*.

Work of the Dáil

The work of the Dáil falls into four broad categories. The Dáil considers proposals for legislation initiated by ministers or by private members; it considers expenditure proposals presented by ministers; it debates motions; and it is a forum in which questions may be addressed to ministers.

Legislation

Proposals for legislation are initiated as bills. Bills fall into various categories: public bills (including private members' bills), private bills, consolidation bills, money bills and bills to amend the Constitution.

Public bills. By far the largest number of bills are public bills, i.e. bills for the benefit of the public as a whole, such as a bill to deal with broadcasting. Public bills may be initiated by either a minister or a private member. The majority of bills that become law are those initiated by ministers. Each bill has five stages, or readings, in the House in which it was initiated, i.e. it is considered on five separate occasions. (Bills other than money bills or bills to amend the Constitution can be introduced in either House.) The first of these stages is when the House is made aware that the bill is on the way. The title of the bill and a short description of its purpose appears on the order paper. This stage is normally a formality and evokes no debate. It leads to the fixing of a date for the second reading, when the minister deals with the general principles of the bill. He indicates why it is necessary and explains the reasons for each of its provisions. These explanations lead to a debate on what is proposed, including suggestions for improved or alternative means of achieving the ends sought. (Those seeking to know the background to any act should study the minister's speech introducing the second reading.) Opposition to the proposals in a bill is expressed by voting against it. Amendments are not permitted at this stage.

At the third (committee) stage the bill is considered in detail – section by section, even word by word – by a committee of the House. This stage is one of relative informality where members may speak more than once on the same aspect. Amendments may be made, to add, delete or substitute words, but these may not be in conflict with the principle of the bill as approved at the previous stage. Amendments to government bills are rarely accepted by ministers. If a bill is going to result in increased public expenditure, a special money resolution authorising such expenditure must be put forward by a minister and passed before committee stage. This is to show that the proposed expenditure has the authority of the government as provided for in the Constitution.

The bill is then 'reported' to the House as its fourth stage. Only amendments arising out of committee stage are in order. If no amendments are offered, there is no debate on the report stage.

The fifth stage is usually a formality, unless a bill is contentious. In that event there may be a debate similar to that which took place on the second reading. The stage is normally taken immediately after the report stage, and the question put to the Dáil is 'that the bill do now pass'. This means that in the case of a bill which has originated in the Dáil it goes to the Seanad for its consideration, or in the case of a bill which has originated in the Seanad it goes to the Dáil.

Another form of public bill is a *private member's bill*, which is a bill initiated by a member who is not a minister, usually a member of an opposition party, with the approval of his party. The party must have at least seven members. The title of the bill, and its purpose, appears on the order paper in the same way as a government bill, as its first stage. If introduction is opposed (in practice, this would be by the government), the member moving the bill has five minutes in which to explain its purpose and the member designated to oppose has five minutes in which to outline objections to it. After that there is a vote which determines whether the bill goes on to a second reading. If a bill is not opposed, the second reading is taken in private members' time, i.e. in the time set aside for business other than government-initiated business. Private members' business is usually dealt with between 7 p.m. and 8.30 p.m. on Tuesdays and Wednesdays. The time normally allowed for debate on the second reading is six hours. If it passes this reading, it is referred for its third reading to a special committee of the House in which it has been introduced. As mentioned earlier, a bill involving expenditure (as most bills do) cannot proceed beyond second stage without a positive money resolution from the government: that is, a resolution to provide the public funds, e.g. salaries or cost of equipment needed to give effect to whatever the bill provides for. Thus, if the money message or financial resolution is not put forward, a bill can, in effect, be made to lapse at this stage. If, however, the bill proceeds, the fourth and fifth stages are taken in government time.

Relatively few private members' bills are passed (although in recent times the number of successful bills has increased), because even if the government accepts the principle of the bill, it usually asks the member to withdraw it on an assurance that the government will itself introduce a measure, officially drafted, to meet the situation. The Judicial Separation and Family Law Reform Act, passed in December 1989, was the first successful private member's bill for thirty years.

When a public bill has been passed in the Dáil, it is sent to the Seanad, where it is regarded as having passed its first stage but is debated at the other stages in the same way as in the Dáil. If the Seanad makes amendments, or recommendations in the case of money bills, these are considered by the Dáil. If the Dáil does not agree with the amendments, the matter is reconsidered by the Seanad, which may decide whether or not to insist on them. If it decides to insist, the Dáil may, after a period of ninety days from the date on which the bill was first sent to the Seanad, pass a resolution deeming the bill to have been passed.

Private bills. These are bills dealing with special interests, such as those of a particular body or locality, as distinct from the public interest as a whole. An example of a private bill is the Limerick Marts Bill 1989, which was deposited in the Private Bill Office in December 1989 and subsequently referred to a select committee of the Dáil and Seanad. (The main purpose of this bill is to increase the number of commodities which may be sold in the Limerick market place and to give the trustees certain powers in relation to tolls, rents and disposal of premises.) The persons who wish to have a private bill passed, known as the promoters of the bill, engage a parliamentary agent (a practising solicitor) to undertake on their behalf the formalities prescribed under standing orders relating to the presentation of such a bill. These include the extensive advertising of its contents, as well as the notification of parties likely to be interested. A private bill is lodged with the Examiner of Private Bills – the Clerk of the Seanad. The bill is introduced in the Seanad at second stage, after which it is referred to a committee of both Houses, consisting of three deputies and three senators, none of whom may have a personal interest in the bill and, in the case of the deputies, none of whose constituents has a personal interest. The committee consults government departments, takes evidence from interested parties and hears counsel on behalf of the promoters and any objectors. The committee makes a report on the bill to both Houses and then sends it to the Seanad for consideration at fourth and fifth stages. After that it goes to the Dáil, also for fourth and fifth stages. It is then enacted in the same way as a public bill, i.e. it is signed by the President and becomes law. Fees must be paid to the state by both promoters and opponents of private bills.

Consolidation bills. These are bills to tidy up the law, i.e. they consolidate existing law. Where, for example, there have been a number of acts passed through the years, each amending and/or adding something to the law relating to a particular subject, it may be considered desirable, for ease of reference, to get all of the up-to-date provisions into one act. A consolidation bill does not contain any new legislative provision. After its second reading it is referred for examination to a joint committee of both Houses. The bill is then considered on fourth and fifth stages in the initiating House, after which it is sent to the other House, where the first, second and third stages are waived and it is considered on fourth and fifth stages only. Such bills are rare because neither ministers nor officials are enthusiastic about devoting scarce time to them unless there is a very obvious need and supporting pressure. The most recent consolidation act was the Social Welfare (Consolidation) Act 1993.

Money bills. These may be initiated in the Dáil only. They are bills which deal only with taxation, public debt, loans and such matters and are dealt with in the same way as public bills. When they go to the Seanad for consideration, that body has only twenty-one days to consider them, and it may make recommendations only; it cannot amend them. If a money bill is not returned within twenty-one days, or is returned with recommendations which the Dáil does not accept, it is deemed to have been passed by the Dáil at the end of that time.

Bills to amend the Constitution. Any proposal to amend the Constitution must first be passed in the form of a bill, which may not contain any other proposal. Such a bill may be initiated in the Dáil only. When passed there, it is considered in the Seanad in the same way as a public bill.

Financial Procedures

Article 28.4.3 of the Constitution obliges the government to prepare estimates of receipts and of expenditure for each year and to present these to the Dáil. The document containing these estimates, which is known as the White Paper on receipts and expenditure, is usually published by the Department of Finance on the weekend before the annual budget, which as from November 1997 will be in November each year. In his annual budget statement the Minister for Finance outlines, among other things, his taxation proposals for the years ahead. As it is desirable that some of these, such as excise duties on petrol or tobacco, come into operation on the day they are made public, the proposals are voted upon on budget day. They are put forward in the form of budget resolutions which, under the Provisional Collection of Taxes Act 1927, have immediate effect and continue in operation for up to four months from the date of passing. The main debate on the budget proposals continues over a number of weeks. When it is concluded, the Finance Bill is introduced by the Minister for Finance. Its enactment gives final legislative effect to the taxation measures in the budget. The Dáil, through a number of select committees, then considers the estimate for each individual department, which is presented by its minister. In his speech the minister reviews the work of his department in the previous year, outlines his programme for the year ahead and explains the need for the money he is seeking. The estimates are presented in the form of a number of spending items called subheads, which enumerate clearly the various items of expenditure. Thus in all departments the A subheads represent the administrative costs, viz. pay, travel, equipment, postal and telephone expenses, etc. The other letters of the alphabet are used for the specific needs of individual departments. When the Dáil has approved the expenditure of the total sum, the estimate then becomes known as the vote for the relevant department. (See Appendix 5 for the estimate for the Department of the Marine for 1997.)

Under the terms of the Central Fund (Permanent Provisions) Act 1965, the Minister for Finance is empowered to make available to a department four-fifths of the sum which it had in the year before, to enable it to carry out its work, i.e. to enable public services to be carried on during that part of the year when the estimates for these services are being considered. When the estimates for all departments have been agreed by the Dáil, normally by May or June of each year, the Minister for Finance introduces the Appropriation Bill to give statutory effect to the individual estimates for each department and to transfer moneys voted for them.

If in the course of a year a minister finds that for some unforeseen reason he needs more money to run his department than the Dáil has allowed under the procedures described above, he must seek the Dáil's approval of a supplementary estimate. The debate on this occasion is confined to a discussion of the particular items for which the extra money is being sought. Up to recently, the expenditure of each department was voted on an annual basis. It is planned, however, to move to a position where individual departmental spending allocations over a three-year time-frame will be decided upon and presented in the budget.

Motions

A motion is a proposal made by a member (a minister or an ordinary TD) to do something, order something to be done or express an opinion with regard to some matter. It must be phrased in such a way that, if passed, it will be seen to express the judgment or will of the House. Motions may be conveniently classified into (1) *substantive motions*, which are self-contained proposals drafted in such a way as to be capable of expressing the will of the House, for example the motion 'that Dáil Éireann approve the terms of the Convention on the Physical Protection of Nuclear Material done at Vienna on 26 October 1979, copies of which were laid before Dáil Éireann on 27 March 1990' (proposal of the Minister for Energy); and (2) *subsidiary motions*, which are purely procedural in character, such as 'that the debate be adjourned'.

Parliamentary Questions

Deputies may address questions to a minister about matters connected with his department or about public affairs for which he is officially responsible. There is no formal obligation on ministers to answer such questions, but in practice, they do so. One hour and three-quarters is set aside each sitting Tuesday and Wednesday and one hour and twenty minutes on Thursday for parliamentary questions.

The procedure is that a deputy submits his question in writing to the general office in the Dáil before 11 a.m. on the fourth preceding day for questions seeking an oral reply and on the third preceding day for questions nominated for priority and for written replies. The question is examined in the office (and ultimately by the Ceann Comhairle) to ensure that its purpose is genuinely to seek information or clarification on matters of fact or policy; that such information has not been provided within the preceding four months; that it contains no argument or personal imputation; that it does not deal with a matter which is sub judice; and that it does not seek to anticipate a matter of which the Dáil has been given notice on which the Ceann Comhairle is satisfied a debate will take place within a reasonable time.

Questions for oral reply may be divided into three main categories: questions nominated for priority, questions not so nominated and private notice questions. Priority questions are confined to groups in opposition (parties of not less than seven members), and no more than five such questions may be tabled to any minister. The party decides what questions may be tabled in any one day, what questions are to be designated as priority and the members in whose names they are to be asked. Only the members in whose names the questions are tabled may ask *supplementary questions* seeking elaboration of the information provided in the answer to the question. Although a member of the government may group questions put down for oral answer and questions put down for written answer for the purposes of reply, he is not permitted to group priority questions with other oral questions.

Private notice questions must relate to matters of urgent public importance. They may be tabled up to 2.30 p.m. and, given the time constraints, do not appear on the order paper.

Oral questions are answered by ministers on a rota system. Under this system, ministers present themselves in the Dáil in sequence to answer the questions addressed to them. This means that each minister answers oral questions about once in every five weeks. Where a question put down for oral answer is of such a nature as to require a lengthy reply, or a reply in the form of a tabular statement, the minister may not wish to answer it orally. In such a situation the Ceann Comhairle must accept a request from the minister that the answer be provided in the official report for that day. The deputy gets a copy of the reply in advance of publication.

In addition to the questions to which deputies seek an oral reply (so that they may ask a supplementary question to press for additional information if not satisfied with the reply), deputies also ask questions for written reply. The vast majority of these written questions relate to constituents' problems, such as when payments are expected to be made under social welfare and grant schemes of various kinds.

Presentation of Documents

Many kinds of documents are presented to the Dáil under the provisions of legislation, for example the annual reports and accounts of state-sponsored bodies and statutory regulations made by ministers. Rarely are these documents debated. Statutory regulations may, however, be revoked by the passage of a resolution to that effect, but such a resolution is also rare. The purpose of presenting these documents is to make their existence known and to make them available in the library for interested members of the Oireachtas.

Dáil Reform

In recent years there has been considerable criticism from academics, other interested observers and politicians themselves about the procedures and practices under which the Dáil conducts its business. These have been generally regarded as belonging to another, more leisurely age, having been largely adopted from those obtaining in the British parliament at the time of the foundation of the Irish state. The accepted view is that there has been a failure to adapt and develop the system so that it reflects adequately the changes that have taken place over the past few decades. C.H. Murray, a former secretary of the Department of Finance, writes: 'It is doubtful whether a parliamentary Rip Van Winkle who was familiar with the Dáil procedures of 1922 would discern any major changes in the Dáil procedures of 1989' (Murray 1990: 149).

In considering what changes should be made, all commentators are conscious of individual deputies' perception of their role. In general, the latter do not see this as helping to formulate policy by contributing to debates on legislation, as monitoring the performance of ministers and public bodies and as giving leadership to the community. They regard themselves mainly as welfare officers for their constituents, and as having a need to preserve their image with a view to protecting their seats. They are forced into this situation largely because of the multi-seat proportional representation system, which generates competition not only between deputies of different parties but between deputies of the same party. The system places a premium on welfare politics as each candidate seeks to woo the constituent. Gemma Hussey, a former Minister for Education and for Social Welfare, noted: 'Dáil sittings merely interrupt the business of the TDs in looking after their constituents rather than being the central part of their political lives' (*The Irish Times*, 16 August 1989). A backbench TD is recorded as acknowledging that the existing electoral system leads to mediocrity, which inevitably affects the quality of debate in the Dáil chamber. What we need, he said, 'in order to free TDs to carry out more work at parliamentary level is a different electoral system' (*Irish Independent*, 15 December 1989). On the other hand, Pádraig Flynn, when Minister for the Environment, in response to Mrs Hussey's comments, said: 'I am wary of calls for reform which would depersonalise the process of political representation so that our TDs and ministers were dealing only with issues and concepts and large umbrella groups.'

Proposals for Reform

The most recent proposals for the reform of Dáil procedures are contained in the report of a subcommittee of the Committee on Procedure and Privileges, published in June 1996. These relate in the main to the standing orders and more specifically to the procedures regarding the presentation of legislation and the debates thereon, Dáil divisions, Dáil committees, parliamentary questions, televising/broadcasting debates and members' privileges. Agreed changes in existing procedures are being made.

The Seanad

The theoretical case for having a bicameral legislature is that the upper House (Seanad Éireann) provides (1) a system of checks and balances on the main legislative chamber; (2) representation for particular areas or interest groups; (3) an additional input of expertise into policy formation and legislation. The Constitution of 1937 introduced a new concept, that of a vocational Seanad, to draw on the knowledge of persons from a wide range of vocations. The concept has remained merely a concept, since, in practice, the emphasis in the election of members is on political affiliation rather than on professional knowledge.

The Seanad has no independent life. An election for the Seanad must take place not later than ninety days after dissolution of the Dáil, and the first meeting of the new Seanad takes place on a day fixed by the President on the advice of the Taoiseach. Outgoing senators hold their seats until the day before polling day for the new Seanad.

Seanad Éireann

Membership

The Seanad is provided for in Articles 18 and 19 of the Constitution. The same conditions apply in relation to eligibility for membership as in the case of the Dáil. The Seanad consists of sixty members, of whom forty-nine are elected and eleven are nominated by the Taoiseach. Of the forty-nine elected members, forty-three are selected from vocational panels of candidates. Of the remaining six, three represent the National University of Ireland and three the University of Dublin.

The five vocational panels contain the names of persons having knowledge and practical experience of:

(1) the national language and culture, literature, art, education, law and medicine;
(2) agriculture, fisheries and allied interests;
(3) labour matters;
(4) industry and commerce;
(5) public administration and social services.

Each panel is divided into two sub-panels. One of these (the Oireachtas sub-panel) contains the names of candidates nominated by not less than four members of the Houses of the Oireachtas. The other (the nominating bodies' sub-panel) contains the names of those nominated by bodies on the register of nominating bodies. The method of compilation and revision of the register, and the provisions relating to eligibility, are laid down in the Seanad Electoral (Panel Members) Acts 1947 to 1960. The register is the responsibility of the Clerk of the Seanad.

The electorate for the forty-three members from the panels consists of the members of the Dáil, Seanad, county and borough councils, a total of about 960, all of whom are practising politicians. Election is by proportional representation and by secret ballot. Appendix 6 reproduces an extract from *Seanad General Election, 1997* which shows the voting for candidates on the administrative panel in that year.

The six university representatives are elected by the graduates of the two universities indicated. This provision has frequently been criticised as being curiously out of date in the present day. Apart from its overtones of elitism, there is a considerable imbalance in the two electorates. The National University, with four constituent colleges, had in 1993 an electorate of about 81,240, while the University of Dublin has one constituent college only (Trinity College) and an electorate of 22,549. Furthermore, the two new universities established in 1989, Dublin City University and the University of Limerick, do not have representation in the Seanad.

The nomination of eleven members by the Taoiseach under Article 18.3 of the Constitution enables persons of special calibre to reach parliament without going through the electoral process. The Taoiseach, however, tends to nominate party candidates who failed to get elected in the preceding Dáil election, those who seem to stand a good chance of being elected at the next Dáil election or persons who have worked well for the party over the years. As well as rewarding the worthy, this helps to strengthen the voting power of the government party (or parties) in the Seanad.

Functions

While the Seanad does have a role in initiating legislation, relatively few bills (though the number is increasing) begin their life in the upper House. Traditionally, the main function of the Seanad has been to review legislation passed by the Dáil. In practice, however, the Seanad exerts no significant control on the business of the Dáil. Bills passed by the Dáil are normally passed by the Seanad and it is only occasionally that it suggests any significant amendment. This is because the manner of electing senators results in the Seanad having the same political complexion as the Dáil. While those elected by the universities are seldom members of any political party, and are therefore independent, the vast majority of the remainder are, inevitably, members of one or other of the political parties.

The low level of Seanad activity has sometimes been adversely commented upon. The number of days on which the Seanad was in session in each of the years 1986–96 is as follows: 78 in 1986; 47 in 1987; 63 in 1988; 42 in 1989; 61 in 1990; 68 in 1991; 68 in 1992; 64 in 1993; 52 in 1994; 75 in 1995; 73 in 1996. Clearly, the upper House is neither overused nor overworked, and this has led to a questioning of the need for such a body, almost since the beginning of the state. Speaking in the Dáil in 1928, Seán Lemass expressed his party's belief that the Seanad should be abolished, and declared that, failing this, it should be 'a group of individuals who dare not let a squeak out of them except when we [the Dáil] lift our fingers to give them the breath to do it'; he also concurred with the description of the ideal Seanad as 'a penny-in-the-slot machine' (Dáil Debates, 14 June 1928, col. 614). Subsequently, in the 1930s there was a long-drawn-out feud between Eamon de Valera's government and the Seanad, culminating in its abolition in 1936. It is clear that in the formulation of the 1937 Constitution Mr de Valera had serious doubts about the desirability of having an upper House at all, or at least of giving it any effective role in legislation.

In 1966 a committee of nine TDs and three senators was set up to review the constitutional, legislative and institutional bases of government. It reported in 1967 and in regard to the Seanad it recommended, in essence, no change in the status quo.

In more recent years there have been calls to make changes in the manner of electing the Seanad and to find ways to make it more effective. Indeed one of the parties in the government formed in 1997, the Progressive Democrats, openly supports the abolition of the Seanad. These calls, however, receive very little support from politicians generally.

In April 1995 the government established a Review Group under the chairmanship of Dr T.K. Whitaker to review the Constitution. Its report, made in May 1996, recommended 'a separate, comprehensive, independent examination of all issues relating to Seanad Éireann'. For this reason, it made no substantive or technical recommendations relating to the Seanad. The government established an all-party committee on the Constitution to consider the Review Group's report. The all-party committee commissioned a report, *Options for the Future of Seanad Éireann*, from John Coakley, Department of Political Science, University College, Dublin, and Michael Laver, Department of Political Science, Trinity College, Dublin. This report observed that 'There is a case for looking carefully at the capacity of the Seanad to act as a voice for special groups that might otherwise be kept at a distance from Irish political life, such as representatives of the Irish abroad, and of marginal groups within Irish society'.

The all-party committee's own report on the Seanad, published in April 1997, commented: 'The Committee is persuaded by the argument in Coakley/Laver that the Seanad does make a useful contribution to the democratic life of the state. The Committee also agrees with Coakley/Laver that the Seanad is a resource that could be deployed for greater effect if it were reformed.'

It concluded that, on balance, the Seanad should continue to exist but that a fresh innovative approach needed to be taken to what the Seanad should do and who the senators should be. It also concluded that the proper function of the Seanad is to act as a consultative body where people with knowledge, experience and judgment over the whole spectrum of public affairs should be available in a broadly non-partisan way to help the Dáil to carry out its functions more effectively and efficiently. It went on to identify a number of tasks which the Seanad could undertake to increase the productivity of the legislative process. It could carry out special reviews of government programmes, debate policy reports and maintain a focus on Northern Ireland relationships, thus enriching the political system by helping the Dáil.

The committee then made recommendations in regard to the composition of the Seanad, that membership should remain at sixty, that there should be directly and non-directly elected members, that some should be elected by the incoming Dáil and some by county councils, that there should be provision for gender balance and that the Taoiseach should retain the power of appointing eleven senators.

This report of the all-party Oireachtas committee is under examination.

The Infrastructure

Oireachtas Committees

The Oireachtas has established a number of committees to deal with aspects of its work. Some of these are joint committees; others contain members of the Dáil only. Party representation on committees is determined by reference to their relative strengths in the Houses. Generally, committees are set up to do work for which either House, as a large assembly, would not be suited, for example detailed inquiry or the examination of witnesses. They may engage any legal, economic or financial consultants they require to assist them in their work. Committees have not the power to make decisions in their own right. They prepare reports on the matters they have examined for presentation to the Oireachtas and for publication.

The development of the committee system provides greater opportunities for deputies and senators to become involved in all aspects of the parliamentary process. The committees are formed early in the lifetime of each new Dáil and Seanad. The number and range of committees have expanded greatly in recent years, enabling the Houses to deal in a detailed manner with an ever-increasing range and complexity of business. Most committees meet in public session throughout the year, save for August, and may be attended by members of the public.

There are three broad categories of committee: namely, standing, select and special. Standing committees include the Committee on Selection (to nominate members to sit on all committees), the Committee on Procedure and Privileges, and the Committee on Public Accounts, which reports on the accounts prepared by the Comptroller and Auditor General on the manner in which moneys granted by the Dáil to meet public expenditure have been spent – this is, perhaps, the most important committee of all. Other standing committees are the Joint Committee on Consolidation Bills, already referred to, the Broadcasting Committee, and the Liaison Committee, which allocates funds to the other committees for travel, consultancy and so on. Standing orders require that the standing committees be set up as soon as possible after each general election.

On the other hand, select committees are set up at the discretion of the House and vary as to number and type. In general, they are investigatory or legislative and deal either with a specialised subject that is referred to them by the Dáil or with the committee stages of bills. The terms of reference of some select committees may give them powers to send for persons, papers or records under the provisions of the Committees of the Houses of the Oireachtas (Compellability, Privileges and Immunities of Witnesses) Act 1997. This act provides a substantial increase in committee powers to require

Joint Committee of the Houses of the Oireachtas

witnesses to attend hearings and to respond to questions. As a corollary of this increase in powers there are concepts of privilege and immunity. Accordingly, committees are able to grant witnesses who are compelled to give evidence before them the equivalent of High Court privilege.

Special committees are set up to consider a particular bill at its third, or committee, stage. These committees cease to exist when their work has been completed and a report made to the Dáil. In recent years, however, the practice is to refer bills to select committees responsible for a particular area of government activity.

Joint committees are, essentially, select committees of each House, sitting and voting together. They are set up for specific purposes, for example to oversee the administration and provision of services to both Houses. A joint committee may also function as a specialised committee of experts, for example the Joint Committee on European Affairs.

The committee system is a feature of parliamentary life in many countries, including the USA and several member states of the European Community. The system has, however, come late to Ireland, and it is not clear that members of the Oireachtas yet view participation in the work of parliamentary committees as an integral part of their work. Owing to the priority given by TDs to constituency work with a view to re-election, relatively little importance is attached to service on parliamentary committees, which is of little help in that connection; and this attitude may be responsible for the low numbers of deputies interested in such work, and for the small amount of time they are prepared to devote to it.

No formal evaluation of the cost or worth of the committee system has yet been made public. Advantages generally put forward are that it provides a more relaxed atmosphere with more give and take than obtains in the House itself, where contributions are largely adversarial in nature, and that it enables members to acquire a detailed knowledge of the subject at issue and to discuss it in a minute way.

Remuneration; Expenses; Pensions

The remuneration paid to each deputy, senator and office holder is referred to in the relevant legislation – the Oireachtas (Allowances to Members) and the Ministerial and Parliamentary Offices Acts – as an 'allowance'. The allowances are subject to review from time to time by the Review Body on Higher Remuneration in the Public Sector, which makes recommendations to the government about their appropriate level. The pay rounds, applied on a general basis to the civil service, are normally applied to members of the Oireachtas.

Members of the Dáil and Seanad receive supplementary payments to cover the costs of travel on official business (e.g. to and from meetings of the Houses or committee meetings). These payments are normally by way of mileage allowance for car transport at the rates prevailing for civil servants. However, members who live within ten miles of Leinster House are paid a flat rate travel allowance in lieu of mileage payments. An overnight allowance is payable to members who live more than twenty miles from Dublin. Members receive allowances towards the cost of renting accommodation for and advertising constituency clinics; for the use of their own telephones; and towards the expense involved in establishing and maintaining an office in their constituency.

Official cars with drivers (members of the Garda Síochána) are supplied to the Taoiseach, ministers, the Attorney General and the Ceann Comhairle. The cars are available for private use as if they were the office holders' own cars, but may be used only with their official drivers. The benefit deriving from the private use of these cars is taken into account by the Review Body in determining remuneration. Ministers of state, the Leas-Ceann Comhairle and the Cathaoirleach provide their own cars and are paid mileage allowances for official travel in these cars. In these cases, civilian drivers are engaged by the office holders themselves; the drivers are paid by the state.

Pension schemes apply to members of both Houses, depending on age and length of service.

Allowances to Parties

Under the Ministerial and Parliamentary Offices Act 1938 and the Oireachtas (Allowances to Members) Act 1960, allowances for party expenses are paid to the leaders of political parties which contested the previous general election as organised political parties and had not less than seven members elected.

Secretarial Assistance

Ministers have offices in their departments and in Leinster House. They are assisted in all of their work – parliamentary, departmental, constituency and social – by the civil service. Each deputy has one secretarial assistant, whose salary is paid by the state. Some deputies choose to have their secretaries located in Oireachtas premises, while others prefer to locate them in their constituency offices. Secretarial assistance for senators is on the basis of one secretary for every three senators.

Since the secretaries of deputies devote most, if not all, of their time to constituency work, it follows that any research has to be carried out by the deputies themselves, with voluntary assistance from party supporters. Apart from the library, there is a marked absence of research facilities available to members.

Each deputy and senator is allowed 1,500 ordinary prepaid envelopes each month, which they may post in Leinster House. They also enjoy free telephone facilities, including a constituency telephone allowance of £2,000.

Staff

The staff in the Houses of the Oireachtas are civil servants, but with a legal distinction from the civil servants who serve ministers in government departments. Because they are under the control of the chairmen of the Dáil and Seanad, rather than under that of ministers as other civil servants are, they are properly referred to as *civil servants of the state* under the Staff of the Houses of the Oireachtas Act 1959. The total number of staff is about 240.

The most senior official in each House is called the Clerk of that House, and his deputy is called the Clerk Assistant. These officials are appointed by the Taoiseach on the nomination of the appropriate chairman and the Minister for Finance. The other senior staff are also designated clerks, e.g. principal clerk, committee clerk, etc. The latter officials are interchangeable and are generally referred to as the joint staff of the Houses of the Oireachtas.

The staff includes a Superintendent of the Houses and a Captain of the Guard. Their duties are not prescribed, but, broadly speaking, the former is responsible for members' accommodation and security. The latter is a uniformed officer who can remove disorderly members at the request of the Ceann Comhairle or Cathaoirleach. It rarely comes to this, however, since such offenders usually leave voluntarily when called upon to do so.

Also on the staff is an editor of debates and a number of reporters. As it is stipulated that all acts of the Oireachtas, the daily order paper, the journal of proceedings and other official documents must be published in both Irish and English, the staff also includes several translators. The Public Relations Office provides a service for the Houses of the Oireachtas as a whole, including information for interest groups, schools and members of the public.

Accommodation

Most of the business of the Oireachtas is carried out in Leinster House. In recent years, however, because of the increased use of committees, and the increase in the numbers of secretarial staff, some of the work is now done in buildings adjacent – in the former College of Science in Merrion Street and in the former College of Art in Kildare Street.

Members of the public may gain access to Leinster House only on introduction by a member of either House. This necessitates contacting a member and asking him to make arrangements for access. This having been done, the person may enter in the company of the member, or, more frequently, the member authorises the issue of an admission ticket to the public gallery which is available from the usher's office. A special gallery is reserved for the press, and another for distinguished visitors (indicated in the diagram on p. 57).

REFERENCES

Hussey, Gemma, *At the Cutting Edge: Cabinet Diaries, 1982–87* (Dublin: Gill & Macmillan, 1990)

Murray, C.H., *The Civil Service Observed* (Dublin: Institute of Public Administration, 1990)

APPENDIX 3

Election to the Dáil

Electorate

Every Irish citizen and British citizen over eighteen years who is ordinarily resident in a constituency and whose name appears on the register of electors is entitled to vote at a Dáil election in that constituency. Each elector has one vote only. A new register of electors is compiled by the local county council and county borough corporation and comes into force on 15 February each year. A draft register is published on 1 November each year and is displayed for public inspection in post offices, libraries and other public buildings. Claims for corrections in the register may be made up to 25 November. Claims are adjudicated on by the county registrar who is a legally qualified court officer. There are 2,707,498 Dáil electors on the register for the year 1997/98.

The following categories of elector may vote by post:

- members of the Garda Síochána,
- members of the Defence Forces,
- civil servants (and their spouses) attached to Irish missions abroad,
- persons with a physical illness or disability living at home who are unable to go to a polling station to vote, and
- electors whose service or employment means they are unlikely to be able to get to their local polling station on election day.

Electors with a physical illness or disability living in a hospital, nursing home etc., and who are unable to get to their local polling station may apply for entry on the special voters list in order to vote in the institution concerned. A ballot paper is delivered to such electors by a special presiding officer, accompanied by a member of the Garda Síochána.

General Elections

A general election must be held within thirty days after the dissolution of the Dáil. The Clerk of the Dáil issues a writ to the returning officer in each constituency instructing him/her to hold an election of the prescribed numbers of members. The returning officer is the county registrar except in the county and county boroughs of Cork and Dublin, where the Sheriff is the returning officer. The Ceann Comhairle (chairman of the Dáil) is automatically returned without an election unless he/she signifies that he/she does not wish to continue as a member. The latest time for nominating a person as a candidate is twelve noon on the ninth day after the issue of the writs.

The Minister for the Environment fixes the date of the poll, which must be between the seventeenth and the twenty-fifth day after the issue of the writs (Sundays and bank holidays are not reckoned). He/she fixes the hours of polling, which must be for a period of not less than twelve hours between 8.00 a.m. and 10.30 p.m.

Nomination of Candidates

A candidate may nominate himself/herself or be nominated by a Dáil elector for the constituency. A deposit of IR£300 must be lodged in respect of each candidate. The deposit is refunded if the candidate withdraws, is elected, or if the highest number of votes he/she receives exceeds one-quarter of the quota (see below for explanation of the 'quota'). A candidate may include a party affiliation in the nomination paper which will then appear opposite his/her name on the ballot paper. The party concerned must be entered in the register of political parties maintained by the Clerk of the Dáil which contains particulars of each party which has applied for registration and satisfied the Clerk that it is a genuine political party, organised to contest elections. Alternatively, a candidate may describe himself/herself as 'non-party' or leave the appropriate space blank.

The returning officer must rule on the validity of a nomination paper within one hour of its presentation. He/she is required to object to the name of a candidate if it is not the name by which the candidate is commonly known, if it is misleading and likely to cause confusion, or if it is unnecessarily long or contains a political reference. He/she is also required to object to the description of a candidate which is, in his/her opinion, incorrect, insufficient to identify the candidate or unnecessarily long. The candidate or the returning officer may amend the particulars shown on the nomination paper. The returning officer may rule a nomination paper invalid only if it is not properly made out or is unsigned.

The Poll

Polling places are appointed by county councils or county borough corporations, subject to the approval of the Minister for the Environment. The returning officer provides polling stations at each polling place. Usually schools or other public buildings are used. The returning officer is responsible for organising the poll, printing the ballot papers and counting the votes in each constituency. He/she must send a polling card to each voter, except a postal or special voter, stating the elector's number on the register and the polling station at which he/she may vote. The returning officer sends ballot papers to the postal voters by post and encloses special envelopes for the return of their votes. He/she arranges to have ballot papers delivered to the hospital, nursing home etc., of electors entered on the special voters list. The ballot paper envelopes are placed unopened in a ballot box when returned to the returning officer. Each polling station is supervised by a presiding officer assisted by a polling clerk. A candidate may be represented at a polling station by an agent who assists in the prevention of electoral offence. Before being given a ballot paper, an elector may be asked to produce evidence of identity.

Voting

Voting is by secret ballot and on the system of proportional representation, each elector having one transferable vote. The names of candidates appear in alphabetical order on the ballot paper. The voter indicates the order of his/her choice by writing 1 opposite the name of his/her first choice and, if he/she so wishes, 2 opposite the name of his/her second choice, 3 opposite the name of his/her third choice, and so on. He/she then places the ballot paper in a sealed ballot box. In this way the voter instructs the returning officer to transfer his/her vote to his/her second choice candidate if his/her first choice receives more than the quota of votes necessary for election or is excluded (through receiving so few votes as to have no chance of election). If the same applies to his/her second choice, the vote may be transferred to his/her third choice, and so on.

Counting the Votes

Before the counting of votes begins, the envelopes containing the postal and special voters' ballot papers are opened in the presence of the agents of the candidates and the ballot papers are placed in an ordinary ballot box which is taken with all the other ballot boxes to a central counting place for each constituency. Agents of the candidates are permitted to attend at the counting.

The count commences at 9 a.m. on the day after polling day. Each ballot box is opened and the number of the ballot papers checked against a return furnished by each presiding officer. They are then thoroughly mixed and sorted according to the first preferences recorded for each candidate, invalid papers being rejected. The quota of votes, which is the minimum necessary to guarantee the election of a candidate, is ascertained by dividing the total number of valid papers by the number of seats plus one and adding one to the result; e.g. if there were 40,000 valid papers and four seats to be filled, the quota would be 8,001 i.e.

$$\frac{40{,}000}{4+1} + 1 = 8{,}001$$

It will be seen that in this example only four candidates could possibly reach the quota.

At the end of the first count any candidate who has received a number of votes equal to or greater than the quota is deemed to be elected. If a candidate receives more than the quota, his/her surplus votes are transferred proportionately to the remaining candidates in the following way. If the candidate's votes are all first preference votes, all his/her ballot papers are sorted into separate parcels according to the next preference shown on them. A separate parcel is made of his/her non-transferable papers (papers on which a subsequent preference is not shown). Each remaining candidate then receives from the top of the appropriate parcel of transferable papers a number of votes calculated as follows:

$$\frac{\text{surplus}}{\text{total number of transferable papers}} \times \text{number of papers in that parcel}$$

If the surplus is equal to or greater than the number of transferable votes, each candidate will receive all the votes from the appropriate parcel of transferable papers.

If the surplus arises out of transferred papers, only the papers in the parcel last transferred to that candidate are examined, and this parcel is then treated in the same way as a surplus consisting of first preference votes. If two candidates exceed the quota, the larger surplus is distributed first.

If no candidate has a surplus, or the transferred surplus would not materially affect the progress of the count, the lowest of the remaining candidates is/are excluded and his/her/their papers are transferred to the other remaining candidates according to the next preference indicated on them. If a ballot paper is to be transferred and the second preference shown on it is for a candidate already elected or excluded, the vote passes to the third choice, and so on.

Counting continues until all the seats have been filled. If the position is reached where the number of seats left to be filled is equal to the number of candidates still running, these candidates are declared elected without having obtained the quota.

A returning officer may recount all or any of the papers at any stage of a count. A candidate or the election agent of the candidate is entitled to ask for a recount of the papers dealt with at a particular count or to ask for one complete recount of all parcels of ballot papers. When recounting, the order of the papers must not be disturbed. When an error is discovered which could change the persons elected, the papers must be counted afresh from the point at which the error occurred.

Results

Having publicly announced the results of the election, the returning officer endorses the names of the elected members on the writ issued by the Clerk of the Dáil. He/she then returns the writ to the Clerk of the Dáil.

Bye-elections

Casual vacancies in the membership of the Dáil are filled by bye-elections. On the instructions of the Dáil, the Clerk issues a writ to the returning officer for the constituency concerned, directing him/her to hold a bye-election to fill the vacancy. Procedure at a bye-election is the same as at a general election.

Source: Department of the Environment, July 1997.

APPENDIX 4

Dáil General Election Return: Dublin South, 1997
Electorate 87,994 – Total poll 54,646 – DÚN LAOGHAIRE

Seats 5 Quota 9,043	**1st Count**	**2nd Count** Transfer of **Barrett's** Surplus	**3rd Count** Transfer of **Stokes's**, **Allshire-Tyrrell's**, **Abum's**, **Tyaransen's** and **Madigan's** Votes	**4th Count** Transfer of **Casey's** Votes	**5th Count** Transfer of **MacDowell's** Votes	**6th Count** Transfer of **Andrews's** Surplus	**7th Count** Transfer of **Keogh's** Votes
ABUM, Jog Monster Raving Looney (Ind)	288	— 288	*–288* —				
ALLSHIRE-TYRRELL, Hazel (Ind)	53	— 53	*–53* —				
***ANDREWS**, David (FF)	**8,933**	***+7*** **8,940**	***+255*** **9,195**	— —	— —	***–152*** **9,043**	
BARNES, Monica (FG)	**7,576**	***+125*** **7,701**	***+244*** **7,945**	***+200*** **8,145**	***+633*** **8,778**	***+23*** **8,801**	***+1,056*** **9,857**
***BARRETT**, Seán (FG)	**9,223**	***–180*** **9,043**					
***BHREATHNACH**, Niamh (Lab)	4,698	*+21* 4,719	*+157* 4,876	*+71* 4,947	*+553* 5,500	*+9* 5,509	*+337* 5,846
CASEY, Gerard (CSP)	2,000	*+2* 2,002	*+91* 2,093	*–2,093* —			
***GILMORE,** Éamon (DL)	**7,534**	***+17*** **7,551**	***+268*** **7,819**	***+181*** **8,000**	***+949*** **8,949**	***+18*** **8,967**	***+414*** **9,381**
HANAFIN, Mary (FF)	**5,079**	***+1*** **5,080**	***+165*** **5,245**	***+953*** **6,198**	***+393*** **6,591**	***+77*** **6,668**	***+2,916*** **9,584**
***KEOGH**, Helen (PD)	4,636	*+4* 4,640	*+160* 4,800	*+175* 4,975	*+425* 5,400	*+25* 5,425	*–5,425* —
MacDOWELL, Vincent (GP)	2,762	*+2* 2,764	*+375* 3,139	*+315* 3,454	*–3,454* —		
MADIGAN, Paddy (Ind)	1,082	*+1* 1,083	*–1,083* —				
STOKES, Rory (Ind)	41	— 41	*–41* —				
TYARANSEN, Olaf Paul (Ind)	348	— 348	*–348* —				
Non-Transferable		—	98	198	501	—	702

* outgoing members of previous Dáil

APPENDIX 5

MARINE

I. Estimate of the amount required in the year ending 31 December 1997 for the salaries and expenses of the Office of the Minister for the Marine, including certain services administered by that Office, and for payment of certain grants and sundry grants-in-aid.
Sixty-one million and fifty-nine thousand pounds (£61,059,000)

II. Subheads under which this Vote will be accounted for by the Office of the Minister for the Marine.

	1996 Provisional Outturn £000	**1997 Estimate £000**	Change 1997 over 1996 %
Administration			
A.1. Salaries, wages and allowances	7,271	**7,992**	10
A.2. Travel and subsistence	697	**724**	4
A.3 Incidental expenses	496	**320**	–35
A.4. Postal and telecommunications services	248	**276**	11
A.5. Office machinery and other office supplies	243	**352**	45
A.6. Office premises expenses	190	**498**	162
A.7. Consultancy services	53	**70**	32
Sub-Total	*9,198*	***10,232****	11
Marine Safety, Environment and Shipping Services			
B.1. Marine emergency coastal units *(a)*	192	**236**	23
B.2. Development of coastal radio stations *(b)*	668	**718**	7
B.3. Marine emergency contingency	162	**20**	–88
B.4. Grant to Royal National Lifeboat Institution	100	**100**	–
B.5 Grant to Commissioners of Irish Lights (supplement to light dues) *(c)*	1,853	**2,015**	9
B.6. Marine Emergency Service *(d)*	5,926	**4,258**	–28
B.7. Wreck, salvage and relief of distressed seamen	–	**1**	–
B.8. Marine Environment Protection	17	**90**	429
C. Loran C Navigation System *(e)*	119	**286**	140
Sub-Total	*9,037*	*7,724*	*–15*

(a) Includes capital service 1996 £30,000; 1997 £31,000.
(b) Includes capital service 1996 £128,000; 1997 £255,000.
(c) The books and accounts of the grantee will be made available, if required, for examination by the Comptroller and Auditor General.
(d) Includes capital service 1996 £90,000; 1997 £240,000.
(e) Includes capital service 1996 £20,000; 1997 £250,000.

* Includes carry forward of savings of £315,000 under the terms of the Administrative Budget Agreement.

MARINE *(contd.)*	1996 Provisional Outturn £000	**1997 Estimate £000**	Change 1997 over 1996 %
Harbour Development and Coast Protection			
D.1. Grants for improvements at commercial, secondary and other harbours *(a)*	1,325	**4,100**	209
D.2. State harbours *(b)*	2,518	**3,657**	45
E. Coast protection *(c)*	852	**887**	4
Payment to Arklow Harbour Commissioners	60	–	–
Sub-Total	*4,755*	***8,644***	*82*
Marine Research			
F.1 Marine Institute administration and current development (grant-in-aid) *(d)*	4,051	**4,721**	17
F.2. Marine Institute capital development (grant-in-aid)	1,705	**3,626**	113
F.3. Salmon Research Agency (grant-in-aid) *(e)*	290	**153**	–47
Sub-Total	*6,046*	***8,500***	*41*
Sea Fisheries and Aquaculture Development			
G.1. Development and upgrading of harbours for fishery purposes including payments under the Fishery Harbour Centre Act, 1968 *(a)*	2,949	**2,929**	–1
G.2. Fishery Harbours Centre Fund – Grant under the Fishery Harbour Centres Act, 1968 *(f)*	245	**72**	–71
H.1. An Bord Iascaigh Mhara – administration and current development (grant-in-aid) *(g)*	4,840	**5,212**	8
H.2. An Bord Iascaigh Mhara – capital development (grant-in-aid) *(h)*	2,810	**2,590**	–8
H.3. Repayment of advances *(i)*	–	**1,250**	–
H.4. An Bord Iascaigh Mhara – PESCA Community Initiative (grant-in-aid) *(j)*	272	**468**	72
H.5. Special aid to the shellfish industry (grant-in-aid)	–	**1**	–
I.1. Repayments of compensation for fish withdrawals	–	**1**	–
I.2. Conservation and management of fisheries *(k)*	397	**1,330**	235

(a) Capital service.
(b) Includes capital service 1996 £168,000; 1997 Nil.
(c) Includes capital service 1996 £790,000; 1997 £785,000.
(d) Issues from the grant-in-aid will be made with the consent of the Minister for Finance. The accounts will be audited by the Comptroller and Auditor General and, together with his report thereon, will be laid before each House of the Oireachtas (No. 2 of 1991 Section 12).
(e) The books and accounts of the grantee are audited by the Comptroller and Auditor General.
(f) The accounts of the fund are audited by the Comptroller and Auditor General.
(g) Issues from the grant-in-aid will be made with the consent of the Minister for Finance. The Accounts will be audited by the Comptroller and Auditor General and, together with his report thereon, will be laid before each House of the Oireachtas (No. 7 of 1952 Section 5).
(h) Capital service. Further non-voted Exchequer capital expenditure by the Board, at £100,000 in 1996 and £55,000 in 1997, will be met by way of advances from the Central Fund.
(i) Capital service. Non-programme outlay.
(j) Includes capital service 1996 £88,000; 1997 £250,000.
(k) Includes capital service 1996 £283,000; 1997 £825,000.

MARINE *(contd.)*	1996 Provisional Outturn £000	**1997 Estimate £000**	Change 1997 over 1996 %
I.3. Fish processing *(a)*	241	**100**	–59
I.4. Programme for Peace and Reconciliation *(a)*	–	**200**	–
I.5. Shellfish Monitoring Programme	23	**55**	139
Sub-Total	*11,777*	***14,208***	*21*
Inland Fisheries			
J.1. Payments to the Central Fisheries Board, the Regional Fisheries Boards, the Foyle Fisheries Commission and miscellaneous payments in relation to inland fisheries	9,465	**9,876**	4
J.2. Tourism Angling Programme *(a)*	1,645	**4,570**	178
J.3. Payments in respect of inland fisheries development under Interreg II Programme *(a)*	215	**406**	89
J.4. Fisheries surveillance *(b)*	421	**1,204**	186
J.5. Expenditure in connection with the acquisition of fisheries and other property *(a)*	–	**1**	–
Sub-Total	*11,746*	***16,057***	*37*
Other Services			
K.1. Shipping investment grants *(a)*	–	**1**	–
K.2. Shipboard training of marine cadets	76	**172**	126
L.1. Pensions and allowances to seamen or their dependants and medical expenses of seamen (No. 19 of 1946)	59	**51**	–14
L.2. Ex-gratia payments to certain pensioners of Irish Shipping Ltd	39	**45**	15
L.3. Fund for the payment of ex-gratia awards to certain former employees of Irish Shipping Ltd *(c)*	4	**1**	–75
M. Commissions and Special Inquiries	41	**25**	–39
N. Subscriptions to international organisations	108	**129**	19
O. Technical Assistance Programme	74	**522**	–
Sub-Total	*401*	***946***	*136*
GROSS TOTAL	52,960	**66,311**	25
Deduct:			
P. Appropriations-in-aid (d)	4,567	**5,252**	15
NET TOTAL	48,393	**61,059**	26
		NET INCREASE (£000)	+12,666

(a) Capital service.
(b) Includes capital service 1996 £421,000; 1997 £858,000.
(c) Payments will be made in accordance with Irish Shipping Ltd (Payments to Former Employees) Act, 1994.
(d) Includes capital service receipts 1996 £65,000; 1997 £689,000.

MARINE *(contd.)*

	1996 Provisional Outturn £000	**1997 Estimate £000**
The total expenditure in connection with this Service is estimated as follows:		
Gross provisional outturn and estimate above	52,960	**66,311**
Estimated amounts included in the following Votes in connection with this Service:		
Vote		
7 Superannuation and Retired Allowances	9,701	**10,606**
9 Office of the Revenue Commissioners	140	**142**
10 Office of Public Works	514	**453**
15 Valuation and Ordnance Survey	60	**56**
Central Fund – Ministerial, etc., pension (No. 38 of 1938, etc.)	45	**76**
Total Expenditure	63,420	**77,644**
The receipts in connection with this Service are estimated as follows:		
Appropriations-in-aid above	4,567	**5,252**

III. Details of certain subheads

ADMINISTRATION

A.1. Salaries, wages and allowances:

Numbers 1996	Numbers 1997		1996 Provisional Outturn £000	**1997 Estimate £000**
177	179	Office of the Minister, Minister of State and Administrative Staff	3,769	**3,962**
122	126	Inspectorate engineering and technical staff	2,447	**2,899**
		Payments to volunteer crews in Marine Emergency Coastal Units	93	**110**
		Overtime	289	**320**
		Allowances	457	**473**
		Social Welfare – Employers' contributions	187	**198**
		Payment to the Department of Transport, Energy and Communications for Marine Safety Services	29	**30**
299	305	TOTAL	7,271	**7,992**

ADMINISTRATION *(contd.)*	1996 Provisional Outturn £000	**1997 Estimate £000**
A.2. Travel and subsistence:		
Travelling and subsistence, etc. arising from:		
(i) Home travel	494	**542**
(ii) Foreign travel		
(a) EU	65	**60**
(b) Other	138	**122**
TOTAL	697	**724**
A.3. Incidental expenses:		
1. Entertainment	31	**20**
2. Staff training and development	37	**97**
3. Other	428	**203**
TOTAL	496	**320**
A.4. Postal and telecommunications services:		
1. Postal services	47	**57**
2. Telephones, and other services	201	**218**
3. Miscellaneous	–	**1**
TOTAL	248	**276**
A.5. Office machinery and other office supplies:		
1. Computers and data processing equipment	111	**199**
2. Photocopiers – requisite materials	40	**54**
3. Engineering equipment	12	**10**
4. Other	80	**89**
TOTAL	243	**352**
A.6. Office premises expenses:		
1. Maintenance	104	**400**
2. Heat, light, fuel	59	**48**
3. Furniture and fittings	27	**50**
TOTAL	190	**498**
A.7. Consultancy services		
1. IT consultancy services	–	**5**
2. Other consultancy services	53	**65**
TOTAL	53	**70**
F.1. Marine Institute administration and current development (grant-in-aid)		
1. Administration: Pay	1,251	1,395
Non Pay	1,066	1,090
2. Fish stocks	872	1,033
3. Aquaculture/environment/oceans	377	451
4. Fish Health Unit	101	184
5. Research vessel operational expenses	356	383
6. Dumping at sea	26	154
7. Miscellaneous	2	31
TOTAL	4,051	4,721

Certain administrative costs associated with Fisheries Research Centre staff are now included as part of subhead F.1.

ADMINISTRATION *(contd.)*

	1996 Provisional Outturn £000	**1997 Estimate £000**
Sea Fisheries and Aquaculture Development		
H.3. Repayment of Advances: *(a)*		
Provision for repayment to the Central Fund of advances made under Section 18 of the Sea Fisheries Act, 1952 (No. 7 of 1952), where repayment of An Bord Iascaigh Mhara has been waived under the Sea Fisheries (Amendment) Act, 1963 (No. 21 of 1963)	–	**1,250**
Inland Fisheries		
J.1 Payments to the Central Fisheries Board, the Regional Fisheries Boards, the Foyle Fisheries Commission and miscellaneous payments in relation to inland fisheries:		
1. Payments under the Fisheries (Consolidation) Act, 1959 (No. 14 of 1959) and the Fisheries Act, 1980 (No. 1 of 1980):		
(i) Central Fisheries Board (under Section 21 of the Fisheries Act, 1980)	9,128	**9,376**
(ii) Regional Fisheries Boards (under Section 62 of the Fisheries (Consolidation) Act of 1959)	21	**23**
(iii) Regional Fisheries Boards and the Garda Síochána Reward Fund (under Section 315 of the Fisheries (Consolidation) Act of 1959)	27	**40**
2. Payment to the Foyle Fisheries Commission under Section 16 of the Foyle Fisheries Act, 1952 (No. 5 of 1952)	198	348
3. Miscellaneous	91	**89**
TOTAL	9,465	**9,876**
Other Services		
N. Subscriptions to international organisations		
1. Contributions to the International Council for the Exploration of the Sea	60	**65**
2. Subscriptions to other international organisations etc. . . .	48	**64**
TOTAL	108	**129**
P. Appropriations-in-aid:		
1. Proceeds of fines and forfeitures in respect of fishery offences	787	**695**
2. Charges at state harbours	2,763	**2,666**
3. Receipts under the Merchant Shipping and Mercantile Marine Acts	220	**235**
4. Receipts from radio, telephone and telegraph traffic	105	**180**
5. Receipts under the 1933 Foreshore Act and the 1954 State Property Act *(b)*	295	**459**
6. EU recoupment in respect of expenditure on the conservation and management of fisheries *(c)*	65	**350**

(a) Capital service. Non-programme outlay.
(b) Includes capital receipt 1996 Nil; 1997 £103,000.
(c) Includes capital receipt 1996 £65,000; 1997 £150,000.

ADMINISTRATION *(contd.)*

	1996 Provisional Outturn £000	**1997 Estimate £000**
7. Surveillance (Regional Fisheries Boards) *(a)*	–	**247**
Surveillance (Foyle Fisheries Commission) *(a)*	–	**29**
8. Loran C *(b)*	–	**160**
9. Miscellaneous	332	**231**
TOTAL	4,567	**5,252**

(a) Includes capital receipt 1996 Nil; 1997 £276,000.
(b) Includes capital receipt 1996 Nil; 1997 £160,000.

APPENDIX

An Bord Iascaigh Mhara (Subheads H.1., H.2., H.3., H.4. and H.5.)

	1996 Provisional Outturn £000	**1997 Estimate £000**	Change 1997 over 1996 %
EXPENDITURE:			
Current:			
Administration			
Staff salaries and pension payments	3,002	3,058	2
Other administration expenses	1,139	1,137	–
Development			
Marketing Programmes – Home and Export	642	768	20
Exploratory and experimental fishing	248	310	25
PESCA Community Initiative	220	218	–1
Other	1,142	1,537	35
Special aid schemes	2	1	–50
Capital:			
Grants for the purchase, modernisation and improvement of fishing vessels and decommissioning	3,356	2,417	–28
Mariculture grants	2,112	3,513	66
BIM fixed assets	891	615	–31
Exploratory fishing gear	119	200	68
Write-off loan defaults	–	1,250	–
PESCA Community Initiative	180	791	339
Other	167	363	117
Non-Voted Capital:			
Repayment of Exchequer advances	3,509	3,000	–15
Advances for ice plant development	100	55	–45
Term loans issued by BIM	–	–	–
Total Expenditure	16,829	19,233	14
Sources of Income:			
Subhead H1 (grant-in-aid)	4,840	5,212	8
Subhead H2 (grant-in-aid)	2,810	2,590	8
Subhead H3	–	1,250	–
Subhead H4 (grant-in-aid)	272	468	72
Subhead H5 (grant-in-aid)	–	1	–
Non-voted Exchequer	100	55	–45
Other	8,807	9,657	10
Total Income	16,829	19,233	14

APPENDIX 6

Result of Poll at General Election (Administrative Panel) 1997

Total Electorate: **992** Value of Valid Votes: **974,000** Number of seats to be filled: **7**
No. of Valid Votes: **974** Quota (Value of votes sufficient to secure the election of a candidate): **121,751** Count completed: **14**

NAMES OF CANDIDATES (and placing in Order of Preferences)	First Count		Second Count		Third Count		Fourth Count		Fifth Count		Sixth Count		Seventh Count	
	Number of votes	Value	Transfer of Costello's surplus	Result	Transfer of Byrne's votes	Result	Transfer of McDonald's votes	Result	Transfer of Forde's votes	Result	Transfer of Mulcahy's votes	Result	Transfer of Gilbride's votes	Result
*Byrne	33	33,000	120	33,120	(33,120)	0		0		0		0		0
Coogan	62	62,000	1,260	63,260		63,260	10,360	73,620	2,000	75,620		75,620		75,620
*Costello	129	—	(7,249)	—		—		—		—		—		—
*Doyle	79	79,000	1,500	80,500	60	80,560	10,060	90,620		90,620	1,000	91,620	2,000	93,620
*Finneran	67	67,000	360	67,360	6,000	73,360	1,180	74,540	9,000	83,540	9,000	92,540	11,000	—
Forde	33	33,000	120	33,120	3,000	36,120		36,120	(36,120)	0		0		0
Gilbride	38	38,000	240	38,240	1,000	39,240		39,240	6,000	45,240	2,000	47,240	(47,240)	0
Glynn	83	83,000	60	83,060	9,000	92,060		92,060	7,000	99,060	6,000	—	13,060	—
Kennedy	60	60,000	960	60,960	1,000	61,960	4,060	66,020	60	66,080	1,000	67,080		67,080
Kerrigan	50	50,000	240	50,240	3,000	53,240	1,060	54,300	3,060	57,360	6,000	63,360	6,060	69,420
Kett	91	91,000	60	91,060	3,000	94,060		94,060	2,000	96,060	7,000	—	6,000	—
McDonald	34	34,000	960	34,960		34,960	(34,960)	0		0		0		0
Mulcahy	34	34,000		34,000	3,000	37,000		37,000	3,000	40,000	(40,000)	0		0
*Nolan	57	57,000	120	57,120	3,000	60,120	120	60,240	3,000	63,240	8,000	71,240	8,000	79,240
*O'Connor	60	60,000	240	60,240	60	60,300	3,060	63,360		63,360		63,360		63,360
*O'Dowd	64	64,000	960	64,960		64,960	4,060	69,020	1,000	70,020		70,020	1,060	71,080
Non-transferable value not effective				0	1,000	1,000	1,000	2,000		2,000		2,000	60	2,060
Loss of value owing to disregard of fractions			49	49		49		49		49		49		49
Total	**974**	**974,000**	**0**	**974,000**	**0**	**974,000**	**0**	**974,000**	**0**	**974,000**	**0**	**974,000**	**0**	**974,000**

Elected: Costello, Glynn, Finneran, Kett, Doyle, Coogan, O'Dowd.

* outgoing members of previous Dáil

APPENDIX 6 *(contd.)*

RESULT OF POLL AT GENERAL ELECTION (ADMINISTRATIVE PANEL) 1997

NAMES OF CANDIDATES (and placing in Order of Preferences)	Eighth Count		Ninth Count		Tenth Count		Eleventh Count		Twelfth Count		Thirteenth Count		Fourteenth Count	
	Transfer of O'Connor's votes	Result	Transfer of Kerrigan's votes	Result	Transfer of Glynn's surplus	Result	Transfer of Finneran's surplus	Result	Transfer of Kett's surplus	Result	Transfer of Kennedy's votes	Result	Transfer of Doyle's surplus	Result
*Byrne		0		0		0		0		0		0		0
Coogan	6,120	81,740	4,060	85,800	1,356	87,156		87,156		87,156	30,865	—	7,553	—
*Costello		—		—		—		—		—		—		—
*Doyle	19,180	—	1,000	—		—		—		—	19,000	—	(11,049)	—
*Finneran		—	21,000	—		—	(2,789)	—		—		—		—
Forde		0		0		0		0		0		0		0
Gilbride		0		0		0		0		0		0		0
Glynn	60	—	9,000	—	(5,429)	—		—		—		—		—
Kennedy	9,000	76,080	2,120	78,200		78,200		78,200	50	78,250	(78,250)	0		0
Kerrigan	2,000	71,420	(71,420)	0		0		0		0		0		0
Kett		—	13,000	—		—		—	(309)	—		—		—
McDonald		0		0		0		0		0		0		0
Mulcahy		0		0		0		0		0		0		0
*Nolan		79,240	17,000	96,240	4,068	—	2,780	—	250	—	4,025	—		—
*O'Connor	(63,360)	0		0		0		0		0		0		0
*O'Dowd	26,000	97,080	1,120	98,200		98,200		98,200		98,200	21,120	—	3,486	—
Non-transferable value not effective	1,000	3,060	3,120	6,180		6,180		6,180		6,180	3,240	9,420		9,420
Loss of value owing to disregard of fractions		49		49	5	54	9	63	9	72		72	10	82
Total	**0**	**974,000**	**0**	**974,000**	**0**	**974,000**	**0**	**974,000**	**0**	**974,000**	**0**	**974,000**	**0**	**974,000**

4

THE CONSTITUTION OF IRELAND

The basic law of the state is the Constitution of Ireland (Bunreacht na hÉireann). It is a fundamental document which establishes the state, expresses legal norms and reflects the aspirations, aims and political theories of the people. It is necessarily concerned with guiding principles and guarantees certain basic rights of the people in general terms and imposes limitations on those rights in almost equally general terms.

The Constitution regulates the government and the distribution of the powers of government and, more importantly, limits the power of government and imposes obligations upon those exercising that power; as such, it has been defined as 'a selection of the legal rules which govern the government of that country and which have been embodied in a document' (Wheare 1966: 2). It has a higher legal status and authority than other laws and cannot be changed in the manner of ordinary legislation. In combination with an independent judiciary which has the power to review, it comprises an essential framework to protect the welfare of a liberal democratic country.

The Constitution was adopted by referendum in 1937. Its preamble envisages a system of fundamental law which can absorb or be adapted to changes as society changes and develops. It can therefore be fully appreciated only in conjunction with the legal traditions and precedents and the body of constitutional cases which have evolved since 1937. It should also be considered against the background of the two constitutions which preceded it in 1919 and 1922.

The Constitution of Dáil Éireann, 1919

This was the first Irish Constitution. The definitive text is in Irish and is published in the minutes of the first Dáil. It is a short document with five articles, covering the appointment of a chairman, the competence of the Dáil, the appointment of a Prime Minister and a government and their powers, the provision of funds, the audit of expenditure and provision for amendment. It is written in a clear straightforward manner.

The system of government adopted by this Irish constitution was parliamentary democracy based on the Westminster model then in operation in

Britain. 'The founders of the new state were constitutionalists within a strongly developed parliamentary tradition' (Farrell 1969: 135). The Sinn Féin candidates elected at the general election of December 1918 were in rebellion against British rule in Ireland. They had neither the means, the time nor the inclination to draw up a detailed constitution. The members of the first Dáil saw themselves as completing the work of 1916 by ratifying and establishing the Republic of the 1916 Proclamation. By drawing up a constitution which set out the machinery of government, together with an economic and social programme, the Dáil sought to give practical effect to the declaration of independence and establish the legitimacy of the independence movement.

The Constitution of the Irish Free State, 1922

The Constitution of the new Irish Free State (Saorstát Éireann) was enacted by Dáil Éireann sitting as a constituent (i.e. constitution-making) assembly in the autumn of 1922 and was included as the first schedule to the Constitution of the Irish Free State Act 1922. The Treaty (Articles of Agreement) signed at London on 6 December 1921 between the United Kingdom and the Irish delegation was included as a second schedule to this act. Section 2 of the constituent act stated that 'If any provision of the said Constitution or of any amendment thereof or of any law made thereunder is in any respect repugnant to any of the provisions of the Scheduled Treaty, it shall, to the extent only of such repugnancy, be made absolutely void and inoperative.'

The Constitution acknowledged in its preamble that all lawful authority 'comes from God'. Article 1 declared that 'The Irish Free State is a co-equal member of the Community of Nations forming the British Commonwealth of Nations.' Article 2 declared that 'All powers of government and all authority, legislative, executive and judicial, in Ireland, are derived from the people of Ireland, and the same shall be exercised in the Irish Free State through the organisations established by or under, and in accord with, this Constitution.'

Among the innovative features of the 1922 Constitution was that it provided for the protection of certain fundamental rights and vested the courts with express powers to invalidate legislation adjudged to infringe such rights.

The Constitution guaranteed the liberty of the person, the inviolability of the dwelling of each citizen, freedom of conscience and the free profession and practice of religion, and the right of free expression of opinion, as well as the right to assemble peaceably and the right to free elementary education.

The legislature of the new state was the Oireachtas, which was to consist of the British monarch and two houses, the Dáil and the Seanad. The sole and exclusive power of making laws for the Irish Free State was vested in the Oireachtas, with the Dáil as the dominant partner. It was to be elected by all adult citizens voting by proportional representation. Each of the two universities was to elect two members, and there was to be one Teachta Dála for every 20,000 people. The Dáil was empowered to elect the President of the Executive Council (which was replaced by the office of the Taoiseach in the 1937 Constitution) and to approve his ministers; it could also, in theory, dismiss him, and select his successor.

The Seanad had sixty members, of whom one-quarter were to be elected every three years by popular vote. It could delay bills for 270 days, but could not stop them. Membership of the Seanad was 'composed of citizens who shall be proposed on the grounds that they have done honour to the Nation by reason of useful public service or that, because of special qualifications or attainments, they represent important aspects of the Nation's life' (Article 30). As a result of the very active part played by the Seanad, which frequently brought it into conflict with the government – especially after 1932, when the first Fianna Fáil government came into office – it was abolished in May 1936.

The 1922 Constitution could be amended by referendum and also by the Oireachtas without reference to the people (both provisions of Article 50), so it imposed no effective limitations on the power of the legislature. Article 47 did, however, provide for the reference of bills to the people, but this article was removed by the Constitution (Amendment No. 10) Act 1928, when the Fianna Fáil party sought to have a referendum on the oath of allegiance to the British monarch, provided for in the Constitution. No referendum on a constitutional amendment was held under the 1922 Constitution. Initially, it was intended that all amendments would require a referendum, but during the Dáil debate this was changed to allow for parliamentary amendment of defects that might become obvious during its first eight years. Subsequently, this period of flexible amendment was extended to sixteen years. 'So, during the whole of its life, the Irish Free State Constitution could be changed as easily as any other law, without direct reference to the people. Both the Cosgrave and de Valera governments took full advantage of the latitude, and between 1923 and 1936 twenty-five bills were passed amending many provisions of the original text' (Farrell 1988: 29).

The Free State Constitution reflected some of the major features of the unwritten British Constitution, such as the institution of cabinet government led by a prime minister, accountable to and ultimately controlled by the legislature, and an independent judiciary. It formally defined the separation of legislative, executive and judicial powers. It also sought to qualify the doctrine of ministerial responsibility by creating an additional tier of 'extern ministers' outside the Executive Council. These ministers were placed in charge of departments of a technical or non-controversial nature (e.g. Agriculture, Fisheries, Posts and Telegraphs). This interesting constitutional experiment in enhancing individual responsibility at the expense of collective cabinet responsibility failed and was abandoned in 1927, when the Constitution was amended in such a way that no extern ministers were ever appointed again.

The Constitution contained an inherent conflict between the British monarchical system and Irish republicanism which caused Mansergh (1952: 296) to describe it as 'an essay in frustration'. Examples of the influence of the British monarchy were the oath of allegiance to the British crown to be taken by members of the Oireachtas under Article 17; the monarch's assent to legislation was necessitated, and there was provision for appeal to the British Privy Council, which was a usual feature of Commonwealth constitutions. Ó Briain (1929: 71) described the 1922 Constitution as 'monarchical in external form, republican in substance and, withal, essentially democratic'.

Main Provisions of the Constitution of Ireland, 1937

The basic elements of the 1937 Constitution can be broadly stated as follows. All powers derive, under God, from the people. For the purpose of enacting laws and taking other major decisions the people periodically elect representatives to sit in the principal house of the Oireachtas, the Dáil, which is free to take whatever decisions it thinks proper within the limits set by the Constitution. Every person over eighteen years has the right to vote in these elections, and every person over twenty-one to seek a seat in the Dáil. In addition to the Dáil, the Oireachtas consists of a President elected directly by the people, and an indirectly elected Seanad. The President, who is the head of state, has prescribed functions in relation to the protection of the Constitution. The day-to-day administration of the nation's affairs is entrusted to the executive body known as the government, which is chosen by the Dáil and is responsible to that House only; the government goes out of office on losing support in the Dáil. The interpretation and application of the laws is entrusted to the courts, which are independent and subject only to the Constitution and the laws; these courts also have the function of determining whether any law is repugnant to the Constitution; and trial by jury for ordinary offences is guaranteed.

Certain fundamental rights of the individual are guaranteed, such as personal liberty, equality before the law, freedom of expression (including criticism of the government), freedom of assembly and association, rights relating to the family, education, dwelling and property, and religious freedom. Retrospective legislation may not declare any action to be an offence. Broad principles of social policy are set out for the guidance of the Oireachtas. Certain provisions of the Constitution may be suspended in times of emergency, in accordance with procedures set out in the Constitution; but actual amendments to the Constitution may be effected only by vote of the people in a referendum. As Eamon de Valera put it during the Dáil debate on the draft Constitution, 'If there is one thing more than another that is clear and shining through this whole Constitution, it is the fact that the people are the masters.'

Article 1 refers to the nation's 'sovereign right . . . to determine its relations with other small nations'. While Article 2 states that the national territory consists of the whole island of Ireland, its islands and territorial seas, Article 3 confers reality on the situation by providing that, 'pending the reintegration of the national territory', the laws enacted by the Irish Parliament 'shall have the like area and extent of application as the laws of Saorstát Éireann and the like extra-territorial effect'. Article 4 provides that the name of the State is Éire, or in the English language, Ireland. Article 5 declares that Ireland is a sovereign, independent, democratic state.

Article 6 specifies three powers of government, legislative, executive and judicial, which are the cornerstone of the Irish system of government. This article acknowledges that these powers derive, under God, from the people. The President acts as head of state and the guardian of the people's rights under the Constitution.

The national parliament is referred to as the Oireachtas and consists, as already indicated, of the President, together with the Dáil and Seanad, with the Dáil holding the dominant position. Article 15.2.1 vests the exclusive power of making laws for the state in the Oireachtas. The same article forbids the Oireachtas from enacting any law repugnant to the Constitution.

The status and powers of the government and the Taoiseach (see Chapter 1) are defined in Article 28; and other articles set out procedures for the passage of legislation, e.g. presentation to Dáil and Seanad, signing and promulgation, and reference to the Supreme Court.

Article 27 provides that a bill, other than a bill to amend the Constitution, may be recommended to the President for referral to the people by a majority of the Seanad and not less than one-third of the members of the Dáil. This article has never been invoked.

Article 28.4.2 states that the government shall meet and act as a collective responsibility, and shall be collectively responsible for the departments of state administered by the members of the government.

The Constitution provides for the offices of Attorney General, who advises the government on legal matters, and Comptroller and Auditor General, who audits all moneys administered by the Oireachtas. Under the Constitution, the financial powers of the Dáil are limited. It may not pass any vote or resolution or enact any law for the spending of public moneys unless it has been recommended to the Dáil by a message from the government, signed by the Taoiseach.

Under Article 34, justice is to be administered in courts established by law by judges appointed under the Constitution. The courts comprise courts of first instance, i.e. including courts of local and limited jurisdiction and the High Court, as well as a court of final appeal, the Supreme Court. Judges of the High Court and Supreme Court are appointed by the President on the recommendation of the government. All other judges are appointed by the government. The independence of the judiciary in the exercise of their judicial functions is provided for.

Article 50.1 carries into force laws enacted before the Constitution came into operation, provided that they are not inconsistent with it.

Fundamental Rights

The Constitution firmly establishes the natural law as the basis of many of the rights guaranteed as fundamental rights. It puts outside the reach of the executive or of the legislature the power to act contrary to these rights or to endeavour to suppress them or deny them. One of the most fundamental political rights which the citizen is guaranteed is the right of access to the courts. Another essential civil liberty is the right to vote and to have an electoral system, and 'no voter may exercise more than one vote at an election for Dáil Éireann'(Article 16.1.4).

Under the heading 'Personal Rights' it is declared that 'All citizens shall, as human persons, be held equally before the law.' This is qualified by the statement that 'This shall not be held to mean that the State shall not in its enactments have due regard to differences of capacity, physical and moral, and of social function.' Persons may not be deprived of rights to their liberty save in accordance with law, of the right to express convictions and opinions, to associate with fellow citizens and to assemble. The right of association, the right of assembly and the right of freedom of speech are all subject to the overriding consideration of public order and public morality.

Under Article 40, the state also guarantees in its laws to respect and, as far as practicable, to defend and vindicate the personal rights of the citizen. It guarantees that the state shall, in particular, by its laws protect the citizen as best it may from unjust attack and, in the case of injustice done, vindicate the life, person, good name and property rights of every citizen. Article 40.3 has emerged as the 'due process' clause of the Irish Constitution. Ó Dálaigh C.J. said *In re Haughey* (1971 IR 217, p. 263) that 'Article 40.3 of the Constitution is a guarantee to the citizen of basic fairness of procedures. The Constitution guarantees such fairness, and it is the duty of the Court to underline that the words of Article 40.3 are not political shibboleths but provide a positive protection for the citizen and his good name.'

Article 41 recognises the family as the natural, primary and fundamental unit group of society and as a moral institution possessing inalienable and imprescriptible rights. *Inalienable* means that which cannot be transferred or given away, while *imprescriptible* means that which cannot be lost by the passage of time or abandoned by non-exercise.

The family is also dealt with in Article 42, where it is recognised as the primary and natural educator of the child. That article guarantees to protect the right and the duty of parents to provide, according to their means, for the education of their children. In this context, education is referred to as including religious and moral, intellectual, physical and social training. In the provision dealing with the state's right, as guardian of the common good, to require certain minimum education for all children, the reference is to the moral, intellectual and social elements of education.

Article 43 declares the right to the private ownership of external goods. The state accordingly guarantees to pass no law attempting to abolish the right to private ownership or the general right to transfer, bequeath and inherit property. It goes on to recognise that in civil society the exercise of these rights should be regulated by the principles of social justice, and that the state accordingly, as the occasion requires, may delimit by law the exercise of these rights with a view to reconciling their exercise with the exigencies of the common good.

The guarantee of freedom of conscience and the free profession and practice of religion is made subject to public order and public morality. This consideration is not referred to in Articles 41, 42 or 43.

The Supremacy of the Constitution

The supreme status of the Constitution is reflected in its adoption by the people; in the declaration of its own supremacy in Article 15.4, which states that any laws which are repugnant to its provisions are null and void; in the process of judicial review, which makes independent adjudication possible; and in the process of amendment under Article 46, which states that a proposal to amend must be passed by both Houses of the Oireachtas and then submitted to the people in a referendum.

Constitutional supremacy is, however, qualified in two ways. Firstly, under Article 28.3.3, nothing may invalidate any law enacted by the Oireachtas which is expressed to be for the purpose of securing the public safety and the preservation of the state in time of war or armed rebellion. Secondly, following a referendum in 1972, membership of the EU imposes limitations which provide that laws enacted or measures adopted by the state which are necessitated by membership of the European Union may not be invalidated by the Constitution.

The Constitution is rigid but can be amended. Since coming into operation it has been amended sixteen times; these amendments are briefly outlined below.

Constitutional Amendments

Article 51 of the 'Transitory Provisions' of the original Constitution permitted amendments to be made by the Oireachtas without reference to the people. The first two amendments to the 1937 Constitution were made by this method. These transitional arrangements were superseded in 1941, and all subsequent amendments have required the approval of the people in a referendum.

(1) and (2) took place in 1939 and 1941. Both made changes in Article 28.3.3 to take account of the emergency created by the outbreak of war in Europe.
(3) took place in May 1972 and allowed Ireland's entry to the European Community (Article 29.4.3).
(4) lowered the voting age from twenty-one to eighteen (December 1972).
(5) removed the reference to the 'special position' of the Roman Catholic Church and the recognition of other Churches and religious denominations in Ireland (December 1972).
(6) rendered adoption orders made by the Adoption Board immune from the requirement that justice must be administered by a court (1979).
(7) allowed the redistribution of university seats in the Seanad (1979).
(8) added the right to life of the unborn to the Constitution (1983).
(9) extended the franchise in Dáil elections to non-citizens (1984).
(10) enabled the state to ratify the Single European Act 1986 (1987).
(11) enabled the state to ratify the Treaty on European Union signed at Maastricht (1992).
(12) confirmed the freedom to travel to use an abortion service lawfully operating elsewhere (1992).
(13) confirmed the freedom to obtain or make available information relating to abortion services, subject to conditions laid down by the law (1992).
(14) allowed the introduction of divorce in Ireland (1995).
(15) changed the constitutional provisions on the right to bail (1996).
(16) changed the constitutional provisions on the right to cabinet confidentiality (1997).

Complete lists of referenda, amendments to the Constitution and referendum results are given in the appendices.

There have been five unsuccessful attempts to amend the Constitution. Proposals for electoral reform in 1959 and 1968, both including the replacement of proportional representation by the 'straight vote' system, were defeated; a proposal to change the formation of Dáil constituencies in 1968 was also defeated; and a proposal to legalise divorce was defeated in 1986.

On 25 November 1992 a proposal was made to amend the Constitution by adding the following:

> It shall be unlawful to terminate the life of an unborn unless such termination is necessary to save the life, as distinct from the health of the mother where there is an illness or disorder of the mother giving rise to a real and substantial risk to her life, not being a risk of self-destruction.

While travel and information referenda were passed on the same day, the referendum proposing this change of wording was defeated by a two-to-one majority. The 1996 Report of the Constitution Review Group commented (p. 274): 'It was rejected, apparently, by those who disliked its restrictiveness as well as by those opposed to abortion being legalised here on any ground.'

In November 1995 the Supreme Court held in the McKenna judgment that popular sovereignty, not government preference, is the cardinal principle of constitutional change. The court ruled that the government 'had not held the scales equally' (Chief Justice Hamilton) and declared it unconstitutional for the government to spend public money advocating a particular result in any such context. A Referendum Commission to prepare and disseminate information and to foster, promote and facilitate debate in a fair manner was announced in January 1998.

Directive Principles of Social Policy

Article 45 consists of a number of principles 'for the general guidance of the Oireachtas', presenting a comprehensive vision of society and social policy founded on Catholic social teaching. In the early years this article was largely ignored by the courts, as exemplified by the judgment of Kingsmill Moore J. in the case of *Comyn* v. *Attorney General* (1950 IR 142), when he said that Article 45 'puts the state under certain duties, but they are duties of imperfect obligation since they cannot be enforced or regarded by any court of law, and are only directions for the guidance of the Oireachtas'.

In more recent years Article 45 has become an increasingly important influence, as exemplified by the decision of Finlay J. in *Landers* v. *Attorney General* (109 ILTR 1), in which he held that he was entitled to be guided by these directive principles of social policy which impose upon the state the obligation of endeavouring to meet the common good.

However, Henchy J. in the Supreme Court in *The People (Director of Public Prosecutions)* v. *O'Shea* (1982 IR 384) stated that 'If any person were to institute proceedings in the High Court seeking to compel the state to give effect to any of the specified directives, the High Court would be bound to strike out those proceedings for want of jurisdiction.'

Judicial Review

Judicial review includes the power to invalidate on constitutional grounds acts of any administrative agency and to decide whether any law is in keeping with the provisions of the Constitution. It is an important aspect of the organic process of review and interpretation of the Constitution and ensures that constitutional provisions are observed and that the various political institutions act within their proper sphere of authority. This power is conferred on the High Court and Supreme Court (under Articles 26, 34.3 and 34.4). The process can be used before a bill becomes law if the President, using his powers under Article 26, decides to refer it to the Supreme Court for a decision. The more common practice, however, is to have laws tested in the High Court or Supreme Court in the course of ordinary legislation.

The Irish judiciary have since the mid-1960s become increasingly innovative in their interpretations of the Constitution. This approach included, for example, considerations relating to the Preamble, Article 45 on the directive principles of social policy, the nature of Irish society, and 'concepts of prudence, justice and charity which gradually change or develop as society changes and develops and which fall to be interpreted from time to time in accordance with prevailing ideas' (O'Higgins C.J. in *The State (Healy)* v. *Donoghue* (1976 IR 325, p. 347). In *Tormey* v. *Ireland* (1985 IR 289) Henchy J. said that 'The Constitution must be read as a whole, and its several provisions must not be looked at in isolation, but be treated as interlocking parts of the general constitutional scheme.' The entire body of judicial decisions on constitutional law is regarded as part of the living aspect of the Constitution. The courts are the ultimate guardians of the Constitution, but they cannot move until their powers are invoked. The Attorney General, by virtue of his constitutional office, has also cast upon him, in the appropriate case, the duty of defending the Constitution.

In a wide range of cases the courts have made explicit certain rights and entitlements of citizens that they have found to be implicit in the 1937 Constitution. For example, in the case of *Ryan* v. *Attorney General* (1964 IR 294), which is related to the fluoridation of water, the court held that there are many personal rights of the citizen which follow from the Christian and democratic nature of the state which are not mentioned in Article 40 at all. It instanced as examples of such personal rights the right to bodily integrity, the right to free movement within the state and the right to marry. Speaking fifteen years after his Ryan judgment, Mr Justice Kenny acknowledged in the course of a lecture the significance of the epoch which he inaugurated, when he said, in connection with Article 40.3: 'Judges have become legislators, and have the advantage that they do not have to face an opposition' (1979 NILQ 189, p. 196).

Ó Dálaigh C.J., in delivering the Supreme Court's judgment in this case, said:

> The Court agrees with Mr Justice Kenny that 'personal rights' mentioned in section 3.1 are not exhausted by the enumeration of 'life, person, good name, and property rights' in section 3.2 as is shown by the use of the words 'in particular', nor by the more detached treatment of specific rights in the subsequent sections of the article (pp. 344–5).

In a further case, relating to a law prohibiting the importation or sale of contraceptives, Walsh J. stated in *McGee* v. *Attorney General* (1974 IR 284):

> Articles 41, 42 and 43 emphatically reject the theory that there are no rights without laws, no rights contrary to the law and no rights anterior to the law. They indicate that justice is placed above the law and acknowledge that natural rights, or human rights, are not created by law but that the Constitution confirms their existence and gives them protection.

Since the decision in the Ryan case the courts have defined many other rights which the state is pledged to defend and vindicate even though they are not specifically enumerated in the Constitution. These include the right not to be unconstitutionally restrained from earning one's livelihood (*Murtagh Properties* v. *Cleary* (1972 IR 330)); the right to litigate claims, found to be a personal right of the citizen within Article 40 in *O'Brien* v. *Keogh* (1972 IR 144); the right to work (*Murphy* v. *Stewart* (1973 IR 97)); the right to marital privacy (*McGee* v. *Attorney General* (1974 IR 284)); the right of access to the courts (*Macauley* v. *Minister for Posts and Telegraphs* (1966 IR 345)); the right to avail of such facilities as the state has obtained for its citizens to travel abroad (*The State (M)* v. *Attorney General* (1979 IR 73)); the right to fair procedures (*The State (Healy)* v. *Donoghue* (1976 IR 325)); and the right to privacy in one's communications with others (*Kennedy* v. *Ireland* (unreported, 12 January 1987)).

The Republic of Ireland

The Constitution provides (Article 4) that the name of the state is Éire, or in the English language, Ireland. The normal practice is to use the name 'Éire' in texts in the Irish language and to use 'Ireland' in all English-language texts, with corresponding translations for texts in other languages. The Republic of Ireland Act 1948 provides for the description of the state as 'the Republic of Ireland', but this provision has not changed the usage 'Ireland' as the name of the state in the English language.

Article 5 of the Constitution declares that Ireland is a sovereign, independent, democratic state. It does not, however, proclaim that Ireland is a republic, nor does any other article of the Constitution, despite the fact that many of its provisions have a distinctly republican stamp. The omission of this proclamation of a republic in the Constitution of 1937 was deliberate. Eamon de Valera stated in the Dáil on 14 June 1937 that if the Northern problem was not there, 'in all probability, there would be a flat, downright proclamation of the Republic'.

The Republic of Ireland Act, passed in 1948, repealed the Executive Authority (External Relations) Act 1936 (which had retained the crown for purposes of diplomatic representation and international agreements, in the hope that such an arrangement might, as Mr de Valera put it, facilitate the construction of a bridge 'over which the Northern Unionists might walk') and provided instead for the declaration of a republic. In accordance with this act, on Easter Day 1949 Ireland became a republic.

Constitutional Review

The desirability of revising the Constitution has been discussed from time to time. It is recorded that as early as 1947 Mr de Valera expressed a wish to change the provisions relating to proportional representation, Seanad representation and property rights (Rau 1960: 130). In 1966 an informal all-party committee of TDs and senators was set up to consider possible changes in the Constitution. Its report (December 1967) discussed twenty-seven aspects of the Constitution, leaving it to the government of the day to decide the items which should be selected for inclusion in any legislative proposals that might emerge. It made the unanimous recommendation that Article 44.1.2–3 (on the special position of the Roman Catholic Church and recognition of the other Churches) should be deleted; this was given effect to by the Fifth Amendment in 1972. It also made recommendations for the rewording of Article 3 (on the extent of the application of the laws of the state) and of Article 41 (on marriage). The report commented that the all-party committee was not aware of any public demand for a change in the basic structure of the Constitution and concluded that 'As a general proposition, therefore, it might be said that our inclination was to adhere to the constitutional provisions which have worked so well in practice, and to consider changes only in the case of those provisions which, from experience, might be regarded as not adequately fulfilling their purpose.'

In April 1995 the government set up a Constitution Review Group, composed of fifteen experts under the chairmanship of Dr T.K. Whitaker, 'to review the Constitution and to establish those areas where constitutional change may be desirable or necessary'. The Review Group produced a 700-page report in May 1996, setting forth in a clear and concise manner, with a summary of the relevant arguments, the areas where it considered constitutional change was appropriate. It found that the Constitution has stood the test of time quite well and, as interpreted by many judicial decisions, has shown a considerable degree of adaptability to new circumstances and norms.

Among the recommendations of the Review Group were amendments relating to the following: the name of the state; making the Irish language and the English language the two official languages; describing the President as head of state; the nomination and election of President; providing for a time limit within which a Dáil by-election should be held; the one-judgment rule where the validity of a law is in question; including a time limit for a law enacting a state of emergency and specifying the fundamental rights and freedoms retained; the nomination of a senior minister where the Taoiseach and Tánaiste are unavailable to act; clarifying that Article 29.3 covers public international law; permitting delegation of the Attorney General's functions to another senior lawyer; providing for accountability of the Attorney General to the Dáil through the Taoiseach; giving the Oireachtas greater flexibility to develop different court structures; allowing for regulation by judges themselves of judicial conduct; providing for an impeachment process for judges and other constitutional officers; giving explicit constitutional recognition of, and protection for, enumerated rights in the trial of offences; providing that special courts may be established only for a prescribed period; and regulating the establishment of military tribunals.

The group recommended a separate, comprehensive, independent examination of all issues relating to the Seanad. New provisions recommended by the group for inclusion in the Constitution relate to the placing of all family rights in Article 41, the right of every child to free primary education, new articles on the Ombudsman, local government and the environment, and the establishment of a human rights commission.

At the same time as the publication of the Constitution Review Group Report in July 1996, the government announced the establishment of an all-party committee to undertake a full review of the Constitution and to identify areas where change might be desirable or necessary. This committee is continuing its work and has issued two progress reports.

Conclusion

'Nowhere in the world is the right to personal liberty more fully protected than under the Irish Constitution': so wrote Mr Justice Brian Walsh of the Supreme Court in *The Irish Times* on 29 December 1987 on the occasion of the fiftieth anniversary of the Constitution. He continued:

> The Constitution is a living law. As a document it dates from 1937, as a law from today. It is written in the present tense. It has always been interpreted in

> the light of the circumstances of the contemporary epoch. Therefore it is designed in general principles to look after the future as well as the present. In practice the Constitution of Ireland has worked very well. In many ways the civil service has shown a greater awareness and appreciation of its provisions than has been the case among many politicians. In particular it can be said that the Department of Justice, often the subject of unjust criticism, has in the last twenty years shown great sensitivity to the provisions of the Constitution.

Dr Tom Garvin noted in his contribution to the same edition of the newspaper:

> The great achievement of 1937 was that an arena was established in which the issues of individual *versus* collective interest could be contested. This was the first time such an arena or basic framework had ever been provided in Irish history and was a major step forward in the provision of political order in Ireland. We have come to take that political order so much for granted that we sometimes forget what a formidable achievement it was.

The Constitution gives an incomplete picture of the mechanics of Irish government. What a Constitution says and what actually happens may be quite different things. While the sole power of making laws is vested in the Oireachtas, in practice it is the government that makes the laws, which are then passed by the Oireachtas. Farrell (1987: 162) notes that:

> The Constitution provides not merely an incomplete, but in a number of important respects a misleading, account of the nature, functions and operations of basic political institutions. It enshrines mythologies that bear little relation to the actualities of power. It ignores some real sources of influence, elevates some marginal authorities, distances some relationships and misrepresents the balance of forces that maintain the Irish political system. Political parties are not even mentioned. The role of both Dáil and Seanad in the actual making of legislation is exaggerated. The real dominance of the government is obscured by a pedantic emphasis on parliamentary accountability. The Constitution is a rulebook that has only a tangential connection with the Irish political and governmental game.

Ireland is not unique in having a gap between political practice and constitutional theory. The most important aspect of this is the decline in the power of the legislature. Farrell (1987: 163) notes that the government controls the Dáil rather than the declaration in Article 15.2.1 that 'The sole and exclusive power of making laws for the State is hereby vested in the Oireachtas.' The reasons for this, he suggests, include party politics, the clientist role of deputies, the electoral system of multi-seat proportional representation constituencies, and the government's control over public expenditure.

In his foreword to O'Reilly and Redmond (1980) Mr Justice Brian Walsh observed: 'For so long as the Constitution reflects the politics and social culture of the majority of the people, and there is little real evidence that it does not, it is difficult to justify claims that a drastic overhaul is needed.'

REFERENCES

Farrell, Brian, 'A Note on the Dáil Constitution, 1919', *Irish Jurist*, IV (1969), 127–38

Farrell, Brian, 'The Constitution and the Institutions of Government: Constitutional Theory and Political Practice' in F. Litton (ed.), *The Constitution of Ireland 1937–87* (special issue of *Administration*, vol. 35, no. 4, 1987)

Farrell, Brian (ed.), *De Valera's Constitution and Ours* (Dublin: Gill & Macmillan for RTÉ, 1988)

Government of Ireland, *Report of the Constitution Review Group*, Pn. 2632 (Dublin: Stationery Office, May 1996)

Government of Ireland, *First Progress Report of the All-Party Oireachtas Committee on the Constitution*, Pn. 3795 (Dublin: Stationery Office, April 1997)

Mansergh, Nicholas, *Survey of British Commonwealth Affairs: Problems of External Policy, 1931–39* (London: Oxford Press, 1952)

Ó Briain, Barra, *The Irish Constitution* (Dublin/Cork: Talbot Press, 1929)

O'Reilly, James and Mary Redmond, *Cases and Materials on the Irish Constitution* (Dublin: Incorporated Law Society, 1980)

Rau, Benegal N., *India's Constitution in the Making*, B. Shira Rau (ed.) (Bombay: Orient Longman, 1960)

Wheare, Kenneth C., *Modern Constitutions* (London: Oxford University Press, 1966)

APPENDIX 7

REFERENDA TO AMEND THE CONSTITUTION

There were two amendments of the Constitution made by acts of the Oireachtas under the transitory provision Article 51.1 of the Constitution. The first referendum was held in 1959. There have been nineteen referenda in all (to November 1997). Of these, five were rejected.

Date	Referendum subject	Result
1 July 1937	Plebiscite on Draft Constitution	Passed by Oireachtas
17 June 1959	Voting system	Rejected
18 October 1968	Formation of Dáil constituencies	Rejected
18 October 1968	Voting system	Rejected
10 May 1972	Accession to EC	Approved
7 December 1972	Lowering of voting age	Approved
7 December 1972	Article 44 of the Constitution (special position of RCC)	Approved
5 July 1979	Adoption	Approved
5 July 1979	Seanad representation	Approved
7 September 1983	Rights of unborn	Approved
14 June 1984	Extension of voting rights	Approved
26 June 1986	Dissolution of marriage	Rejected
26 May 1987	Single European Act	Approved
18 June 1992	European Union (Maastricht)	Approved
25 November 1992	Right to life	Rejected
25 November 1992	Travel	Approved
25 November 1992	Information	Approved
24 November 1995	Divorce	Approved
28 November 1996	Bail	Approved
30 October 1997	Cabinet confidentiality	Approved

APPENDIX 8

TABLE OF AMENDMENTS TO THE CONSTITUTION

Title of Amendment	**Date of coming into effect**
First Amendment of the Constitution Act, 1939	2 September 1939
Second Amendment of the Constitution Act, 1941	30 May 1941
Third Amendment of the Constitution Act, 1972	8 June 1972
Fourth Amendment of the Constitution Act, 1972	
Fifth Amendment of the Constitution Act, 1972	5 January 1973
Sixth Amendment of the Constitution (Adoption) Act, 1979	3 August 1979
Seventh Amendment of the Constitution (Election of Members of Seanad Éireann by Institutions of Higher Education) Act, 1979	3 August 1979
Eighth Amendment of the Constitution Act, 1983	7 October 1983
Ninth Amendment of the Constitution Act, 1984	2 August 1984
Tenth Amendment of the Constitution Act, 1987	22 June 1987
Eleventh Amendment of the Constitution Act, 1992	16 July 1992
Thirteenth Amendment of the Constitution Act, 1992*	
Fourteenth Amendment of the Constitution Act, 1992	23 December 1992
Fifteenth Amendment of the Constitution Act, 1995	17 June 1996
Sixteenth Amendment of the Constitution Act, 1996	12 December 1996

* There is no Twelfth Amendment. On 25 November 1992 three proposals were put to the people:

The Twelfth Amendment of the Constitution Bill, 1992
The Thirteenth Amendment of the Constitution Bill, 1992
The Fourteenth Amendment of the Constitution Bill, 1992.

The people rejected the Twelfth Amendment Bill and approved the other two. These were enacted, therefore, as the Thirteenth Amendment of the Constitution Act, 1992 and the Fourteenth Amendment of the Constitution Act, 1992.

APPENDIX 9

REFERENDUM RESULTS

Referendum	Year	Turnout	Votes		
			Yes	No	Spoilt
Draft Constitution	1937	75.8%	51%	49%	–
Voting system	1959	58.4%	46%	50%	4%
Dáil constituencies	1968	65.8%	38%	58%	4%
Voting system	1968	65.8%	38%	58%	4%
Accession to EC	1972	70.9%	82%	17%	1%
Voting age	1972	50.7%	80%	15%	5%
Recognition of religions	1972	50.7%	80%	15%	5%
Adoption	1979	28.6%	97%	1%	2%
Universities/Seanad seats	1979	28.6%	89%	7%	4%
Right to life	1983	53.7%	66%	33%	1%
Voting rights at Dáil elections	1984	47.5%	73%	24%	3%
Divorce	1986	60.8%	36%	63%	1%
Single European Act	1987	44.1%	70%	30%	–
European Union (Maastricht Treaty)	1992	57.3%	69%	31%	–
Right to life	1992	68.2%	33%	62%	5%
Right to travel	1992	68.2%	60%	36%	4%
Right to information	1992	68.1%	57%	39%	4%
Divorce	1995	62.1%	50.1%	49.6%	0.39%
Bail	1996	29.2%	75%	25%	–
Cabinet confidentiality	1997	47.2%	52.6%	47.4%	5.2%

Source: Report of the Constitution Review Group (1996), p. 126.

5

THE PRESIDENT OF IRELAND

The President of Ireland (Uachtarán na hÉireann) is the only officer of state who can be directly elected by all the citizens of the country. He is elected for a period of seven years and can be re-elected only once. His main functions include acting as ceremonial head of state; formalising a number of appointments; summoning and dissolving Dáil Éireann in certain circumstances; signing into law and promulgating bills which have been passed by the Dáil and Seanad; and operating as a check but not as a veto on legislation.

Every citizen over thirty-five years of age is eligible for the office, but a candidate must be nominated by at least twenty members of the Dáil or Seanad or by four county councils. In practice, this confines nominations to the main political parties. This system has repeatedly been criticised and it has been suggested that there should be wider democratic procedures for nominating candidates. In its report of 1996 the Constitution Review Group reached the unambiguous conclusion that 'the constitutional requirements for nominating a presidential candidate are too restrictive and in need of democratisation'. During the 1997 presidential election campaign, Dana, Rosemary Scallon, confounded the pundits by securing nominations from Donegal, Longford, Kerry and Tipperary North Riding councils. Shortly afterwards another candidate, Derek Nally, also secured four nominations. A former or retiring President may become a candidate on his own nomination. A President may not be a member of either House of the Oireachtas or hold any other office or position for which he receives payment; on election to office he must vacate any seat or position.

By virtue of being elected by the direct vote of the people, being head of state and taking precedence over all other people, the President represents all the people of Ireland. The Constitution underlines the non-political, non-partisan nature of the office. From the beginning the President has been described as being 'above politics', in the sense of abstaining from any public statement which could be judged to be politically biased or inconsistent with the fundamental principle that there can be only one executive authority.

The electorate is the same as that for Dáil elections. If only one candidate is put forward, there is no election and the candidate becomes President on the declaration of the returning officer. Elections have in fact been avoided by the nomination of a single agreed candidate on five out of eleven occasions since the office was first filled in 1938.

The role of the President is defined in the Constitution of 1937, and the limitations on that role have been determined not only by the articles of the Constitution but more emphatically by convention. Among the relevant provisions of the Constitution are Article 12.1, which provides for the office of the President of Ireland, 'who shall take precedence over all other persons in the State', and Article 15.1.2, which provides that the Oireachtas shall consist of the President and two Houses. The President is the head of state, and although he is formally a part of the Oireachtas, his primary function is to act as a check on the Houses of Parliament. Under Article 13.8.1, the President is not 'answerable to either House of the Oireachtas or to any Court for the exercise and performance of the powers and functions of his office'. While he is expected to be above and apart from politics, under Article 28.5.2 the Taoiseach is obliged to keep him generally informed on matters of domestic and international policy.

The emoluments of the President are fixed by statute from the Central Fund and cannot be reduced during his term of office. The President is provided with an official residence, Áras an Uachtaráin, in the Phoenix Park, Dublin, which is maintained by the Office of Public Works. The President has the assistance of a number of staff in his duties, including the Secretary to the President. This officer is a civil servant of the state, who is appointed by the government following consultation with the President and does not retire from office with the President. The Secretary to the President is Clerk to the Council of State and ex officio Secretary to the Presidential Commission. The President also has the assistance of an aide-de-camp, who is normally a colonel in the army.

The President has a seal of office, which is referred to in Articles 27, 31, 33 and 35 of the Constitution. The Presidential Seal Act 1937 provides that the President shall have custody and control of this seal, which is affixed to documents issued by him and which must be authenticated by his signature.

The first President of Ireland was Douglas Hyde, a Gaelic scholar who was appointed in 1938 following all-party agreement; Seán T. Ó Ceallaigh became President in 1945 after an election and served a second term after nominating himself in 1952; Eamon de Valera served two terms following election, in 1959 and in 1966; Erskine Childers was elected to the office in 1973; Cearbhall Ó Dálaigh was appointed in 1974 following all-party agreement; as was Patrick Hillery in 1976 and 1983. Mary Robinson became the seventh President in 1990 and was the first woman to hold the office. In November 1997 Mary McAleese became the eighth President of Ireland. A full list of Presidents is at Appendix 10.

Functions and Limitations of the President

The President normally acts on the advice and authority of the government. The Constitution emphasises in several places that the President requires the approval of the government before taking action. Article 13.9 declares that the powers and functions conferred on the President by the Constitution are exercisable and performable by him only on the advice of the government, except where it is provided by the Constitution that he acts in his absolute discretion or after consultation with or in relation to the Council of State, or on the advice of any other person or body. In addition, Article 13.11 provides that 'No power or function conferred on the President by law shall be exercisable or performable by him save only on the advice of the Government.'

In the case of appointments and decisions, the President acts only on the binding advice of the government. For example, members of the judiciary cannot be appointed except on that advice. There are also important provisions in the Constitution which specifically require the initiative of some other person or body before action can be taken by the President. For example, the Attorney General is appointed by the President on the nomination of the Taoiseach (Article 30), and the Comptroller and Auditor General is appointed by the President on the nomination of the Dáil (Article 33). In the case of the removal of persons from these offices, the Constitution obliges the President to act as requested by the appropriate authorities. He must terminate the appointment of the Attorney General and of ministers on the advice of the Taoiseach, and that of the Comptroller and Auditor General and of judges, on a resolution of the Dáil and Seanad.

The primacy of the government is manifest from the provision of Article 12.9, under which the President cannot leave the state during his term of office without the consent of the government. Under Article 13.1, the President appoints the Taoiseach on the nomination of the Dáil, and other members of the government 'on the nomination of the Taoiseach with the previous approval of the Dáil' (Article 13.1.2), while he is required to terminate ministerial appointments on the advice of the Taoiseach only. The Dáil is summoned and dissolved by him on the advice of the Taoiseach under Article 13.2.1.

The President is required by the provision of Articles 13.3 and 25.2.1 to sign bills passed by both Houses of the Oireachtas, thereby giving them the force of law; and in addition he must, under Article 25.4.2 (except in cases where reference to the people or the Supreme Court is involved), promulgate each new legislative measure by publishing in the *Iris Oifigiúil* (the official gazette) a notice stating that the bill has become law.

The President may, after consultation with the Council of State, communicate with the Houses of the Oireachtas and he may address a message to the nation on any matter of national or public importance. Article 13.7.3 states that every such message or address must have received the approval of the government. The Constitution is silent on whether the President can make a statement of a political nature without the consent of the government. Successive governments have tended to believe that the President could not speak publicly on any issue without their approval. While it is not appropriate for the President to be involved in confrontation with the government on legislative or policy matters, Kelly (1984: 65–6) holds that the President retains the ordinary rights of a citizen in regard to freedom in expressing his opinions or, in particular, replying to criticism. President Robinson in a newspaper interview in February 1997 spoke about the fact that the President must work through government, even for rudimentary matters such as clearing speeches in advance. She said:

> It was something that required getting used to, probably on both sides. I think the process of adjustment has worked well because the constitutional framework is very clear in providing that the executive and legislative and judicial power rests elsewhere and that to do this job well you must be in tune with the role of government. I think it has been challenging to develop the role of the Presidency in a way that is compatible with and complements the role of government.

Under Article 13.6, the President has the right to commute the sentences of criminal offenders, but by virtue of Article 13.9 he can exercise this power only on the advice of the government. Only three cases of the receipt of a pardon are reported and all of these occurred during the period in office of Ireland's first President, Dr Douglas Hyde.

The supreme command of the defence forces is vested in the President by Article 13.4, but this is followed by a provision requiring that the exercise of this command is to be regulated by law. Section 17 of the Defence Act 1954 provides that the military command of and all executive and administrative powers in relation to the defence forces shall 'under the direction of the President' be exercisable by the government through the Minister for Defence. Acting under the Defence Act 1954 and on the advice of the government, the President makes appointments to the following offices in the Permanent Defence Forces: Chief of Staff; Adjutant General; Quartermaster General; Inspector General; and Judge Advocate General. Under Article 13.5.2 of the Constitution, all commissioned officers of the defence forces hold their commissions from the President.

While Article 13.10 permits the conferring by law of additional powers and functions on the President, this is qualified by the provision of Article 13.11 referred to above. The Republic of Ireland Act 1948 provides that 'The President on the advice of the government may exercise the executive functions of the State in or in connection with its external relations.' For this reason, it is to the President that foreign ambassadors present their credentials, and it is the President who, on the advice of the government, accredits Irish diplomatic representatives abroad. The President represents Ireland abroad. Finally, in the declaration of war or emergency no function is allotted by the Constitution to the President under Article 28.3.

Among the additional powers which have been conferred on the President by law under Article 13.10 are formal powers of appointment. These include the appointment of council members and senior professors of the Dublin Institute for Advanced Studies (under SS 8 and 9 of the Institute for Advanced Studies Act 1940); of the Governor of the Central Bank (under S. 19 of the Central Bank Act 1942); and of the Ombudsman (under S. 2 of the Ombudsman Act 1980). The Red Cross Act 1944 provides that the President of Ireland shall, by virtue of his office, be President of the Irish Red Cross Society. These additional powers are exercised by the President either on the advice of the government or pursuant to a resolution of the Oireachtas. The President also presents the centenarian's bounty, a once-off payment of £250 made to Irish citizens living in Ireland who have reached the age of one hundred years.

The provisions of the Constitution relating to the impeachment of the President effectively establish the supremacy of the legislature over a President whom it deems to be unfit for office. Article 12.10 provides for the impeachment of the President for 'stated misbehaviour' after a charge made against him by either House of the Oireachtas is sustained by the prescribed two-thirds majority. When such a charge has been preferred, the other House will investigate it or cause it to be investigated. The relevant constitutional provisions are designed to ensure that this serious step will be undertaken only on a matter of widespread public concern.

The Constitution does not define or specify 'stated misbehaviour' or in any way limit the nature of the charge to be brought against the President. It provides, however, that in addition to proving the charge, the House responsible for the investigation must pass a resolution that the misbehaviour that was the subject of the charge was such as to render him unfit to continue in office. This elasticity leaves it to the wisdom of that House to decide whether the particular charge, if proved, is or is not, in the special circumstances of the case, such as to render the President unfit to continue in office (McDunphy 1945: 23).

The Constitution provides at Article 12.3.1 for the removal from office of a President whose permanent incapacity has been 'established to the satisfaction of the Supreme Court consisting of not less than five judges'.

There is no Vice-President of Ireland. The Constitution ensures that there is no gap in continuity as regards the powers, duties and functions of the office. A Presidential Commission discharges the powers and functions of the President in the event of his absence, or his temporary or permanent incapacity, or in the event of his death, resignation, removal from office or failure to exercise and perform the powers and functions of his office. This Commission consists of the Chief Justice, the Ceann Comhairle of the Dáil and the Cathaoirleach of the Seanad. The Commission may act by any two of its number. In the event of the removal from office or death, resignation or permanent incapacity of the President, an election for his successor must take place within sixty days (Article 12.3.3).

Discretionary Powers of the President

While the President acts on the advice of the government and has limited discretion in the making of certain appointments and decisions, he has six independent powers which he may exercise on his own initiative independent of the government. These are outlined below.

(1) Article 26 of the Constitution enables the President, after consultation with the Council of State, to refer any bill (with certain exceptions) to the Supreme Court for a decision as to its constitutionality. Eamon de Valera referred to this when he explained that the President 'in exercising these powers . . . is acting on behalf of the people who have put him there for that special purpose. He is there to guard the people's rights and mainly to guard the Constitution' and is invested with certain functions and powers to do this (*Dáil Debates*, 11 May 1937, col. 51). This power of a President is politically sensitive and has involved one incumbent in controversy which led to a constitutional crisis. The exercise of the power and the crisis of 1976 are examined in detail below.

(2) The second, and arguably most important, independent power of the President is the very wide power under Article 13 which enables him, in his absolute discretion, to refuse to dissolve the Dáil on the advice of a Taoiseach who has ceased to retain the support of a majority in the Dáil. Where he does so refuse, it is presumed the Taoiseach concerned would have to resign, and the Dáil would then have an opportunity of nominating a successor. Mr de Valera explained that the wise exercise of this power 'by the President may mean that he is maintaining the supremacy of the people at a time when it is vital that the people's supremacy should be maintained' (*Dáil Debates*, 11 May 1937, col. 45). Three occasions have arisen when this crucially important power could have been used. Having considered all the options, however, the President on each occasion granted the dissolution (in 1944, in January 1982 and in November 1982). McDunphy (1945: 47, 52) comments:

> Here we find the President endowed with the authority entirely his own, independent of the Taoiseach, independent of the Government, independent

> of the Oireachtas, not answerable even to the Supreme Court, which is the final authority on matters of constitutional validity. The President's power in the matter is absolute; in its exercise he is governed only by his personal judgement of what is best for the people, and his decision, when made, is final and unchallengeable . . . This power is unique in the Irish Constitution. It is the only case in which the President has an absolute and unquestionable right to act in direct opposition to a constitutional request from the Head of the Government, to reject an advice which in other matters is equivalent to a direction, which must be complied with as a matter of course.

There is no evidence that, as regards the dissolution of the Dáil, the President has declined to act on the advice of the Taoiseach on an occasion in which the support of a majority in the Dáil was lost. The President cannot dissolve the Dáil without the request of the Taoiseach. A President who refused such a request from the Taoiseach would invite controversy, yet in McDunphy's words (1945: 51): 'The Constitution gives no indication as to the evidence which would entitle the President to decide that a Taoiseach has in fact ceased to retain the support of a majority in Dáil Éireann.' Clarification of this point might have had a decisive effect in reducing the uncertainty generated by three general elections in rapid succession in 1981–2.

This discretionary power of the President was at the centre of a political controversy which erupted during the presidential campaign of 1990. Following the collapse of the Fine Gael/Labour coalition government in January 1982 after its defeat in the Dáil on a budgetary provision, Fianna Fáil issued a public statement that it was available for consultation with the President if he was going to exercise his absolute right of not dissolving the Dáil, and it was widely reported that efforts were made by senior members of the party to contact the President. Such an attempt to contact the President after the collapse of the government was not necessarily improper, and the President's discretion might be better exercised with full information and advice on the situation. It would, however, be wrong if *advice* became *pressure*; and it was subsequently alleged that telephone calls were made to Áras an Uachtaráin in January 1982 in an attempt to persuade the President to secure a transfer of power without an election. This claim appeared to receive substance from the admission made in the course of an interview in 1990 by Brian Lenihan, a presidential candidate, that he had telephoned Áras an Uachtaráin on the night in question. Mr Lenihan later retracted this statement and requested a meeting with President Hillery to obtain his confirmation that the telephone call had not been made. On the following day, however, he withdrew his request in order to avoid drawing the President into the election campaign.

(3) Article 13 enables the President at any time, after consultation with the Council of State, to convene a meeting of either or both Houses of the Oireachtas. In this situation the President has the freedom to ignore the advice of the government. This power could become important if, for example, an unpopular government tried to avoid criticism by not calling a meeting of the Dáil. The power has never been exercised in the circumstances envisaged by the Constitution (although the President summoned a joint meeting of the Dáil and Seanad on 21 January 1969 to commemorate the fiftieth anniversary of the first meeting of Dáil Éireann). In an interview with the *Cork Examiner* on 8 October 1991 President Robinson envisaged the possibility of using this power, while acknowledging that it had to be a matter of timing and circumstance and that it could not be done at a time of political sensitivity.

(4) Under Article 27, a petition may be addressed to the President by a majority of senators and at least one-third of the members of the Dáil, requesting him not to sign a bill until it has been approved by the people either at a referendum or at a general election. The President then decides whether or not the bill 'contains a proposal of such national importance that the will of the people thereon ought to be ascertained'.

This provision is designed for a situation in which a matter of fundamental national importance is passed in the Dáil but is almost unanimously rejected in the Seanad. It applies to bills in respect of which the Seanad has been overruled by the Dáil in exercise of the powers given by Article 23. The President can act only after consultation with the Council of State. Where the President accepts a petition, the bill cannot become law until it has been approved by the people at a referendum or by resolution of the Dáil passed after a dissolution and reassembly. No bill has so far been referred to the people under these provisions.

(5) Article 22 enables the President, at the request of the Seanad, to refer the question as to whether a bill is or is not a money bill (a bill relating to the finances of the state) to a Committee of Privileges, a committee consisting of an equal number of members of the Dáil and of the Seanad with a judge of the Supreme Court as chairman. For the discussion of money bills, the Seanad has only twenty-one days, although it has three months for the discussion of an ordinary measure. Mr de Valera explained:

> To prevent any fraud upon the Seanad by compelling them to discuss within twenty-one days and practically not to interfere with the bill which they would have a perfect right to discuss if it came in the guise of an ordinary measure, and to prevent the possibility of mistakes by the Chairman of the Dáil, there is

an appeal to the President against a certificate of the Ceann Comhairle. There can be an appeal made by the House affected, that is the Seanad (*Dáil Debates*, 11 May 1937, col. 49).

The Seanad may complain to the President that the bill was certified a money bill in error and may accordingly ask him to set up a Committee of Privileges to determine whether the bill was or was not a money bill. This function has not been exercised.

(6) The final independent power of the President relates to the need to get legislation passed quickly during a state of emergency. Under Article 24, when a bill is 'urgent and immediately necessary for the preservation of the public peace and security, or by reason of the existence of a public emergency whether domestic or international', the time for its consideration by the Seanad may be shortened. There may be occasions in which the very safety of the state may depend upon making a quick decision. The President has to agree with the government's view that a bill is in this category before this procedure can be adopted. The Dáil can then compel the Seanad to reach a decision within a very limited period; and if the Dáil does not accept this decision, the law can be enacted without the approval of the Seanad.

It is in order to diminish the chances of a misuse of this power that the President's consent has to be obtained. He has to agree with the Dáil before the power of the Seanad can be curtailed. He is put in a very responsible position to act as umpire to see that the Dáil acts in accordance with the spirit of the Constitution. It would have to be a clear and an obvious abuse of power before the President would interfere. No attempts appear to have been made to avail of the powers given by this article.

The Constitution Review Group, 1996 considered the question of whether the powers of the President should be expanded. It recommended against such an extension, as likely to embroil the President in party politics and to reduce accountability, since the President, unlike the government, is not answerable to the Oireachtas and the courts.

The Council of State

The Council of State aids and counsels the President. It plays a vital role when the President opts to use his discretionary powers listed under (1), (3) and (4) above. The Council of State is composed of: (1) (as ex officio members) the Taoiseach, the Tánaiste, the Chief Justice, the President of the High Court, the Ceann Comhairle of the Dáil, the Cathaoirleach of the Senate and the Attorney General; (2) every able and willing person who has held office as President, Taoiseach and Chief Justice; (3) a maximum of seven other persons whom the President may appoint at his own discretion. Members in the third category serve only during the term(s) of the President who appoints them, and he has the power to remove them for any reason he deems sufficient. Their appointment enables the President to make the Council of State 'as representative as possible' (*Dáil Debates*, 13 May 1937, col. 430). The term of office of the Council of State is the same as that of the President who appointed it.

Members of the Council of State take an oath to 'conscientiously fulfil duties' as members and meet only when summoned by the President. The meetings are held in camera, and the President is not bound to follow the advice he receives; the final decision on the matter in question is his alone – Article 32 of the Constitution states that 'The president shall not exercise or perform any of the powers or functions which are by this Constitution expressed to be exercisable or performable by him after consultation with the Council of State unless, and on every occasion before so doing, he shall have convened a meeting of the Council of State and the members present at such meeting shall have been heard by him.'

President Robinson called together the Council of State on eight occasions, more often than any other President in any single term in the history of the state. Two of the occasions were not connected with legislation, but related to advice being sought from the Council of State on issues which the president would raise in addresses of the Houses of the Oireachtas. The other six meetings were in regard to legislation.

Article 14 provides for the establishment of a Presidential Commission, consisting of the Chief Justice, the Ceann Comhairle and the Cathaoirleach, to exercise the powers and functions of the President in the event of his absence, temporary incapacity or at any time when the office of the president may be vacant. In any contingency not provided for in the situation envisaged by Article 14, the Council of State may exercise its sole power to make such provisions as to it may seem necessary for the exercise and performance of the President's powers and functions. A full listing of the meetings of the Council of State is at Appendix 11.

Reference of Bills to the Supreme Court

Under Article 26 (referred to earlier), the President is given the special function of highlighting the fact that a particular bill, or section of a bill, may be against the Constitution and of stopping it before it becomes law. If the President is of the opinion that the measure, if passed, might be invalid by being contrary to the Constitution, he has the power of referring that measure for decision to the Supreme Court. It is not the President who decides whether it is against the Constitution or not. His function is simply one of referral to the Supreme Court, which makes the ultimate decision. It is an important power, because if the President did sign the bill into law, some of its consequences might well be irreversible.

Every reference of a bill to the Supreme Court by the President must be made not later than the seventh day after the date on which the bill is presented to him by the Taoiseach for signature. The President is not permitted to refer money bills, bills to amend the Constitution or bills whose time for consideration by the Seanad had been abridged under Article 24. The Supreme Court must deliver a single decision, with no dissenting or separate judgments, not later than sixty days after the date of reference.

The advantages of the Article 26 procedure are that it allows the President to take action in good time to prevent legislation which is unconstitutional from getting on to the statute book. Furthermore, it saves the citizens from the trouble and expense of contesting the legislation later in the courts. It has the further advantage of deterring governments from introducing legislative proposals which might be repugnant to the Constitution.

The disadvantages are, firstly, that testing at this stage may be unsatisfactory, as there is no experience of operating the legislation. Furthermore, Article 34.3.3 provides that 'no court whatever shall have jurisdiction to question the validity of a law' which has been cleared through the Article 26 procedure. This means that although the act may have disclosed highly objectionable aspects in its operation, which were unforeseen at the time of the Article 26 reference, it cannot subsequently be challenged. In addition, commentators have noted that the leading constitutional court decisions have been taken in the course of ordinary proceedings brought in the courts. It is also argued that the Supreme Court is the ultimate arbiter and, as such, is the real guardian of the people's rights in the Constitution.

In the case of a reference of a bill under Article 26, the Attorney General (or counsel on his behalf) argues the case in favour of the constitutionality of the bill, and counsel assigned by the court argues the case that the bill is repugnant to the Constitution, largely by drawing attention to hypothetical results of its enactment. Such hypothetical argument is often difficult because it is not always possible to envisage the consequences of the bills if enacted.

Twelve bills have been referred by the President to the Supreme Court under Article 26. These were:

(1) the Offences Against the State (Amendment) Bill 1940;
(2) the School Attendance Bill 1942;
(3) the Electoral (Amendment) Bill 1961;
(4) the Criminal Law (Jurisdiction) Bill 1975;
(5) the Emergency Powers Bill 1976;

(6) the Housing (Private Rented Dwellings) Bill 1981;
(7) the Electoral (Amendment) Bill 1983;
(8) the Adoption (No. 2) Bill 1987;
(9) the Matrimonial Home Bill 1993;
(10) the Regulation of Information Services Outside the State for Termination of Pregnancies Bill 1995;
(11) the Employment Equality Bill 1996;
(12) the Equal Status Bill 1997.

Six of these were declared to be repugnant to the Constitution. They were: the School Attendance Bill, which, in the opinion of the court, infringed the rights of parents to decide how their children should be educated; the Housing Bill, which was deemed to interfere with the property rights of owners of particular dwellings; the Electoral (Amendment) Bill 1983, which, in extending voting rights, was deemed to conflict with other basic provisions of the Constitution; the Matrimonial Home Bill; the Employment Equality Bill; and the Equal Status Bill. The bills of 1940 and 1961 were amendments of legislation which had already been declared unconstitutional. A full listing of bills referred to the Supreme Court by the President is at Appendix 12.

The 1967 Report of the Committee on the Constitution stated in relation to Article 26: 'We feel that, on the whole, this kind of provision is useful in the Constitution, and we are unable to agree, therefore, that it should be deleted. While we are unanimous in this opinion that Article 26 should be retained, we feel that some changes are necessary, but we have been unable to agree on the best approach to the problem.'

The 1996 Constitution Review Group favoured the retention of the reference procedure of Article 26, but considered that, on balance, the unchallengeability provision under Article 34.3.3 should be deleted in its entirety.

The Emergency Powers Bill 1976

In September 1976 President Cearbhall Ó Dálaigh referred the Emergency Powers Bill 1976 to the Supreme Court under Article 26 of the Constitution, as he was entitled to do, for a decision as to its constitutionality as the bill conferred great powers on the authorities. The government's view was that the exemption provided by Article 28.3.3 meant that the bill could not be declared unconstitutional as the Supreme Court did not have jurisdiction to review the bill, because it was for the purpose of securing the public safety of the state. The Supreme Court found that the bill was not repugnant to the Constitution, but stated:

> As to the right of the President to refer the bill to this Court, it is clear that he has power to do so notwithstanding that the bill is one passed by both Houses of the Oireachtas by reference to the provisions of subsection 3.3 of Article 28. The power of the President to do so has not been questioned in these proceedings.

The exercise of this independent power under Article 26 involved the President in political controversy. The Minister for Defence, Patrick Donegan, publicly criticised the President 'in a clearly improper manner' (Chubb 1982: 200) in a speech delivered at Columb Military Barracks, Mullingar, on 18 October 1976 when he referred to him as 'a thundering disgrace', adding: 'The fact is that the army must stand behind the state.' The President in a letter to Mr Donegan dated 19 October 1976 asked the question, 'Can this sequence be construed by ordinary people otherwise than as an insinuation that the President does not stand behind the state?'

The Taoiseach, Liam Cosgrave, referred to the Minister for Defence's outburst as no more than 'excessive verbal exuberance', and a Dáil motion calling on the minister to resign was defeated by 63 votes to 58 on 21 October. On the following day, moved by the government's failure to take action against the minister, President Ó Dálaigh resigned. He took this course of action to assert publicly his personal dignity and independence as President of Ireland and – a matter of much greater importance for every citizen – to endeavour to protect the dignity and independence of the presidency as an institution. The Minister for Defence had apologised by letter for what he had said, telling the President that he deeply regretted the use of the words 'thundering disgrace'. Immediately after resigning, Mr Ó Dálaigh published the correspondence exchanged between himself and the minister, in the course of which he had written:

> The President's role in relation to the Defence Forces is honorary in character; nevertheless, a special relationship exists between the President and the Minister for Defence. That relationship has been irreparably breached not only by what you said yesterday, but also because of the place where, and the persons before whom, you chose to make your outrageous criticism.

Thus the combination of the roles of guardian of the people's rights under the Constitution and the ceremonial head of state can involve the President in political controversy in the exercise of the independent powers bestowed on him by the Constitution, particularly in so far as they have been designed and fall to be exercised at times of crisis and where a conflict of opinion may emerge.

Conclusion

The President of Ireland is head of state with very few powers or functions which may be exercised independently of government control. This accords with constitutional practice in most other countries where the government is led by a prime minister; it differs radically from the United States, where the powers usually found in the hands of the nominal head of state are vested in the President together with the real executive power of government. In Ireland the Taoiseach is the head of the government and the President is ceremonial head of state.

The President, freed from executive functions and the divisiveness of party politics, serves as a personification of the state. From the President the people seek a reflection of their higher values and aspirations. In return, the President takes precedence over all persons in the state.

The Constitution spells out the President's powers in detail so that conflict over spheres of authority between the cabinet and the President should not arise. The President's powers are directly circumscribed, and he normally acts on the advice and authority of the government. Any appointments which he makes under the Constitution (with the exception of the seven appointees to the Council of State, a purely consultative body) are made following the advice of a third party. Such independent powers as he possesses are intended for use only in emergencies, and to date only two of these independent powers have been exercised. The constitutional crisis of October 1976 which led to the resignation of President Ó Dálaigh resulted from the exercise by him of one of his independent powers under the Constitution.

From time to time there has been discussion as to how far it is possible or desirable to develop, within the existing constitutional controls, a new and more open style of presidency in which each individual incumbent can make a distinctively personal contribution. In this connection, Erskine Childers, on the announcement of his candidature for the office of President in 1973, declared: 'I have learned by experience that outside the party political field, some leaders should give guidance to the people, some leaders should reflect the most reasonable aspirations of the people on matters where discussion and debate will not create fundamental national division, but will encourage enlightened examination.' President Childers did not follow this strategy with much vigour, partly because of the generally unfavourable reaction among politicians of all parties to this suggestion, and partly because of his untimely death. Clearly, it would be extremely difficult for a President to combine the diverse roles of titular head of state, guardian of people's rights under the Constitution and advocate of enlightened examination of social issues without falling foul of political controversy, criticism and misunderstanding.

In her inauguration speech on 3 December 1990 President Robinson described her aim as a presidency of 'justice, peace and love'. President McAleese, at her inauguration on 11 November 1997, said:

> I am honoured and humbled to be successor to seven exemplary presidents. Their differing religious, political, geographical and social origins speak loudly of a presidency which has always been wide open and all-embracing. Among them were presidents from Connacht, Leinster and Munster, to say nothing of America and London. It is my special privilege and delight to be the first president from Ulster.

The 1967 Report of the Committee on the Constitution considered a proposal that the separate office of President should be abolished and set out the arguments advanced for and against. The committee was divided on the question. The arguments put forward in favour of abolition include: (1) that the President is largely a figurehead; (2) that the President's formal duties as head of state could without difficulty be discharged by the Taoiseach, who could act as both head of government and head of state; (3) that the abolition of the separate office of President would give rise to substantial financial savings. However, it can be reasonably argued that it would be neither desirable (in view of the President's function as guardian of the Constitution) nor practicable to combine the offices of Taoiseach and President; nor would it result in any significant financial saving. The 1996 Report of the Constitution Review Group considered that there was no public demand or good reason for the abolition of the office: 'A State requires a Head of State; the President's function as guardian of the Constitution requires that the office be separate from the executive.' The Review Group considered that the Constitution should be amended to describe the President as head of state.

The President is in constitutional theory elected by the people to safeguard their rights under the Constitution and is an important part of the system of checks and balances on the power of the legislature. While the President has very few independent powers under the Constitution, it is clear that these independent powers are potentially very important because they are designed to act as a check in circumstances of conflict or crisis. The fact that these powers have not often or never been exercised does not diminish their potential importance.

REFERENCES

Chubb, Basil, *The Government and Politics of Ireland*, 2nd ed. (London: Longman, 1982)

Chubb, Basil, *A Source Book of Irish Government* (Dublin: Institute of Public Administration, 1983)

Farrell, Brian, 'The Constitution and the Institutions of Government: Constitutional Theory and Political Practice' in F. Litton (ed.), *The Constitution of Ireland 1937–87* (special issue of *Administration*, vol. 35, no. 4, 1987)
Government of Ireland, *Report of the Constitution Review Group*, Pn. 2632 (Dublin: Stationery Office, 1996)
Kelly, John M., *The Irish Constitution* (Dublin: Jurist Publishing, 1984)
McDunphy, Michael, *The President of Ireland: His Powers, Functions and Duties* (Dublin: Browne & Nolan, 1945)

APPENDIX 10

Presidents of Ireland

	President
25.6.38–25.6.45	Douglas Hyde
25.6.45–25.6.59	Seán T. Ó Ceallaigh
25.6.59–25.6.73	Eamon de Valera
25.6.73–17.11.74	Erskine Childers
19.12.74–22.10.76	Cearbhall Ó Dálaigh
3.12.76–3.12.90	Patrick Hillery
3.12.90–12.9.97	Mary Robinson
11.11.97–	Mary McAleese

APPENDIX 11

Meetings of the Council of State

	Date of meeting	Purpose	Outcome
1	8 January 1940	Offences Against the State (Amendment) Bill 1940 To repeal Part VI of the Offences Against the State Act 1939, and to make other provisions in relation to the detention of certain persons	Referred to Supreme Court and subsequently signed
2	25 February 1943	School Attendance Bill 1942 To amend the School Attendance Act 1926	Referred to Supreme Court and found unconstitutional
3	13 August 1947	Health Bill 1947	Bill signed without referral
4	14 June 1961	Electoral (Amendment) Bill 1961 To fix the number of members of Dáil Éireann and to revise their constituencies and to amend the law relating to the election of such members	Referred to Supreme Court and subsequently signed
5	6 March 1967	Income Tax Bill 1966	Bill signed without referral
6	20 December 1968	The President to address the Houses of the Oireachtas on 21 January 1969 on the occasion of the fiftieth anniversary of the first meeting of the First Dáil Éireann	
7	10 March 1976	Criminal Law (Jurisdiction) Bill 1975 To extend the criminal law of the state to certain acts done in Northern Ireland. To provide for	Referred to Supreme Court and subsequently signed

→

	Date of meeting	Purpose	Outcome
7	10 March 1976 *contd.*	the admission of evidence obtained by the examination of witnesses in Northern Ireland at trials for offences in respect of those acts, to enable evidence to be obtained by the examination of witnesses in the state for trials in Northern Ireland for corresponding offences under the law of Northern Ireland in respect of acts done in the state, to reform the criminal law in other respects and to provide for related matters.	
8	23 September 1976	Emergency Powers Bill 1976	Referred to Supreme Court and subsequently signed
		For the purpose of securing the public safety and the preservation of the state in time of an armed conflict in respect of which each of the Houses of the Oireachtas has adopted a resolution on the first day of September 1976, pursuant to subsection 3° of Section 3 of Article 28 of the Constitution	
9	23 September 1976	Criminal Law Bill 1976	Bill signed without referral
10	22 December 1981	Housing (Private Rented Dwellings) Bill 1981	Referred to Supreme Court and found unconstitutional
		To provide for the promotion by the Minister for the Environment of a limited company to provide finance either directly or indirectly, for the acquisition and construction of houses, to provide for the guaranteeing by the Minister for Finance of borrowings by the said company and to provide for other connected matters	

→

	Date of meeting	Purpose	Outcome
11	20 December 1983	Electoral (Amendment) Bill 1983 To provide for the number of members of Dáil Éireann and for the revision of constituencies and to amend the law relating to the election of such members	Referred to Supreme Court and found unconstitutional
12	5 December 1984	Criminal Justice Bill 1983	Bill signed without referral
13	22 June 1988	Adoption (No. 2) Bill 1987 To provide, in exceptional cases, where the parents for physical or moral reasons have failed in their duty towards their children, of the place of the parents and for that purpose and other purposes to amend and extend the Adoption Acts 1952 to 1976	Referred to Supreme Court and subsequently signed
14	30 October 1991	Fisheries (Amendment) Bill 1990	Bill signed without referral
15	29 June 1992	The President to address the Houses of the Oireachtas on a matter of national importance – 'The Irish Identity in Europe'	
16	1 December 1993	Matrimonial Home Bill 1993 To make provision, in the interests of the common good, in relation to the ownership of matrimonial homes, to provide for certain other matters affecting spouses in relation to property and to provide for related matters	Referred to Supreme Court and found unconstitutional

⟶

	Date of meeting	Purpose	Outcome
17	1 March 1994	Criminal Justice Public Order Bill 1993	Bill signed without referral
18	24 January 1995	The President to address the Houses of the Oireachtas on a matter of public importance – 'Cherishing the Irish Diaspora'	
19	16 March 1995	Regulation of Information Services Outside the State for Termination of Pregnancies Bill 1995 To prescribe the conditions subject to which certain information relating to services lawfully available outside the State for the termination of pregnancies and to persons who provide such services may be given to individual women or the general public, to amend the Indecent Advertisements Act 1889, and the Censorship of Publications Acts 1929 to 1967, and to provide for related matters	Referred to Supreme Court and subsequently signed
20	1 April 1997	Employment Equality Bill 1996	Referred to Supreme Court and found unconstitutional
21	6 May 1997	Equal Status Bill 1997	Referred to Supreme Court and found unconstitutional

APPENDIX 12

BILLS REFERRED TO THE SUPREME COURT BY THE PRESIDENT

	Date of meeting of Council of State	Bill	Outcome
1	8 January 1940	Offences Against the State (Amendment) Bill 1940 To repeal Part VI of the Offences Against the State Act 1939, and to make other provisions in relation to the detention of certain persons	Referred to Supreme Court and subsequently signed
2	25 February 1943	School Attendance Bill 1942 To amend the School Attendance Act 1926	Referred to Supreme Court and found unconstitutional
3	14 June 1961	Electoral (Amendment) Bill 1961 To fix the number of members of Dáil Éireann and to revise their constituencies and to amend the law relating to the election of such members	Referred to Supreme Court and subsequently signed
4	10 March 1976	Criminal Law (Jurisdiction) Bill 1975 To extend the criminal law of the State to certain Acts done in N. Ireland. To provide for the admission of evidence obtained by the examination of witnesses in N Ireland at Trials for Offences in respect of those Acts, to enable evidence to be obtained by the examination of witnesses in the State for Trials in N Ireland for corresponding offences under the law of N Ireland in respect of Acts done in the State, to reform the Criminal Law in other respects and to provide for related matters	Referred to Supreme Court and subsequently signed

→

	Date of meeting of Council of State	Bill	Outcome
5	23 September 1976	Emergency Powers Bill 1976 For the purpose of securing the public safety and the preservation of the State in time of an armed conflict in respect of which each of the Houses of the Oireachtas has adopted a resolution on the first day of September, 1976, pursuant to subsection 3° of Section 3 of Article 28 of the Constitution	Referred to Supreme Court and subsequently signed
6	22 December 1981	Housing (Private Rented Dwellings) Bill 1981 To amend the Rent Restrictions Acts on foot of the decision in *Blake* v. *Attorney General* [1982] IR 177	Referred to Supreme Court and found unconstitutional
7	20 December 1983	Electoral (Amendment) Bill 1983 To extend the franchise to British citizens resident in Ireland	Referred to Supreme Court and found unconstitutional
8	22 June 1988	Adoption (No. 2) Bill 1987 To provide, in exceptional cases, where the parents for physical or moral reasons have failed in their duty towards their children, of the place of parents and for that purpose and other purposes to amend and extend the Adoption Acts 1952 to 1976	Referred to Supreme Court and subsequently signed
9	1 December 1993	Matrimonial Home Bill 1993 To make provision, in the interests of the common good, in relation to the ownership of	Referred to Supreme Court and found unconstitutional

→

	Date of meeting of Council of State	Bill	Outcome
9	1 December 1993 *contd.*	matrimonial homes, to provide for certain other matters affecting spouses in relation to property and to provide for related matters	
10	16 March 1995	Regulation of Information Services Outside the State for Termination of Pregnancies Bill 1995 To prescribe the conditions subject to which certain information relating to services lawfully available outside the State for the termination of pregnancies and to persons who provide such services may be given to individual women or the general public, to amend the Indecent Advertisements Act 1889, and the Censorship of Publications Acts 1929 to 1967, and to provide for related matters	Referred to Supreme Court and subsequently signed
11	1 April 1997	Employment Equality Bill 1996 To counter discrimination in employment	Referred to Supreme Court and found unconstitutional
12	6 May 1997	Equal Status Bill 1997 To provide for protection against discrimination for, among others, travellers, certain religious groups, homosexuals and people with some disabilities	Referred to Supreme Court and found unconstitutional

6

THE CIVIL SERVICE

The civil service comprises that body of persons who have been selected by the Civil Service Commission to serve the organs of state defined by the Constitution, namely the President, the Houses of the Oireachtas, the judiciary, the Taoiseach and his ministers, the Attorney General and the Comptroller and Auditor General. The term can be used roughly to describe those who work in government departments. The legal basis for the civil service is provided in the Ministers and Secretaries Act 1924. That act authorises each minister to appoint the civil servants in his department (except the secretary general) in such numbers and grades as the Minister for Finance approves. The secretary general of each department is appointed by the government on the recommendation of the minister concerned. The procedure by which appointments are made is described below.

Technically, there are two categories of civil servants. Those employed in parts of the civil service not under the direct control of ministers are *civil servants of the state*, for example the staff in the Houses of the Oireachtas. All other civil servants – the vast majority – who are employed in the government departments are *civil servants of the government.*

There were 31,015 civil servants on 1 January 1997. The table at Appendix 13 shows the number in each department/office. Although this is less than the number of persons employed in the local authorities, the health services or the state-sponsored bodies, the civil service occupies a key position in the public service in that it is the part of that service which is closest to ministers and government and, therefore, more immediately involved in the making of policy. Moreover, its supervisory influence extends to the various other parts of the public service, on whose activities it impinges in one way or another, whether in matters of policy, finance, organisation, pay or personnel management. It is at the hub of the wheel of government, so to speak.

The prime purpose of the civil service as a whole is, of course, to serve the public, and the first duty of a civil servant is to help his minister meet his responsibilities to the Oireachtas. He works continuously for, with and under politicians in a system which responds to a complex series of demands which emerge in various ways: from political parties, organisations, groups and the media; from administrators themselves through their perception of needs, their appreciation of the problems hindering development and their concern to get these resolved; from decisions of the courts and other appellate bodies; from Ireland's membership of international organisations, such as the EU; and from developments abroad generally, such as economic recession or war.

An interesting aspect of the Irish civil servant is that although politicians and ministers change, the civil service is permanent. There is something of a paradox in this, in that the civil service is at one and the same time the permanent servant of the state and the servant of the administration which is for the time being in power.

Recruitment

Civil servants (with some exceptions noted beneath) are recruited as a result of competitions held by the Civil Service Commission under the Civil Service Commissioners Act 1956. The commissioners are the Ceann Comhairle of the Dáil, the Secretary to the Government and an assistant secretary in the Department of Finance. The commission operates under the aegis of the Department of Finance, but is independent of the minister in its selection procedures, though it is the minister who answers parliamentary questions relating to the policy of the commission.

The competitions can be of different kinds and may consist of one or more of the following: a written, oral or practical examination, an interview, or any other test considered appropriate. Candidates fall into two broad categories. The first category is that of persons seeking admission on the basis of the school certificate examinations or tests specially set by the commission. In addition to an examination, such candidates are usually obliged to undergo an interview before being appointed, as, for example, potential executive officers. The second category comprises persons who have technical qualifications usually acquired after some form of third-level education or who have certain prescribed experience. Generally, persons in this category (for example, engineers) are selected after interview. These competitions are described as open competitions, i.e. they are open to persons outside the civil service who fulfil the conditions laid down.

For each competition by interview, a special interview board is set up, normally consisting of three members. The commission uses the services of interviewers drawn from all sections of the community. A detailed scheme of marking is provided by the commission for each board so as to give it a framework within which it may make its assessments.

Canvassing on behalf of competition candidates is prohibited, and this is a rule which is rigidly enforced. No matter what criticism may be levelled against the commission for its seemingly bureaucratic procedures, there has never been any suggestion that these are anything other than completely fair. Even politicians, who spend a great deal of their time making representations to other civil service offices, have discovered the waste of time in approaching the Civil Service Commission.

As the minister in charge of each department is legally the employer of all the staff in that department, the names of those selected by the commission are submitted to departments to get ministers' approval to their appointment. No alternative names are provided, and invariably those recommended are appointed.

The exceptional appointments referred to above relate to persons appointed in the public interest, to those in the broad category of skilled worker, porter and cleaner, and to short-term or contract appointments such as temporary seasonal staff for the Passport Office. Those appointed in the public interest are usually persons who have particular skills or talents which the civil service lacks, for example a geologist with special experience or an expert in nuclear energy. Where such appointments are made, the Civil Service Commissioners have no function to perform. The procedure is that the minister to whose department the person is to be appointed obtains first the consent of the government, after which a notice must be published in *Iris Oifigiúil*, the official gazette. If any questions are raised in the Dáil or elsewhere, the minister and the government must be prepared to defend the appointment. For other types of non-competitive appointment specified above, the manner of recruitment is left to individual departments. The usual procedure is for the jobs to be advertised and then filled by interview.

Career Structures

The civil service may be divided into three main career structures: general, departmental and technical. Within these categories are the grades (described below).

General Service

The general service grades are described by the Devlin Report (1969) as consisting of

> a central core of general service officers who are recruited to perform the general duties of departments from the routine clerical operations to the higher policy, advisory and managerial work. These officers are recruited at varying educational levels from primary school to university degree standard. The emphasis is on a general education, and every recruit can, if he obtains the necessary educational qualifications and experience, aspire to the highest positions in the civil service.

Departmental

Departmental grades are confined to a few departments or offices, such as the Department of Foreign Affairs, the Houses of the Oireachtas and the Office of the Comptroller and Auditor General.

Technical

There are technical officers employed in nearly all departments. They are recruited to the civil service for the performance of specialised work and already possess a qualification related to the work to be performed. The qualification is usually a formally recognised degree, diploma or certificate. In so far as it is possible to generalise, their role is to bring expert knowledge, skill and experience in specialist fields to bear on the determination and execution of government policy, for example in advising on the interpretation of the law, on health schemes, on environmental issues or on the development of natural resources. These are the solicitors in the Office of the Chief State Solicitor, the doctors in the Department of Health, the engineers in the Department of the Environment, and the geologists in the Department of Public Enterprise.

Grades

The civil service is divided into about 700 grades: that is to say, within the three categories outlined above there are about 700 job titles. There are not, however, that many pay scales, since many grades have the same scales, and there are many grades with only one person in them, such as the Director of the Meteorological Service or the Registrar of the Supreme Court.

There is no legal definition of a grade; persons are appointed to what are called 'positions' in the civil service. What happens is that positions requiring broadly the same level of qualifications and with comparable levels of work, responsibility, pay and conditions of service are grouped by the Department of Finance into grades. Examples of grades are the executive, engineering, librarian and draftsman grades. The general service is made up of grades which are common to two or more departments; these are described below.

The work of the general service grades has not, even at this remove from the beginning of the state, yet been closely defined, with the result that the lines of demarcation between contiguous grades are far from clear. The confusion which this causes for outsiders is compounded by the fact that job descriptions are not common in the civil service. Persons moving from one job to another within a grade, or moving to a higher grade on promotion, seldom get a statement showing what their new duties are. For the absence of job descriptions there are two main reasons. The first is the tedium of preparing them, when there is no rule saying they should be prepared. The second is that to have them could reduce the freedom of managers at all levels in allocating tasks and could lead to claims for increases in pay where the work done was not exactly in accord with that set down in the job description. Those in the various general service grades are expected to be able to perform efficiently any work assigned to them. This arrangement has, however, enabled the civil service to take in its stride, more or less, the various restrictions on recruitment which have led to many officials at all levels having to carry out tasks not appropriate to their grade because there was no one else available to do so.

Clerical Staff

Clerical staff perform work which includes filing, the operation of machines, the recording of information, checking accounts and making payments, less difficult analysis and presentation of findings, and the drafting of letters and memoranda which follow established practice and seek or give factual information. In general, they deal with work which requires substantial dependence on acquired knowledge and experience. The receptionists in public offices are generally from the clerical grades.

Executive and Higher Executive Officers

The executive grades, which are generally referred to as the middle management grades, could be regarded as the most central to the smooth working of every government department. At entry level they include the brightest of the school leavers, while each year a certain number of places are reserved for university graduates.

The work of executive officers includes presenting all the important aspects of complicated cases in a logical and readable sequence, summarising accurately the particular issues, recommending a course of action where there are a number of options, preparing briefs for, and reports of, meetings, analysing statistical material and accounting for unusual developments.

The work of higher executive officers is an extension, at a higher level, of the work of the basic grade. Higher executive officers have to make more difficult decisions and give directions where there are exceptions to standard procedures.

They and their staff perform a wide range of tasks. Some are charged with large areas of responsibility, such as the payment of salaries in the Department of Education (teachers), Justice (Gardaí) or Defence (army); travelling expenses of the advisers and inspectors employed by the Department of Agriculture and

Food; social welfare allowances; and housing grants. Many are engaged in what is known as case work: for example, examining proposals and making suggestions about the provision of a new school or health clinic; the introduction of a youth help scheme; a new measure to deal with an environmental problem. Some are engaged in monitoring the progress of ongoing measures such as fisheries protection, energy conservation or projects to attract tourists. Many, such as those in the Transport and Aviation Divisions of the Department of Public Enterprise, oversee the operations of state-sponsored bodies. Very many are involved in EU work. Some are engaged in the work of the other international organisations of which Ireland is a member, such as the World Health Organization, the World Trade Organization or the Organization for Economic Co-operation and Development, and regularly attend meetings of these bodies abroad. Very many also are engaged in the operation, maintenance and enhancement of computerised systems, as, for example, those who are responsible for the processing and payment of claims in the Department of Social Welfare. They implement the provisions of legislation (such as the collection of taxes) and assemble information for new legislation, consulting the legal officers as required on this and on the taking of prosecutions under existing legislation. Officers in the Department of Justice ensure the smooth operation of the judicial system and the daily running of the courts. Nearly all officers in all departments at one time or another have to prepare replies to parliamentary questions. The above examples are only a small and random selection of the varied work undertaken by higher executive officers.

The Higher Civil Service

Those in the general service grades from assistant principal upwards, sometimes referred to, following British practice, as the administrative grades, constitute the higher civil service. Their work is broadly concerned with the formulation of policy, pursuing and examining proposals for change, offering alternative lines to ministers, preparation of legislation, organisation of projects or schemes and the general management of large blocks of executive work. They are responsible for the administration of the state and for the execution of policy and are expected, on a continuous basis, to devise ways of improving efficiency. These grades also supply the advisers who accompany ministers when meeting deputations or attending meetings abroad.

In general, the higher an officer moves up the administrative grades, the greater and wider will be his policy role, while his executive role will be correspondingly diminished.

Civil Service Grade Structure

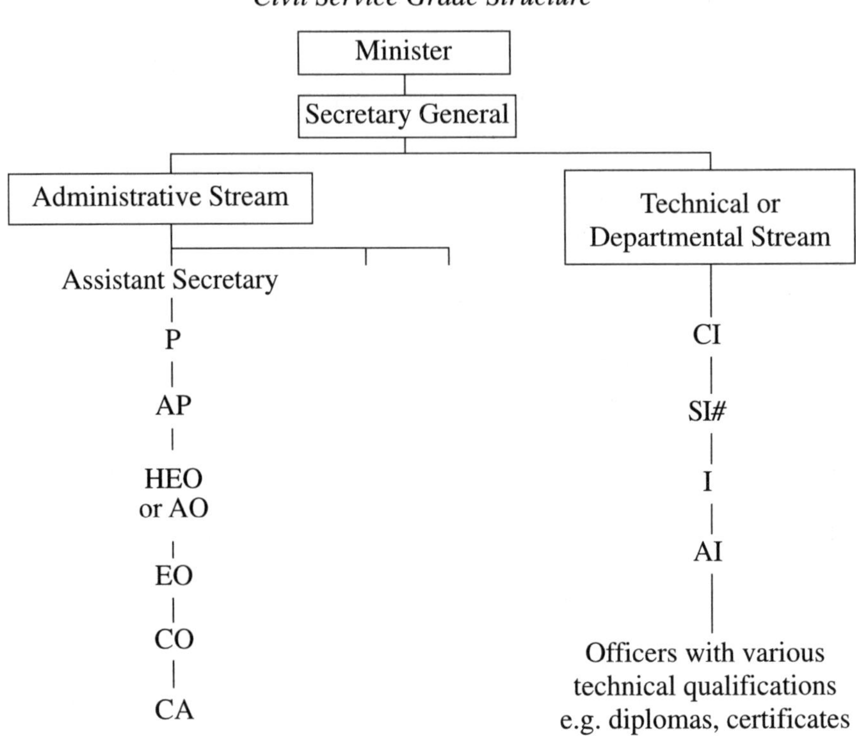

P: Principal (4 or 5 to each Assistant Secretary)
AP: Assistant Principal
HEO: Higher Executive Officer
AO: Administrative Officer (Graduate Entry Grade)
CO/CA: Clerical Officer/Assistant
AI: Assistant Inspector (Graduate Entry Grade)

CI: Chief Inspector (Engineer, Doctor, Architect, Veterinary Surgeon)
SI: Senior Inspector (as above)
#: Number varies up to about 6 Senior Inspectors to each chief
I: Inspector

Principal and Assistant Principal

The grade of principal is a central one in the sense that principals are in charge of large blocks of their departments' work. Each department has a finance and a personnel division. Other examples of divisions are those dealing with old-age benefits, national school buildings and petroleum products in the relevant departments.

Where a principal is engaged on policy work relating to broad national issues, the work is typically divided into sub-areas with an assistant principal in each, putting forward proposals for dealing with the issues in his sub-area. Where the work involves national schemes, it could be divided on a geographical basis. Each principal has, in the normal course, the help of at least two assistant principals. The area of work controlled by an assistant principal is normally called a *branch*.

The officials who accompany ministers on their appearances in the Dáil in connection with routine parliamentary business are usually in the grades of assistant principal or principal.

Assistant Secretary

The duties of assistant secretaries are rather similar to those of principals, but on a higher level of responsibility and usually in a broader field. A main feature of the assistant secretary's role is his access to the minister; the terms and frequency of this access depend on the attitudes of individual ministers and secretaries general.

On major parliamentary occasions, such as the presentation of the budget or of departmental estimates, or when the issues being debated are otherwise politically important or sensitive, the official accompanying the minister in the Dáil is usually an assistant secretary.

Secretary General

The secretary general is the chief adviser to the minister and is the apex of the pyramid. He is, in effect, the managing director of the department. All of the policy proposals which have been formulated within the department, all of the matters on which the minister's views or directions are sought or which it is considered desirable to bring to his notice are submitted to the secretary general for presentation to the minister. The secretary general is personally responsible to the minister for the overall management of the department, including the regularity and propriety of all transactions and the efficiency and economy of administration in the department.

The secretary general is also the accounting officer for his department's vote. What this means is that he has primary responsibility for the administration of the money voted each year by the Dáil for the department. This is an important exception to the principle of ministerial responsibility. At the end of each year he must prepare an account, called the appropriation account, showing how the money voted by the Dáil for the department has been spent – in effect to show that it has been properly spent in the manner approved by the Dáil. (The appropriation account of the Department of Finance for 1995 is reproduced in Appendix 14.) The secretary general must be satisfied that adequate arrangements exist to ensure the correctness of all payments from the vote under his control and the bringing to account of all receipts connected with the vote. This account is presented to the Comptroller and Auditor General and subsequently to the Public Accounts Committee (PAC). When the committee is examining the report, the secretary general is the principal witness. He answers the questions of the committee and otherwise explains matters as requested.

Work of the Civil Service

The Principle of Accountability

Under the Ministers and Secretaries Act 1924, ministers are responsible for administering their departments and for exercising the powers, duties and functions thereof. The act confers also on the minister, as head of the department, the status of corporation sole, that is perpetual succession enabling the minister, as an office, to sue and be sued, and acquire, hold and dispose of land for the purpose of the powers, duties and functions of his department. These two provisions, taken together, have had the effect that the acts of a department are seen to be the acts of its minister, for which he alone is responsible; and that, legally speaking, unless there is an exception provided by law (which there is, for example, in the case of civil servants determining tax liabilities in the Office of the Revenue Commissioners), no civil servant can in law give a decision. In effect, the minister is the department, and his servants have no separate existence. Every decision made by a government department comes, strictly speaking, from the minister. As it is obvious that ministers cannot personally make all decisions, owing to the demands on their time and the lack of the necessary detailed knowledge, the vast majority of the decisions are in fact made by the civil servants. How the system works in practice is that the civil servants' decisions are regarded as being those which the minister would have made had the issues been brought to his personal notice. The work is carried on through a system of implicit delegation from the minister to the secretary general of the department and on down through the various grades. Hence the conventional opening phrase in letters from government departments: 'I am directed by the Minister for X to state . . .'

The system has had a major impact on the way in which the civil service does its work. It is the minister who is answerable to the Dáil and ultimately to the electorate for all the activities of his department; and as he may be questioned in the Dáil about them, the discretion and freedom of action of civil servants is limited. As a result, they are often regarded as being over-cautious. This caution arises from their anxiety to ensure that none of their actions/decisions is such as to cause the minister any embarrassment which could in turn reflect on the individual official. There is, in particular, a need for consistency in dealing with individual cases; and this in turn leads to a reliance on precedents, which may not be quite apt in every instance. The overriding emphasis on equity and impartiality is marked in all aspects of civil service work.

Following a review of the Ministers and Secretaries Act, in the context of a programme of change for the civil service designed to bring about a greater focus on service delivery, performance and the achievement of results, the Public Service Management Act 1997 was enacted. Though this act also is founded on the principle of ministerial accountability to the Dáil, it provides for the formal assignment to the secretary general of authority, responsibility and accountability for carrying out specified functions and duties on behalf of the minister. In turn, there is provision for the secretary general to assign responsibility and accountability for functions to civil servants at other levels within the department. The act provides also for civil servants to appear before parliamentary committees duly authorised to examine the exercise of any such function. These provisions are significant additions to the arrangements in the Ministers and Secretaries Act, which did not provide for the formal assignment of statutory responsibility to secretaries or their subordinates for the exercise of functions on behalf of the minister.

The accountability of the minister to parliament and to the public is an integral part of the daily life of many civil servants. This entails keeping detailed records, taking decisions at a higher level than may appear necessary, documenting discussions and negotiations leading to decisions, carefully drawing up and meticulously observing the rules relating to the making and receipt of payments, and having more centralised arrangements for financial control than are found in the private sector. Commenting on this aspect of the work, FitzGerald noted (1991: 54): 'I came to appreciate also the commitment to thoroughness which, while sometimes frustrating in the slow tempo it imposes on change, protects the system against egregious error.'

The Non-Commercial Principle

A large part of the work of the civil service has no commercial counterpart. Drafting and applying legislation, taking measures to protect the environment, making social welfare payments and arranging for the certificate examinations in second-level schools are typical of the tasks which are unique to government. Government is judged not on its profitability but on its social, political, cultural and economic achievements, subject to some overall limitation upon its total demands for taxation. The level of taxation is judged in general terms; it is seldom linked to specific outputs. Thus, up to the present time, the efficiency and effectiveness with which departments conduct their business have not been the dominant factor in determining the flow of funds towards them. Hence departments have not generally found much benefit in deploying the kinds of management system common in the private sector. This situation is, however, changing, albeit slowly.

Basic Functions

The civil service has two main tasks: to assist ministers in the making of policy, and to carry out policy decisions. Policy formulation means analysing the problems that exist, defining the issues they present and finding out how they should be dealt with. Among the major questions to which civil servants have addressed themselves in recent years are: keeping beaches free from pollution; amendment of the criminal justice laws; the welfare of children; neutrality; changes in secondary education.

Having thoroughly examined all aspects of the problems laid before them, civil servants then inform their ministers of the various alternatives open to them, making a recommendation as to which should be selected. Thus the decisions of a minister are considerably influenced by what has gone on before. The calibre of mind that civil servants bring to their appraisal of the facts of a specific problem influences, and often determines, the character of the minister's decision. The nature and importance of the policy-making process illustrate the necessity for civil servants to have ability, professional knowledge, integrity, and independence of thought. Generally, ministers have a relationship with their advisers in which no one feels restrained from freely expressing their views. FitzGerald, however, adverts to an occasion on which he considered that the Department of Finance attempted to challenge a government decision. He went on to say that this action was, nevertheless, untypical, noting that

> civil servants rightly consider it to be their duty to advise ministers fully of the possible adverse consequences of proposed political decisions; they would be failing in their duty were they to do otherwise. It is also humanly understandable that they should often tend to feel that the status quo, the product largely of their own and their predecessors' efforts, has a certain merit and deserves to be preserved unless very cogent arguments are put forward for altering it. Some resistance to change is thus to be expected from the civil service, each department of which tends to have its own attachment to policies developed in the past (1991: 301).

When decisions are taken, civil servants at all levels seek faithfully to implement them, irrespective of whether or not they accord with the advice given. The situation is neatly expressed in the well-worn phrase 'minister on top, civil servant on tap'. The relationship between a civil servant and his minister is one in which the former is publicly silent and the latter generally has little to say. In the course of their work in advising ministers and in seeing that decisions are implemented, the types of task are many and varied. Some typical examples follow.

Legislation

When legislation is needed to implement some new policy or to change an existing policy, one of the senior officials in the field of work where the new measures are to be taken usually has the task of preparing a background memorandum setting out why the legislation is necessary; why the present position in regard to the matter at issue is regarded as unsatisfactory; what benefits will accrue from passing the legislation (and what disadvantages, if any); what parties or activities are likely to be affected and in what respects; what changes will be required in existing cognate activities as a result of the new legislation; what the cost will be, and so on.

When the proposals have been approved by his minister and by the government, the civil servant then attends on the Attorney General during their drafting into the form of a bill for presentation to the government and subsequently to the Dáil or Seanad. He prepares the speeches which the minister delivers on the various stages of the bill, and waits on the minister during all stages of the debates. He takes notes on the points made by members, arranges for the inclusion in the bill of any amendments accepted, and prepares the minister's concluding speech, which deals with the various points raised.

When legislation has been passed by the Oireachtas (or otherwise when decisions have been taken by the government) requiring the introduction of new schemes or changes in existing schemes, a number of consequential matters have to be considered. These might include staffing, publicity, forms and procedures, discussions with bodies and groups who will be affected, and systems to provide management information.

Meetings Abroad

Over the last thirty years or so civil servants have increasingly taken part in the work of numerous international organisations, most notably the European Union. Attendance at meetings abroad is now a feature of the work of many civil servants, mainly those at middle and senior level. As far as possible, attendance is shared evenly among those engaged on a particular aspect of their department's work, and staff transfers take account of the desirability of providing this type of experience for as many persons as possible.

The EU process involves the representatives of national governments in the preparatory and decision-making functions of the Council of Ministers. Officials from the Departments of Foreign Affairs, Finance, Agriculture and Food, Enterprise, Trade and Employment, and Environment attend frequently and regularly at meetings in Brussels (and officials of the other departments less regularly). There they advance the views and interests of their departments and respond to initiatives from others. In a typical instance the Commission initially invites member countries, in effect officials from the departments concerned, to bilateral discussions on some proposal it hopes to put forward for the ultimate approval of the Council of Ministers. Typical examples of proposals are a project to reduce unemployment, the tightening of regulations about the use of heavy lorries, the revision of the Common Agricultural Policy, and provision for Union-wide recognition of architects. After the bilateral discussions a draft regulation or directive is examined, first by a working group consisting of officials of the member states, and then by higher-level committees – the Special Committee on Agriculture if it is of an agricultural nature, and the Committee of Permanent Representatives (COREPER) when it relates to any other issue – which seek to resolve any conflicts.

This involvement in a wide range of issues for debate at EU level as well as the scope for 'package deals' calls for co-ordination and agreement at national level. Overall co-ordination is achieved through a committee of senior officials from the departments concerned meeting frequently in Dublin. During the period of the Irish presidency of the EU in 1996 the Irish officials served as chairmen of over 2,000 working groups. The work calls for a thorough knowledge of the subject matter and for the negotiating and diplomatic experience necessary to know when to stand firm, when to concede and when to support an alternative viewpoint.

General

Other activities which help to give an insight into the work of the civil service (in addition to those already mentioned and others more obvious) include the operation of the national scheme for the eradication of bovine tuberculosis; the inspection of primary and secondary schools; the erection and upkeep of public buildings; the meteorological service; the valuation of land and buildings; the protection of wildlife; the issue of passports and visas; the national archives, library, gallery and museum; consumer affairs; the geological survey; grant of patents; the state laboratory; driver testing – all these in addition to constantly meeting deputations, replying to letters from politicians on behalf of their constituents, and liaising with other public service bodies. The list is endless!

A useful general description of the work of an Irish civil servant is provided by the account of his own work given by a senior officer in Britain:

> You will spend a fair amount of time in your office writing and answering letters to members of the public, other civil servants, outside bodies with which your department deals; preparing memoranda, writing minutes, suggesting how to initiate, implement or alter policy; telephoning or being telephoned; interviewing visitors; discussing informally with colleagues how or what to do; consulting with specialists with whom the administrative civil servant has more and more contact: architects, engineers, cost accountants, doctors, inspectors of several kinds. In many departments of government, principals and some assistant secretaries have territorial responsibilities which necessitate periodic visits away from the office. These visits can refresh as well as inform.

> In this age of government by committee you will have to attend at committees or at an outside body's committees as your department's representative. An ability to speak intelligibly, briefly and cogently is needed as much in the Home Civil Service as in the Foreign Office. The opportunities for travel tend to grow, even in the social service departments; for we are all internationally minded now (William Reid, quoted in Chapman 1970: 60).

Code of Conduct

Integrity

Civil servants are bound by the Corruption Acts 1889–1916. These provide penalties for corrupt acceptance of gifts or other considerations as rewards or inducements for doing or not doing some act or for showing favour or disfavour in relation to the business of their departments. The use of official information for private gain is also regarded as a corrupt practice. In addition to their statutory obligations, civil servants are expected to preserve a proper sense of integrity in all their work, whether in relation to their advisory or their executive role.

It must be noted, however, that the fundamental concept of public service has for some years been in a state of change, reflecting the general atmosphere of change prevalent throughout Irish society as a whole. The old conventional practices such as the unquestioning acceptance of rules and regulations and the instinctive obedience to authority are now being challenged in a way unthinkable to previous generations of civil servants. Former certainties now seem less well established and increasingly irrelevant, and changing values and priorities are giving rise to new and less restrictive attitudes regarding what is right, important and acceptable in the conduct of public affairs.

Civil servants are now covered by the Ethics in Public Office Act 1995. Under this act senior civil servants must make written statements on an annual basis in respect of personal interests which could materially influence them in the performance of their official duties.

Confidentiality

The obligations here derive from the Official Secrets Act 1963, which prohibits civil servants from communicating official information unless authorised to do so. Such information includes not only documentary material such as papers, minutes, briefs, letters and so on, but views, comments and advice acquired or transmitted verbally. The prohibition also applies to those who have retired, in relation to information to which they had access before retirement.

Further, a civil servant may not publish without the agreement of the head of his department any material touching on the business of his own or any other department. To a certain extent, no doubt, this accounts for the paucity of written information generally available on the workings of government departments. It also largely accounts for the fact that civil servants are very rarely heard on radio or television programmes discussing matters for which their departments are responsible.

Party Politics

The rules on this subject are of very long standing. Their purpose is, generally speaking, to prohibit civil servants from participating in party politics. They originally applied to every civil servant but were modified in the 1970s along the lines indicated below, following representations from some staff associations. Essentially, the argument of the associations was that all civil servants, because of their experience of the administrative machine, are particularly well qualified for service in parliament; and that it is inconsistent with the natural rights of a civil servant as a citizen, and harmful to the public interest, if he is not allowed to offer himself for this other form of public service and to serve the community in another capacity, without being expected to sacrifice his career, security of employment and pension rights. They pointed to the practice in a number of other member states of the European Union where even senior civil servants are allowed to pursue political activities, including standing for parliament. Civil servants there may resume their posts if unsuccessful in an election or when they wish to retire from parliament.

Successive governments and the Department of Finance, on the other hand, have long been apprehensive of the results of civil servants playing an active role in party politics. They point out that it is in the public interest that civil servants should be politically impartial and that confidence in their impartiality is an essential part of the structure of government in Ireland.

The modification referred to above permits clerical staff, analogous grades in the technical area and industrial workers to engage in politics (though not to stand for election to the Oireachtas), subject to the proviso that the permission could be revoked in the case of officers engaged on a particular category of work. Civil servants engaged in the framing of policy proposals remain completely barred from political activity. In practice, this means the executive, middle and senior grades. Civil servants in these grades seem, in general, happy with the present position, and there are no apparent moves to change it. They rarely discuss party politics, and the vast majority of civil servants do not know how their colleagues vote at elections. They tend to be very critical of the occasional colleague who may be seen to be overtly political. Civil servants in Ireland display a total loyalty to the minister of the day, no matter what party he belongs to.

Outside Occupations

Those in technical grades such as engineer, doctor or solicitor are prohibited from engaging in private practice or from having connections with outside business. In other cases, civil servants are not actually prohibited from taking on other work for remuneration outside office hours, for example teaching or taking part in a business. They are, however, obliged to ensure that any outside business activities do not conflict with their official duties and are not of such a nature as to hinder the proper performance of such duties. (Thus a civil servant would probably be debarred from doing any work for a firm with which his department did business.) Where there is any doubt, an officer is obliged to reveal his position to the secretary general of his department and to abide by the latter's decision on the matter.

Employment Arrangements

Pay

Civil servants generally have pay scales which provide for a number of annual increments. There are long scales for the basic recruitment grades (up to fourteen points in some cases); medium-length scales for those in the middle grades (about seven points); short for lower grades and also for grades at the highest levels (three in the case of paper-keepers and assistant secretaries). Secretaries general have flat salaries. The secretaries of the Departments of the Taoiseach, Finance and Agriculture and Food have higher salaries than the others, as has the Chairman of the Revenue Commissioners. The system of increments is designed to provide incentives, and before an increment is granted the head of the department or someone on his behalf (usually the head of the personnel section) must certify that the officer has done his work satisfactorily during the preceding year.

The civil service is divided into broad groups for the purpose of determining pay. The first and largest group is that comprehended within the conciliation scheme for the civil service. This scheme embraces those having salary scales up to the maximum of principal. The arbitrator is normally a lawyer and is appointed by the Minister for Finance after consultation with the staff associations. The second largest group is that of the industrial workers, whose rates are dealt with by a joint industrial council under the aegis of the Labour Court. The smallest group contains those with salaries higher than principal. Recommendations on the pay of this group are made to the government by the Review Body on Higher Remuneration in the Public Sector. The ultimate decision on matters of pay rests with the government, but in practice the rates are fixed by the Minister for Finance under the powers conferred on him by the Civil Service (Regulation) Act 1956.

The pay structure in the civil service is much less flexible than the pay arrangements in ordinary commercial employment. With a view to providing more incentives and encouragement towards greater effectiveness, the White Paper *Serving the Country Better* (1985) announced the introduction of merit pay. It indicated that measured, outstanding performance would be rewarded by a cash bonus. To preserve the incentive element, merit payments would be made to not more than 10 per cent of staff in any grade or department. The size of payment would vary with the degree of outstanding performance within a range equivalent to 5 to 10 per cent of annual salary. In 1986 the Review Body on Higher Remuneration in the Public Sector was asked to consider the application of performance-related pay to the senior grades of the civil service. Having set out all the arguments for and against, the Review Body concluded that the potential advantages of properly designed and appropriately introduced performance-related pay schemes outweighed the possible disadvantages, for all the civil service grades within its remit except that of secretary general. (This exception was made in order to avoid involving ministers as appraisers, which would be undesirable for reasons of practice and principle.) Accordingly, in reply to a parliamentary question in May 1991, the Minister for Finance indicated that a merit pay system for assistant secretaries and some other grades at that level had been introduced. The system is based on variable progression through a pay range by reference to annual assessment of performance against predetermined work objectives. The minister further indicated that he had no proposals to extend this system to other grades. In general, the proposal for merit pay has not received a welcome from either civil servants themselves or their unions. They point to the difficulties of performance assessment and the dangers of favouritism.

More recently, in reply to a parliamentary question on 13 March 1997 the Minister for Finance stated, 'The only formalised scheme of merit pay which applies in the civil service is the performance-related bonus scheme for assistant secretaries, and some departmental and professional post-holders at that level, which was introduced with effect from 1 May 1995.'

The minister went on to say that

> under the programme of change, *Delivering Better Government*, a system of performance management is currently being designed and developed in order to underpin the achievement of objectives set out in the day-to-day work programmes for staff at all levels in each Department and thereby to promote a high-performance, results-oriented civil service. Recognition and reward for good performance, and a constructive approach to the management of under-performance, are essential features of an effective performance management process. Rewards, including performance-related pay, will be addressed, therefore, as an integral part of the overall design of the system. A firm of consultants has been engaged to assist with the design and development of the system.

> I should also mention an arrangement introduced a few years ago whereby heads of Departments and offices have a very limited discretion, within their administrative budgets, to reward exceptional performance by persons in grades below assistant secretary level by means of *ex gratia* payments or other awards. The operation of these arrangements and the number and amounts of awards are matters left entirely to the discretion of the heads of Departments and offices.

It would appear that there is no formal set of arrangements but that in some departments/offices 1 per cent of the pay element of their budget is set aside for this purpose and that rewards are being made.

Promotion

Promotions are technically regarded as appointments and are, therefore, governed by the Ministers and Secretaries Act 1924 and, as already indicated, made by the minister in charge of the department concerned. Promotions to the more senior posts require also the concurrence of the Minister for Finance. Where promotions are not done in the customary way, that is in the normal grade-to-grade progression, the approval of the Civil Service Commission must be obtained. Promotions not in the customary way are very rare. Examples would be promotion from executive officer to assistant principal (skipping a grade) or from engineer to assistant principal (crossing a work category barrier).

The principle is accepted that those seeking promotion should be selected on merit. Before an officer is promoted, the head of the department must certify not only that he is fully qualified for the vacant position but that he is the best qualified of all those eligible. Up to recent years it had been left to the head of each department to select the most meritorious persons for the promotion to vacancies occurring in his own department. Increasingly, however, particularly in the general service grades, the net is now being cast wider than the officers serving in the department where the vacancy exists. Thus, for promotion to the clerical officer grade about a quarter of the vacancies arising are filled from interdepartmental competition, and for the executive, higher executive, assistant principal and principal grades nearly one-half of the vacancies are so filled.

For the highest posts in the civil service a new system was introduced in 1984. Since then, appointments to posts at the level of secretary general and of assistant secretary (including technical posts at the same level) are made by the government (in the case of secretaries) or by the appropriate minister, with the approval of the Minister for Finance (in the case of other grades). These appointments are made on the basis of reports from the Top Level Appointments Committee (TLAC), established in 1984. Secretaries general may serve for a period of not more than seven years; if, on appointment as secretary, a person is between fifty-six and sixty years of age, the government may, at its discretion, (a) waive that person's obligation to retire at sixty; and (b) permit the person to serve as secretary for a period not exceeding four years in any case.

Conditions

The Civil Service (Regulation) Act 1956 makes provision for the regulation, control and management of the civil service and empowers the Minister for Finance to make such arrangements to this end as he sees fit. The act provides that every established civil servant holds office at the will and pleasure of the government. What this meant (until modified by recent legislation, discussed below) was that only the government could dismiss such a civil servant. In practice, however, this power is used very rarely and then only for a grave reason involving serious misconduct. Civil servants are rarely dismissed because of poor work performance, partly because of the difficulties of assessment, partly because job descriptions do not exist and partly because of a tendency to make generous allowances for incapacity. It is sometimes said that an Irish civil servant's tenure is, legally, the most insecure in the world, but that, in practice, it is the most secure.

Among the other provisions of the act are that civil servants must retire at the age of sixty-five years, but that they may be required to retire at the age of sixty; that they may be suspended without pay for grave misconduct; and that they may be reduced in pay or in grade.

Under the Public Service Management Act 1997, the secretary general of a department has the authority, responsibility and accountability for managing all matters pertaining to appointments, performance, discipline and dismissals of staff below the grade of principal or its equivalent, subject to the Civil Service Commissioners and the Civil Service (Regulation) Acts, 1956.

Job-Sharing and Career Breaks

A scheme to facilitate the sharing of jobs was introduced in 1984. In general, job-sharers have the same arrangements pro rata as their full-time colleagues in regard to pay and other conditions of employment.

Career breaks (in addition to those granted for domestic or educational reasons) of between one and five years are available where the demands of the work permit, excluding grades with specialist skills. Those returning to the civil service after a career break have a guarantee of re-employment in a relevant grade (but not necessarily in their original department) within a period of twelve months of the date on which they planned to return to work.

These arrangements bring a measure of flexibility and opportunity in a time of scarcity of promotional outlets. Changes in this area are anticipated following the report of an interdepartmental group on work-sharing.

Redeployment

This important concept and practice which had hitherto proved virtually impossible has been a feature of civil service manpower policy since 1982 for all grades and in all work categories of the civil service. Persons in grades such as those of executive officer, customs and excise officer and building inspector who were found to be surplus in certain work areas of their own departments were, for example, transferred to priority work relating to the collection of revenue and to the making of social welfare payments. In addition, persons in certain of the state-sponsored bodies which had surplus staff were redeployed into the civil service following competitions arranged by the Civil Service Commission.

Disabled Persons

The employment target set by the government is 3 per cent. Information available suggests that this target has been achieved. The majority of disabled persons are employed in the clerical or subordinate grades.

Local Offices

In accordance with government policy, the work of the civil service is increasingly being carried out from local offices, and numbers of civil servants have been transferred from Dublin to these offices. This development is frequently referred to as decentralisation, though some commentators prefer to call it dispersal or relocation, since nearly all the decisions continue to be made at departmental headquarters.

REFERENCES

Chapman, Richard A., *The Higher Civil Service in Britain* (London: Constable, 1970)

FitzGerald, Garret, *All in a Life* (Dublin: Gill & Macmillan, 1991)

Government of Ireland, *Report of the Public Services Organisation Review Group, 1966–69* [Devlin Report] (Dublin: Stationery Office, 1969)

Government of Ireland, *Serving the Country Better: A White Paper on the Public Service* (Dublin: Stationery Office, 1985)

APPENDIX 13

Total Numbers of Civil Servants – 1 January 1997

Department	Number of non-industrial civil servants	Number of industrial civil servants	Total
Agriculture, Food and Forestry	3,961.0	41.0	4,002.0
Arts, Culture and Gaeltacht	551.0	805.0	1,356.0
Attorney General	61.5	–	61.5
Central Statistics Office	776.0	–	776.0
Chief State Solicitor	159.5	–	159.5
Civil Service Commission	96.5	–	96.5
Comptroller and Auditor General	127.0	–	127.0
Defence	422.5	–	422.5
Director of Public Prosecutions	30.5	–	30.5
Education	905.0	1.0	906.0
Enterprise and Employment – Head Office	806.5	–	806.5
Enterprise and Employment – Labour Relations Commission	33.0	–	33.0
Environment	800.0	–	800.0
Equality and Law Reform	84.5	–	84.5
Finance	513.0	–	513.0
Foreign Affairs – Head Office	1,037.0	–	1,037.0
Foreign Affairs – International Co-operation	19.0	–	19.0
Health	439.5	–	439.5
Justice – Charities Office	8.0	–	8.0
Justice – Courts	824.5	–	824.5
Justice – Data Protection Commissioner	8.0	–	8.0
Justice – Garda Civilians	886.5	–	886.5
Justice – Garda Complaints Board	16.0	–	16.0
Justice – Land Registry	511.0	–	511.0
Justice – Office Headquarters	486.0	16.0	502.0
Justice – Probation and Welfare Service	240.0	–	240.0
Marine	298.5	108.0	406.5
National Gallery	19.0	34.0	53.0
Office of Public Works	581.5	730.0	1,311.5
Oireachtas	241.0	32.0	273.0
Ombudsman	38.5	–	38.5
Ordnance Survey	276.0	–	276.0
President's Establishment	12.0	–	12.0
Prisons	2,469.0	–	2,469.0
Revenue Commissioners	6,040.5	12.0	6,052.5
Social Welfare	4,267.0	–	4,267.0
State Laboratory	72.0	–	72.0
Tánaiste	23.0	–	23.0
Taoiseach	179.0	–	179.0
Tourism and Trade	116.0	–	116.0
Transport, Energy and Communications	655.0	–	655.0
Valuation Office	145.5	–	145.5
Totals	29,236.5	1,779.0	31,015.5

APPENDIX 14

Vote 6

Office of the Minister for Finance

Account of the sum expended, in the year ended 31 December 1995, compared with the sum granted and of the sum which may be applied as appropriations in aid in addition thereto, for the salaries and expenses of the Office of the Minister for Finance, including the Paymaster General's Office, and for payment of certain grants, grants-in-aid and for the Ad Hoc Commission on Referendum Information.

Service	Estimate Provision £'000	Outturn £'000	Closing Accruals £'000
Administration			
A.1. Salaries, Wages and Allowances	13,180	12,733	–
A.2. Travel and Subsistence	256	337	27
A.3. Incidental Expenses	823	693	31
A.4. Postal and Telecommunications Services	650	723	32
A.5. Office Machinery and Other Office Supplies	1,360	917	108
A.6. Office Premises Expenses	734	763	103
A.7. Consultancy Services	447	414	18
A.8. Central Information Technology Service	591	411	(21)
Other Services			
B. Consultancy Services	1,102	992	–
C. Information Technology, Training Initiatives and Strategic Management Fund	800	503	(52)
D. Economic and Social Research Institute – Administration and General Expenses (Grant-in-Aid)	1,375	1,375	–
E. Institute of Public Administration (Grant-in-Aid)	1,375	1,375	–
F. Losses in respect of certain loans for Industrial Development Purposes advanced by ICC Bank plc	880	645	500
G. Gaeleagras na Seirbhíse Poiblí *(National Lottery Funded)*	110	109	–
H. Civil Service Arbitration Board and Civil Service Appeals Board	20	5	1
I. Review Body on Higher Remuneration in the Public Sector	115	28	–
J. Contribution to the Common Fund for Commodities	100	–	–
K. Management Expenses of Assets and Liabilities of Foir Teoranta transferred to ICC Bank plc	370	388	300

Service	Estimate Provision £'000	Outturn £'000	Closing Accruals £'000
L. Emergency Services Network	3,000	53	–
M. Fund for Community Initiatives (Grant-in-Aid)	10,000	–	–
N. Community Support Framework and INTERREG Technical Assistance and Other Costs	907	277	175
O. Determination Committees	85	–	–
Q. Referendum Information			
Original *£Nil*			
Supplementary *215,000*	215	202	8
R. Irish Institute for European Affairs (Grant-in-Aid) *(National Lottery Funded)*			
Original *£Nil*			
Supplementary *250,000*	250	250	–
Gross Total			
Original *£38,280,000*			
Supplementary *465,000*	38,745	23,193	1,230*
Deduct:			
P. Appropriations in Aid	230	339	1**
Net Total			
Original *£38,050,000*			
Supplementary *465,000*	38,515	22,854	1,229
SURPLUS TO BE SURRENDERED		**£15,661,408**	

The Statement of Accounting Policies and Principles and Notes 1 to 13 form part of this Account.

Transferred to Statement of Current Assets and Liabilities as:
* Accrued Expenses £1,358,000 and Prepayments (£128,000)
** Accrued Income (£1,000)

Notes

1. Memorandum Statement of Current Assets and Liabilities as at 31 December 1995

	£'000	£'000
Current Assets		
Stocks (Note 12)		39
Prepayments		128
Accrued Income		1
Other Debit Balances:		
GTN Payments	807	
Recoupable Salaries	133	
Recoupable Travel Expenses	43	
Other Suspense Items	12	995
PMG Balance & Cash	2,425	
Less: Orders Outstanding	1,183	1,242
Exchequer Grant Undrawn		14,364
		16,769
***Less* Current Liabilities**		
Accrued Expenses	1,358	
Other Credit Balances:		
Payroll Deductions	84	
Due to State (Note 13)	856	
Surplus to be Surrendered	15,661	17,959
Net Current Assets – Deficiency		(1,190)

2. Memorandum Statement of Capital Assets as at 31 December 1995[1]

	Hardware/ Software £'000	Furniture and Fittings £'000	GTN[2] £'000	Office Equipment £'000	Total £'000
Cost of Valuation at 1 January 1995	2,079	1,650	1,241	232	5,202
Additions	690	204	38	262	1,194
Disposals	(93)	–	–	(14)	(107)
Revaluations	–	–	–	–	–
Gross Assets at 31 December 1995	2,676	1,854	1,279	480	6,289
Accumulated Depreciation					
Opening Balance at 1 January 1995	1,027	800	877	157	2,861
Depreciation for the Year	516	186	149	78	929
Depreciation on Disposals	(89)	–	–	(9)	(98)
Cumulative Depreciation at 31 December 1995	1,454	986	1,026	226	3,692
Net Assets at 31 December 1995	1,222	868	253	254	2,597

NOTES:

1. The opening balances for 1995 differ from the closing balances of 1994 because of the inadvertent omission of certain assets from the 1994 statement.
2. Government Telecommunications Network.

3. Explanation of the Causes of Variation between Outturn and Estimate Provision

Subhead	Less/(More) than Provided £'000	Explanation
A.1.	447	The saving arose because a number of posts in various grades remained unfilled for short periods during 1995.
A.2.	(81)	The excess occurred due to an increase in EU and foreign travel during the year.
A.3.	130	Expenditure on training was lower than had been expected.
A.4.	(73)	The Department purchased a new telephone system in 1995, the cost of which exceeded that originally provided for in the estimate.
A.5.	443	Provision was made for the purchase of a cheque scanning storage and retrieval system for the Paymaster General's Office. This will not now be purchased until 1996.
A.7.	33	Certain consultancy projects were not completed in 1995 and will not be paid for until 1996.
A.8.	180	Expenditure was below the demand because of: (1) progress being slower than expected in specifying and completing modifications to the new computerised payroll package – £76,000; (2) reduced expenditure on the Government Telecommunications Network (GTN) consequent on deferred investments pending clarification of the implications of adopting an alternative approach (Telecom Éireann's Virtual Private Network) – £84,000; (3) postponement of enhancements to the Personnel Administration System (PAS) – £20,000.
B.	110	Provision was made in this subhead for costs associated with the sale and restructuring of the State Banking Sector and costs arising from the disposal of the State's remaining shareholding in Irish Life. Decisions about the sale and restructuring of the State Banking Sector are still pending and consequently no expenditure was incurred in this regard. The excess required in respect of costs associated with the sale of the State's remaining shareholding in Irish Life was covered by savings on the State Banking Sector element of the subhead.

→

Subhead	Less/(More) than Provided £'000	Explanation
C.	297	Lower than expected demands were received from Departments for assistance on information technology initiatives (£140,000), training initiatives (£32,000) and strategic management consultancy (£125,000). Subhead C is used to subvent such initiatives across all Departments.
F.	235	The savings arose because many of the companies involved in the scheme performed better than expected. As the scheme continues to wind down variations from budget estimates become unavoidable since the cost becomes more dependent on the varying business performance of a smaller number of borrowers.
H.	15	There were fewer sittings of the Arbitration Board in 1995 than were expected and fewer cases for the Appeals Board.
I.	87	The Review Body was not reconstituted until the end of March 1995. The expected general review of remuneration of top public servants (which would have required the engagement of specialist assistance) was postponed, with precedence being given to a review of medical consultants.
J.	100	The contingency provided for part payment of Ireland's voluntary contribution of $250,000 to the Second Account of the Common Fund for Commodities, demand for which did not arise in 1995.
K.	(18)	This subhead provides for the management expenses of ICC Bank associated with its administering of the Foir Teoranta portfolio. Precise expenditure levels are difficult to predict as they depend on the relative performance of the companies within the portfolio which varies from year to year.
L.	2,947	Expenditure was less than expected because of the need to undertake further study of a possible alternative approach to that originally envisaged in relation to the provision of voice and data telecommunications for the civil and public service. Consequently, preparatory work which would have necessitated some initial investment was not proceeded with. The alternative in question relates to the possible use of Telecom Éireann's Virtual Private Network technology which is currently the subject of a joint study with Telecom Éireann. This study is now almost complete.

→

Subhead	Less/(More) than Provided £'000	Explanation
M.	10,000	A global provision of £10 million was made in respect of expected expenditure under the EU Community Initiatives for 1995. In the event, the appointment of intermediary bodies was not completed until late 1995 and no Departments drew down funds in time to incur expenditure.
N.	631	Savings arose because of delays in the following: (1) the approval of the INTERREG 2 and Maritime programmes and the appointment of the INTERREG Development Officer, and (2) the setting up of the Central Evaluation Unit and appointment of a Structural Funds Information Officer. In addition, expenses of the Regional Authority EU Operational Committees were less than expected.
O.	85	The saving arose because the panels from which determination committees are to be drawn under Section 65 of the Stock Exchange Act, 1995 and Section 74 of the Investment Intermediaries Act, 1995 had not been established.
Q.	13	Expenditure on the Ad Hoc Commission on Referendum Information and on the related publicity campaign was lower than expected, and certain payments will accrue in 1996.

4. Appropriations in Aid

	Estimated £	Realised £
1. Receipts from An Post and Telecom Éireann	16,000	26,180
2. Receipts from computer services rendered by Central Information Technology Service	13,000	9,737
3. Recoupment of salaries, etc., of officers on secondment	87,000	115,538
4. Recoupment of certain travelling and subsistence expenses from the EU, etc.	14,000	65,761
5. Miscellaneous	100,000	122,217
Total	£230,000	£339,433

Explanation of Variations

1. Payments from An Post in respect of services provided by the Chief Medical Officer (CMO) in 1992 and 1993 were not received until 1995. The provision of services by the CMO to An Post and Telecom Éireann was terminated in November 1994.
3. The excess arose because salary costs that were paid out in the latter part of 1994 were not received until 1995.
4. Outstanding EU Receipts in respect of 1994 and airline discounts received in 1995 were higher than provided for.
5. The surplus was mainly due to unexpectedly high receipts from the sale of publications and redundant PCs.

5. Commitments

Global Commitments

(i) Subhead F

Under this scheme, the Exchequer assumed part (50% in respect of loans issued before 30 September 1985, 40% thereafter) of the credit risk on certain loans in the manufacturing and tourism sectors advanced by ICC Bank plc from its own funds. Although the scheme, which was initiated in 1980, was terminated in 1990, losses under it will continue to be drawn on the Vote pending the working through of the outstanding loans. It is not possible to estimate how much will fall to be met from the Vote during this period. At the end of 1995 the principal outstanding was £3.4 million.

(ii) Subhead K

The Exchequer is committed to paying ICC Bank plc a fee, calculated according to an agreed formula, for its management of the Foir Teoranta portfolio. This fee will be payable as long as the portfolio is under active management. This will be approximately £350,000 per year for a number of years.

(iii) Commitments on other subheads at year end amount to £257,000.

6. Details of Extra Remuneration

	Total Amount Paid £	Total No. of Recipients	Recipients of £5,000 or more	Max. individual payment of £5,000 or more £
Higher, special or additional duties	170,964	152*	3	5,949
Overtime and extra attendance	256,457	217	8	10,278
Shift and roster allowances	73	2	–	–
Miscellaneous	27,196	19	–	–
Total extra remuneration	**454,690**	**326***	**12***	**12,239***

* Certain individuals received more than one allowance.

7. Miscellaneous Items

This account includes expenditure of £159,415 in respect of nine members of staff on loan without repayment, £56,457 of which is in respect of one officer on loan to the European Institute of Public Administration.

Subhead D (ESRI) – In addition to the sum expended under this Subhead, a sum of £31,000 was received from the Vote for Increases in Remuneration and Pensions (No. 45).

Subhead E (IPA) – In addition to the sum expended under this Subhead, a sum of £39,000 was received from the Vote for Increases in Remuneration and Pensions (No. 45).

A subvention of £5,203 was expended directly from the Training Initiatives Fund, Subhead C of the Vote, for the running of a service-wide training course on behalf of the Internal Audit Network of the Civil Service.

A total of £7,340 was spent on merit awards (i.e. seven individual awards ranging from £114 to £2,600 and two group awards of £83 and £343).

The 1996 Estimate Provision includes carry forward of savings of £684,000 from 1995 under the terms of the Administrative Budget Agreement.

Subhead F – The end of year for these loans is October. The 1995 outturn of £645,000 relates to the period 1 November 1993 to 31 October 1994. The accrued liability of £500,000 at end 1995 is for the period 1 November 1994 to 31 December 1995.

Subhead K – The end of year for these expenses is March. The 1995 outturn of £388,005 relates to the period 1 April 1994 to 31 March 1995. The accrued liability of £300,000 at end 1995 is for the period 1 April 1995 to 31 December 1995.

8. EU Funding

Subhead N – The outturn of £276,524 in this Subhead (Community Support Framework and INTERREG Technical Assistance and Other Costs) is assisted by the European Regional Development Fund (ERDF).

9. Commissions and Inquiries etc.

The cumulative expenditure in respect of Commissions etc. to 31 December 1995 on account of which payments were made in the year is as follows:

Commission, Committee or Special Inquiry	Year of Appointment	Expenditure in 1995 £	Cumulative Expenditure to 31 December 1995 £
Civil Service Arbitration Board . .	1950/51	2,272	385,784
Review Body on Higher Remuneration in the Public Sector	1969/70	107,480	1,112,415
Civil Service Appeals Board	1993	3,486	6,339

10. Miscellaneous Accounts

Western Development Fund

Responsibility for the Fund was transferred to the Vote for Enterprise and Employment (No. 34) with effect from 5 June 1993. The balance of £303,821 on hands at 4 June 1993 remained in the Account until December 1995 when it was surrendered to the Exchequer.

11. National Lottery Funding

Subhead G – The expenditure of £108,943 out of a provision of £110,000 in respect of Gaeleagras na Seirbhíse Poiblí is entirely funded by the National Lottery.

Subhead R – The Grant-in-Aid of £250,000 to the Irish Institute for European Affairs is entirely funded by the National Lottery.

12. Stocks

Stocks at 31 December 1995 comprise:

	£'000
Stationery	30
IT Consumables *etc.*	9
Total	**39**

13. Due to the State

The amount due to the State at 31 December 1995 consisted of:

	£'000
Income Tax	285
Pay Related Social Insurance	52
Pension Contributions	2
Retention Tax	517
Total	**856**

P.H. MULLARKEY
Accounting Officer
DEPARTMENT OF FINANCE
29 March 1996

Certificate of the Comptroller and Auditor General

I have audited the Appropriation Account of the Vote for the Office of the Minister for Finance for 1995 in accordance with Section 3 of the Comptroller and Auditor General (Amendment) Act, 1993. I have obtained all the information and explanations that I have required. As the result of my audit, it is my opinion that the Account properly presents the receipts and expenditure of the Vote for the year ended 31 December 1995.

JOHN PURCELL
Comptroller and Auditor General

7

THE LEGAL OFFICERS

The Attorney General

The Attorney General is one of the great officers of state. According to Article 30 of the Constitution:

1. There shall be an Attorney General who shall be the adviser of the Government in matters of law and legal opinion . . .
2. The Attorney General shall be appointed by the President on the nomination of the Taoiseach.
4. The Attorney General shall not be a member of the government.
5. 2° The Taoiseach may, for reasons which to him seem sufficient, request the resignation of the Attorney General.
   3° In the event of failure to comply with the request, the appointment of the Attorney General shall be terminated by the President if the Taoiseach so advises.
   4° The Attorney General shall retire from office upon the resignation of the Taoiseach, but may continue to carry on his duties until the successor to the Taoiseach shall have been appointed.
6. Subject to the foregoing provisions of this Article, the office of the Attorney General, including the remuneration to be paid to the holder of the office, shall be regulated by law.

In practice, the Attorney General is a member of the same party as the Taoiseach. No specific qualifications for the post are required but he is normally a senior counsel. Once appointed, he performs his duties in an independent manner; he is not the servant of the Taoiseach or of the executive and does not take directions from them.

Though he may not be a member of the government he may be either a TD or a senator and may vote with the government in the Dáil or Seanad. In practice, very few Attorneys have been members of the Oireachtas – only six since the foundation of the state, the last being J.M. Kelly in 1977.

He attends meetings of the government where he advises on all the constitutional and legal issues which arise prior to, or at, the government meetings, including acts and treaties of the European Union and other international treaties.

The Attorney General's remuneration is the same as that of a minister. That remuneration is recommended to the government by the Review Body on Higher Remuneration in the Public Sector, the standing body whose primary function is to advise the government every four years on the general levels of remuneration appropriate to members of the Houses of the Oireachtas, members of the government (including the Attorney General), the judiciary and senior public servants. It is for the government to take the decisions on payment.

There is no legal objection to the Attorney General engaging in private practice. Some do and some do not; some regard the office as full-time and some do not.

Responsibility for the office of the Attorney General rests with the Taoiseach and it is the Taoiseach who answers parliamentary questions about its activities.

Apart from advising the government as a collectivity, the Attorney General is also the adviser of ministers and departments. While he is the central source of legal advice to government departments, some departments have their own legal advisers (see below). The division of labour between these persons and the Attorney General's office follows a practical working arrangement. The primary recourse of such departments is to their own legal advisers but the Attorney General's office is consulted in certain situations, for example in connection with litigation or in relation to matters which involve the Constitution or which may have to be submitted to the government.

Because of the doctrine of separation of powers, the Attorney General does not furnish legal advice to the other branches of government, that is to say the President and the legislative and judicial branches. Neither does he furnish advice to individual members of the public.

The Attorney General is ex officio a member of the Council of State. He is also leader of the bar and he takes precedence, for example, in court appearances. This leadership does not give him any regulatory or disciplinary functions. The former are exercised by the Bar Council (of which the Attorney General is an ex officio member), the latter by the Benchers of the King's Inns (of which body the Attorney General is normally a member).

The Office of the Attorney General

The Office of the Attorney General is composed of three parts. It includes the legal assistants, who are primarily responsible for the legal advisory work; the parliamentary draftsmen; and the office of the Chief State Solicitor.

On the legal advisory side, activities include representing the state in all legal proceedings involving the state, defending the constitutionality of bills referred to the Supreme Court and making decisions in regard to extradition.

The range is broad, including constitutional and administrative law, commercial law, public international law and criminal law.

Requests for advice by the government or ministers are usually made directly to the Attorney General himself. Most requests for advice, however, come from civil servants in departments or offices, either directly to the office or via the Chief State Solicitor's Office.

Generally, the office is not involved in criminal matters, which, instead, are dealt with by the Director of Public Prosecutions.

The office has about twenty-one legal assistants, who may be solicitors or barristers. The principal players in the Attorney General's office in relation to the drafting of legislation are the draftsmen, with the legal assistants having an auxiliary role in the actual drafting process. Essentially, the tasks of the office of the parliamentary draftsman are to draft government bills and statutory instruments and various other types of ancillary documents. It is responsible also for drafting government amendments to bills, as each bill proceeds through the Dáil and Seanad. In addition, it prepares the indexes to the statutes and to the statutory instruments. There is a legal staff of about eighteen, supported by the usual executive and clerical staff.

Both the parliamentary draftsmen and the legal assistants are involved in the work of the Legislation Committee, which monitors progress in the drafting of legislation approved by the government. This committee is chaired by the Government Chief Whip.

It is understood that the name of the office is likely to be altered to that of 'office of parliamentary counsel', to accord with the title used in other, similar jurisdictions.

The Office of the Chief State Solicitor

This office has been in existence since the foundation of the state, when it replaced the then Crown Solicitor's Office. As indicated above, it is one of three law offices within the remit of the Attorney General. Two of these are located in Government Buildings. Possibly because of this geographical fact, the Chief State Solicitor's Office (CSSO), located until recently in Dublin Castle, tends to be regarded as a separate entity.

In general terms, the litigation functions, the responsibility of the Attorney General, are provided by the CSSO. This office also provides services to the Director of Public Prosecutions (DPP) in relation to crime.

Reflecting changing times, the total staff of the office has increased from about fifty-five in 1970 to about three times that number today.

The work of the CSSO includes the following tasks, set out in broad, and very brief, terms:

- Providing legal advice to government departments as well as any necessary accompanying legal documents.
- Conveyancing of state property.
- Prosecutions initiated by ministers/government departments.
- Acting as agent of the government before the European Court of Justice.
- Functions under the Hague Convention.
- Providing a solicitor service in all civil courts in which departments/ state authorities are involved.

The work includes dealing with personal injury claims taken by individuals against government departments, compensation claims by members of the Gardaí and the army for injuries sustained in the course of their duties, appeals to higher courts and applications for judicial review of decisions made by government departments. The foregoing provides a short summary only; to describe the work in detail would be tedious. A flavour may be obtained by mentioning landlord and tenant law, competition law, company law, labour law, merchant shipping law and so on, the type of work which comes within the ambit of any large legal practice.

Solicitors from the office appear in all of the courts from District to Supreme and their functions embrace all of the varied types of case with which the courts deal. For example, up to 9,000 new District Court files are opened each year in the office while about 850 new Dublin Circuit Criminal Court cases arise. Factors affecting the work include recent increases in the number of judges, new legislation and the lengthening of the court calendar.

State Solicitors

These are solicitors in private practice in each county who are appointed by the state on a part-time basis to conduct cases which if occurring in the Dublin Metropolitan area would be undertaken by the Chief State Solicitor's Office.

The Director of Public Prosecutions

Introducing the second stage of the Prosecution of Offences Bill 1974 in the Dáil, the parliamentary secretary to the Taoiseach said that the bill had two aims:

> The first is to ensure, as will be generally agreed to be desirable, that our system for the prosecution of offences should not only be impartial but should be seen to be so and that it should not only be free from outside influence but should be manifestly so.

The second is to enable the Attorney General more effectively to discharge his primary function of giving legal advice to the government and government departments on matters of law and legal opinion.

The ever-widening field of government activity, both in domestic and international affairs, requires legal advice and assistance on matters of a breadth and complexity not envisaged until recently. Our accession to the EEC, as Deputies will certainly appreciate, has given rise to a large volume of time-consuming work, involving new responsibilities for the Attorney General's office. It will be appreciated that a considerable amount of the legal advice which the Attorney General is called upon to provide must be furnished urgently. The burden of increased responsibility which has been imposed on the office makes it a matter of practical necessity to relieve the office of its present responsibility for directing and supervising criminal prosecutions.

The division of the present responsibilities of the Attorney General, which the bill proposes, should also remove any grounds for thinking that political considerations influence the Attorney General in carrying out his functions as regards criminal prosecutions. I do not accept that such considerations have, in practice, exercised any such influence. However, the fact that the office of Attorney General has a political aspect gives rise to a danger that members of the public may harbour suspicions, however misconceived, on this score.

The bill's main provisions, designed to achieve these two aims, are for the creation of an office of Director of Public Prosecutions and for the conferring on the Director of the powers, duties and functions of the Attorney General in relation to criminal and certain other matters . . .

The Government are aware of criticisms made over the years by members of the public, in the media, and amongst members of the legal profession of the method which has operated in the retention of counsel on behalf of the State both in criminal and civil matters. Allegations of lack of impartiality and of undue preference to the political supporters of the Government in office have been made. Whether true or false these allegations are not conducive to confidence in the administration of our legal system. The assignment of counsel in relation to criminal prosecution will be one of the responsibilities of the Director of Public Prosecutions and, undoubtedly, the independence which will be afforded to the Director will ensure his impartiality in the retention of counsel . . .

The Director will have the same security of tenure enjoyed by civil servants and, in addition, can only be removed from office by the Government after consideration of a report received from a committee consisting of the Chief Justice, a judge of the High Court, whom the Chief Justice shall nominate, and the Attorney General. Furthermore, the Director will not be accountable to or in any way subject to the direction of the Attorney General in relation to the performance of his functions. This differs from the legislation establishing similar offices in England and Wales and in Northern Ireland. The English Act provides for the carrying out of the Director's duty under the superintendence of the Attorney General. Under the provision applying to Northern Ireland, the

> Director is responsible to the Attorney General for the due performance of his function. Neither of these concepts has been adopted in the bill before the House. Instead, subsection (6) of section 2 provides merely for 'consultation' between the Attorney General and the Director in relation to matters pertaining to the functions of the Director.

The main opposition party welcomed the creation of a post of Director of Public Prosecutions.

The Director is a civil servant of the state. He must have been a practising barrister or solicitor appointed following a selection interview by a board consisting of the Chief Justice, the Chairman of the Bar Council, the President of the Incorporated Law Society, the Secretary to the Government and the senior legal assistant in the Attorney General's office.

The main function of the DPP's office is to examine files, almost always submitted by/on behalf of the Gardaí, and, on occasion, by other agencies, such as the Revenue Solicitor (see below), to see if a case is a proper one for prosecution. The staff of the office dealing with the files are professional civil servants, barristers or solicitors, with civil servants in various other grades dealing with administrative matters. The total staff of the office is about forty, of whom about ten are in the legal grades.

Despite the length of time that the office is established, there would appear from public comment to be some uncertainty about the actual role of the DPP; the narrowness of the remit given to him by the 1974 act is not well understood and he attracts occasional public criticism for not carrying out activities which, he maintains, are outside his remit. Unlike such offices as District Attorney, Examining Magistrate or Public Prosecutor which may be known to the public through films or television programmes concerning other jurisdictions, the DPP has no investigative role in relation to crime. Responsibility for an investigation lies with the Gardaí. It is for them to investigate crime, to establish if a crime or crimes have occurred and to identify a suspect or suspects. He has no direct relationship to the Gardaí; they do not answer to him directly concerning their investigations and he does not direct these investigations. If the Gardaí consider there is any chance of a prima facie case they put their evidence before the DPP.

The decision to prosecute or not to prosecute a criminal action is one of major importance. Even if he is eventually acquitted, the initiation of a prosecution may have significant adverse consequences for the person prosecuted, leading to substantial expense, loss of reputation or loss of employment. Certain issues may be prosecuted in the District Courts by the Garda Síochána but decisions as to the initiation of cases involving murder and sexual, subversive and other serious crimes are taken centrally by the DPP, who nominates counsel for court appearance on behalf of the state. From 1922 to 1974 these functions in relation to the prosecution of offences were exercised by the Attorney General.

The DPP has no general duty to assist the victims of crime, other than to make a decision, based on the information properly before him, to prosecute or not to prosecute a suspect or suspects. This decision is made on the basis of the strength of the case against the suspect. The DPP is not an agent of the court service or of the Minister for Justice. In some cases where he decides not to prosecute, there are demands from the public, and even from politicians, that he provide the reasons for such decisions. In a statement issued in 1983 (*The Irish Times*, 23 July), the DPP explained his position thus:

> If reasons are given in one or more cases, they must be given in all. Otherwise, wrong conclusions will inevitably be drawn in relation to those cases where the reasons are refused, resulting either in unjust implications regarding the guilt of the suspect or former accused, or in suspicions of malpractice or both.
>
> If, on the other hand, reasons are given in all cases, and those reasons are more than bland generalities, the unjust consequences are even more obvious and likely. In a minority of cases, the reasons would result in no damage to a reputation or other injustice to an individual. In the majority, such a result would be difficult or impossible to avoid.
>
> The reason for non-prosecution often has little or no relevance to the issue of guilt or innocence. It may be, and often is, the non-availability of a particular proof, perhaps purely technical, but nevertheless essential to establish the case. It may be the sudden death or departure abroad of an essential witness. To announce that such a factor was the sole reason for non-prosecution would amount to conviction without trial in the public estimation, and to depriving the person involved of the protection afforded by the careful analytical examination in open court of the case against him which judicial criminal procedure affords.
>
> In other cases, the publication of the particular reasons for non-prosecution could cause unnecessary pain and damage to persons other than the suspect, as where certain types of aberration become apparent in an intended witness.
>
> If some method can be devised whereby the Director could, without doing injustice, inform the public of the reasons for his decisions, he will very willingly put it into operation. From time to time his office is subject to criticism arising from its inability to respond to inquiries from interested parties such as the victim of a crime or the family of such victim.
>
> Unfortunately, the Director is unaware of any method in which reasons can be given without, in many cases, doing injustice. He considers that any departure by him from the firmly established practice would be improper, in the absence of a specific requirement to that effect imposed on him by law. It would also be fraught with very serious legal consequences.

The Office of the Revenue Solicitor

The Office of the Revenue Solicitor was established during the reign of Charles II (1660–85). A royal warrant of 12 March 1685 appointing the 'Commissioners and Governors of all Revenues . . . arising in Ireland' goes on to say that in order 'that the Commissioners may in no wise be diverted or hindered from giving their daily attendance upon this service', one John Thompson was appointed to be the commissioners' 'agent and solicitor in all causes and matters'.

Up until 1841, there were at various times one and two solicitors dealing with issues relating to customs and excise. In that year, the office was expanded and became, as the Law Department, a separate department in the Office of the Revenue of Excise. In 1849, when the Offices of the Commissioners of Excise, Stamps and Taxes were merged in the Board of Inland Revenue, the Law Department remained a discrete entity within that office, with the solicitor also being a Special Commissioner for Income Tax.

A separate Law Department has obtained up to the present day, with various changes in the nature of the duties performed by the solicitor. Today the office is known as the Office of the Revenue Solicitor. It has a staff of thirty-six, comprising eight solicitors, eighteen legal executives and ten administrative staff, all civil servants. In the words of the corporate plan of the Revenue Commissioners, the tasks of the office are to 'provide a professional, comprehensive, efficient and cost-effective legal service to the Revenue Commissioners'. In practice, what this means is that the Revenue Solicitor's office supports and advises virtually all areas of the Office of the Revenue Commissioners on issues ranging from court actions for breaches of tax and customs and excise legislation to recommendations on employment-related issues for Revenue staff. In very broad terms, the work of the office falls into two broad categories, litigation and advice. Court actions are taken and defended on behalf of all the Revenue divisions but mainly for:

- the Collector General for debt collection and cases of insolvency;
- Inspectors of Taxes for tax appeals and compliance procedures;
- Customs to deal with smuggled and prohibited goods; and
- Excise for duties and licences.

In addition to the foregoing, which might be considered, more or less, the traditional work of the Revenue Solicitor's office, the advent of the Single Market, developments in jurisprudence in the fields of administrative law and constitutional law, together with evolving practice and procedure have led to more varied tasks. These include:

(1) dealing with issues arising from EU legislation, especially in the customs and indirect tax areas, and also from the free movement of goods, people, capital and services;
(2) consideration of the concept of 'proportionality' emanating from the EU, which requires that a balance be struck between the rights, liberties and interests of citizens in the exercise of discretionary powers by an administrative authority such as the Revenue Commissioners;
(3) the regulation of trade, for example vehicle registration tax, VAT information, exchange systems and duty suspension arrangements;
(4) the issue of warning letters and the taking of prosecutions under the self-assessment programme and arising from the non-submission of the well-known form P35;
(5) carrying out a greater role in the licensing field, as a result of changes in the functions of the courts since 1988 and the introduction of tax clearance requirements in 1992. The commissioners are responsible for the issuance of a range of licences, such as intoxicating liquor licences and bookmakers' licences.

As with all employers of large numbers of people (the Revenue Commissioners have 6,000 employees), there are inevitable claims for damages of various kinds arising from accidents and from the corpus of employment law.

In sum, the Revenue Solicitor's office assists the Revenue Commissioners over the whole range of their activities.

Department of Foreign Affairs

The first legal adviser was appointed to this department in 1929. Today the legal division has a staff of six. Article 29.3 of the Constitution reads: 'Ireland accepts the generally recognised principles of international law as its rule of conduct in its relations with other States.' The task of the department is to advise the minister as to these principles, their interpretation and application, and, more specifically, the task of the legal division is to ensure that Ireland's conduct of foreign relations is carried out with due regard to international law.

The advice and information provided falls into four main areas of law:

Public international law. This includes treaty law, human rights, the law of the sea, diplomatic privileges and immunities, the negotiation and conclusion of bilateral international and extradition agreements, membership of international bodies.

EU law. This governs issues relating to Ireland's membership of the Union, the powers of the Union's institutions and the Union's relations with third countries (i.e. non-EU countries). When revisions of the core treaties of the European Union are being negotiated, for example during the Intergovernmental Conference in 1997, which resulted in the Amsterdam Treaty, the legal division provides supportive collaboration to the divisions within the department which has the overall responsibility.

Private international law. Ireland is a member of a number of international organisations which promote development in private international law, for example the Hague Conference on Private International Law. These organisations are involved in the preparation of numerous conventions in this area, and the legal division monitors their activities.

Domestic law. The issues which arise under this heading include passports, citizenship and consular matters.

The legal division represents Ireland in international legal proceedings, for example before the European Commission and before the European Court of Human Rights.

The division drafts statutory instruments, as required, and also the various other instruments relating to the legal formalities arising in connection with international agreements.

Requests from foreign countries (except from the United Kingdom, where a different system applies) for the extradition of persons from Ireland are transmitted through diplomatic channels. The legal division arranges for them to be communicated to the appropriate Irish authority and continues to liaise between the foreign authorities and the Irish authorities until the request has been dealt with.

Equally, the division may be involved in the preparation of requests for extradition or mutual assistance issuing from Ireland to other countries.

Responsibility for the publication and registration of international agreements to which Ireland becomes a party, save for those published in the *Official Journal of the European Communities*, rests with the legal division.

Department of the Environment

The post of legal adviser in this department, which had its origin in the Irish Local Government Board, dates from 1879. The board itself was the successor, founded in 1872, to the Irish Poor Law Board, established in the famine year of 1847. The appointment of the first full-time legal adviser coincided with a massive increase of work in the board, occasioned by the passing of the historic Local Government Act 1898. Shortly thereafter, an assistant legal adviser was appointed and this situation obtained until relatively recent years. The adviser performed services also for the Department of Health.

The advisory duties cover a wide range and include issues such as electoral matters, motorway schemes, compulsory purchase, local authority staffing matters (such as discipline and superannuation) and fairs and markets. Since local authorities act largely by statute and by statutory instrument, a considerable amount of the legal officer's time is spent on the drafting and settling of legislation.

Department of Health and Children

A separate legal section in the Department of Health is a new development. Since the establishment of the department in 1947, it shared advisers until recently, with the Department of Local Government, now the Department of the Environment and Local Government.

With the increase in the range of activities of the Department of Health, the advantages of having an 'in-house' legal adviser specialising in the administration of the health legislation became more evident.

Specifically, the legal section provides assistance on issues arising under the law relating to family, child care, food and medicines; on the initial preparation of legislation relating to drugs, infectious diseases, health insurance and so on; in the settlement of statutory instruments under the various acts operated by the department; and on health matters arising from membership of the EU. More general work arises from, *inter alia*, court decisions, appeals, contracts and agreements.

REFERENCES

Casey, James, *The Irish Law Officers* (Dublin: Round Hall, Sweet & Maxwell, 1996)

Department of Foreign Affairs, *Strategy Statement 1997*

Office of the Attorney General, *Strategy Statement 1997–1999*

Office of the Revenue Commissioners, *Seventy-Second Annual Report of the Revenue Commissioners* (Dublin: Stationery Office, 1994)

8

LOCAL GOVERNMENT

Ireland has had local government since the Middle Ages. The original authorities charged with its administration were the county sheriffs, assisted by the grand juries. In later years these were supplemented by a number of ad hoc bodies established to meet the needs created by various social and economic changes (town commissioners, poor law guardians, sanitary authorities, boards of governors of hospitals and asylums, harbour authorities and so on). The old system was essentially judicial in its mode of operation and thoroughly unrepresentative in character. It survived until 1898, when the Local Government (Ireland) Act inaugurated a comprehensive reform based on the principles of efficiency and democracy. It set up a number of multi-purpose authorities and extended the franchise to householders; these provisions, with subsequent modifications, form the basis of the local government system of today.

The system as it now operates is made up of elected and non-elected statutory bodies. The elected local authorities consist of town commissioners (26), boroughs (5), urban district councils (49), county boroughs (5) and county councils (29). (See map at Appendix 15.) The non-elected bodies include vocational education committees, joint library committees and harbour authorities.

Chairpersons of local authorities are known as Cathaoirligh, save in the case of county boroughs and boroughs where they are lord mayor or mayor, as appropriate. Councillors' expenses have been consolidated into an allowance based on the individual's distance from headquarters and an assumption about the number of meetings. In addition, the chairperson may, and usually does, receive an allowance for his term of office.

The county councils and the county boroughs exercise the full range of local government functions. The boroughs and urban district councils have responsibility for most of these functions within their areas. The town commissioners have limited responsibilities. Each local authority has two arms: the elected council, which makes policy, within limits prescribed by legislation; and the executive, which carries out the policy.

Powers

Local authorities receive their powers through legislation. That legislation specifies what they can, or must, do and in some cases how they must do it. It also specifies whether, and to what extent, they are responsible to central government or, more specifically, to particular ministers. Irish local government in design is similar to the British system, where a local authority may do only what the law empowers it to do. However, a departure from this has been made by the Local Government Act 1991, which confers a general competence on them, similar to that enjoyed by continental local authorities, which are commonly involved in public transport, police, primary and second-level education and municipal undertakings of various kinds, such as, for example, the provision and operation of theatres.

Irish local authorities, however, are, in carrying out their functions, enjoined to have regard to policies and objectives of the government or any minister of the government in so far as they may affect or relate to their functions. Tight financial resources have tended to restrict local authority functions to the traditional ones.

Elections

All counties, county boroughs and the larger boroughs and urban districts (Bray, Drogheda, Dundalk and Sligo) are divided into electoral areas under orders made by the Minister for the Environment and Local Government. The smaller urban districts and towns with commissioners constitute single electoral areas. The number of councillors in each local authority is determined by order (except in the case of boroughs and county boroughs, where the number is fixed by statute), as also is the number of councillors to be elected for each electoral area. County councils have between 20 and 48 members; county boroughs between 15 and 52; boroughs usually 12; urban district councils usually 9, and town commissioners the same number. There are 1,627 elected members in all. There is no prescribed councillor/population ratio; in practice, the ratio varies considerably, even within one class of local authority.

The law provides that elections are to be held every five years. However, they have been postponed on a number of occasions. For this to happen from 1998 on, new legislation will be required. The system of voting, as for national elections, is by proportional representation. Those over eighteen years of age on the date the electoral register comes into force (15 April each year) are entitled to vote, irrespective of nationality. Polling day must, by law, be in June; the actual date is fixed by the minister. Each candidate must lodge a deposit – £50 for county council and county borough elections and £25 for other local authorities – which is forfeit if the candidate fails to reach one-third of the quota at some stage. As for Dáil elections, political party affiliations may be shown on the ballot paper.

Certain persons are disqualified from being elected, including those who have served, or are serving, prison sentences, those guilty of misconduct while members of local authorities, and persons who are active members of the defence forces. In addition, certain officials of local authorities – generally those above the grade of clerical officer – may not retain their employment if they are elected to and wish to serve on their own or a neighbouring local authority. Restrictions also apply to civil servants: those in the executive grades and upwards may not put themselves forward.

From 1998 on, other disqualifications will include being an EU Commissioner or a member of the European Parliament, a European judicial or audit office holder, minister or minister of state, Ceann Comhairle, Cathaoirleach of the Seanad, chairman of an Oireachtas committee, judge or Comptroller and Auditor General.

Meetings

A local authority may make its own standing orders to regulate its meetings. Members of the public have no legal right to attend; it is a matter for each local authority to decide whether or not to admit them. The press is not entitled as a matter of right to attend meetings of the borough councils. In the case of other elected local authorities, the press may not be excluded from council meetings unless the Minister for the Environment and Local Government so authorises. As in the case of the Dáil, there is usually a control mechanism to restrict numbers, especially at times of heightened tension, e.g. rezoning decisions affecting local areas, street demonstrations and so on.

Council meetings are presided over by the Cathaoirleach or, in the case of a borough, by the mayor. These officers are elected annually by the council; a Leas-Cathaoirleach may also be elected. They have no executive role and are not responsible for administration. This is the responsibility of the manager. The Cathaoirleach has, however, special power to obtain information from the manager – a right which no other individual councillor has – and the manager normally meets him regularly to keep him informed.

The Management System

The city and county management system owes its origin to the United States of America. There in the early part of the century the idea of running municipal affairs in the same manner as business affairs took hold. This was the idea that, instead of elected members being in charge of activities, they and a manager should operate in the same way for a city as a board of directors and a general manager for a business. This idea spread rapidly in the United States and reached Ireland in the early 1920s. Thus, when the Dublin and Cork Corporations, which had been dissolved in 1924 and replaced by commissioners, came to be reconstituted in 1929, legislation provided for a city manager in each case to run the cities with the elected members. Roche (1982: 101) notes that the original dissolution in Dublin, at any rate, was received with equanimity by the citizens, who seemed to share the accepted view of the corporation as a combination of corruption and inefficiency. Subsequently, Limerick and Waterford got city managers, and the counties got county managers.

The functions of local authorities are, under the management system, divided into *reserved functions*, discharged by the elected members, and *executive functions*, performed by the city or county manager. While the law provides for an exact division of the functions so that responsibility may be defined, in practice they are complementary; managers and councillors do not act independently of each other. The relationship is outlined below. The manager is the experienced whole-time administrator responsible for the efficient discharge of day-to-day business without making an undue demand on the time of the elected members, who are part-time.

The Manager: Appointment and Area

City and county managers are appointed by the local authority on the recommendation of the Local Appointments Commission, the three-man body set up in 1926 to select and recommend to local authorities persons for appointment to the principal offices. Internal promotions to the post of manager are not permitted. Nearly all managers have had previous service with local authorities, and it is exceptional when a person outside the local authority service succeeds in being recommended by the commission.

The same person acts as manager for the county council and all boroughs, urban districts and towns in the county. Managers appointed since 1991 have a maximum term of office of seven years.

Reserved Functions

The main functions which are reserved to elected members include the adoption of the annual estimate of expenses, the fixing of the annual rate to be levied to meet these and the amount to be borrowed, the making of development plans and by-laws, house-building programmes, and assisting other local bodies in providing services and amenities. The various functions can be exercised only on the passing of a resolution. The manager may not, save with the consent of the members, exceed the amount provided for any particular purpose.

Executive Functions

Executive functions are in practice all of those not reserved. They include arrangements made by the manager in relation to staff, acceptance of tenders, making contracts, fixing rents, making lettings, and deciding on applications for planning permissions.

Manager/Council Relations

The sharp legal distinction made between the reserved and the executive functions does not, however, quite reflect the way in which business is actually carried out. Managers and councillors work in close co-operation, and the manager attends and participates in council meetings as if he were a member (though he has not the right to vote). The councillors appreciate that the manager is the expert in administration, having normally spent his whole life in local government. Indeed the manager has often been described as the powerhouse of local government. Even in policy areas, therefore, which are their prerogative, they rely on him for guidance as to what can and cannot be done. He has a greater knowledge than they have because of his wider experience of the forming and execution of policy. Collins (1987: 59) writes of the advantage enjoyed by the manager

> because he is the centre of a wide communications network involving the central government, other managers, his staff, the public and other politicians. A manager is liable to be in contact with the local business community, state agencies for economic development and a range of social institutions. Such a network keeps the manager abreast of possible sources of advantage or difficulty for his own plans. He is also able to use his administrative and technical staff to store and assess the information available to him.

For his part, the manager goes beyond the mere legal obligation to keep his councillors informed about the business of the council, about new works or about the way in which he proposes to carry out any particular executive function. Because they now hold the power formerly vested in the council, managers generally are careful to retain the goodwill of members, and they like to keep them informed about matters affecting their constituents. Managers recognise the brokerage role expected of the individual councillor, and recognise also that their own overall policy responsibilities are not compromised by the occasional marginal adjustment to facilitate individual citizens.

Council policy is articulated by the manager. In doing so he is normally careful to be circumspect about appearing influential and freely refers to the assistance of the individual councillors in helping the council to arrive at decisions. Such a line of action reflects the manager's recognition of the wealth of local knowledge and collective wisdom of his council. Real conflict is rare, though there may frequently be a semblance of conflict when councillors at meetings may wish to be seen as championing the interests of those who elected them against the tyranny of the bureaucracy. Certainly the conflict anticipated at the introduction of the management system is not in evidence today: both sides have learned to live in harmony with the system.

The manager has absolute authority in regard to control and suspension of staff, and this is an authority which the councillors are happy to leave with him.

However, if the number of staff or their remuneration is to be changed, council must agree.

Staff

In many ways the local authority service is a single service with a standard pattern of grades and uniformity in methods of recruitment, pay and conditions of service. Local authorities employ about 30,000 people. About 10,000 of these are in managerial, clerical and technical grades. The officials in these grades have uniform conditions of appointment and, in general, have the same permanent tenure of office as established civil servants.

The standard county administrative organisation is: county manager; assistant county manager in the larger counties; county secretary; finance officer; administrative officer; senior staff officer; staff officer; assistant staff officer; and clerical officer. Four grades are appointed following competitions conducted by the Local Appointments Commission. (The commissioners are the Ceann Comhairle of the Dáil and the secretaries general of the Departments of the Environment and Local Government, and Health and Children. The commission is staffed by civil servants and is housed in the same building as the Civil Service Commission; the staffs are interchangeable.) The promotions to the four intermediate grades are made by competitions held locally and usually open to the whole local government, health and vocational education sectors.

On the technical side, the grades include engineers, architects, planners, solicitors, technicians and fire officers.

Dublin Corporation and the three county councils in the Dublin area are exceptions to the general rule about appointments. Vacancies in some senior, but not the top, posts are filled by promotion from among eligible officers serving with these bodies.

About 20,000 people are employed in the skilled, semi-skilled and manual grades. These have, in general, the same conditions as people in equivalent jobs outside the public service.

Functions of Local Government

Almost all of the functions of local authorities derive from legislation emanating from the Department of the Environment, whether acts of the Oireachtas or statutory instruments made by the minister. There are, however, some tasks carried out on behalf of other departments, such as the dipping of sheep against scab, vocational education and grants for higher education, and certain traffic control measures.

In the day-to-day work there is constant contact between the officials in the department and the managers and other staff of the local authorities. Managers and departmental staff meet frequently. Information is exchanged, plans are discussed and new proposals are sounded out. Managers themselves hold monthly meetings to compare experiences and discuss common business. The minister occasionally addresses county managers collectively on policy issues.

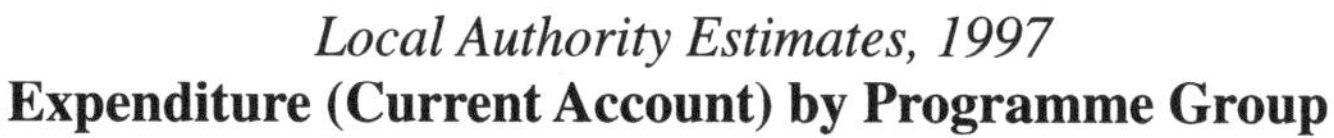

Local Authority Estimates, 1997
Expenditure (Current Account) by Programme Group

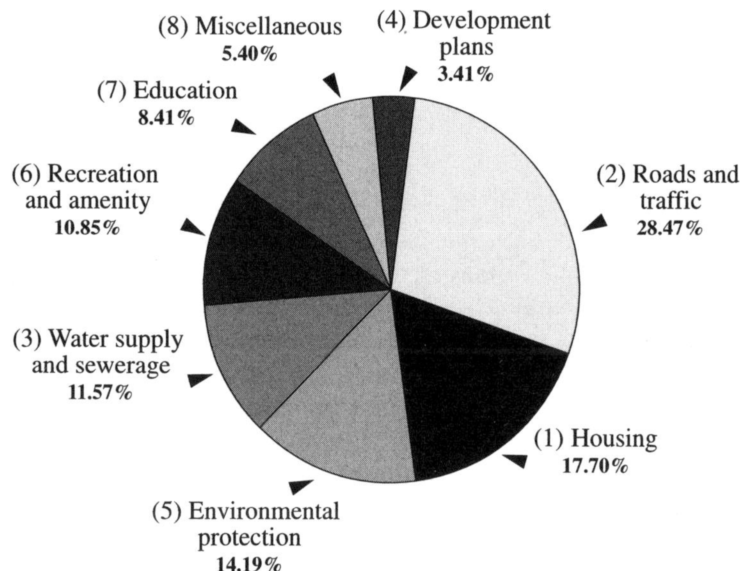

The services provided may be classified under eight broad headings: (1) housing; (2) roads and traffic; (3) water supply and sewerage; (4) development plans; (5) environmental protection; (6) recreation and amenity; (7) education; (8) miscellaneous. The total estimated expenditure on current account for 1997 under these headings was £1,358.3 million. The percentage allocated to each heading is shown in the above diagram.

(1) Housing

National housing policy is that, as far as resources permit, every family should have a house of a good standard in an acceptable environment at a price or rent the family can afford.

There are, of course, many bodies as well as local authorities involved in housing. These include building societies, the associated banks, assurance companies, and the Housing Finance Agency (a specialised agency through which local authorities fund house purchase loans). The role of the local authorities can be regarded as a residual one – to provide access to housing for those who cannot afford to get their own houses or who have difficulty in qualifying for loans from the recognised lending agencies. Local authorities may assist in providing houses by administering loans financed by the Housing Finance Agency; by building houses for letting and possible subsequent sale to the tenants; by providing serviced sites for individuals or co-operatives who wish to build their own houses; by supporting the work of voluntary housing associations with grant and loan assistance; and by providing, in addition to what might be termed normal housing, special-category accommodation such as sheltered housing for the elderly and serviced halting sites for travellers. The provision of sites for travellers has a high political profile, with the result that the management acts have been amended to give the manager rather than the council the greater control in this area.

(2) Roads and Traffic

County councils, county boroughs, boroughs and urban district councils are road authorities under the various road legislation acts and are responsible in law for maintaining the public roads system. In practice, however, the state has accepted responsibility for the national primary roads (the main routes from Dublin to the principal cities and towns) and the national secondary roads (the routes between the major national centres) and makes 100 per cent grants to the roads authorities to cover the cost of maintaining and improving these. The upkeep of the other roads in the country, which are classified as regional, county and urban, is financed from local authorities' own resources and from government grants. Through the grant mechanism, the minister largely controls the location and timing of road works, especially on the larger roads.

Two recent developments have been the introduction of tolls to finance road construction and the establishment of the National Roads Authority. The legal basis for the former type of venture is contained in the Roads Act 1993, which allows road authorities to enter agreements with private interests for the construction, maintenance and management of toll roads and bridges. A formal toll scheme must be made (this is a reserved function of the elected members), and if there are objections, a public local inquiry must be conducted by a person appointed by the minister, after which the minister may confirm or refuse to confirm the scheme. The tasks of the National Roads Authority are (1) to plan the roads of the future, to recommend how they should be paid for and then to make the payments; and (2) to arrange for the design of road improvement projects, the placing of construction contracts and the promotion of private investment in roads.

The local authorities, however, continue to have a major role in the development of national roads; they continue to own, maintain and manage them. They also continue to have responsibility for non-national roads, which account for 94 per cent of total road mileage.

Responsibility for road traffic matters generally, such as the specification of standards for vehicles and the preparation of 'rules of the road', rests largely with the Department of the Environment and Local Government in consultation with the Department of Justice, Equality and Law Reform and the Gardaí. Local authority responsibilities include the provision of traffic signs and road markings, the preparation of traffic studies and the application of traffic management techniques, the employment of road safety officers and co-operation in road safety campaigns, the operation of meter-parking schemes and the employment of traffic and school wardens. Recent regulations have devolved other significant traffic management and parking functions on local authorities from both the Minister for the Environment and the Gardaí.

Motor taxation and the licensing of drivers are carried out by the local authorities as agents of central government. The moneys collected are paid to a central fund after the deduction of administrative costs. The central fund is now a dedicated fund for local government expenditure but the precise application of the fund has been the subject of changing policies in 1997 and 1998; this is dealt with below.

Public lighting is provided by the county councils and the urban authorities, through arrangements made with the Electricity Supply Board. Only Dublin Corporation has its own public lighting department. Grants are available from the Department of the Environment towards the provision of new and improved lighting on main roads in built-up areas but not towards maintenance or operating costs.

(3) Water Supply and Sewerage

County councils, county borough and borough corporations and urban district councils are designated sanitary authorities with an obligation to provide adequate supplies of water for domestic, agricultural and industrial uses, and systems for the safe and environmentally acceptable disposal of sewage and other water-borne wastes. Technical advice and other assistance (for example, access to a public mains supply) is provided to groups who organise their own supply of water through group schemes. The Public Capital Programme provides each year for investment in water and sewerage facilities. This money is divided by the department among the various authorities in accordance with proposals on hand and the needs of each area.

Local authorities have charged for water supplies for many years, mainly to commercial users and to those domestic users connected to a public water supply. However, up to 1983 the charges did not apply to domestic users in urban areas. (Since the vast majority of houses in urban areas had a water supply, they were regarded as paying for this through their ordinary rates.) With the abolition of rates on private dwellings in 1978, the position changed, and subsequently in 1983 the powers of local authorities were extended to enable them to charge for services generally. A decision to levy charges is a function reserved to the elected members. In 1997 the government decided to abolish charges to domestic consumers for water supply and sewage disposal. Legislation was enacted in that year for that purpose.

(4) Development Plans

The Local Government (Planning and Development) Act 1963 constituted county councils, county boroughs, boroughs and urban district councils as planning authorities and obliged them to prepare a development plan within three years of the passing of the act and to review the plan at five-yearly intervals. A development plan is a statement of development objectives, supported by maps. The objectives must include the zoning of land for different uses, the development of roads and public utilities such as water and sewerage, the preservation and extension of amenities, and urban renewal. It may include a wide range of additional objectives to assist local interest groups, for example provisions for community and recreational development and measures to encourage the local economy.

The plan is the framework within which development, both public and private, is to take place. Its adoption is a reserved function of the elected council. Before adoption it must be prepared in draft form and displayed publicly for three months in order to give the public the opportunity to make representations. These representations must be considered (but not necessarily accepted) by the local authority before it formally adopts the plan.

While the development plans are not subject to the approval of a central authority, the Minister for the Environment nevertheless has power to take whatever measures are necessary to co-ordinate the development plan objectives of the eighty-eight separate planning authorities and to resolve any conflicts that may arise between them. For example, he may require a number of authorities to work together, or he may direct that the provisions of a plan be varied. This power has never been used.

Control of development is ensured through the operation of a system of planning permissions and refusals. Most developments may not proceed without permission from the authority or, on appeal, from An Bord Pleanála (the body set up by statute in 1976 to deal with appeals). Certain classes of development are exempt from the requirement of planning permission, for example small extensions to domestic dwellings, and agricultural and forestry development. Decisions on planning applications are a matter for the city or county manager, but the council may intervene in very restrictive circumstances to alter managers' decisions. Planning permissions lapse after a period of five years if the development is not undertaken.

An area of growing importance for local authorities in recent years is urban renewal. They can require works to be carried out to remove the appearance of dereliction, or, in extreme cases, acquire the property compulsorily. The minister may designate urban areas for the application of tax incentives to encourage development. Further, under the 1994–9 tranche of European Structural Funds, grants are available to local authorities for environmental upgrading works in run-down areas, which, in turn, act as a catalyst for private development.

Following the controversies in the early 1990s over the construction by the Office of Public Works of interpretative centres, development by government departments, which up to then had been considered to be outside planning control, became subject to such control as a result of a court decision. Legislation subsequently regulated the application of the planning code to developments by state authorities.

(5) Environmental Protection

The role of local authorities in environmental protection has been changing significantly since the 1980s as demands for protection – driven largely by EU legislation – intensify and become more complex. The emergence of the Environmental Protection Agency as a specialised agency taking over some of the functions of the local authorities has been a significant feature of the 1990s. Nevertheless, local authorities retain a large number of functions in regard to, for example, air and water pollution, flood relief, the provision of notices and the erection of fencing at dangerous places such as quarries, rivers and cliffs. They must collect refuse and clean streets, or arrange for this to be done. Litter wardens may be appointed and offenders prosecuted.

Other responsibilities undertaken by the local authorities include the inspection of buildings to prevent fire hazards, civil defence arrangements (under the guidance of the Department of Defence) and the control of dogs, including their licensing.

(6) Recreation and Amenity

Under this heading the services include the provision of libraries and museums and the giving of assistance to local festivals and exhibitions. Facilities for sport and for community development include the provision of parks and open spaces and of land free or at reduced prices for sports grounds or community halls. Some local authorities provide direct amenities such as golf courses, tennis courts and swimming pools, and some also provide caravan and camping sites directly, such as Dublin, Wexford and Wicklow.

(7) Education

County councils, county borough corporations, the borough corporations of Drogheda, Dún Laoghaire, Galway, Sligo and Wexford and the urban councils of Bray and Tralee are each required by law to establish a Vocational Education Committee to provide and manage vocational schools. The committees, which have their own corporate status, do not come within the city and county management system. The main funding for these schools comes from the Department of Education, but the local authorities also provide some.

Under the national scheme of higher education grants, the local authorities make the payments. The cost of the grants is met, in the first instance, by the local authority, but all expenditure over and above the amount provided in the year 1967–8 by local authorities themselves for certain former scholarship schemes (post-primary and university) is refunded by the Exchequer.

Local authorities in urban areas and in towns may provide school meals. County councils can provide meals in Gaeltacht areas only.

In the county boroughs of Cork, Dublin and Waterford and in Dún Laoghaire, school attendance committees comprising representatives of the local authority, the Minister for Education, parents and managers enforce the School Attendance Act 1926. Elsewhere the act is enforced by the Gardaí.

(8) Miscellaneous

The activities under this heading include administration, purchase of plant, the preparation of the list of electors for all elections, and the appointment (in the Dublin area only) of inspectors to check weighing scales used in shops and such places.

Finance

Local authority expenditure is divided into capital and current. Capital expenditure, generally speaking, represents expenditure on fixed assets such as housing, including loans to house purchasers, water and sewerage schemes, libraries and swimming pools. Among the items in the Public Capital Programme of the government each year are sums to meet the needs of local authorities. The Minister for the Environment and Local Government allocates these sums between the individual authorities, on the basis of proposals from them, the level of need in each area, and the state of ongoing works. Where borrowing is necessary, for example for the provision of offices, recourse is had to the Local Loans Fund or, more frequently, to the banks. The vast bulk of capital expenditure by local authorities – on roads, housing, sanitary services, fire stations and libraries – is now financed by 100 per cent grants from the Exchequer.

Sources

There are changes to be made in the sources of funding for local authorities' current expenditure from 1 January 1999. The present position is that current expenditure is defrayed from four main sources of income: government grants, which are almost wholly earmarked for specific expenditure programmes (about 26 per cent); income from goods and services (about 28 per cent); rates on business property (about 22 per cent); and, since 1997, the proceeds of motor taxation (about 19 per cent). For 1997 and 1998, motor tax has replaced charges for water to domestic consumers, which were discontinued in 1997, and the rate support grant, a government grant given in lieu of rates on houses and land. Local authorities are entitled to retain 80 per cent of the tax they collect on cars and motorcycles and must surrender the rest to an Equalisation Fund. This fund is then distributed to local authorities on the basis of their respective needs and resources (equalisation).

For 1999, however, the Minister for the Environment and Local Government has announced a new system. A Local Government Fund will be created, which will be ringfenced in legislation for local government use. The fund, amounting to £590 million in 1999, will be made up in part of the full proceeds of motor tax (£320 million), which local authorities will continue to collect but will have to surrender to the fund. This part of the fund will be used mainly to finance expenditure on the non-national roads – thus replacing a significant portion of the government grants given for specific purposes. The remaining £270 million in the fund will be provided by the Exchequer and will be distributed to local authorities on the basis of needs and resources, to be spent at their discretion. The minister also announced that he would be using existing powers available to him to cap increases in rates on business.

Local Authority Finance, 1997

Expenditure and Receipts

A summary of the estimated expenditure and receipts for 1997 is as follows, with comparative out-turn figures for 1996.

Estimated Current Receipts and Expenditure of Local Authorities, 1997

	County councils £'m	County boroughs £'m	Urbans £'m	Miscellaneous bodies[1] £'m	Total 1997 £'m	Provisional out-turn '96 £'m
Expenditure	906.4	344.1	108.7	2.1	1,358.3	1,270.7
Financed by government grants/subsidies	295.73	48.36	11.96	–	356.05	491.5
Goods/services	228.74	106.77	41.83	1.4	378.74	444.9
Commercial rates ...	172.8	139.2	46.4	0.6	359.0	338.6
Motor tax[2]	192.63	42.97	21.81	–	257.41	–
County demand	17.0	–	(16.2)	–	0.8	–
Total receipts	906.9	337.3	105.8	2.0	1,352.0	1,275.0

NOTES

1. Includes town commissioners, Joint Drainage Boards, Burial Boards and other miscellaneous bodies.
2. The figures for 1997 have been adjusted to reflect the fact that motor tax was, for that year, a dedicated source of revenue for local authorities.

The new system will involve significant additional resources for local authorities. In terms of discretion over their spending, they will continue to have full discretion over how to spend existing income sources such as the income from goods and services (house loan repayments, rents, refuse collection charges, water charges to non-domestic consumers, planning application fees, employees' pension contributions and so on); rates; and the £270 million mentioned above. There is less discretion in the spending of motor tax revenues – since they have to be spent mainly on roads – and grants such as for higher education scholarships and FÁS schemes.

Rates are levied on the basis of valuations placed annually on all immovable property by the Commissioner for Valuation. Certain places are exempt from valuation, such as places of religious worship, or from rating, such as secondary schools, domestic dwellings or land. The remaining buildings which attract rates are primarily those used for industrial or commercial purposes. The aggregate property valuation in each local authority area forms the basis for the levy of rates. The procedure is that each local authority is required to prepare and adopt an estimate of expenses for the year ahead. The estimate shows projected gross expenditure and the anticipated receipts available to meet that expenditure. The gap is bridged (on each of the eight programmes outlined) by dividing the residual amount by the aggregate valuation, thus producing a rate in the pound. Town commissioners are not rating authorities. They prepare an estimate, and the cost of their services is sought from the county council. The county council then levies 'town charges' on the county rate and applies that higher rate in the town only.

Audit

Accounts of receipts and expenditure are audited by auditors from the Department of the Environment and Local Government. The auditors have power to disallow payments made without authority and to surcharge those responsible for making them. On occasion, councillors, generally for political reasons of their own, vote against the advice of the manager for some project which is not lawful or not approved.

Surcharges may, and usually are, appealed to the minister, who has the power to remit them and often does so. Managers are obliged to warn council members about the loss of money through decisions arising from the use of their reserved powers which lack legal authority.

Local Government Reform

Fundamental Considerations

Any consideration of the local government system must be influenced by two basic determinants. On the one hand, local authorities are providers of services involving very substantial public expenditure (in excess of £2 billion in 1997, counting current and capital). It is necessary, therefore, that local authority structures should be such as to ensure the efficient and effective operation of the local government system. This implies fairly large authorities having the necessary resources to meet this requirement.

On the other hand, the local government system is not merely a provider of services, but is one of the essential elements that go to make up the democratic nature of the state. In Irish terms, local democracy connotes small units, which may, however, be so small as to be unable to perform effectively and efficiently in the major services areas, but which must nevertheless be financed from public funds.

The arguments for reform, therefore, tend to turn on these two principles of efficiency and local democracy and on the relative importance attached to each.

Reform Proposals

Reform of local government has been on the political agenda since about 1971. However, little change has occurred in the structure of the system, with the exception of Galway city being upgraded to county borough status in 1986 and Dublin County Council being divided into three separate county councils in 1994, each with its own manager; and also the establishment in 1994 of eight regional authorities to promote co-ordination of public services at the regional level and to monitor and advise on the implementation of EU funding by the constituent local authorities with support from the Department of Finance in respect of EU-related functions.

The main changes have been in the finance area, with the abolition of domestic rates, the ending of farm rates as a result of a court decision, the full funding of most capital schemes, the abolition of domestic water and sewerage charges, and the use of motor tax revenues in place of the rate support grant and service charges.

Operationally, there have been a number of changes wrought by the Local Government Acts 1991 and 1994, including a seven-year tenure for managers (already mentioned), an adjustment in the balance of the councillor/manager relationship in regard to the planning laws, the virtual elimination of petty controls on local authorities and the granting of a power of general competence. Further changes are envisaged under *Better Local Government – A Programme for Change*, published in December 1996, much of which has been explicitly endorsed by the government which came into office in June 1997. Change is necessary, the programme states, because:

- Local authority functions are too narrow, inhibiting comprehensive and integrated responses to problems.
- The system as it has operated has not allowed councillors to realise fully the policy role which was always envisaged for them.
- Local authorities have tended to be bypassed by new approaches to local development which have been pursued through the creation of a wide range of disparate organisations (these are the County Enterprise Boards, the Partnership Companies, the LEADER Groups, the County Tourism Committees and the County Strategy Committees).
- There have been too many central controls on local authorities, stifling local initiative and self-reliance.
- Resources have been so scarce as adversely to affect performance of the traditional functions and to prevent proper use of discretionary powers to act in new areas of endeavour for the benefit of the local community.

On the face of it, then, local government in Ireland is on the verge of a new era.

REFERENCES

Collins, Neil, *Local Government Managers at Work* (Dublin: Institute of Public Administration, 1987)

Government of Ireland, *Local Government Reorganisation and Reform* (Dublin: Stationery Office, 1991)

Government of Ireland, *Devolution Commission – Interim Report* (Dublin: Stationery Office, 1996)

Government of Ireland, *Better Local Government – A Programme for Change* (Dublin: Stationery Office, 1996)

Roche, Desmond, *Local Government in Ireland* (Dublin: Institute of Public Administration, 1982)

APPENDIX 15

LOCAL AUTHORITY AREAS

9

THE STATE-SPONSORED BODIES

Definition

The description of state-sponsored bodies provided by FitzGerald (1963: 5) remains perhaps the most succinct. He defined them as autonomous public bodies, neither temporary in character nor purely advisory in their functions, whose staff is not drawn from the civil service but to whose board or council the government or ministers in the government appoint directors etc. They exclude bodies which (1) have some autonomy vis-à-vis government departments and which are staffed by civil servants, such as the Adoption Board or the Civil Service Commission; (2) are mainly advisory in function and permanent in character, such as the Animal Remedies Consultative Committee; (3) are advisory and temporary in character, such as the Constitution Review Group; and (4) are local authorities. Each body operates under the general control of a minister, who is responsible for ensuring that the body carries out the tasks for which it is set up but who does not intervene in the day-to-day carrying out of these tasks.

State-sponsored bodies are therefore part of the system of government, and the government is ultimately responsible for their performance. This situation underlines the fundamental difference between private sector companies, who are responsible to shareholders, and state-sponsored bodies, whose shareholder is ultimately the Minister for Finance, and it leads to endless debate on the degrees of freedom and control appropriate in the case of these bodies.

The state-sponsored bodies form a large part of the public sector. They may be divided into two broad categories according to their basic purpose: the commercial (trading) bodies and the non-commercial. Both categories, and the reasons for their establishment, are discussed below, and a full list of them is given in Appendix 16.

There is no standard framework for the setting up of state-sponsored bodies; their legal status, terms of reference and mode of operation tend to be determined empirically as the need arises. Each is established by means of a constituent document (act, statutory instrument or some other form of written directive) which deals with such matters as functions, board membership, staff, funding, and the relationship between the minister and the board. It is possible to distinguish six different methods of incorporation; these too are briefly outlined below.

Reasons for Establishment

The 'corporation sole' concept introduced in the Ministers and Secretaries Act 1924 meant that civil servants would be the employees of the ministers and would carry out all the functions of government in the name of ministers. After only three years, however, it became clear that if certain tasks desirable in the national interest were to be undertaken, and if the only body in a position to undertake these was the state, it would become necessary to loosen the control of ministers. The rigidity of the civil service system was considered unsuitable for the running of the commercial operations which were becoming necessary. Thus, in order to cut through the red tape that often constrains speedy direct action by government, the first of the commercial bodies (the Electricity Supply Board and the Agricultural Credit Corporation) were established in 1927: many others followed, one of the most recent being Temple Bar Properties in 1991. Ministers were placed at one remove, so to speak, from these bodies; they were responsible for what the bodies were set up to do (i.e. for their policy) but not for the details of the way in which they did their work.

From the beginning these bodies have been established for practical reasons. Something needed to be done, and the best, or sometimes the only, way of having it done was through direct public intervention. Thus the system of state-sponsored bodies emerged in a haphazard fashion in order to perform certain specific tasks which could not readily or appropriately be undertaken within the structure of government departments or local authorities, such as the manufacture and sale of products, marketing, or the provision of transport services. There has been little of the ideological motivation common elsewhere, as, for example, in Britain.

The management of the semi-state bodies is also determined by practical considerations. In contrast to the civil service (whose structure is designed essentially for the purpose of assisting ministers), they have freedom to adopt the structures most suitable for the efficient performance of the duties assigned to them. They also have greater freedom in matters such as recruitment. A further advantage is that the system enables the state to assemble boards of directors who have experience in the private sector.

Up to recent years, the tendency was to set up a new body to meet each new need or opportunity as it arose. In many cases, these new bodies engaged in tasks which were formerly carried out by government departments. For example, the work of Telecom Éireann and An Post was formerly carried out by the Department of Posts and Telegraphs, much of the work of An Bord Glas by the Department of Agriculture and Food, and the work of Coillte by the Department of the Marine and Natural Resources. In recent years, however, following close financial scrutiny, some state-sponsored bodies have been abolished and their work assigned to government departments (as in the case of Bord na gCapall and An Foras Forbartha). In other cases, tasks have been amalgamated, as in the instance of Teagasc (merger of the Agricultural Research Institute and the National Agricultural Advisory and Training Service).

Commercial Bodies

These bodies are sometimes called public enterprises because they operate in the market place, providing goods and services from whose sale they derive the greater part of their revenue. There are about twenty-five of these enterprises, employing about 62,000 people. They include bodies which provide an infrastructural base for the whole economy, the undertaking of which the private sector found either unattractive or beyond its resources at the time the need for the activities arose (e.g. Aer Lingus and the ESB). They also include bodies to develop natural resources (e.g. Bord na Móna and An Bord Gáis); bodies set up as a rescue operation by the state when a private undertaking was threatened with financial difficulties (e.g. the former Irish Life Assurance Company); and bodies to provide finance for certain sectors (e.g. the Agricultural Credit Corporation) or to promote a particular industry (e.g. the Irish Horseracing Authority and Bord na gCon).

The basic assumption behind the establishment of the commercial bodies is the belief that the business and entrepreneurial skills employed in the private sector may be utilised to equal effect in the service of the state. In accordance with this view, it is maintained that a business task is best performed by a body with a definition of objectives and a clear mandate which, because of the changing political scene, government departments do not generally have; that a board of directors which includes people who have what is termed 'outside experience' brings such experience, freshness and skills to augment the civil service in the conduct of public service tasks; and that the practice results in the harnessing of the talents of persons who might wish to give public service and who might not otherwise have the opportunity of doing so. In this way, the argument runs, the best of both worlds is achieved.

Non-Commercial Bodies

These bodies carry out a wide variety of tasks such as the promotion of Irish goods (An Bord Tráchtála), agricultural and industrial advice (Teagasc and Forfás), the provision of health services (the Blood Transfusion Service and

Dublin Dental Hospital) and the regulation of certain professions (the Opticians Board and the Nursing Board). Other areas of activity include industry (the Industrial Development Agency), training and employment (FÁS), education (the Higher Education Authority), tourism (Bord Fáilte), culture (the Arts Council) and research (the Health Research Board).

These are all activities which in some other countries are carried out by government departments. The Public Services Organisation Review Group (in the Devlin Report, 1969, still the most comprehensive account of the public service) noted that most of the activities of the non-commercial state-sponsored bodies are such as are, were or could be carried out within the civil service. The group referred to a tacit acceptance by ministers, officials and the public generally that functions such as the bodies carry out are best performed outside the civil service with its existing organisation and constraints. It pointed out, however, that every decision to allocate a new function to a state-sponsored body while similar functions are left in the civil service structure represented a failure to face the problems of the efficiency of the machinery of government or at least to think through the roles of the parts of that machinery. This critical reappraisal of the role of the non-commercial bodies may have been partly responsible for some of the terminations and amalgamations referred to earlier.

Methods of Establishment

State-sponsored bodies are set up in various ways, as follows:

(1) the statutory corporation which derives its powers and authority directly from the act which sets it up. Its relationship with the sponsoring minister, its functions and powers are laid down in the act. Examples of bodies set up in this manner are Teagasc and FÁS.

(2) the public company set up pursuant to a statute and incorporated by registration under the Companies Act. In these cases, the act provides for the setting up of a company which is subsequently established by memorandum and articles of association issued under ministerial authority. Examples are the National Stud and Telecom Éireann.

(3) the private company incorporated by registration under the Companies Act in accordance with company law. The objects of the company and the special conditions governing its operations are contained either in the memorandum and articles of association or in administrative directions from the parent department. Examples of companies set up in this way are Aer Rianta and the Irish National Petroleum Corporation.

(4) the corporate body set up under a statutory instrument made by a minister. For example, the Health (Corporate Bodies) Act 1961 and the Local

Government (Corporate Bodies) Act 1971 provide for the establishment, by orders issued by the Ministers for Health and the Environment respectively, of bodies to provide health and environmental services – the National Rehabilitation Board and the National Safety Council.

(5) bodies set up as private companies limited by guarantee and thus legally independent of ministers, but which, because of their dependence on the state for some of their finance, are sometimes regarded as being state-sponsored bodies. Organisations in this category include the Institute of Public Administration and the Economic and Social Research Institute.

(6) bodies which have no governing legislation or articles of association, whose constitution amounts to a statement from the government or the minister concerned as to what their tasks are, such as the Combat Poverty Agency.

Clear criteria as to when some of the above methods should be used are not discernible. The company mould, at least in the earlier days when the commercial bodies were being set up, seems to have been preferred for the reason that the public might be encouraged to take up some of the shares. (There has, however, been no large take-up though some of the bodies, for example Arramara Teo. and the Industrial Credit Corporation, have private shareholders.) There was also the consideration that changes in direction could be more flexibly provided for without going through the elaborate procedure of an amending statute.

Prescribed Functions

The functions are normally prescribed in such a way as to enable board and management to exercise a certain amount of discretion. Sometimes the prescription can be so broad as to lead to problems of interpretation as to what the functions really are; such problems do not, however, normally emerge into public view, being dealt with between the department and the body concerned. A broad prescription can lead to such wide diversification of activities that it raises questions about state bodies entering into competition with private firms, for example in the case of the hotel and catering services of Aer Lingus or the sale of appliances by the ESB. On other occasions the functions can be prescribed in such detail as to leave little discretion with the body and to raise the question why the sponsoring department did not itself carry them out. For example, the functions of FÁS, the body set up under the Labour Services Act 1987 to provide training and employment schemes and job services, are set out in considerable detail, amounting to about 1,000 words.

Boards

Board members are all part-time, save for those bodies where the chief executive is a member. The number of directors is normally prescribed in the governing legislation and varies from board to board. In general, six is about the lowest membership and ten or twelve the norm.

Selection

In the selection of directors, ministers have almost unlimited discretion and choice. In practice, ministers notify their colleagues informally at the meetings of the government of appointments they propose to make. In some cases, however, the legislation provides that certain organisations must be represented on the board: for example, in the case of FÁS, employers and unions must be represented; and in the case of Teagasc, farming organisations. But even in such circumstances ministers may choose from names submitted to them. Members of the Oireachtas and of the European Parliament are debarred from board membership.

In order to meet persistent criticism that many directors owed their appointments to their services to a political party rather than to professional competence, a scheme to regulate the selection of board members was announced in December 1986. It involved, on the one hand, the introduction of a register of suitable appointees, to be prepared in consultation with bodies such as the Irish Congress of Trade Unions and the Irish Management Institute; and, on the other hand, the drawing up by ministers of a range of required competences for boards under their aegis, so that these could be matched with the abilities of prospective appointees. Although such a register has been formed, the criticism persists. The Programme for Economic and Social Progress (1991) stated:

> The primary considerations which should apply in the appointment of directors to state companies are the experience and expertise of the individuals concerned. The chairman should be consulted prior to the appointment of directors in order to provide the minister concerned with the necessary information on the experience, talents and qualifications required for the board of the company in question.

This principle is accepted by government.

Worker Representation

Worker representation on the boards of a number of state bodies (Aer Lingus, Aer Rianta, Bord na Móna, CIE, ESB, NET, An Post, Telecom Éireann and the National Rehabilitation Board) is provided for under the Worker Participation (State Enterprise) Acts 1977–88. The reasons for worker participation were given by the Minister for Labour when introducing the arrangement in 1977. These were: the entitlement of workers to participate in company decision-making, the need to harness the total resources of a company, and the beneficial effect on industrial relations. In introducing the 1988 bill, which added Aer Rianta and the National Rehabilitation Board (the only non-commercial body in the list) to those provided for in 1977, the minister referred to the need to extend what the European Commission described as the 'democratic imperative' to representative arrangements in the workplace.

Under these arrangements, one-third of the seats on the boards of the designated bodies are reserved for worker representatives. Elections among the workers employed by the bodies are held every four years under the auspices of the body concerned. The successful candidates are then appointed by the minister.

The contribution of workers' representatives to the business of boards has not yet been substantively evaluated. Clearly, ministers and trade unions are happy with the arrangements. Not so happy – though it is difficult to get firm evidence on this – may be some of the chairmen and chief executives of the bodies concerned. They have referred to conflicts of interest, and also to problems of confidentiality which can arise, for example when worker representatives return from a board meeting to their fellow workers (i.e. their own electorate), who may not fully appreciate the need for discretion regarding the proceedings at the meeting. On the other hand, a summary report of the National Productivity Centre in 1982 in relation to seven bodies pointed to certain benefits such as the provision of two-way communication between shop floor and boardroom, the bringing of practical experience to discussions, and improved industrial relations.

Civil Service Representation

In some cases, ministers have appointed senior officials in their departments to boards under their aegis. The practice is, however, neither common nor uniform. The arguments for it have not been openly advanced by ministers, but they are accepted as being the desirability of providing a direct and useful flow of information between the body concerned and the department, to the advantage of both.

The appointment of civil servants to boards is not always acceptable to some chief executives or to some of the other members. They regard such appointments as inhibiting and interfering, and point out that they can cause conflicts of role in that civil service appointees are often called upon, as part of their departmental responsibilities, to evaluate and adjudicate on proposals from boards of which they are members. They also point to the risk of such appointments cutting across the lines of communication that should normally obtain between the chairman of a board and the minister.

Fees

Membership of boards generally carries a fee, but, again, the practice is not uniform, nor is the amount of the fee. Fees, where payable, are in the range of £3,000 to £7,500 a year for the chairman (but there are a few exceptions where the fee is higher) and £2,000 to £5,000 for ordinary members. Fees are not payable to civil servants for board membership, on the grounds that their work on the board is merely an extension of their work in their departments. Travelling and subsistence expenses at the highest rates applicable to the civil service are in all cases paid for attendance at meetings on the business of the board.

Finance

Commercial Bodies

The commercial bodies are financed in three main ways: from the Exchequer, from internal sources, and through borrowing from the banks and other financial institutions at home and abroad.

The Exchequer provides loans, share capital and subsidies. In the case of statutory corporations, the financial structure is subject to statutory control. Limits on the aggregate of loans for individual corporations are prescribed in the establishing legislation and increases over these limits require further legislation.

The sole or main shareholder in many of the commercial state-sponsored bodies is the Minister for Finance; in others it is the responsible minister. The share capital structure is prescribed in the establishing statutes and increases in that capital also require legislation.

It is government policy that the commercial state-sponsored bodies should operate, as far as possible, without Exchequer assistance, i.e. that they should make ends meet from their own resources, for example from the fares charged by the transport bodies and from the sales of products and services in other cases. Some of them, such as the Electricity Supply Board and the Voluntary Health Insurance Board, are required by law to break even, taking one year with another. Despite these aspirations and legal imperatives, however, it is not unusual that for other reasons, of a social or political nature, one finds that the policies of the government make attainment of these more difficult. This happens, for example, when the government delays price increases, as it does sometimes in the case of CIE, or when it seeks to delay the termination of a loss-making activity, as in the case of the closure of some post offices by An Post.

Some of the bodies raise a proportion of the capital they need through borrowing abroad, since in many recent years the interest rates available there have been lower than those available in Ireland. (The bodies have to weigh the advantages of the lower rates available against the possible disadvantages of exchange rate fluctuations and devaluation.) In some instances, the borrowing is guaranteed by the state. The incidence of guarantees is being greatly reduced in line with current government policy. Where guarantees are given, the Department of Finance must be satisfied that the money to be borrowed is to be used for properly authorised projects and that the terms of the loans are reasonable. What this means, in effect, is that no state body has the authority to incur obligations that ultimately fall upon the Exchequer unless the Minister for Finance agrees. (The collapse of the previously successful Irish Shipping in 1984 was due to its having entered a number of highly speculative, long-term, fixed-rate agreements fundamental to the future of the company, without the knowledge of the Minister for Finance. The government refused to underwrite the massive costs arising from these unauthorised agreements.)

Non-Commercial Bodies

The non-commercial bodies employ about 8,700 people and depend mainly on the Exchequer for their funds. As indicated earlier, these bodies were not set up to trade and in very many cases are performing tasks which could be carried out by government departments. The normal procedure is that they get a specific sum of money called a grant-in-aid from their parent department. The sum is arrived at by consultation between officials of the body concerned, the parent department and the Department of Finance. The final determination is made by the government. Some bodies such as FÁS, Bord Fáilte and SFADCo have received moneys from the European Union.

Accounts

All state-sponsored bodies prepare annual statements of accounts. In some cases, these are certified by the Comptroller and Auditor General and in others, mainly the commercial bodies, by auditors in the private sector. In the latter cases, the accountants responsible for certification must be approved by the Minister for Finance, who can also prescribe the format of the accounts. In all cases, the accounts must be submitted to the parent department; and, where the establishing legislation so provides, they must be submitted to the government prior to subsequent presentation to the Dáil (in effect making them available in the Oireachtas library).

The Mechanism of Control

Ministerial Control

Ministerial control derives mainly from the act or other document setting up the body, but also from the fact that the minister is a member of the government, which has ultimate control. The constituent document, in addition to prescribing the functions of the board, normally lays down that certain powers may not be exercised except with the approval of the minister, and that such reports and information as he requests must be made available to him.

Individual sections within the departments concerned are responsible for carrying out the duties directly arising from the operations of the state bodies under their aegis. These duties can range from the preparation of warrants of appointment of directors to examining new proposals and answering parliamentary questions. The normal lines of communication are between the chairman of the board and the minister, between the chief executive and the assistant secretary in charge of that work, and otherwise between officials in the body and in the department at various levels, exchanging information and making suggestions.

The degree of ministerial control depends to some extent on the attitude of individual ministers. Some are very interested in the performance of the bodies under their aegis and meet their boards frequently; some meet them only occasionally; some never meet them.

On the rare occasions when boards are reluctant to accept government policy they can earn themselves a ministerial reprimand, as when in April 1978 the Agricultural Credit Corporation did not accept that government pay policy applied to its chief executive; or removal of the chairman and the board, as when in November 1972 RTÉ did not accept a government ban on a broadcast interview with an IRA leader. The latter is a power that a minister will feel able to apply only in the last resort.

Oireachtas Control

The state-sponsored bodies are answerable to the Oireachtas in a number of ways:

(1) They are obliged to present annual reports and accounts. Even though, as with the annual reports and accounts of most companies, these may not reveal a great deal about the thinking behind the bodies' policies, the

presentation nevertheless affords members of the Oireachtas an opportunity to have discussion initiated by way of a motion in either House.

(2) Parliamentary questions may be asked. In answering, however, ministers seek to ensure that the bodies are not subjected to such degree of scrutiny as would disclose commercial information or undermine their proper managerial prerogative. Usually, therefore, ministers do not answer questions which relate solely to day-to-day matters; the conventional reply is that the minister has no function in these.

(3) When amending legislation in relation to a particular body is being debated, deputies and senators have wide scope for raising issues relating to the body concerned.

(4) The annual presentation by ministers of the estimates for their departments affords members of the Dáil an opportunity of commenting on the affairs of those bodies for which funds are being provided in the estimate.

(5) Individual members of the Dáil or Seanad may at any time table motions relating to the affairs of individual bodies or of the bodies as a whole.

By and large, however, the above means of inquiring into the affairs of state bodies are not greatly availed of, that task being left mainly to the joint committee on these bodies.

Joint Committee on Commercial State-Sponsored Bodies

This committee was originally appointed by the Dáil and the Seanad in 1976. The life of each committee is coterminous with the life of the Dáil which appointed it. It normally consists of eleven members – seven deputies and four senators – with a chairman who is a member of the party in government. Its task is to examine the reports and accounts and overall operational results of specified bodies, as well as matters relating to responsibility, structure and organisation, accountability and financing, together with relationship to central government and to the Oireachtas, and to report on these to the Oireachtas, with recommendations as appropriate. The committee may also undertake more general studies of the common problems of the bodies and make such reports as it sees fit.

The committee itself selects the bodies for its examination, normally taking them in rotation. The body selected is asked to submit a memorandum on its activities, current and envisaged. A similar memorandum setting out the government's views and concerns is requested from the relevant department, and the public is also invited to make submissions. In addition, the committee takes account of previous reports on the body concerned made by organisations such as the Economic and Social Research Institute or the National Economic and Social Council or by consultants, and of debates in the Dáil or Seanad or in the media. Having established the key issues and questions, the committee conducts a formal examination of representatives of the state-sponsored body (usually the chairman and two or three members of the board, together with the chief executive). The committee has the power to demand, and be provided with, reports and documents. The questioning can be intensive and, when considered of interest to the public at large, is widely reported in the media. In addition, a full report of the proceedings is published. It is difficult to measure the impact of this publicity, but there is little doubt that in so far as it bears directly on consumer affairs, both the body and the relevant minister take note.

The question of privilege for witnesses appearing before the committee is governed by the Committees of the Houses of the Oireachtas (Compellability, Privileges and Immunities of Witnesses) Act 1997.

The Ombudsman

Only the two largest of the commercial bodies come within the remit of the Ombudsman, namely An Post and Telecom Éireann. Where the Ombudsman receives a complaint about either of these bodies he can investigate it at no cost to the complainant. However, the latter must have pursued the matter fully with An Post or Telecom Éireann before approaching the Ombudsman.

The Debate on Accountability and Control

As the state-sponsored bodies have been established in the national interest, it is accepted that the government and the Oireachtas should be in a position to measure adequately whether they are carrying out efficiently the tasks assigned to them. At the same time, it is accepted also that the very fact of the setting up of such bodies to carry out specific functions outside the civil service structure and without direct ministerial responsibility is an indication of an intention to give them a reasonable amount of freedom and scope for initiative. There is something of a dilemma here, and it is reflected in a general lack of definition concerning the relationship between the bodies and their departments. The accountability and control of the state-sponsored body is as yet an unsolved problem, and the failure to devise a precise and comprehensive system has meant that the level of control tends to depend on such factors as the political visibility of an organisation (e.g. RTÉ), its geographical spread (e.g. CIE), its financial performance (e.g. Aer Lingus) and the attitudes of individual ministers and boards.

Government policy over the years has, in broad terms, been to allow the state-sponsored bodies as much freedom as possible consistent with the achievement of the objectives for which they were established. More recently, it has been explicitly indicated that the commercial bodies must achieve commercial results within a competitive framework, without benefit of financial help from the state. In so far as the non-commercial bodies are concerned, performance is to be measured not so much financially as by innovativeness in generating revenue, increasing industry involvement in their task, and achieving set targets and improved productivity. They can no longer rely on incremental increases in their annual grants.

The question of the appropriate nature and degree of control over the state-sponsored bodies has long been debated. The debate has become more intensive in recent years because of the severe strain on the Exchequer imposed by some of the bodies in the general context of a relentless national drive for efficiency and economy. The respective cases for freedom of action and constant government intervention were set out in the NESC report *Enterprise in the Public Sector* (1979). Accountability and control and the problems of performance associated with them also received considerable attention in the government programmes *The Way Forward* (1982) and *Building on Reality* (1984), in the report *Proposals for a Plan, 1984–87*, and in a White Paper on industrial policy published in 1984. This last document cited a number of reasons for the worsening financial performance of many of the commercial bodies. Among them were the lack of clarity of objectives and confusion between social and strategic roles.

This concern led to the government deciding in 1986 that a system of information to enable ministers to anticipate problems rather than have problems thrust upon them was necessary and, accordingly, that each commercial body should prepare a corporate plan for its activities for a period of five years ahead which would be rolled over on an annual basis. It was indicated that such a plan would encourage a systematic approach to planning and would provide standards for the evaluation of performance, especially in such areas as finance, investment and employment. The plans were submitted to the parent departments, where they were evaluated in consultation with the Department of Finance. Other ameliorative measures, mainly providing for a more strictly regulated system of submission of reports and accounts, were also put in place. Difficulties in this area persisted, however. In 1991, for example, Telecom Éireann and An Post found themselves, as a result of the intervention of the Minister for Communications following public outcry, unable to implement certain proposals concerning, respectively, revised telephone charges and the closure of some local post offices.

In 1992 the Department of Finance found it necessary to issue guidelines to the state bodies for the conduct of their operations. These provided, *inter alia*, that all such bodies should have adequate internal audit arrangements; that competitive tendering should be normal practice; that the establishment of subsidiaries and participation in joint ventures should be subject to the approval of the relevant minister and the Minister for Finance; that a written code of conduct should be put in place, of which an essential element would be disclosure of interest; that chairmen of boards were responsible for the implementation of government policy in relation to the remuneration of the chief executive; and that all chairmen should furnish comprehensive annual reports to ministers on significant developments during the preceding year in which they would confirm that the above-mentioned matters are being complied with.

The chief executives of the commercial bodies do not like some of these arrangements. They maintain that what they describe as the dead hand of bureaucracy is creeping more and more relentlessly into the management of the bodies. They are unhappy also about government control over remuneration, which, they say, should be left free for their boards to determine. This is a long-standing grievance. The chief executives point to what they call the illogicality of giving boards responsibility for spending millions of pounds and yet not giving them responsibility for the pay of their staff. The government answer to this is that all parts of the public service must conform to its guidelines on pay, which, because of the relative size of public sector employment to total employment in the country, are vital to the economy because of the spin-off effects. It is, in addition, sometimes pointed out that when control over pay was not exercised centrally, many boards were excessively generous in rewarding their staff.

The Comptroller and Auditor General (C & AG) carries out the annual audit of most non-commercial state-sponsored bodies. This is a standard financial/regularity type of audit carried out in accordance with the relevant accounting standards. The Comptroller and Auditor General (Amendment) Act 1993 extended the powers of the C & AG and allowed him to examine the economy, efficiency and management effectiveness of the non-commercial state bodies. The C & AG's reports on these bodies are considered by the Public Accounts Committee, thereby improving accountability.

The commercial state bodies are audited by private sector firms. The 1993 act did not extend the powers of inspection of the C & AG to these bodies.

As regards the corporate plans specifically, the chief executives say that they have got little response from departments, and that, where responses were received, they were lacking in depth. In their view, this is not surprising, since departments have little experience in this area.

In 1995 a Task Force comprising officials of the Departments of Finance and Transport, Energy and Communications and of the larger bodies under the aegis of the latter department reviewed the efficiency of the existing controls governing those bodies. Its stated objective was to strike the correct balance between necessary public accountability and commercial freedom. The review placed particular emphasis on corporate governance – the system of directing and controlling companies. Because of its overriding importance, corporate governance should, the Task Force said, be the subject of a separate review. In advance of such a review it made certain recommendations. These included the following:

- People appointed as chairpersons and directors of the boards of the commercial state companies should be appointed solely on the basis of their experience, competence and expertise, other than elected directors. The system of selection and remuneration of directors should be reviewed.
- The Task Force supported the strongly held view of chairpersons and chief executives that consideration should be given to the appointment of chief executives and civil servants to the boards of the commercial state companies. The wider question of executive board representation should be addressed as part of the review of corporate governance to which it referred.
- The minister should consult with the chairperson prior to the appointment of new directors to seek the chairperson's views on the skills mix needed on the board.
- Board appointments should be of such a period so as to ensure that, in normal circumstances, large numbers of board replacements are not effected at any one time.
- Directors should be provided with a brief by the minister on appointment or reappointment as director, which would outline the mission statement of the company to which they are being appointed, their responsibilities as directors, relevant legislation and other appropriate material.

The Task Force elaborated each of the foregoing recommendations.

The Debate on Privatisation

An issue which is debated from time to time in the media, in academia and in the Dáil is that of privatisation. Privatisation may include: charging for services previously supplied by government agencies at prices not reflecting the true commercial cost; injecting private non-voting capital into the financial structures of nationalised undertakings; opening up their markets to competition from private sector firms; full-scale denationalisation, involving the sale of a majority shareholding to the private sector.

It is this last concept of privatisation which has been the main focus of debate in Ireland to date. Normally, behind a debate such as this there is a clash of ideologies, a clash of views as to the role of the state in society. One view is that government is a burden on society, that all creative forces are in the market place and that the state is largely an obstacle to economic progress. The other view is that the state is a moral system superimposed on the disorder of nature and that the mission of government is to bring order and justice to an unjust world. The state, according to this view, has to provide social justice. It has to make up for market failure.

Apart from Irish Sugar and the Irish Life Assurance Company, which were privatised in 1991, the bodies mentioned in the debate about privatisation have included Telecom, Aer Lingus, Aer Rianta, the Agricultural Credit Corporation and the Industrial Credit Corporation.

The arguments in favour of privatising the state bodies include:

(1) Efficiency. Public sector enterprises have difficulty in measuring their efficiency, since they have to satisfy conflicting social and commercial objectives. Such enterprises are inevitably constrained in their actions by political considerations. Greater speed and flexibility in decision-making could be possible if there were not the need for frequent reference to government departments or to the government.
(2) Funding. Public ownership would provide companies with opportunities for further development by means of funding secured in the private sector if national budgetary considerations precluded the financing of such developments by the Exchequer.
(3) Wider public interest. Providing shares to the general public would increase their interest in the companies, would be to the benefit of democracy and would provide better for the interests of the consumer.
(4) Improved performance. The sale of shares to employees, sometimes by means of preferential offers, is said to increase the sense of employee involvement in the concern and to act as a stimulus to improved performance on the part of employees and, consequently, of the firm.
(5) The public sector borrowing requirement. The reduction of this requirement could help in dealing with the problem of high taxation and the national debt.

The arguments against privatisation include:

(1) There is no certainty that the free market will automatically lead to the optimum economic out-turn, nor that it will lead to social equality. The only way in which these goals can be achieved is through state intervention; otherwise the profit motive will prevail.
(2) Benefits for private investors. Potential purchasers in the private sector will be interested only in those state concerns which are profitable and will leave the state with the bodies which continue to be a drain. Such private investors will reap the benefit of large amounts of taxpayers'

money which over the years have been injected into the state sector. Thus privatisation would bring profit to the few at the expense of the community.

(3) Employment. Employment is a vital part of community interest. Its provision would not, however, be given its due importance should a state enterprise be privatised.

(4) Efficiency. There is no evidence that state bodies are any less efficient than private business, as witness the collapse of the Private Motorists' Protection Association and of the Insurance Corporation of Ireland.

(5) Removal of constraints. The question is asked why the state bodies were set up in the first place and whether the situation has changed. Any weakness caused by the constraints of state ownership could be remedied by dealing with such constraints, while retaining the bodies in state ownership.

Successive governments have adopted a pragmatic view on the question of the privatisation of state-sponsored bodies. What is important is that state-sponsored bodies work, that they contribute to economic activity and growth, and that they compete fairly in the open market place.

The EU and State Bodies

The Treaty of Rome sees market forces as the prime motor of a transnational economy. It regards these forces as being capable, subject to adequate supervision, of bringing about 'harmonious development of economic activities, a continuous and balanced expansion, an increase in stability, an accelerated raising of the standard of living and closer relations between the states belonging to it' (Article 2). There is no 'community role' for public enterprise.

Essentially, the EU requires both private and state commercial organisations to be bound by the same rules of competition, i.e. that there be no discrimination in favour of state bodies. It points to the fact that the state in relation to its bodies is generally looking for results, among which profit may not always be the major consideration, and that a state body can be in direct competition in its activities with those of other undertakings, whether public or private, in its own or other countries. The risk (as far as the EU is concerned) of distortions of competition between undertakings becomes real at this point and is highlighted by the difficulty of defining normal market behaviour.

It was against this background that the Union adopted in 1980 a directive on the transparency, or openness, of the financial relations between member states and their public enterprises. The directive imposes on member states the obligation to supply on request certain information on these relations; it also defines certain types of financial relationship to which the EU considered it particularly important that transparency should be applied. Examples of these relationships are the forgoing of a normal return on public funds and the compensation for financial burdens imposed by the state. The directive was not acceptable to some member states (Ireland did not object), who challenged it in the European Court of Justice; this challenge was unsuccessful.

It was in the light of this general situation that, even before the directive, Bord Bainne (the Dairy Board) had to change its status from that of a state-sponsored body to that of a co-operative. An Bord Gráin (the Grain Board), the Pigs and Bacon Commission and the Dublin and Cork District Milk Boards were forced to terminate their activities.

Conclusion

It is difficult to disagree with the assessment given by Barrington (1980: 65):

> Overall [the Irish state-sponsored body] has shown itself to be a very considerable instrument for development. It has played a big part in raising the level of management in this country. In an unstructured, unplanned sort of way, the state-sponsored bodies have contributed very effectively to the development of the country, and represent a most interesting adaptation of a form of organisation from the private business world to the needs of public administration. This has not been without its problems, and there are other problems still to be faced; but, overall, one cannot but be impressed by the record. This record, if accepted, poses major challenges, and opportunities, for the future of Irish public administration.

REFERENCES

Barrington, T.J., *The Irish Administrative System* (Dublin: Institute of Public Administration, 1980)

Department of Finance, *State Bodies Guidelines*, 1992

FitzGerald, Garret, *State-Sponsored Bodies*, 2nd ed. (Dublin: Institute of Public Administration, 1963)

Government of Ireland, *Report of the Task Force Established to Review the Controls in the Commercial State Companies Operating under the Aegis of the Minister for Transport, Energy and Communications* (Dublin: Stationery Office, 1995)

APPENDIX 16

List of State-Sponsored Bodies

This comprehensive list of Irish state-sponsored bodies (both commercial and non-commercial) is based on information supplied by ministers in response to parliamentary questions in March 1997. The bodies are listed under the relevant government department, together with dates of establishment.

Agriculture, Food and Forestry

Commercial

Bord na gCon 1958
Coillte Teoranta 1989
Irish Horseracing Authority 1994
National Stud 1946

Non-Commercial

An Bord Bia 1994
An Bord Glas 1990
National Milk Agency 1994
Teagasc 1988

Arts, Culture and the Gaeltacht

Bord na Gaeilge 1978
Bord na Leabhar Gaeilge 1952
Bord Scannán na Éireann
Established 1981
Re-established 1993
Broadcasting Complaints Commission 1977
An Ceoláras Náisiúnta 1981
An Chomhairle Ealaíon 1951
An Chomhairle Oidhreachta ... 1995
Independent Radio and Television Commission 1988
National Gallery of Ireland 1865
National Museum of Modern Art .. 1991
Radio Telefís Éireann 1960
Údarás na Gaeltachta 1979

Education

Dublin Institute for Advanced Studies 1940
Higher Education Authority 1968
Institiúd Teangeolaíochta Éireann .. 1972
National Council for Educational Awards 1972
Royal Irish Academy 1785
Royal Irish Academy of Music .. 1848

Enterprise and Employment

FÁS Training and Employment Authority 1988
Forbairt 1994
Forfás 1994
IDA Ireland 1994
Kilkenny Design Workshops Ltd (non-trading) 1963
National Authority for Occupational Safety and Health 1989
Nitrogen Éireann Teoranta 1961
Shannon Free Airport Development Company 1959

The thirty-five city and county enterprise boards are autonomous local development companies which operate under the aegis of my Department and could be considered analogous to non-commercial state-sponsored bodies.

The boards were established in September–October 1993, with the exception of Galway County and City Enterprise Board, which was established in 1992. All the boards have been incorporated as companies limited by guarantee and the status of the county enterprise initiative was confirmed by section 10 of the Industrial Development Act 1995. The date of incorporation of each CEB is set out in table 2, which I am circulating in the Official Report.

ENTERPRISE AND EMPLOYMENT *(contd.)*

Carlow	23–6–95
Cavan	22–3–95
Clare	27–10–94
Cork City	22–3–95
Cork North	18–11–94
South Cork	18–8–95
West Cork	27–10–94
Donegal	12–12–94
Dublin City	14–3–95
Fingal (Dublin North)	17–11–94
South Dublin	24–3–95
Dún Laoghaire–Rathdown	1–4–95
Galway City and County	11–7–95
Kerry	30–11–94
Kildare	3–8–95
Kilkenny	10–4–95
Laois	27–10–94
Leitrim	12–12–94
Limerick City	27–10–94
Limerick County	26–9–94
Longford	28–2–95
Louth	8–12–94
Mayo	31–5–95
Meath	28–2–95
Monaghan	6–6–95
Offaly	30–11–94
Roscommon	7–12–94
Sligo	23–5–95
Tipperary North	16–11–94
Tipperary South	30–11–94
Waterford City	23–5–95
Waterford County	27–7–95
Westmeath	1–3–95
Wexford	29–6–95
Wicklow	8–6–95

ENVIRONMENT

Commercial

Custom House Docks Development Authority	1986
Housing Finance Agency	1982
National Building Agency	1960
Temple Bar Properties Ltd	1991

Non-Commercial

An Bord Pleanála	1976
Building Regulations Advisory Body	1992
An Chomhairle Leabharlanna	1947
Dublin Transportation Office	1995
Environmental Protection Agency	1993
Fire Services Council	1983
Local Government Computer Services Board	1975
Local Government Management Services Board	1997
Medical Bureau of Road Safety	1968
National Roads Authority	1994
National Safety Council	1987
Rent Tribunal	1983
Temple Bar Renewal	1991

EQUALITY AND LAW REFORM

Employment Equality Agency	1977
Legal Aid Board	1979

FINANCE

ACC Bank plc	1927
ICC Bank plc	1933
An Post National Lottery Company	1986
National Treasury Management Agency Advisory Committee	1990

FOREIGN AFFAIRS

Agency for Personal Service Overseas	1973
Cultural Relations Committee	1949
Irish Aid Advisory Committee	1993
National Committee for Development Education	1994
Refugee Agency	1991

HEALTH

Commercial

Voluntary Health Insurance Board	1957

Non-Commercial

Beaumont Hospital Board	1977
Blood Transfusion Service Board	1965
Board for the Employment of the Blind	1957

Board of the Adelaide and Meath Hospitals 1996
Bord na Radharcmhastóirí 1956
An Bord Altranais (Nursing Board) 1985
An Bord Uchtála (Adoption Board) 1952
Comhairle na Nimheanna 1961
Comhairle na nOspidéal 1970
Dental Council 1985
Disability Federation of Ireland (formerly Union of Voluntary Organisations for the Handicapped) 1992
Drug Treatment Centre Board . . . 1988
Dublin Dental Hospital Board . . . 1963
Food Safety Advisory Board 1995
Food Safety Board of Ireland . . . 1996
General Medical Services (Payments) Board 1972
Health Research Board 1986
Health Service Employers' Agency 1996
Hospital Bodies' Administrative Bureau 1973
Hospitals Trust Board 1938
Irish Medicines Board 1995
Leopardstown Park Hospital Board 1979
Medical Council 1978
National Association for the Mentally Handicapped 1961
National Cancer Registry 1991
National Council for the Elderly . 1990
National Rehabilitation Board . . 1967
National Social Service Board . . 1984
Pharmaceutical Society of Ireland 1875
Postgraduate Medical and Dental Board 1978
St James's Hospital Board 1971
St Luke's and St Anne's Hospital Board 1988
Tallaght Hospital Board 1980

HEALTH BOARDS All 1971

Eastern Health Board
Midland Health Board
Mid-Western Health Board
North-Eastern Health Board
North-Western Health Board
South-Eastern Health Board
Southern Health Board
Western Health Board

MARINE

Bord Iascaigh Mhara 1952
Foyle Fisheries Commission 1952
Marine Institute 1992

CENTRAL FISHERIES BOARD 1980

REGIONAL FISHERIES BOARDS All 1980

Eastern Regional Fisheries Board
Northern Regional Fisheries Board
North-Western Regional Fisheries Board
Shannon Regional Fisheries Board
Southern Regional Fisheries Board
South-Western Regional Fisheries Board
Western Regional Fisheries Board

HARBOUR AUTHORITIES UNDER HARBOUR ACTS 1946 All 1946

Annagassan Harbour Commissioners
Arklow Harbour Commissioners
Baltimore and Skibbereen Harbour Commissioners
Ballyshannon Harbour Commissioners
Buncrana Harbour Commissioners
Dingle Harbour Commissioners
Dundalk Harbour Commissioners
Kilrush Urban District Council
Kinsale Harbour Commissioners
River Moy Harbour Commissioners
Sligo Harbour Commissioners
Tralee and Fenit Pier and Harbour Commissioners
Waterford Harbour Commissioners
Westport Harbour Commissioners
Wexford Harbour Commissioners
Wicklow Harbour Commissioners
Youghal Urban District Council
Bantry Bay Harbour Commissioners 1976

PORT COMPANIES UNDER HARBOURS ACT 1996 All 1997

Port of Cork Company

Port Companies under Harbours Act 1996 *(contd.)*

Dublin Port Company
Dún Laoghaire Harbour Company
Drogheda Port Company
Foynes Port Company
Galway Harbour Company
New Ross Port Company
Shannon Estuary Ports Company

Arramara Teo. and the Salmon Research Agency, private companies to whose boards the Minister for the Marine appoints directors, were incorporated in 1947 and 1955 respectively.

Social Welfare

Combat Poverty Agency	1986
Pensions Board	1990

Taoiseach

Law Reform Commission	1975
National Economic and Social Council	1973

Tourism and Trade

Bord Fáilte	1952
An Bord Tráchtála*	1991
CERT	1963

* In 1991 Córas Tráchtála was merged with the Irish Goods Council to establish An Bord Tráchtála.

Transport, Energy and Communications

Aer Lingus Group plc	1993
Aer Rianta cpt	1937
Bord Gáis Éireann	1976
Bord na Móna	1946
CIE	1950
Electricity Supply Board	1927
Irish Aviation Authority	1994
Irish National Petroleum Corporation	1979
An Post	1984
Radiological Protection Institute of Ireland	1992
Telecom Éireann	1984

There are no state-sponsored bodies under the aegis of either the Department of Defence or the Department of Justice.

10

THE HEALTH SERVICES

The role of the state in health care has been evolving since the late eighteenth century from the locally funded provision of essential basic services, mainly for the very poor, to the wide and sophisticated range of services provided on a national basis for the whole community in the latter part of the twentieth century. The rationale for the dominant role now adopted is that health is perceived in the modern state as a basic human right, the protection of which is accepted as a valid function of the state.

The current role of the state in relation to health services might be described as involving three aspects: that of regulating and setting standards for inputs to the health system; that of providing services (health services staff are, in the main, state employees, and many hospitals, health centres and so on are in the ownership of the state); and that of funder of services. The dominant source of funding is currently the Exchequer.

The Irish health care system has a unique structure. It is a mixture of a universal health service, free at the point of consumption, and a fee-based private system where individuals subscribe to insurance for coverage of medical expenses. While health status indicators have improved substantially, they remain relatively low compared to many other European countries, with a lower life expectancy suggesting that health care outcomes could be improved. Services are recognised internationally to be of high quality.

The major responsibility for health policy in Ireland lies with the Minister for Health and the Department of Health, established in 1947. The Department of Health and Children is primarily a policy-making unit with the great bulk of publicly funded health services provided by other health agencies, which have varying reporting relationships to the department. The present organisation of the service results in significant day-to-day management functions continuing to reside in the department, notably in relation to voluntary hospital and voluntary mental handicap agencies. It has been stated government policy, for a number of years, that this aspect of the department's work should be transferred to health agencies at local level so as to allow the department to concentrate on policy formulation and the overall monitoring of services.

The mission of the Department of Health and Children is: in a partnership with the providers of health care, and in co-operation with other government departments, statutory and non-statutory bodies, to protect, promote and restore the health and well-being of people by ensuring that health and personal social services are planned, managed and delivered to achieve measurable health and social gain and provide the optimum return on resources invested.

The department is now arguably facing the most challenging period in its history. There are unprecedented demands on the health and personal social services. At the same time, there is a greatly enhanced capacity to improve the health and quality of life of many people.

Legislation and regulations setting the broad structure within which better health services for the nation can be developed are introduced by the minister and department and approved by the Dáil and Seanad.

The General Register Office, which is responsible for the registration of births, marriages and deaths, is staffed and managed as part of the department. The secretary general of the department is the Registrar General.

Figure 1: The General Structure of Ireland's Health Care System

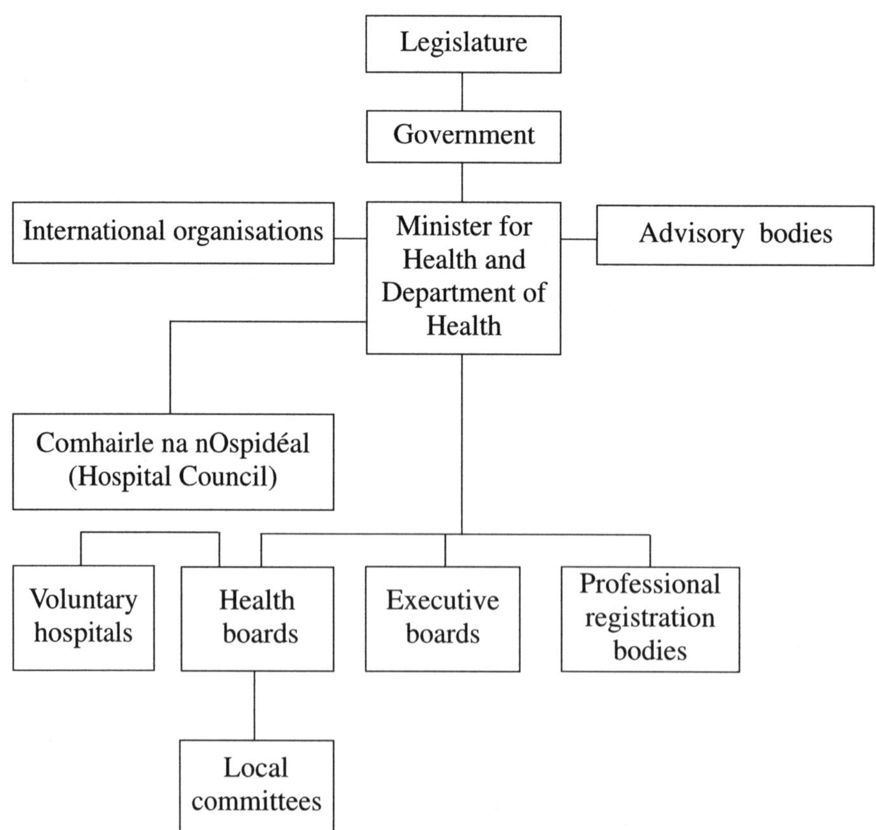

The Irish health service is a large and complex service employing a vast range of expertise and skills in over 300 grades in approximately 150 hospitals, which provide acute in-patient care. In addition, mental handicap homes, psychiatric hospitals, community health centres and general practitioners provide essential health services. The system encompasses a mix of public and private care, involving the same institutions and personnel, and with a degree of interaction in funding arrangements. The administrative structure of the system is shown in Figure 1.

There are over 65,000 people employed in the public health services in Ireland, and expenditure on staff represents about 70 per cent of current public expenditure on the health services. The well-qualified, committed and caring staff trained to the best international standards are one of the most important strengths of the system. Public health expenditure accounts for almost one-fifth of total government spending and represents about 6.8 per cent of GNP. An estimated further 2 per cent is accounted for by private health expenditure. Health services represent the fastest-growing claims on the resources of the community within the social services.

The Policy Framework

The health strategy *Shaping a Healthier Future*, published in April 1994, sets out the national strategy for the development of the health services. The health strategy is underpinned by three key principles: equality, quality of service and accountability. The main theme of the strategy is the reorientation of the system towards improving the effectiveness of the health and personal social services by reshaping the way that services are planned and delivered. The strategy sets out the three dimensions involved in this reorientation.

The Services: to focus prevention, treatment and care services more on measurable improvements in health status and quality of life ('health gain and social gain').

The Framework: in management and organisational structures, to provide for more decision-making and accountability at regional level, allied to better methods of performance measurement.

The Participants: to develop a greater sensitivity to the right of the consumer to a service which responds to his needs in an equitable and quality-driven manner and greater recognition of the key role of those who provide the services and the importance of enabling them to do so to their full potential.

Since the publication of the strategy, the Department of Health, with its partners in the delivery of health care, has been pursuing that vision of the health service. Further policy documents have been produced, which deal in greater detail with aspects of the implementation of the strategy. These include:

a Health Promotion Strategy; a National Policy on Alcohol; a White Paper on mental health; a Plan for Women's Health; the Mental Health Action Plan; the Report of the Review Group on Health Services for Persons with a Physical or Sensory Disability; a Management Development Strategy; a Cancer Strategy; Services for Persons with Mental Handicap.

The health strategy signalled a significant change in direction for the department and the health services. It required the department to redefine its role, to divest itself of various activities and functions which are not directly related to that role and to redefine its relationship with the health agencies.

The Freedom of Information Act 1997 has major implications for the health service. Under this legislation people have the right of access to medical records and other matters on file. Eligibility for medical cards is an example, and people are now able to ask about the criteria used in the decision-making process. There are also implications for people being able to look at their own patient cards and medical records.

The Comptroller and Auditor General (Amendment) Act 1993 extended the remit of the Comptroller and Auditor General (C & AG) to the health boards. Prior to this legislation the C & AG had no direct role in the auditing of these bodies, which were audited by the local government auditors. The C & AG is empowered to carry out discretionary examinations of the economy, efficiency and management effectiveness of the boards.

According to a new strategy statement published in 1997 as part of the overall Strategic Management Initiative in the civil service, the Department of Health will no longer be involved in the detailed management of services, although the Minister for Health will continue to have ultimate accountability to the Oireachtas for all health services. The health boards and agencies will be responsible for providing, directly or indirectly, all health and personal social services in their functional areas.

The change in role of the department is expected to take several years. It will involve:

- ending direct funding by the department of voluntary hospitals and certain agencies;
- devolving executive work to other agencies – health boards will be responsible for providing, directly or indirectly through other agencies, all health services;
- redefining the department's relationship with the agencies it funds;
- internal reorganisation and a new system of performance appraisal for higher grade staff.

The challenge for the department now is to divest itself of activities which are not directly related to its role and to reposition itself for the attainment of its objectives.

The key objectives of the Department of Health and Children are:

- to support the minister in the formulation, development and evaluation of health policy and in the discharge of all other ministerial functions;
- to plan the strategic development of services, through partnership and consultation with health boards, the voluntary sector, other relevant government departments and other interests;
- to encourage the attainment of the highest standards of effectiveness, efficiency, equity, quality and value for money in the health delivery system;
- to strengthen accountability at all levels of the health service;
- to encourage the continuing development of a customer service ethos in the delivery of health services;
- to optimise staff performance, training and development;
- to represent the Irish interest in EU, WHO and international fora relating to health matters.

The scope of the international responsibilities of the department has extended significantly, particularly since the signing of the Maastricht Treaty, which provides a framework for the development of public health within the European Union (under Article 129).

The Role of the Health Boards

The eight health boards, established under the Health Act 1970, are the statutory bodies responsible for the provision of health and personal social services in their respective functional areas. They are also the main providers of health care at regional level. The health boards serve populations ranging from 200,000 to 1.3 million, with annual budgets of between £118 million and £475 million in 1998. Membership of the boards comprises elected local representatives, ministerial nominees and delegates of consumer and health professional organisations. They replaced the former system, under which health services were administered on a county basis by twenty-seven main local authorities. The boards decide and administer the practical details and working of the health service at local level and are the largest employers of staff in the health service. In order to ensure that central policy decisions are implemented in a way acceptable to local interests, a majority of their members are appointed by the relevant local authorities for the areas served by each board.

The 1970 legislation arose from the necessity to make the organisation and administration of the health services as efficient and economic as possible. As the state had the major financial interest in the health services and this interest was increasing, it was desirable that a new administrative framework combining national and local interests should be developed for services. It was also necessary to broaden both the geographical and the representational basis of the local bodies in charge of the health services so as to get a more balanced approach towards desirable changes such as the reorganisation of the general hospital services. Developments in professional techniques and equipment and management methods indicated that the county was too small an administrative unit to be the basis for health services and that better services could be provided on an inter-county basis. This was particularly true in relation to the hospital service.

While the health board system has served the country well, *Shaping a Healthier Future* summarised the findings of a number of reviews which identified several key weaknesses in the structure of the health boards. These included a lack of clarity with regard to the respective roles and responsibilities of health boards and their Chief Executive Officers; inadequate accountability within the structure; and over-involvement by the Department of Health in the detailed management of the services.

The Health (Amendment) (No. 3) Act 1996 tackled these weaknesses, significantly enhancing the role and responsibilities of the health boards. The respective roles of health boards and their Chief Executive Officers have been clarified, and financial accountability within the system has been strengthened by a range of measures, including the requirement that each health board produce an annual service plan and publish an annual report.

The act has defined more clearly the remit of a health board, imposing on it an obligation in carrying out its functions to:

- secure the most beneficial, effective and efficient use of resources;
- co-operate with voluntary bodies providing services in its area;
- co-operate and co-ordinate its activities with other health boards, local authorities and public bodies; and
- give due consideration to the policies and objectives of ministers and of the government.

Health boards are working together more closely on issues which are of national importance but not appropriate to the Department of Health. One major initiative, in co-operation with the voluntary hospitals and the agencies providing services for people with a mental handicap, has been the establishment of the Health Service Employers' Agency.

Responsibilities of Health Boards

In addition to their responsibilities for health services, the health boards are responsible for a long and diverse list of functions under the health acts and various other acts ranging from the Rats and Mice (Destruction) Act 1919 to the State Lands (Workhouse) Act 1930. Certain welfare services are also provided by the boards; for example, they have responsibility for the payment of cash allowances, for the home help service, and for welfare homes for the aged. Health boards administer the supplementary welfare allowance scheme on an agency basis for the local authorities, thus facilitating co-ordination of health and welfare services. The boards also co-ordinate the work of voluntary organisations working in their areas.

The division between public, voluntary and private health agencies, however, means that a health board has limited power in determining overall health policy for its area, particularly if the major hospitals serving its catchment area are under private or voluntary control and funded directly by the Department of Health.

The mission statement of the Eastern Health Board, including its goals and the principles and values which underpin its work, is set out in Appendix 17.

Structure of Health Boards

The total number of persons on a health board ranges from twenty-seven on the North-Western Health Board to thirty-five on the Eastern Health Board. The membership is a combination of three main interests as follows: (1) elected representatives from county councils and borough councils, who account for more than half the membership; (2) professional representatives of the medical, nursing, dental and pharmaceutical interests, who are mostly officers of the boards; (3) nominees of the Minister for Health, of which there are three on each board; these were formerly used to represent excluded professional groups, but now tend to represent the consumers of medical services.

Each health board has a Chief Executive Officer (CEO) who has responsibility for day-to-day administration. The Health Act 1970 provides for the appointment of this statutory officer, who has specific responsibilities in the areas of staff appointments and pay, determining eligibility for health services and ensuring that budget allocations are not exceeded.

The board generally holds its meetings on a monthly basis. Business is conducted by means of various subcommittees, such as visiting, financial and other appropriate committees.

Management of Health Boards

The management structure of the health boards was devised in accordance with the recommendations of the McKinsey Report (1970). It is based on the idea of a management team with a Chief Executive Officer supported by programme managers and functional officers such as the Finance Officer and the Personnel Officer. These are full-time officers. The management team usually meets weekly under the leadership of the CEO.

Under the 1970 act, only a limited range of decisions, mainly relating to eligibility of individuals for services and personnel matters, are reserved to the Chief Executive Officer of a health board. Otherwise he and other officers of the board are required to act in accordance with the decisions of the board. In practice, however, the health boards have recognised the need for substantial delegation to their Chief Executive Officers of the day-to-day management of the services, while retaining ultimate control in their own hands.

For administrative purposes, the work of the board is divided into three broad programmes covering community care services, general hospital services and special hospital services (mainly the hospital services for the mentally ill). Each of these programmes is in the charge of a 'programme manager'. In the larger boards there is a separate programme manager for each of the three programmes, while in the three smaller boards there are two programme managers, one of whom deals with the two hospital programmes. In addition, there are functional officers in charge of finance, personnel, planning and management services. This group of officers, under the Chief Executive Officer, forms the management team for the health board. Each member of the team has his own specific responsibilities, but they act together as a group in evolving policy and advising the board on future lines of development. An outline of the three programmes is as follows:

Community care contains three components: community protection; community welfare; and community health. Responsibilities for community protection include the prevention of infectious diseases, food hygiene, child health examinations and health education. Community welfare provision is more assistance than health related and covers a wide range of services including provision for the disabled, home helps, meals on wheels, support for homes for the elderly and home nursing services. Community health includes general practitioner services provided for low-income families through the General Medical Service (GMS) scheme and home nursing services.

General hospitals cover the treatment of patients in medical, surgical and maternity hospitals, including the treatment at outpatient consultant clinics associated with these hospitals. Depending on the size of the health board, the general hospital programme may incorporate regional, general or community and district hospitals. The services are provided either directly by the board in hospitals under its own control or by voluntary and private hospitals.

Special hospitals cover services provided for the mentally ill and the mentally handicapped. Services for the mentally ill are provided mainly by consultant clinics or by liaising with professionals in the relevant voluntary bodies.

Services for the mentally handicapped are frequently provided by voluntary and religious organisations, and patients are maintained in their institutions by the board on a contract basis. There has been a gradual movement away from the programme structure in recent years towards provision of services on a care group basis, for example the elderly, children, travellers and people with disabilities.

The health board and the Minister for Health can each delegate functions to the Chief Executive Officer. The 1970 Health Act distinguished between functions reserved to the health board and functions delegated to the Chief Executive Officer. This reflects a similar type of distinction in the local government area. Among the functions reserved to the board are: the drawing up of objectives for improved health services; deciding the allocation of the budget; selecting and starting capital projects; the decision on numbers and categories of staff appointed to the board; dealing in property and land.

Among the functions delegated to the Chief Executive Officer are: advising the board; executing its decisions; deciding on eligibility for services; responsibility for personnel matters and other functions as may be prescribed. Among the responsibilities of programme managers are the determination of the needs and targets for the services in their programme; the proposal of plans and estimates of the resources required for the services provided; the implementation and review of the plans; ensuring a high level of efficiency in service provision.

The Health (Amendment) (No. 3) Act 1996 clarified the respective roles of health boards and their Chief Executive Officers by making boards responsible for certain defined functions relating to policy matters and major financial decisions and Chief Executive Officers responsible for executive matters. The act also imposed on health boards, for the first time, a statutory obligation to develop and implement health promotion programmes. Service planning in the Irish health services became a legal requirement under this act. The legislation makes provision in relation to income, expenditure and indebtedness of health boards. The service plan is part of the contract between the department and health boards in relation to service provision. The act's principles are also being applied on an administrative basis to other agencies funded by the department.

Specialist Health Agencies

Specialist agencies are significant partners in the health sector. Outside of the Department of Health, there are a number of bodies established on a permanent basis, such as Comhairle na nOspidéal, the Postgraduate Medical and Dental Board, the Medical Council, the Dental Council, the Irish Medicines Board and the Adoption Board, which provide a wide range of services and advice on their relevant areas of activity. For those aspects of the work of the health services not suited to localised operation, the practice has evolved of setting up special central executive agencies such as the Blood Transfusion Service Board.

In 1961 the Health (Corporate Bodies) Act introduced a new, more easily used procedure for the Minister for Health to set up specialist bodies. This enabled the minister by order to 'establish a body to perform functions in, or in relation to, the provision of a health service or two or more health services'. Such an order, which is liable to annulment by either House of the Oireachtas, specifies the constitution and functions of the body established and includes provision for the appointment of staff. The Blood Transfusion Service Board is an example of a body established under this procedure.

In addition, as required, special broadly based working parties and committees are established from time to time to advise on specific aspects of the services. Notable among these are reports on the psychiatric services, the general medical services, and the care of the mentally handicapped, the elderly and the disabled.

The statutory responsibility for the regulation of the number and type of appointments of consultant medical staff and senior registrars in hospitals is vested in Comhairle na nOspidéal. It also specifies qualifications for such appointments and regulates the appointment of certain hospital staff, such as senior biochemists, and advises the Minister for Health on matters relating to the organisation and operation of hospital services. It is not involved in the day-to-day administration of hospitals but rather in co-ordination and control of service development and long-term medical manpower planning.

Comhairle na nOspidéal was an innovative mechanism, involving devolution of authority to medical experts for the provision of technical inputs into the hospital policy-making process. Fourteen of its twenty-seven members (each of whom is appointed for a three-year term of office) must be members of the medical profession.

The Office for Health Gain was founded in 1995 by the Chief Executive Officers of the eight health boards. Its mission is 'Working Together to Achieve Measurable Health Gain'. The purpose of this office is to facilitate joint working, between health boards themselves but also between health boards and service providers such as voluntary and public hospitals and voluntary agencies in the mental handicap or other service areas, with the aim of achieving measurable health or social gain.

The government health strategy *Shaping a Healthier Future* is founded on the concepts of health gain and social gain and the principles of equity, quality and accountability. The Office for Health Gain concentrated initially on the three major causes of death or disability identified in the health strategy, on the risk factors associated with them and on the targets for reduction in mortality from these causes. These are cardiovascular disease, cancer and accidents. Smoking, exercise and the causes of accidents were chosen as the subjects for the first joint initiatives. These initiatives involved not only the health sector but the participation of the voluntary sector, the business sector and other public sector partners. This emphasises that the aim of working together to achieve measurable health gain will be realised only through the participation and support of all those involved in the health and social services.

The management of the health service, in particular the development of the management capacity in the system, is an important issue. With a budget of £2.5 billion and over 65,000 working in the service, a considerable investment has been made in education, training and the provision of services. There is general agreement on the need to improve the management of the health and personal social services. A report entitled *A Management Development Strategy for the Health and Personal Social Services in Ireland* was produced in 1996. Its main features are:

- an overhaul of selection, recruitment and training;
- the introduction of performance measurement;
- continuing management development and career development;
- health services management education.

An Office for Health Management has been set up and a separate budget has been provided for its operation. It involves health boards, unions, professional bodies and education providers in making progress in this area.

The Report of the Review Body on Higher Remuneration in the Public Sector (Report No. 36) set out a series of recommendations for greater involvement of medical consultants in the management of hospitals, including responsibility for the development of a hospital plan within the overall framework of national and regional plans for setting hospital priorities, establishing service and quality targets and defining the responsibilities of the unit leaders which are proposed under the plan.

The Voluntary Sector

The health strategy acknowledged the vital role played by the voluntary sector in the delivery of health and personal social services in Ireland. Agencies in the voluntary sector range from major hospitals and national organisations to small community-based support groups set up in response to local needs. The voluntary sector is a most important provider of health and personal social services.

The health service has a unique mix of public and voluntary involvement. There are considerable numbers of voluntary organisations which on a national or local basis provide health services with the financial support of the Exchequer. Voluntary hospitals, many of which are owned and controlled by religious orders or by lay boards of governors, have traditionally played a major role in the Irish health services. Most of these hospitals enjoy teaching hospital status and retain significant autonomy in management. While the state, through the Department of Health and the health boards, provides most of the finance for hospitals in Ireland, only a proportion of these are managed and controlled by public authorities. When the health boards were established in 1971, the voluntary public hospitals were allowed to maintain their direct financial links with the Department of Health.

About half the acute hospital beds in the country are provided in non-statutory voluntary and joint board hospitals with a range of private forms of management and control. In the Eastern Health Board area (Cos. Dublin, Kildare and Wicklow) over 80 per cent of acute beds are outside the direct management of the health board as voluntary organisations have played, and will continue to play, a major role in the development of services in the Dublin region.

Numerous voluntary organisations serving the elderly, the physically and mentally handicapped, the mentally ill and many other groups provide very valuable services both locally and often on a national basis. They include the voluntary hospitals and councils and associations for specific diseases or conditions and bodies concerned in the organisation of social services. Their role involves not just the delivery of services but also participation in the process of policy development. Statutorily, the hospitals and institutions involved, many of which are owned and run by religious bodies, provide services on behalf of health boards. Even the use of the term 'voluntary' is a misnomer for the most part, as these voluntary bodies are dependent for virtually all their funding on Exchequer sources.

Owing to the range and nature of the services it provides, the voluntary sector is a significant spender of money and employer of labour. Personnel employed by the sector enjoy broadly similar conditions of employment, including pension arrangements, pay rates and grading structures, to their health board counterparts.

The Department of Health is committed to continuing to respect and protect the independence and operational autonomy of voluntary agencies. However, the direct funding of some voluntary agencies by the department has impeded the effective co-ordination, development and evaluation of services at a local level and reduced the department's capacity to achieve its objectives. Voluntary agencies will in future receive funding from the health boards, to which they will be accountable for the public funds they receive. The larger voluntary agencies will have service agreements with the health boards linking funding to agreed levels of service. In order to improve the linkages between the voluntary and statutory sectors, the voluntary sector will be represented on the health boards. The operational independence of the voluntary sector will be fully respected under these arrangements and it will continue to have a direct input to the overall development of policy at national level.

The Private Health Insurance Market

There has been considerable debate, in Ireland as in other countries, on the appropriate public/private mix in health care. In Ireland private insurance and private providers of services are integral parts of the health care system, with a close, complementary relationship with the public sector. Many people choose to supplement their statutory entitlements to health services by taking out private health insurance cover. The state pays a significant part of the cost through tax relief, while much of the income of these schemes is, in turn, spent on the services of public hospitals. The state also pays private providers, such as general practitioners and pharmacists, for their services to certain categories of patient.

Under the 1994 Health Insurance Act, the Minister for Health is the regulator of the private medical insurance market and ensures that the health insurance market is operated within the statutory framework. This act introduced competition into the market for private health insurance, as Ireland was required to do on foot of the Third EU Directive on Non-Life Insurance. The Health Insurance Act 1994 and the 1996 Health Insurance Regulations provide the regulatory framework for the operation of the competitive private medical insurance market in Ireland.

The legislation requires insurers offering medical insurance to comply with the principles of community rating (an insurer must charge the same premium for a given level of benefits irrespective of age, sex or health status), open enrolment (an insurer is required, with certain qualifications, to provide cover to any individual under the age of sixty-five who wishes to enrol) and lifetime cover (an insurer may not, except in prescribed circumstances, refuse to renew cover once an individual has enrolled).

Insurers offering cover for hospital in-patient services are also required to provide minimum benefit (i.e. minimum level of cover) across a range of services, including general hospitals, outpatient and maternity benefits, convalescence, psychiatric treatment, substance abuse and day care.

Insurers are also required to participate in a Risk Equalisation Scheme, which is an essential feature of a competitive market that operates under the principles of community rating and open enrolment. It provides for the equitable distribution of risk between insurers, thereby ensuring that insurers will not benefit from preferred risk selection ('cherry-picking'); and without it the system of community rating/open enrolment would be inherently unstable.

Only insurers listed on the Register of Health Benefits Undertakings, which is maintained by the Minister for Health, are permitted to carry on the business of private medical insurance in this country. Of the insurance companies registered there, two, i.e. VHI and BUPA, offer health insurance products to the public.

The Voluntary Health Insurance Board was established in 1957 following the report of an advisory body. It is a state-sponsored body whose members are appointed by the Minister for Health. It provides for persons who wish to supplement their entitlement to health services. The board is non-profit-making and is mainly concerned with hospital costs, for which it provides a range of plans. In 1997 BUPA, a UK health insurance company, became the first overseas insurer to enter the new Irish competitive market. It has affirmed its commitment to community rating.

Other than the VHI and BUPA there are fourteen licensed health insurance schemes which cater mainly for a workplace or union membership (such as, for example, the largest scheme, the ESB Staff Medical Provident Fund).

The private medical insurance market plays a pivotal role in the delicate mix between public and private care in Ireland. At the end of 1997 there were in excess of 1.4 million persons (almost 37 per cent of the population) covered by schemes operated by these companies.

Health Expenditure

In common with other Western countries, Ireland has experienced substantial increases in health expenditure over the last thirty years. The main reasons for this may be summarised as: technological advances which have been expensive and complement (rather than replace) existing facilities, thereby increasing total costs; demographic factors, particularly the proportion of elderly people in the population, since they account for a significant part of total health spending; personnel increases due to higher demands for services and growing specialisation; expanded scope of services, with an increased emphasis on welfare services for disadvantaged groups such as the disabled, the elderly and children at risk; the growth in coverage of services with extensions in eligibility; and the appearance of new diseases, most notably AIDS.

As a result of rapid economic growth in recent years and a major downsizing of the hospital network during the 1980s, Ireland is one of the few OECD countries that has experienced a reduction in the share of GNP devoted to health. Per capita spending on health is still markedly lower than in other European countries though the average share of GNP devoted to public health spending is only slightly below average. The OECD economic survey of Ireland in 1997 notes that the share of GNP devoted to public health care fell to a low of 6.8 per cent in 1996 from a high of 8.1 per cent in 1980, without jeopardising the high quality of service provided. It said that public health costs have been contained because a significant proportion of the population hold insurance for hospital care and because first-level medical care is publicly funded only for the least advantaged members of society.

Eligibility for Health Services

Successive Irish governments have been committed to having a public/private mix in the health care system. This mix of public and private services facilitates complementary roles rather than conflict. The health strategy does not seek to alter the mix of public/private health service provided in any radical fashion but rather to enable it to contribute to the achievement of the overall objectives. The strategy is clear, however, in stating that 'the co-existence of public and private practice within the public system must not undermine the principle of equitable access'. In fact, prior to the publication of the strategy, it had already been agreed in the context of the Programme for Economic and Social Progress to separate the two strands within the system, through the designation of specific beds for public and private patients, so as to achieve greater transparency. This system does not restrict the admission of patients who need emergency treatment, but ensures that private patients requiring elective procedures are admitted only to private beds.

The primary aim of the eligibility criteria is to ensure that no person in need is denied access to a health service which he is unable to afford from his own resources. Health promotion is encouraged by making certain community protection services available to all persons without charge.

The 1966 White Paper on the health services and their further development outlined the then thinking on health service eligibility. It stated that the government did not accept the proposition that the state had a duty to provide unconditionally all medical, dental and other health services free of charge to everyone without regard to individual need or circumstances. On the other hand, it stated that no service was designed so that a person must show dire want before he could avail of it. The preventative services designed to protect the community as well as to help the individual were available to all without regard to means.

The structure of eligibility for most of the major health services is clearly specified in legislation, which also governs the charges which can be made. Every Irish resident falls into one of two eligibility categories:

- those in Category One, known as medical card holders, who are entitled to a comprehensive range of health services free of charge;
- those in Category Two, who are entitled to public hospital services subject to statutory charges, and who are also entitled to certain other services (mainly relating to assistance towards any excessive drugs costs). They are not entitled to free general practitioner services.

However, there are a number of services for which no eligibility criteria, or rules governing charges, are set down in legislation. In many cases, this is because the services have developed since the Health Act in 1970. These include services which now play a very important role in providing appropriate care in the community to people who might otherwise need residential care, for example community paramedical services, home helps, meals on wheels and day care centres. The strategy outlines the need for national guidelines on eligibility and charges, which will be applied in a uniform manner in all areas, to be introduced in respect of all health services.

The Eastern Regional Health Authority

Structural problems in the delivery of services in Dublin, Kildare and Wicklow have been identified for many years. The core problems identified in the eastern region by successive reports are:

(1) the absence of a single authority with responsibility for planning the delivery and co-ordination of services for the region;
(2) overcentralised decision-making within the health board and the lack of an appropriate management structure at district level, given the increase in the population over the last twenty-five years;
(3) the need for better communication and co-operation between the voluntary sector and the health board.

A brief summary of the main points of relevance from earlier studies is contained in Appendix 18.

Since the establishment of the Eastern Health Board in 1971, the population in its area has increased by almost one-third. The period since its establishment has also seen a marked increase in the range and extent of social problems (such as drug abuse, child abuse and homelessness) which come under the aegis of the health board. In spite of these significant changes, the organisational and management structure of the Eastern Health Board has remained virtually unchanged.

It is now generally accepted that the management structure of the Eastern Health Board is no longer suitable for the size of region it serves and the scale and complexity of the issues it deals with. A map showing the Eastern Health Board Community Care areas is at Appendix 19.

In November 1996 the Minister for Health announced that the government had agreed to his proposals for the establishment of an Eastern Regional Health Authority which would have responsibility for the funding of all health and personal social services in Dublin, Kildare and Wicklow.

> Under the new arrangements, all services, both voluntary and statutory, will be funded by the new authority, facilitating more integrated planning, delivery and evaluation of health and personal social services in the area. I believe this will enable the Authority to promote a more effective, efficient and patient/consumer-friendly delivery system in the region.

These proposals were brought forward in response to the health strategy *Shaping a Healthier Future*, which identified the need for substantial changes in the administration of services in the Eastern Health Board region. At present, the Eastern Health Board is formally responsible for services in Cos. Dublin, Kildare and Wicklow. However, in practice, the bulk of the general hospital services and much of the mental handicap provision are funded directly by the Department of Health and do not have any formal links with the board. As a result, there is insufficient integration and co-ordination in relation to service delivery and little integrated planning of services for the region.

The primary objective of this reorganisation of health service structures is to achieve real improvement in health and personal social service delivery to patients, clients and service users. The new Eastern Regional Health Authority, managed through three areas, will result in greater co-ordination and integration of services and bring decision-making closer to the local community.

Conclusion

The overall health of the Irish people has improved considerably over the last forty years. Life expectancy at birth in Ireland has increased substantially. By 1993 it was 72.7 for men and 78.2 for women, having increased by eleven years for women and nine years for men since 1950. The fact that heart disease and cancer each accounted for approximately one-quarter of all deaths in Ireland in the mid-1990s suggests that there is still considerable room for improvement.

The health services are facing new challenges as we head into the next century. The population is beginning to age, the number of elderly people will rise significantly over the next ten to twenty years and the health services will have to provide increasingly for high-dependency groups in the population such as adults with mental handicap and persons with AIDS.

Successive governments have tried to meet these challenges through the improvement and development of services, through the provision of additional resources to areas of special need and by striving to deliver services in an equitable and cost-efficient manner.

REFERENCES

Government of Ireland, *Proposals for Plan, 1984–87* (Dublin: National Planning Board, 1984)

Government of Ireland, *Report of the Commission on Health Funding* (Dublin: Stationery Office, 1989)

Government of Ireland, *Ireland: Shaping a Healthier Future – A Strategy for Effective Healthcare in the 1990s* (Pn. 0658) (Dublin: Stationery Office, 1994)

Organization for Economic Co-operation and Development, *OECD Economic Surveys: Ireland 1997* (Paris: OECD, 1997)

Towards Better Health Care: Management in the Health Boards (Dublin: McKinsey & Company Incorporated, 1970)

APPENDIX 17

MISSION STATEMENT OF THE EASTERN HEALTH BOARD

The Eastern Health Board strives to enhance and maintain the health and well-being of all people in its region.

Goals

In pursuit of our mission of health and social gain, we will strive:

- In co-operation with other sectors, to identify and address the barriers to the achievement of full health and well-being by individuals, their families and local communities.
- To generate a sense of ownership and responsibility for personal health and well-being among the community.
- To ensure the provision of accessible treatment and care of the highest standard at the most appropriate level in response to identified need.
- To ensure the provision of comprehensive personal social services aimed at meeting the special needs of vulnerable groups for protection and support.
- To develop constructive partnerships with and amongst our staff, voluntary agencies and other service providers.

The principles and values which underpin the work of our Board are:

Equity – addressing inequalities in the health status of different population groups, as well as equal access to services within a reasonable time regardless of ability to pay or geographic location.

Quality – a constant striving for excellence through the application of the highest professional and technical standards as well as a commitment to the development of 'best practice' and a culture of lifelong learning within the organisation.

Accountability – by staff at all levels in the organisation for meeting agreed objectives in relation to the delivery of services and for the use of available resources in the most efficient and effective manner.

Appropriateness – ensuring that treatment and care is delivered at the lowest service level appropriate to need and in the most appropriate setting.

Responsiveness – being responsive to the needs of individuals and their families and reflecting this in service responses which are timely and helpful.

Openness – ensuring a free flow of information regarding service provision, entitlements and the establishment of a fair appeals system.

Respect – for the uniqueness, dignity and potential of the individual whether service users or staff.

APPENDIX 18

STUDIES ON HEALTH SERVICE DELIVERY IN IRELAND

Health – The Wider Dimensions (1986)

While not dealing specifically with the eastern region, this report was one of the first to identify the need within the health system for greater accountability, closer integration between the statutory and non-statutory sectors and a more structured planning cycle to incorporate, *inter alia*, the monitoring of quality of care.

Commission on Health Funding (1989)

This report did not deal exclusively with the eastern region, but carried out an evaluation of health services generally. It did, however, identify specific problems in the east, stating:

> There is now widespread recognition that a cost-effective health service, providing care at the least complex level appropriate to the particular case, requires integration of responsibility of all levels of service within a particular catchment area. In the absence of this, there are practical difficulties in the co-ordination of hospital services with community-based services in the most efficient and effective manner. This problem is particularly marked in the Eastern Health Board area, where most hospital services are provided by the voluntary sector (p. 248).

Hospital Efficiency Review Group (1990)

This group focused mainly on the internal management arrangements of acute hospitals to determine whether greater efficiencies could be achieved. It concluded that acute hospital services could be delivered more efficiently if mechanisms could be developed to 'better co-ordinate services, more intensively use facilities and improve resource management' (Summary of Recommendations, p. 1).

Dublin Hospital Initiative Group (1990)

This group, chaired by David Kennedy, was critical of the existing organisational structure for delivery of health services in the eastern region. It said that the present fragmented arrangements should be replaced with 'an integrated and comprehensive health service, based on a systematic evaluation of patients' needs, with decision-making located as close as possible to the point of delivery of service, and with a continuation and development of the voluntary contribution to health care in the region' (p. ix).

The Kennedy group (as it became known) made recommendations for new structural arrangements which included a new regional policy board and a strengthened management executive based on an area management structure.

Examining the role of the voluntary sector, the group stated its conviction that the independence and operational autonomy of the voluntary agencies should continue. It recommended that 'the best way to achieve an integrated service to patients while maintaining the contribution of the voluntary ethos would be for the funding and service role of each agency to be expressed in detail in a contract between the area unit and the agency or hospital concerned' (p. 24).

Shaping a Healthier Future (1994)

The health strategy *Shaping a Healthier Future* was the culmination of the policy development process which had commenced in 1986 with *Health – The Wider Dimensions*. The strategy described the particular problems of the eastern region, where, 'to a greater extent than elsewhere, significant services are provided by voluntary agencies, but there is no single authority with an overall responsibility to co-ordinate all services and to ensure appropriate linkages between them' (p. 30). It put forward proposals for legislation to provide for a new authority in the eastern region.

APPENDIX 19

EASTERN HEALTH BOARD COMMUNITY CARE AREAS

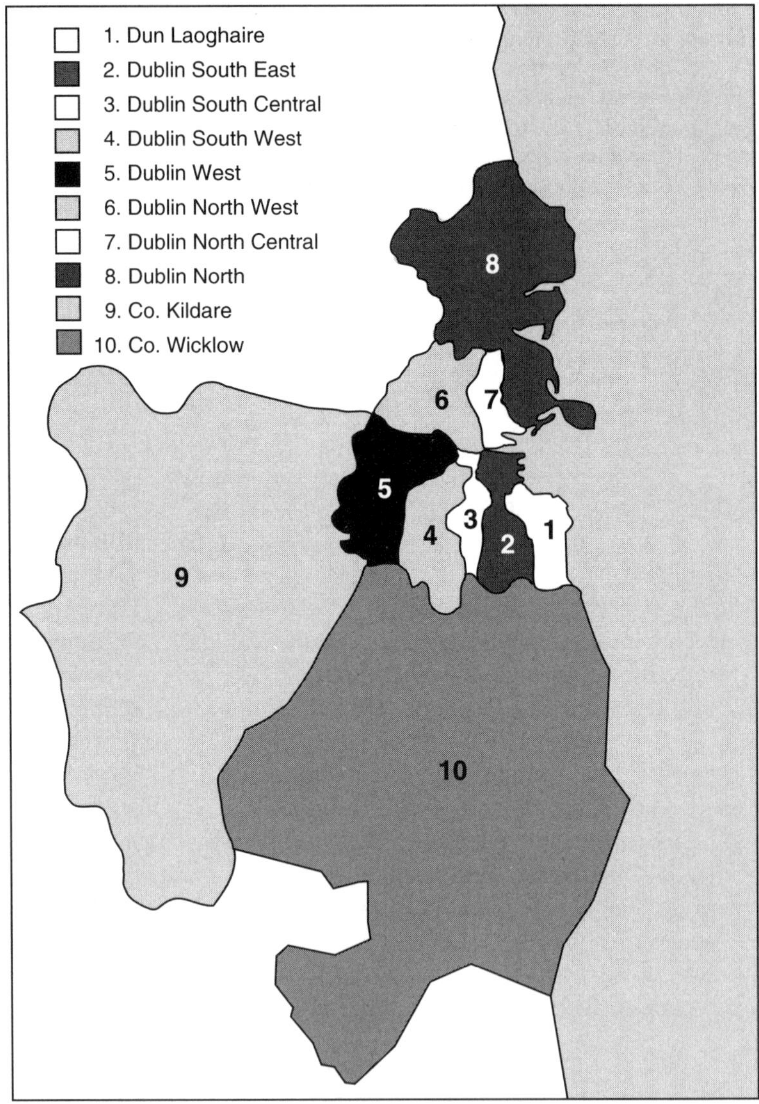

The Eastern Health Board is the largest of the eight regional health boards in the state in terms of population.

The board provides health and personal social services for 1.3 million people in Dublin, Wicklow and Kildare. It has a budget of approximately £400 million for health services and a further £100 million for other personal social services.

11

APPEALS

Every day officials in government departments and public bodies make hundreds of discretionary decisions which deprive people of entitlements and benefits or impose on them restrictions. Inevitably, many of those adversely affected by these decisions feel that they have not been treated fairly. Frequently, they complain that they have not been given reasons for a decision, that they have not been given a chance to provide their side of the story, that there has been unreasonable delay, or simply that a mistake has been made. In addition, there are occasions when the actions of public bodies appear to exceed their legal and constitutional rights.

Since public servants are not the best judges of their own conduct, it is clearly desirable that there should be independent systems of review under which the grievances of citizens against public bodies can be effectively examined and, if well founded, remedied. By this means it would be possible to ensure that the exercise of discretionary power is not abused, that natural justice obtains, that there are not wrong motives or irrelevant grounds, that decisions are not taken arbitrarily, unreasonably or erroneously, and that, in short, the activities of public bodies are controlled in the interests of the people.

A formalised system of complaints and redress is not as well developed in Ireland as in many European countries. The reason for this relative lack is that Ireland has followed the British tradition, in which all executive powers are vested by parliament in individual ministers, who are accountable to parliament for their actions and those of their officials. This concept is enshrined in the Ministers and Secretaries Act 1924, which makes ministerial responsibility central to the Irish form of democracy; and it means that, in Ireland as in Britain, the idea of political rather than legal protection for citizens who have a grievance against the administration is embedded in political tradition. As a result, the development of appeals bodies has been both limited and patchy; for example, Ireland did not get an Ombudsman until 1984. The High Court has, of course, always been available to complainants, but the situations in which it is employed to intervene in relations between the executive and the citizen are rare. This is largely because of its long delays and prohibitive costs, not to mention its reluctance to get involved in administrative decisions.

The need for adequate appellate institutions and procedures was stressed by the Public Services Organisation Review Group. In this connection, it also recommended that ministers should shed their executive functions, making them over to executive agencies, a number of which would be created in each department. These agencies would be responsible for day-to-day work, including detailed operations such as the payment of grants, issue of licences and award of contracts (i.e. the type of activities frequently involving controversial decisions). Successive governments have, however, proved extremely reluctant to adopt this recommendation, thereby exemplifying the preference of politicians for the established practice of seeking political remedies.

The idea was discussed again in 1985 during the preparation of the White Paper *Serving the Country Better*, but the proposal was dropped by the government in response to the general desire that ministers should retain their existing responsibilities and that politicians should continue to be the main channel for constituents' complaints. In the event, the White Paper facilitated the voluntary establishment of executive agencies; but although some (for example, the Social Welfare Services Office) have been set up informally, no minister has legally adopted the system.

In Ireland there are a number of informal methods and systems of a more formal kind for obtaining the investigation and, if appropriate, redress of grievances. The informal methods include approaches to public representatives (who may air the grievance by means of a parliamentary question), to interest groups and trade unions, and even directly to the decision-making body concerned, as well as publicity in the press and on the radio. The formal systems include the courts (both domestic and European), legally established tribunals and the Ombudsman.

A recent development in this area was the passing of the Freedom of Information Act 1997. It asserts the right of members of the public to obtain access to official information to the greatest extent possible consistent with the public interest and the right to privacy. It has helped public servants to be more open in their dealings with people. The act established three new statutory rights:

- a legal right for each person to gain access to information relating to himself held by public bodies;
- a legal right for each person to have official information relating to himself amended where it is incomplete, incorrect or misleading;
- a legal right to obtain reasons for decisions affecting oneself.

In addition, the act provided for the establishment of an independent office of Information Commissioner to review decisions relating to freedom of information made by public bodies.

Another recent development has been the establishment of complaints sections. Certain public bodies like the Revenue Commissioners and the Eastern Health Board have already set up their own complaints sections. The Ombudsman has said that he would like to see most public bodies following this lead.

Another method of complaint is the petition to the European Parliament. This is a written request or complaint submitted to the Parliament by any citizen of the European Union, either individually or jointly with other citizens, and examined by the European Parliament Committee on Petitions. Petitions to the Parliament often concern implementation at local or national level of European legislation. In a majority of cases, the Parliament decides that it requires either further information or the Commission's opinion. Petitions are forwarded to the competent Commissioner and Directorates General for further action. In recent years, petitions to the Parliament and subsequent referrals to the Commission have increased significantly. The parliamentary petitions procedure was enshrined in the Treaty on European Union, the Maastricht Treaty.

Public Representatives

By far the most frequently used of the informal remedies is the approach to a politician, usually a TD, who then uses his influence with the minister or with others who are responsible for making decisions. Such approaches are encouraged by the politicians themselves, who do not generally regard themselves as legislators and are more at home in dealing with constituency issues. The Dáil itself has long been regarded as a watchdog against government, and the handling by TDs of individual grievances could be regarded as a natural extension of this. Furthermore, because of the Irish system of multi-seat constituencies, where members of even the same party are in competition with each other for election, there are considerable benefits to be gained from services provided for constituents.

For these reasons, little interest has been shown in other forms of remedy: for example, only four deputies took part in the debate on the bill to establish the office of Ombudsman, and after its enactment four years elapsed before an appointment to the vacant office was made. At an earlier stage, in 1966, the then Minister for Finance had stated: 'The basic reason we do not need the Ombudsman is because we have so many unofficial but nevertheless effective ones.'

This preference for the use of representatives is shared by the general public. A survey of the factors influencing electors during the 1989 general election confirmed emphatically the relevance and importance of looking after constituency matters: 73 per cent of those polled considered that it mattered a lot, and 17 per cent considered that it mattered somewhat.

Extent of Influence of Factors on Voting Intentions

	A lot %	Some-what %	Not really %	Not at all %	No opinion %
Look after constituency needs	73	17	6	3	1
Perform well on national issues	57	27	9	4	3
Policies of the party	42	26	21	9	2
Choosing a Taoiseach	26	27	28	17	2

Source: The Irish Times, 2 June 1990.

There are a number of ways in which this informal system works. By far the most widely used is that which is known as 'representations'. A politician belonging to a government party makes a request by letter on behalf of his constituent to the minister responsible. Those in the opposition parties who have previously held office write personally to the secretary general of the department, while ordinary backbenchers write to him formally or to an official whom they have got to know. Letters to the minister are, in the first instance, acknowledged by the minister himself, with an additional copy of his reply for the politician to send to his constituent. The original letter is then sent from the minister's private office to the appropriate section of the department for preparation of a final reply. Normally, this reply will be prepared by the official who either recommended or made the decision complained of. Thus, unless a minister takes a personal interest (which he usually does only when personally approached by the party member making the representations) and the decision is one of a discretionary nature, it is unlikely that it will be altered.

Officials are not impressed by representations, to which they are well accustomed. The matter may or may not be re-examined, depending on the issue, the nature of the examination already made, and the political standing of the person making the representations. The reply, prepared for signature by the minister on his own personal headed paper, may, however, contain a fuller restatement of the reasons for the original decision and generally includes a soothing last sentence to the effect that 'the minister regrets that he cannot be of more assistance on this occasion'. It is then sent back to the minister's private office, where it is scrutinised by his private secretary before presentation to the minister for his signature. Again, an extra copy of the reply is sent to the politician concerned. In the vast majority of cases this ends the correspondence.

A minister receives directly all the grievances and all the requests for favours from his own constituents, irrespective of whether they are members of his own party or not. If the subject matter relates to the work of his own department, the procedure is as outlined above. If it does not, the letter is transmitted over the minister's signature to whichever of his colleagues has the responsibility, with a request for favourable consideration, and the constituent is informed accordingly. In due course a final reply is received from the investigating minister, whose investigation has been the same as that referred to in the preceding paragraph. This reply is sent by the minister to his constituent, who thus has evidence of the high level at which his letter has been dealt with.

Occasionally, politicians, especially those who have been in the Oireachtas for some time and may have got to know many of the senior officials, inquire on the telephone about constituency affairs. This practice is not common, however, since it does not produce any written matter to show the constituent that action has been taken on his behalf.

Officials generally regard this elaborate and expensive representations procedure with a degree of cynicism, since it very rarely has the effect of having administrative decisions reversed. They complain that it has detrimental effects on their work. Since ministers demand that priority be given to representations, official resources are diverted away from dealing with the issues which the representations are intended to ameliorate. Officials who should be engaged full-time on, for example, paying grants have to detach themselves to deal with representations about delays in payment of the same grants. They also point out that the system distracts ministers and senior officials from the policy-making activities in which they should more properly be engaged. A further undesirable feature of the system is the creation of an impression among the public that everything can be fixed.

Another type of public representative, the local councillor, can play a role as intermediary between the citizen and the administration at local authority level.

Councillors have a certain advantage over TDs in following up individual complaints because of their close involvement with the administrative process and their more ready access to local offices.

Parliamentary Questions

The procedures relating to the tabling and answering of parliamentary questions have been dealt with in Chapter 3. Questions may be divided into two broad categories: those which relate to policy matters and those which relate to matters of day-to-day administration. It is those in the latter category with which we are concerned here, and specifically those where TDs seek to have grievances ventilated.

By far the most numerous of these are the questions relating to matters such as the non-payment, inadequate payment or delay in payment of grants and allowances. The TD conveys his question to the Dáil office, whence it is sent to the minister's office and thence to the appropriate section of the department. The main difference in the treatment of this type of complaint and that of the 'representations' is that the reply to the parliamentary question is normally seen and approved by the assistant secretary concerned before transmission to the minister's office for presentation to the Dáil. Copies of the replies to all parliamentary questions are normally seen also by the secretary general of the department, but not necessarily for clearance by him. Only on very rare occasions does this procedure result in any alteration of the reply at the insistence of one of these senior officials. What the procedure does ensure is that the reply will be technically correct and will be in such terms as to protect the minister from criticism by way of supplementary questions (where the question is for oral reply) or from other questions on the same issue on a subsequent occasion. Replies must arrive in the minister's private office at least twenty-four hours before they are due for answer; this rule, however, is not always adhered to, especially if there is an amount of information to be collected for the reply.

The replies to all questions which he has to answer orally are examined by the minister himself before he goes to the Dáil to present them. In these cases he will have the benefit of an accompanying note giving the background to the question, together with sufficient information to enable him to deal with supplementary questions. To change the nature of the reply, i.e. to approve some benefit already rejected, is normally within his prerogative. However, this prerogative is very rarely exercised, and the minister normally accepts the judgment of his officials.

The replies to written questions are generally seen by the senior officials only, and are rarely seen by the minister. Copies of the reply are provided by the minister's private secretary to the Dáil to be passed on to the TD concerned and for subsequent publication in the record of Dáil debates.

Parliamentary questions have little effect on the work of civil servants beyond the amount of time taken up in the administrative procedure which the careful preparation of replies and notes entails. There is always a sense of urgency, since the standing orders of the Dáil provide that three clear days' notice only need be given, i.e. that deputies are entitled to, and invariably receive, answers to their written questions (by far the most numerous) on such short notice. The officials preparing the replies to parliamentary questions are obliged under their own standing departmental regulations to drop all other work and attend to parliamentary questions. Information about the problems of individual constituents can, of course, be obtained by deputies, through either a telephone call or a letter, especially now that members of the Oireachtas have secretarial assistance. However, civil servants are aware that the main reasons for questions on constituency matters are, firstly, to allow politicians to represent themselves openly as advocates of the defenceless citizen against the powerful minister and soulless bureaucrat, and, secondly, to provide them with written material which they can send to their constituents and to their local newspapers as evidence that they are about their constituents' business. Questions are, nevertheless, an essential element of democracy.

The value of the parliamentary question as a means of resolving grievances, however, is questionable. Neither ministers nor civil servants are disposed to admit readily that they have been remiss in the exercise of the discretion vested in them, particularly given the adversarial manner in which question time is conducted in the Dáil. Thus ministers tend to defend themselves against what they regard as attacks on them and their departments and to justify decisions rather than admit error, and civil servants tend to seek additional arguments to support the decisions taken, rather than seek compromise.

Furthermore, Dáil standing orders contain a number of restrictions which greatly reduce the efficacy of the parliamentary question as a way of having decisions altered. Questions may be asked only about matters for which a minister has direct responsibility; thus any questions raised on matters connected with the day-to-day work of local authorities, health boards and state-sponsored bodies are automatically rejected. Debates or statements at question time are prohibited, and votes are not taken on issues raised. Moreover, the Dáil has no sanctions: it cannot alter a decision or punish decision-makers. The only course still open to a deputy dissatisfied with a reply is to seek the permission of the Ceann Comhairle to raise the matter again on the adjournment. Thus, unless he is in a position to make a forceful and detailed case on the basis of information not hitherto disclosed, he is unlikely to succeed in having a decision altered.

One effect that the raising of grievances through parliamentary questions may have, however, is to ensure that similar cases are handled more sympathetically in the future. To this extent, the parliamentary question could be regarded as being better at preventing rather than remedying grievances. An analysis of parliamentary questions asked between the general elections of 1992 and 1997 indicates that most questions are asked by opposition TDs. Government backbenchers, with more direct access to ministers, rarely need to. The average cost per question is £165 for the time spent on research work by civil servants. Many of the 65,366 parliamentary questions asked during this period, at a total cost of £10.8 million, could have been dealt with more effectively by other means. Given the growth in influence of the European Parliament, the expanding volume of parliamentary questions in the Parliament, both written and oral, is becoming increasingly important. The questions are sent to the Commissioners, Cabinets and Directorates General concerned, and the replies are transmitted back to the Parliament.

Miscellaneous Informal Remedies

An informal, though very effective, means of redress is provided by the media, both newspapers and radio. Many newspapers and some radio programmes provide facilities whereby people may bring to attention instances of what they consider to be unfair treatment by public bodies. On occasion, the media follow up the complaints directly with the bodies concerned. Otherwise the publicity itself often results in the bodies re-examining the cases complained of.

Another informal means is through pressure groups or through trade unions, particularly in cases related to employment-linked social welfare and health entitlements. No matter how formal a relationship may appear to be, the reality is that the officers in pressure groups and unions normally have good personal relations with the officials with whom they deal on a daily basis, thus enabling matters in which either side is interested to be discussed informally.

Everyone may, of course, use the hierarchical method of appeal. They may make a written complaint about a matter of concern to them directly to the chief executive of the organisation concerned. In general, this method is used by the more articulate and well-informed section of the community. It is perhaps as effective as any of the means described above.

The Irish Courts

While the courts have no concern with the vast majority of the administrative decisions of public bodies, since it is not their function to entertain appeals against such decisions, they are concerned to ensure that actions and decisions are within the law. The High Court is available to citizens in certain circumstances to contest decisions with which they are not satisfied. The area of judicial review is somewhat complex, and the remedies provided are frequently hedged about with restrictions as to the type of person eligible to apply and the type of body against whom the remedy will lie. It is sometimes difficult even for lawyers to determine which remedy is appropriate to the particular circumstances.

Generally speaking, individual citizens acting alone in their own interest do not seek the help of the courts. The technicality and complexity of the law, referred to above, can be a deterrent, as can the long delays involved, and the inaccessibility to citizens of the case law and precedents on which so many of the legal decisions depend. The uncertainty of the law, owing to the fluidity of judicial interpretation, is a further factor. But above all, perhaps, is the prohibitive cost of legal proceedings, which is well beyond the reach of the ordinary citizen; even if he wins his case, he may be left with substantial costs to pay.

Types of Appeal

There is an extensive literature on all aspects of appellate procedures conducted in the Irish courts. It is possible here only to indicate in broad terms the three most usual situations in which the courts will intervene to provide remedies.

Constitutional rights infringed. A citizen may resort to the courts if he considers that an act of the Oireachtas infringes his constitutional rights. An example of this case is that of a farmer (Brennan) in Co. Wexford who contested the constitutionality of the rating system as it applied to him. Under the Valuation Acts 1852–64 his farm was valued by reference to the price of certain crops in the years 1849–52. The amount of the valuation determined his liability for rates and his eligibility for certain kinds of state assistance. He pleaded that this method of valuation violated his personal and property rights under the Constitution. The court found in his favour in 1984, because the use of the 1852 valuation long after farming methods had changed was an infringement of his property rights in that he was paying more in rates than neighbours with better land. The fact that there was no other source of review of the valuation open to him was a further attack on his property rights.

Constitutional justice disregarded. The second type of situation is where a public body making a decision did not observe the principles of justice provided for each citizen by the Constitution, i.e. that the decision-maker must not be biased or be seen to be biased, that an opportunity be given to the person whose case is under review to know what evidence has been given against him so that he can give his side of the story, and that no body should be a judge in its own case. The requirement to follow fair procedures binds ministers and officials to act in good faith and to listen carefully to both sides of the case. Court decisions suggest that when a citizen has a legitimate expectation that, for example, his application for a discretionary benefit such as a licence or a permit will not be refused without a chance for him to put his case, then he is entitled to some kind of hearing. Where he already enjoys the benefit, the expectation that he should not be deprived of it arbitrarily and unheard by the decision-maker makes his case legally and morally stronger. An example of this type of case is that of E.P. Garvey, former Commissioner of the Garda Síochána, who was removed from office and who brought proceedings before the High Court. The removal was struck down because he had been given no reason for it and no opportunity to indicate why he should not be removed.

Ultra vires. Cases under the third situation, i.e. where public bodies have gone beyond the powers conferred on them by statute, are by far the most numerous. The body, for example, might not have observed prescribed procedures, or it might have taken extraneous matters into account in arriving at its decision. The courts have no concern with the vast majority of administrative decisions, since they assume, reasonably, that when the legislature allocates the power to make such decisions to a public body, it does not intend that the power should be taken over by the courts. On the other hand, the courts are concerned that decisions are taken within the law. Therefore, the courts are available to citizens who contest the legality of decisions taken in their cases, and a number of remedies are provided.

Types of Remedy

Apart from damages, what the aggrieved citizen wants from the courts in the case of administrative decisions which adversely affect him is relief by way of an order of the court under one or more of the following headings: (1) invalidating the administrative decision; (2) requiring the public body to desist from or discontinue some course of action; (3) commanding the fulfilment of a legal obligation. The difference between an appeal and a judicial order or review is that the first involves a new decision while the second does not. There are five different orders which may be sought to meet the needs broadly outlined; these are briefly discussed below.

(1) Certiorari. This type of order presupposes a duty to act judicially. A judicial act comprises an act done by any competent authority, such as a public body, upon consideration of facts and circumstances, which imposes liability or affects the rights of others. An order of certiorari may be sought by a citizen who seeks to have a decision made by a public body declared invalid because the body acted in excess of its legal authority. The excess may be due to the fact that the body had no legal authority to make the decision it did, because the procedures adopted by it in coming to its decision were vitiated by its failure to observe constitutional or natural justice, as already defined, or because there was an error on the face of the record. Such an error would arise where there was a misinterpretation of a statute or where there was a failure to follow a procedure laid down in a statute. A failure of the latter kind would arise, for example, if the statute said that the body making the decision should consist of two lawyers and a layman and if instead it consisted of two laymen and a lawyer, or if a local authority was empowered to purchase land compulsorily for housing and if instead it could be shown to have been purchased for the making of a road.

Certiorari is a discretionary remedy in the sense that even though the complainant may prove his case, he may, in the exercise of its discretion by the court, be refused the remedy he seeks. This discretion is exercised not in an arbitrary but rather in a judicial manner. If an order of certiorari is granted by the court, its effect is to quash the decision and to leave the body which took it free to consider the matter afresh. Such an order may not attract damages, however. A person who wishes to obtain damages for any loss occasioned must seek a different kind of order, a declaratory order with damages.

(2) Declaration. The court may be asked to declare the rights and duties of parties before it. In some respects a declaration is wider than certiorari in that its reach is not confined to situations where there is a duty to act judicially. It is widely availed of in cases such as the withholding of discretionary benefits and the revocation of licences. It is a defence against the unlawful exercise of administrative power. It entitles the aggrieved person to take the initiative where the alternative would be to await action on foot of the unlawful act of the public body and, at that stage, to dispute its lawfulness. A declaration, as its name implies, declares the true legal position in regard to the rights and duties of the parties. It does not quash the original decision as an order of certiorari does. Nevertheless, the effect may be the same, since a public authority is unlikely to ignore a judicial declaration of the law.

(3) Prohibition. The issue of this order restrains an administrative body which has a duty to act judicially and whose decisions affect rights or impose liabilities from embarking upon or continuing a given course of action which would be in excess of its jurisdiction. The order has, therefore, a close affinity with certiorari, and essentially the difference between them is one of timing. Prohibition issues to restrain the making of a decision in excess of jurisdiction; certiorari issues to quash such a decision where it has already been made.

Prohibition does not apply if a public body is acting administratively, and it must be said that the difference between acting judicially and acting administratively is not always clear. Where it is acting administratively, its proceedings may, however, be restrained by injunction.

(4) Injunction. This is a coercive order from the court to stop the recipient from taking some particular action against a person who can show virtual certainty of its taking place and that it will cause irreparable injury. An injunction may be interlocutory, requiring interim cessation of the action so as to maintain the status quo pending final determination of a case.

(5) Mandamus. This remedy exists to enforce the performance of its duty by a public authority where neglect in the performance is adversely affecting some person. The authority may be pleading that it is not under a legal obligation to perform a certain duty. Persons affected may test the matter in

the courts by seeking an order of mandamus. This order may also be the appropriate remedy in the case of failure to implement a judicial decree of damages given against the state.

European Commission for Human Rights

The promotion and development of human rights is one of the main tasks of the Council of Europe, of which Ireland is a member. The European Commission for Human Rights, which is under the auspices of the Council, examines complaints by individuals who consider that an entitlement under the European Convention for Human Rights and Fundamental Freedoms has been violated in their case. If the Commission finds merit in the complaint and does not succeed in arriving at a settlement between the complainant and the government body concerned, it may refer the case to the Court of Human Rights at Strasbourg.

European Court of Justice

The task of the Court of Justice at Luxembourg is to ensure observance of the law in the interpretation and application of the treaties setting up the European Union and in implementing regulations issued by the Council of Ministers of the European Commission. The Court may review the legality of acts of the Council or Commission on the grounds of lack of competence, infringement of an essential legal requirement, infringement of a treaty or of any legal rule relating to its application, or misuse of power. A person may appeal any decision given against him or against other persons which is of direct and individual concern to him.

Tribunals

There is a wide variety of bodies which have the word 'Tribunal' in their title, such as the Valuation Tribunal, the Employment Appeals Tribunal, the Rent Tribunal and the Pensions Tribunal. There is also a variety of tribunals set up to resolve disputes or to discipline members within the public service, for example those in the Garda Síochána, the Permanent Defence Forces and the prison service. Most of these have been established by law and operate in the field of public law, assisting in the dirigiste and welfare aspects of the state's responsibilities. Typical of the vague terminology which obtains in regard to tribunals are what might be termed domestic tribunals, set up by professions, organisations, clubs and so on, which may have rules for dealing, themselves, with the discipline of their own members. The lack of uniformity extends to nomenclature. Hogan and Gwynn-Morgan (1991) note:

not only do the names of tribunals differ – Board, Commission, Tribunal, Officer, Registrar, Controller, Referee, Umpire – but different authorities use different titles for the entire species. Thus one finds tribunals described as: administrative tribunals; special tribunals; statutory tribunals; or even quasi-judicial tribunals.

Administrative Tribunals

A number of tribunals have been set up to which aggrieved people may bring their complaints about the discretionary decisions made by public bodies. The tribunals may be individual persons or groups of persons who have been designated by law to adjudicate in these situations. Some examples are those where an application for a social welfare allowance has been rejected or where the valuation placed on a property for rating purposes is regarded as excessive. In those cases an appeal lies to the Social Welfare Appeals Office and to the Valuation Tribunal respectively.

Appeal tribunals in Ireland cannot be said to constitute a formal system. They have been established by individual ministers on a more or less ad hoc basis over a number of years, and there are inconsistencies in their composition, their procedures and the areas in which they operate. As regards the last point, there is, for instance, provision for an appeal against assessment to income tax but not against assessment to customs duty; yet both of these functions are under the same jurisdiction, that of the Revenue Commissioners. Their total number, including bodies set up to adjudicate on issues arising between parties in the private sector such as the Employment Appeals Tribunal or the Rights Commissioners (which do not concern us directly here), is about 80. This number is a small fraction of those in the United Kingdom, where there are over 2,000, supervised by a General Council on Tribunals.

Features of tribunals which they have in common are:

(1) Independence of the administration and the power to decide cases impartially as between the parties before them. This makes the tribunal form of remedy different from that of an internal administrative review of a decision, which may sometimes be offered by a public body and may be carried out by the official who made the decision in the first place.

(2) Binding decisions reached by a person or persons who are not engaged full-time on this work and who are not judges. The members may represent opposing interests with, perhaps, some neutrals and a chairman who is often a lawyer.

(3) Flexible procedures, generally less formal than those in the courts. Tribunals can formulate their own standards and depart from these if the situation so warrants.

(4) A facility to acquire considerable expertise in a particular and generally limited area.
(5) Less rigid attitudes towards precedents.

Other features are speed and the absence of the heavy legal costs entailed in court appearances, where counsel can spend a whole day explaining to a judge how a particular scheme is designed to operate.

The Devlin Report, as part of its proposal to establish executive agencies, recommended that tribunals with unlimited scope of appellate jurisdiction should be set up within every agency or for groups of agencies. There would thus be a right of appeal to a single, independent, fully trained person attached to the body by which the decision was given; in cases of particular complexity two experts in the matter under examination might be brought on to the tribunal. This recommendation has not been adopted.

Examples of Tribunals

In some instances the tribunal is one person only, for example in the area of social welfare, where about 12,000 cases are dealt with every year. The Social Welfare Act 1952, which set up the system of adjudication in that area, provides for the appointment of a number of deciding officers and appeals officers. A case is decided in the first instance by a deciding officer on the basis of the information before him, without an oral hearing. His decision may be appealed to an appeals officer, who operates under prescribed procedures. These include the power to take evidence on oath and to require persons to give evidence and produce documents. Appeals officers have power to award costs and expenses and the award must be paid by the minister. It has been established by the High Court (*McLoughlin* v. *Minister for Social Welfare* (1958 IR 5)) that an appeals officer is independent of the minister in the exercise of his functions, which are judicial functions, and that it would be improper for the minister to give him instructions as to how he should decide a particular case, or for him to accept such instructions. Thus appeals officers are different from other civil servants, who are answerable to their ministers for actions taken in the ordinary course of administration, such actions being invariably taken in the name of the minister, who accepts both legal and political responsibility for them.

The social welfare tribunals now operate under the Social Welfare Appeals Office following the recommendation in the Report of the Commission on Social Welfare, which had noted a perception that the existing appeals procedure was not independent of the workings of the Department of Social Welfare. The commission recommended also that the reasons for the rejection of appeals be given. This is also now being done and has greatly reduced the number of appeals.

Another example of a one-person tribunal is the Minister for the Environment and Local Government, who may be appealed to by an officer of a local authority against a decision in his case, e.g. suspension. Similarly, the Minister for Enterprise, Trade and Employment may be appealed to by a person aggrieved by a decision of the Controller of Industrial and Commercial Property (the Patents Office) not to register a trade mark.

An example of a two-person tribunal is that of the Office of the Appeals Commissioners, to which appeals against assessments to income tax may be made. The commissioners are full-time, appointed by the Minister for Finance; one of them is normally a lawyer or an accountant and the other a revenue official. The appeals are held orally and are attended by the inspector who made the assessment, the aggrieved taxpayer and (if he wishes) his professional adviser.

The Valuation Tribunal, which was set up in 1988, has thirteen members, lawyers and property valuers, who are part-time. Appeals can be made to this tribunal against the valuation placed by the Commissioner of Valuation on buildings and other fixed property as a basis for the levying of rates by local authorities. It deals with about 250 appeals a year.

An Bord Pleanála, which deals with appeals against the grant of planning permissions in some cases and against the refusal of others, has six members, all full-time. The Levy Appeals Tribunal, set up by the Minister for Labour to determine appeals by employers against assessments to training levies imposed by FÁS, the Training and Employment Authority, has sixteen members. Four of those must be lawyers, the chairman and three deputy chairmen. The other twelve must be representatives of employer organisations and trade unions.

Tribunals of Inquiry

These are set up under the Tribunals of Inquiry (Evidence) Act 1921 (as adapted) and the Tribunals of Inquiry (Evidence) (Amendment) Act 1979. There have been several occasions in recent years when the public disquiet at some event has been such that some form of inquiry has been necessary.

Tribunals of inquiry are tribunals established for inquiring into a definite matter of urgent public importance and with power to enforce the attendance and examination of witnesses and the production of documents. The Tribunals of Inquiry (Evidence) Act 1921 provides extensive powers to these bodies. It is based on the unspoken, but unbroken, assumption that the public respect enjoyed by the judiciary should be drawn upon to engender confidence in the impartiality of the inquiry. A tribunal of inquiry may consist of one or more persons, sitting with or without an assessor or assessors; an assessor is not a *member* of the tribunal. The Tribunals of Inquiry (Evidence) (Amendment) Act 1979 updated these provisions.

A tribunal may make such orders as it considers necessary for the purpose of its functions and in that respect has the powers, rights and privileges which are vested in the High Court. A statement or admission by a person before a tribunal of inquiry is not admissible as evidence against that person in any criminal proceedings.

A tribunal which has been appointed to inquire into matters of public interest pursuant to resolutions of the Oireachtas may inquire into all matters within its terms of reference, including matters which are the subject of current civil proceedings or allegations of breaches of the criminal law or matters which involve allegations attacking the good name of a citizen (*Goodman International* v. *Mr Justice Hamilton* (HC & SC) (1992)).

Among the tribunals of inquiry held in recent times have been the tribunal on moneylending in Dublin (1970); on the Betelguese tanker disaster in Bantry Bay – Whiddy Inquiry (1979); on the Stardust fire (1981); the Kerry Babies Inquiry (1985); the Inquiry into the Beef Processing Industry (1991–3); the Blood Transfusion Service Board Hepatitis C Tribunal (1997); and the Payments to Politicians by Dunnes Stores Tribunal (1997).

The Ombudsman

Ireland has been behind many European countries in adopting the institution of Ombudsman. The reason for being late into this field is the preference for political remedies noted above. The necessary act was passed in 1980, but the first Ombudsman was not appointed until 1984. Discussion on the creation of the office began in the mid-1960s and received a further impetus with the publication of the Devlin Report in 1969. It was not until 1975, however, that the matter began to be considered by the Oireachtas – both then and subsequently only as a result of the efforts of private members. These efforts eventually led to the introduction of a government bill which became the Ombudsman Act 1980. This act provided for the establishment of the office of the Ombudsman, the appointment to the post to be made by the President upon resolutions passed by the Dáil and Seanad. Under the act, the Ombudsman has the same remuneration as a judge of the High Court, holds office for a period of six years and may be reappointed for a second and subsequent terms.

The Ombudsman may act either on a complaint made to him or where he himself considers that an investigation would be warranted. He may investigate the actions of any officials in the organisations within his remit where it appears

> (a) that the action has or may have adversely affected a person . . . and (b) that the action was or may have been taken without proper authority or on irrelevant grounds; the result of negligence or carelessness; based on erroneous or incomplete information; improperly discriminatory; based on undesirable administrative practice; or otherwise contrary to fair or sound administration.

In short, he is responsible for ensuring decent standards of behaviour in all areas of administration. In his own words, 'I see my role as being concerned with not only the legal aspects of the complaint but also with the question of equity and fair play.'

In general, complaints have to be made within twelve months of the action complained of taking place. In general also, complaints are not accepted for investigation unless the complainant has already taken up the matter unsuccessfully with the public body concerned and has already used whatever appeal facilities are open to him. The services are free, and no lawyers are required. The Ombudsman's staff investigate on the citizen's behalf, and all the latter needs to do is to set out his complaint in a letter. The organisations within the Ombudsman's remit are government departments and offices, local authorities, health boards, Telecom Éireann and An Post. There is provision for extending the list of organisations by ministerial order. All matters relating to public service personnel (e.g. their pay, promotion or transfer) are excluded from the Ombudsman's remit.

For the purpose of his investigations the Ombudsman must be provided with all documents which he considers relevant. The Official Secrets Act does not apply to the supply by civil servants of documents or information to the Ombudsman. He may also require persons to appear before him for examination. Investigations are conducted in private, but he must give an opportunity to all parties concerned to comment. Where he finds that the action complained of has had an adverse effect on the complainant, he can recommend to the organisation concerned (1) that the matter in relation to which the action in question was taken be reconsidered, (2) that measures be taken to remedy the adverse effects of the action or (3) that the reason for taking the action be given. The Ombudsman is empowered to require the body concerned to notify him within a specific time of its response to his recommendations. He has not, however, the power to overturn decisions; his power of recommending is considered adequate.

There is provision for a ministerial veto on investigations. If a minister so requests in writing, the Ombudsman may not investigate an action specified in the request. The minister must provide the Ombudsman with a written statement setting out the reasons for his request. The purpose of the provision is to provide a means whereby the discretionary decisions of a minister can be exempted from the scrutiny of the Ombudsman. It was never intended that the provision would be widely used, and the Ombudsman can, if he feels the provision is being abused, refer to this in his annual report. In fact, no minister has to date vetoed an investigation.

To facilitate the work of the Ombudsman in dealing with government departments, each department nominates an officer in the grade of principal to act as liaison officer with the Ombudsman's office. It is this officer's duty to ensure that written or oral inquiries are directed to the appropriate section for attention, that time limits applying to requests for information are met, and that the relevant documents and files are made available for inspection as required. Much of the work of the office is done on an informal basis as a result of discussions between the investigators and the officials concerned in the various bodies. Where these discussions are not concluded to the satisfaction of the investigators, and where there is prima facie evidence of maladministration, the investigation moves to a more formal stage. The Ombudsman writes formally to the chief officer of the body concerned, enclosing a written summary of the complaint and requesting written observations thereon. Such inquiries are dealt with as a matter of priority, and replies are issued within two weeks of receipt. If a department does not accept that a complaint has been properly referred to it (i.e. if it is of the view that the matter is not one for the Ombudsman, or if it considers that the complaint is not appropriate to the department), the chief officer conveys the departmental view to the Ombudsman within seven days.

The Ombudsman's annual report presents statistics and detailed particulars of complaints dealt with during the year and gives typical examples, together with information on general issues arising from the work of the office. Some material from the 1996 report is reproduced in Appendix 20. The report must be laid before both Houses of the Oireachtas. The Ombudsman may also make such other reports with respect to his functions as he sees fit. A 25 per cent increase in complaints to the Ombudsman and a greater awareness of his office in 1996 has prompted him to publish a guide to *Standards of Best Practice for Public Servants*. This states that 'public bodies should strive for the highest standards of administration in their dealings with the citizen, they should be dealt with properly, fairly and impartially'.

The question of extending the powers and remit of the Ombudsman to bodies such as the non-commercial state bodies, the public voluntary hospitals, the Vocational Education Committees, FÁS and the Health and Safety Authority is being considered by government. An Administrative Procedures Bill has also been proposed which would set down for public bodies minimum response times for dealing with correspondence and the level of guidance to be given to the public on the basis for decisions and on rights of appeal. It is intended that the Ombudsman would have a monitoring role under the proposed act.

REFERENCES

Curran, Dermot, 'An Ombudsman for Ireland', *Seirbhís Phoiblí*, vol. 1, no. 2

Doolan, Brian, *Constitutional Law and Constitutional Rights in Ireland*, 2nd ed. (Dublin: Gill & Macmillan, 1988)

Hogan, G. and D. Gwynn-Morgan, *Administrative Law in Ireland*, 2nd ed. (London: Sweet & Maxwell, 1991)

Komito, Lee, 'Voters, Politicians and Clientelism: A Dublin Survey', *Administration*, vol. 37, no. 2

Roche, Richard, 'The Ombudsman Proposals: A Critique', *Journal of Irish Business and Administrative Research*, vol. 1, no. 1

Office of the Ombudsman, *Annual Report of the Ombudsman 1996* (Dublin: Stationery Office, 1997)

APPENDIX 20

ANNUAL REPORT OF THE OMBUDSMAN 1996

Statistics – Complaints received within jurisdiction

1996 Total 2,536 – **1995** Total 2,250 – **1994** Total 2,489

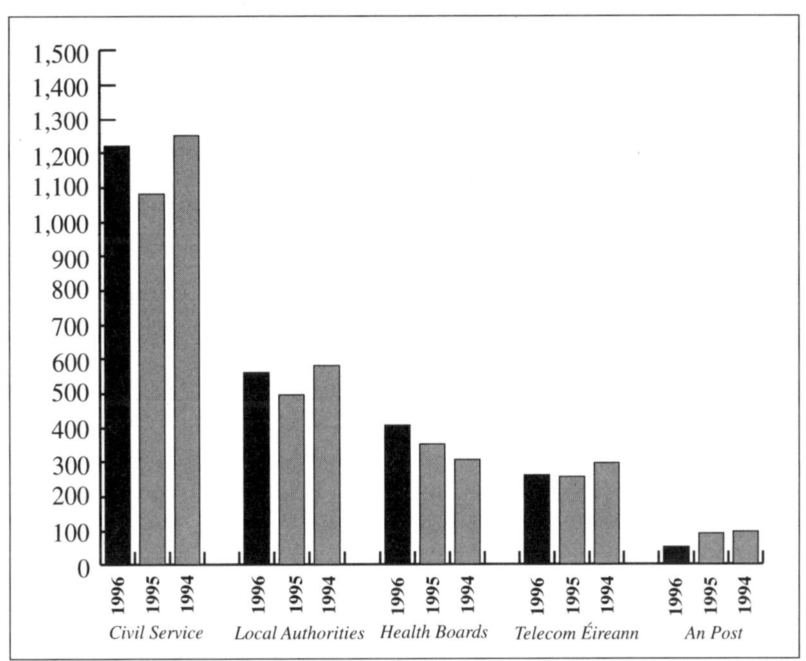

Geographical distribution of complaints within jurisdiction received in 1996

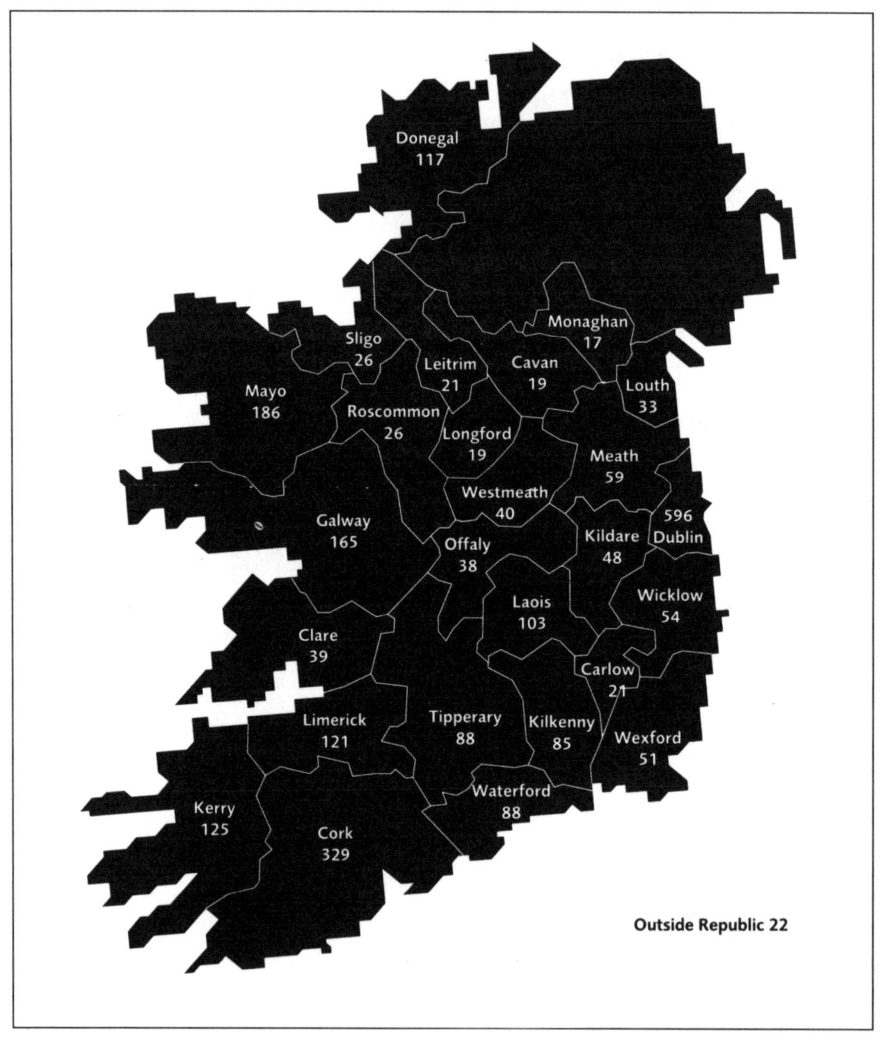

12

THE IMPACT OF THE EUROPEAN UNION

Introduction

Ireland became a member of the European Economic Community on 1 January 1973, joining at the same time as Britain and Denmark. The European Community dates from 1951, when the six founder members signed the Treaty of Paris to found the European Coal and Steel Community in July 1952. The Rome Treaties of 1957 established the European Economic Community (EEC) and the European Atomic Energy Community (Euratom). In 1967 the institutions serving the three communities were merged and were termed 'The European Community' (EC), from 1993 known as the European Union (EU). Ireland's membership of the EU affects every citizen of the state. It has had a profound impact on every aspect of Irish life, and the development of the country over the past twenty-five years owes much to membership of the European Union. The Irish people have historically been well disposed to our membership, on three occasions – in 1972, 1987 and 1992 – overwhelmingly endorsing our place in Europe. Such a decisive result, recorded on three separate occasions, is indicative of a people satisfied and at ease with Ireland's position in Europe. The process of European integration continues to spread into even more aspects of national life in an increasing number of member states. Over the next number of years decisions will be made which will decide the shape of the Union well into the twenty-first century. The EU, as a supranational organisation, represents a distinct approach to international relations that is of profound significance for the member states in the economic, legal, social and political areas.

Ireland has drawn significant economic benefit from its membership of the EU. At about £IR400 per head per annum, Ireland's citizens are the most heavily subsidised in Europe. The costs of integration have been more than offset by the scale of transfers under different headings. At each successive stage of integration new common policies have been introduced which allowed the economy to overcome difficulties and to sustain growth above the level which would otherwise have been achieved.

The Treaty on European Union

The Treaty on European Union was signed in Maastricht on 7 February 1992 by the member states. Viewed against the backcloth of the history and evolution of Europe, the decisions on integration taken at Maastricht are a significant step forward. Europe set for itself a clear strategy to achieve economic and monetary union. In the area of political union, 'Maastricht' clearly increased the EU's competence. The Treaty strengthened the EU's decision-making capacity by providing for increased majority voting in the Council of Ministers and by significantly enlarging the direct and indirect powers of the European Parliament over law-making.

The European Parliament emerged as the most important institutional 'winner' in the Maastricht process. The Article 189b 'co-decision' procedure in effect gives the European Parliament veto powers over a range of policy issues. The Parliament's growing influence arose from its increased role in the appointment of the new President and the new Commission as well as the synchronisation of its new five-year cycle with that of the Commission. The Parliament can withhold approval of the full Commission if it is not satisfied with the programme presented by the President.

The new direct and indirect powers of the European Parliament have given it a greater political influence than it has ever enjoyed. These reforms have enabled MEPs to make a bigger impact on the decision-making process of the Community.

The increased volume of EU legislation which is already proceeding through the institutions and being implemented in the member states, as well as the further expansion of EU law-making, has given the European Court of Justice an enhanced role in the life of the Union.

The Council of Ministers (as opposed to the member states) emerges as a substantially stronger institution in the complex of decision-making processes embodied in the Maastricht Treaty.

EU Constitutional Cohesion

The separate decision-making institutions – or 'pillars' – set out in the Maastricht Treaty, covering foreign and security policy as well as justice and home affairs co-operation, undoubtedly complicate the EU's constitutional cohesion.

There are powerful practical pressures pushing member states towards the adoption of a genuine common foreign policy.

At the same time, the taboo in dealing with defence has been broken. The goal of a common defence policy has been agreed in principle. For the present, responsibility for defence matters will rest with the Western European

Union (WEU), of which Ireland is not a member but has observer status. The WEU retains close links with NATO and can dispatch forces to security or peacekeeping operations outside Europe.

There are seventeen Protocols attached to the Maastricht Treaty. These Protocols have legal force as they clarify or elaborate on provisions of the Treaty on European Union. The first Protocol, for example, permits Denmark to maintain its existing legislation on the acquisition of second homes. The seventeenth Protocol expressly provides that the application in Ireland of Article 40.3.3 of our Constitution, which bans abortion, shall not be affected by the EU Treaty or any previous treaties or acts relating to the European Communities. This Protocol is unique in being annexed not only to the treaty establishing the European Community (the EC Treaty), i.e. the Treaty of Rome as amended by the Single European Act and the EU Treaty, but to the European Coal and Steel Community, Euratom and Union Treaties.

Constitutional Implications for Ireland

Accession to the EU heralded a new era in the context of the work of government and the public service in Ireland. The shaping and execution of Union policies is now an everyday part of that work.

The Constitution had not anticipated membership by Ireland of a supranational organisation such as the European Union. It was clear during the negotiations prior to accession that several articles were incompatible with EU membership (e.g. Articles 5, 15.2, 28, 29.4.1 and 34–8). An amendment in the following terms was accordingly put before the people in a referendum on 10 May 1972:

> No provision of this Constitution invalidates laws enacted, acts done or measures adopted by the State necessitated by the obligations of membership of the Communities or prevents laws enacted, acts done or measures adopted by the Communities, or institutions thereof, from having the force of law in the State.

There was a relatively high turnout of 71 per cent, with a total of 82 per cent voting in favour of membership. Thus the government and public service was given a clear mandate by the people in the context of membership of the EU.

The European Communities Act 1972 provided that the treaties of the European Communities and the existing and future acts of their institutions were binding on the state and thus brought European law into the Irish legal system. Since 1973 the Rome Treaty, as amended, has become part of the Irish Constitution and the exclusive law-making power of the Oireachtas provided for in Article 15 has been removed. As Henchy J. said in *Doyle* v. *An Taoiseach* (1985 ILRM 135), Community law 'has the paramount force and effect of constitutional provisions'.

This was exemplified by the Supreme Court's ruling in *Crotty* v. *An Taoiseach* and others (1986 no. 12036P) that the Single European Act could not be ratified by Ireland unless the Constitution was amended, since the SEA contained provisions which were in contravention of the Constitution. The necessary amendment was approved by the people on 26 May 1987 and allowed the state to ratify the Single European Act.

Another constitutional amendment was required for the ratification by Ireland of the Treaty on European Union. On 18 June 1992 the Irish people voted two to one in a referendum in favour of ratification. Whatever new arrangements emerge from the 1997 Intergovernmental Conference will require another amendment to the Constitution, and another referendum.

European Union Law

The law-making power of the EU is extensive and unique. The three founding treaties of the EC, the later Single European Act and the Treaty on European Union are the primary sources of EU law, laying down principles and rules that are binding on the member states. The legal acts of the EU are the secondary source of law. EU legal instruments have direct applicability in the member states, and in a conflict between national and EU law the latter predominates. Membership of the EU has qualified the exclusive role of the Irish courts, since the body ultimately responsible for the interpretation of the Treaty of Rome is the EU Court of Justice.

The Court of Justice of the European Union ensures that EU law is applied uniformly in the same way in every member state and that the rule of law applies within the EU. The Court has laid down rules on how the body of European law relates to the national legal system of the member states. It has assisted national courts in developing a standard approach to the interpretation of EU legislation. The Court has heard cases brought against the nationalism and protectionism of member states.

The operation of the Court of Justice of the European Union shows that EU law is 'like an incoming tide. It flows into the estuaries and up the rivers. It cannot be held back' (Lord Denning (H.P.) in *Bulmer Ltd* v. *J. Bollinger SA* (1974) 1 ch. 401 at 418). Membership of the EU has in fact resulted in a diminution of national sovereignty by placing legal restrictions on what an Irish government can do in a wide range of social and economic areas. The obligation to implement EU law and the resulting impact on Irish law have been of crucial significance in the operation of government and public administration in Ireland.

For the purpose of carrying out their tasks under the treaties, the Commission and the Council have three legally binding instruments available. These are collectively described as EU secondary legislation and comprise regulations, directives and decisions.

Regulations are of general application and immediate effect, and are binding in their entirety. They are directly applicable in all member states, requiring no implementing measures by the national authorities, and become part of Irish law as soon as they have been formally adopted by the Council or Commission. They are the most common type of secondary legislation and generate rights and obligations for every person in the Union.

Directives are EU acts adopted by the Council or the Commission. They are binding on any member state to which they are addressed as to the objectives to be achieved but leave the choice of method of implementation to the member state. They indicate the reasons on which they are based, are communicated to the countries to which they are addressed, and state in the text the date on which they come into effect. They are normally used in the harmonisation of legal provisions where the end is not specific. Directives are addressed only to the governments of member states; they create rights but do not create obligations for individuals in a member state. Directives can be implemented domestically in either of two ways: by primary legislation, which involves the passing of a bill by the Oireachtas; or by secondary legislation, which involves ministerial regulations. The majority of directives are implemented through this latter method.

Decisions are legally binding instruments designed to achieve administrative aims and may be directed to a member state, a corporation or an individual. They are used to fill out the framework of regulations where necessary.

The Political Impact: Institutional Innovations

Most of the important EU issues come before the full cabinet, either formally or informally. In addition, from time to time special government subcommittees are formed to deal with EU affairs. Three ministers in particular are intensively involved in EU business (Finance, Foreign Affairs, and Agriculture and Food), and are obliged frequently and regularly to attend meetings at EU headquarters in Brussels. Other ministers attend when their areas of responsibility are discussed. The government is fully aware of all developments in the EU affecting Ireland. The members of the Oireachtas are advised of such developments by the obligation on the government to report on these matters and by the existence of a joint Oireachtas committee to monitor this area (see below). Many opportunities exist for them to discuss and debate EU policy issues. Such matters can be raised, and are raised, in both Houses of the Oireachtas, either in the form of special motions or on the adjournment. The annual debate on the estimate for the Department of Foreign Affairs, the presentation of the statutory twice-yearly reports on developments in the European Union, reports on meetings of the European Council and Dáil question time all provide opportunities for debate and discussion.

The Dáil and Seanad have developed more effective means of supervising the executive activities of government, particularly as regards the executive activities of the EU.

There is almost unanimous agreement among member states that national parliaments should be given a greater role in the supervision of European legislation. Some member states have introduced more effective mechanisms to ensure that national parliaments are informed and consulted about developments in policy-making at EU level. This supervision is seen as particularly important given the view of the then President of the European Commission:

> I find it extraordinary that the national parliaments with the exception of those in the Federal Republic of Germany and the United Kingdom should have failed to realise what is going on. Ten years hence 80 per cent of our economic legislation and perhaps even our fiscal and social legislation as well will be of Community origin (Jacques Delors, speech to the European Parliament, 6 July 1988).

In Ireland's case, some considerable progress has been made in securing greater involvement of the Dáil and Seanad in European affairs. The establishment of the Joint Committees on Foreign Affairs and European Affairs, together with the greater emphasis now being placed generally on the role of committees, means that policy and legislation are subject to greater scrutiny on a continuous basis. The direct participation of MEPs is a welcome development. Extracts from the orders of reference of the Joint Committee on European Affairs and of the Joint Committee on Foreign Affairs are included at Appendix 21.

The Joint Oireachtas Committee on European Affairs considers proposed EU programmes and legislation. It monitors and reports on matters arising from Ireland's membership of the EU. It usually meets in plenary session once a fortnight and has one subcommittee, which deals with secondary legislation of the European Union. Members of the European Parliament may attend meetings of the Joint Committee.

The Joint Oireachtas Committee on Foreign Affairs examines legislation and expenditure relating to foreign affairs and international co-operation. It monitors and reports on Ireland's international relations, including co-operation with developing countries and EU matters generally. It usually meets in plenary session once a fortnight and has four subcommittees. Members of the European Parliament may also attend meetings of this joint committee.

The 1996 White Paper on foreign policy noted that these committees 'have significant powers and are important instruments for maintaining the democratic accountability of foreign policy in Ireland' (p. 333). They make a valuable input to the examination of the key foreign policy and EU issues of the moment.

Further European integration will result in changed roles and institutional relationships for many parts of the machinery of government. With more and more decision-making occurring in Brussels, and with an ever-growing body of EU law coming into effect, the role of the civil service will increasingly be that of translating EU directives into national law. This highlights the importance of procedures for monitoring the activities of the Council of Ministers as the competence of the EU expands.

The 1996 Report of the Review Group on the Constitution examined the transposition of EU directives into domestic law. It did not recommend any constitutional amendment but suggested that consideration be given to a re-examination of the role of the Oireachtas and public information in this area. This report considered the decision of the Supreme Court in *Meagher* v. *Minister for Agriculture* (1994) 1 IR 329. In that case, the applicant had challenged the validity of a statutory instrument which had amended an earlier statute. The statutory instrument in question gave effect to a number of EU directives in Irish domestic law. The Supreme Court held that the sheer number of EU directives was such that membership of the Union necessitated the possibility of implementing directives in Irish law by means of statutory instrument rather than by act of the Oireachtas, even where amendment of an act of the Oireachtas was involved.

The Review Group (1996: 115) noted that

> the present situation is not entirely satisfactory. The extensive use of statutory instruments to implement directives has meant that hundreds of statutory provisions, some important, have been expressly or impliedly repealed by statutory instruments often with a minimum of publicity. The use of statutory instruments ensures speedy and effective implementation of EC law but often at the expense of the publicity and debate which attends the processing of legislation through the Oireachtas.

Ireland has a good record in compliance with EU legislation. For example, according to the European Commission's twelfth annual report, Ireland has notified the Commission of implementing measures for 97 per cent of EU environmental directives, second only to Denmark in compliance.

The European Co-ordinating Committee

The European Co-ordinating Committee, which looks after day-to-day co-ordination of EU matters within the national government, pre-dates EC membership. Until 1987 it was chaired by the Department of Foreign Affairs and was composed of the assistant secretaries of the Departments of the Taoiseach, Foreign Affairs, Agriculture and Food, Finance and other relevant departments. Other departments were represented when the agenda covered matters relating to their area of competence. It was replaced by a new committee which was chaired by the Minister of State for European Affairs and is now chaired by an appropriate assistant secretary. The creation of a ministerial post for EU affairs is an indication of the importance of this area. (A previous Taoiseach, Dr FitzGerald, had proposed, but not implemented, the division of the Department of Foreign Affairs and the creation of a Minister for European Affairs and Development Co-operation as a separate ministry with full departmental structures.)

In June 1997 the Taoiseach, Bertie Ahern, scrapped plans for a special European ministry. He removed the portfolio of European Affairs from the Minister for Defence and dropped the idea of giving him an office in the Department of Foreign Affairs. This was in response to claims that this plan would breach collective cabinet responsibility and the spirit of the Constitution. Given the importance of Northern Ireland and some European issues, the Taoiseach did not want to have a junior minister filling in for the Minister for Foreign Affairs in his absence abroad. He wanted to have a fully briefed senior minister available at short notice.

Meetings of the committee are attended, as occasion affords, by Ireland's Permanent Representative to the EU so as to maintain close relations between COREPER (the Committee of Permanent Representatives of the Member States) and the domestic civil service. Much of the co-ordination takes place directly with other government departments, particularly through the officers of those departments who are seconded to Foreign Affairs, on post at the Permanent Representation. It provides a forum for the most senior officials to exchange views on an interdepartmental basis, to discuss broad policy issues, to prepare regular reports for the cabinet and to recommend national priorities in relation to the EU. During the 1996 Irish EU presidency the European Co-ordinating Committee was suspended in favour of the Ministers' and Secretaries' Group. The European Co-ordinating Committee established an Interdepartmental Co-ordinating Committee in April 1994, chaired by the Department of Foreign Affairs, to prepare the EU presidency agenda. The participation by the Permanent Representation to the EU at these meetings in Dublin proved to be extremely important as a channel of communication between Dublin and Brussels.

It is interesting to look at the situation in some member states. France, for example, has a Secrétariat Général and Comité Interministériel (SGCI), a 175-strong team, which co-ordinates France's interministerial initiatives and has sole co-ordinating responsibility for all negotiations between Paris and Brussels.

The Ministers' and Secretaries' Group on EU Policy

Given the increasing importance of EU matters, a special committee known as the Ministers' and Secretaries' Group on EU Policy was set up in 1989. This committee is chaired by the Taoiseach. Originally, it was concerned with issues relating to the internal market and structural funds, but its remit was extended to include an examination of more general EU matters. The group is composed of the ministers and secretaries general of the key relevant departments and co-ordinated Ireland's negotiating strategy on issues such as the Intergovernmental Conference and enlargement.

The Political Impact: Government and Administration

The Civil Service

Adaptation to the demands of EU membership has been perhaps the greatest challenge faced by the Irish civil service since the foundation of the state. Not alone has participation in the European Union increased the range and complexity of the issues facing Irish civil and public servants by the addition of a new dimension to national policy-making, but membership has greatly increased the workload of the public service. As more and more issues fall within the ambit of the EU, a wider range of civil and public service agencies are becoming involved. All government departments and state agencies have been affected to varying degrees by membership. In the civil service the impact has perhaps been greatest in the central departments of Finance, Taoiseach and Foreign Affairs. Of the other departments which have responsibility for policy formulation and execution in specific sectors, the impact has been greatest in the Department of Agriculture and Food, which has been predominantly concerned with administering the Common Agricultural Policy.

Irish officials, reflecting the views of the Irish people, adopt a positive approach to the progressing of EU business.

Ireland, as a net beneficiary of all EU policies, has consistently adopted a positive role towards the development of the Union. It has tried to look at the totality of the relationships involved in EU membership and to be part of the development of these relationships. FitzGerald (1975: 5) noted that 'European idealism and Irish national interest have tended to coincide in Ireland's case.' This emphasis on what is often termed the communautaire approach connotes strong support of the EU's institutions and processes and of their further development as the most effective safeguard of the interests of a smaller member state.

A well-established feature of Ireland's policy on EU institutions is support for the role of the Commission. Irish politicians and policy-makers regard it as the key protector of the interests of small states in the Union, and experience since membership supports this policy inference. The principle of one Commissioner per state is therefore an important one from an Irish perspective since without a full Commissioner Ireland would have little influence at the highest political level in the one institution charged with representing the overall interest of the Union.

The Irish Permanent Representation in Brussels (in effect, the Irish embassy to the EU) is the largest Irish overseas mission and arguably the most important. It consists of about sixty officials, of whom almost thirty are of diplomatic status. Its task is to act as a channel of communication from the Commission and the Council and to advise the government and departments about the strategies of other member states. It co-ordinates a coherent Irish position across the entire public service. The Permanent Representation services the meetings of COREPER and of many working parties of the Council.

The relatively small size of the European Commission means that the civil and public service has the responsibility for the implementation in Ireland of directly applicable EU legislation. The relatively small size of the Irish civil service facilitates informal and loosely structured administrative arrangements for the co-ordination of EU business; this enables a less formal and less institutionalised approach which can respond quickly. The civil and public service also evaluates the impact of EU policy in Ireland across a broad range of economic and social spheres. The greater use of qualified majority voting (see Appendix 22) has speeded up the progress of directives through the Council hierarchy, so that national officials have now less time to prepare a response to Commission proposals and to ensure that Irish organisations are aware of the implications of proposed legislation.

Department of Finance

The Department of Finance played a central role in negotiating Ireland's entry into the EC, and since the beginning it has had a large involvement with EU matters. While its co-ordinating role was gradually taken over by the Department of Foreign Affairs in the late 1970s, it continues to occupy a unique and prominent position in that it must be consulted by all other departments on proposals that have expenditure implications. However, it has not overriding authority among government departments, and although it can advise, support and persuade, it cannot order; disagreements between departments have to be resolved at cabinet level.

The Department of Finance has retained responsibility for the important major sources of funds, together with control of the central economic issues such as Economic and Monetary Union (EMU), Ireland's financial contributions, financial regulation and monetary policy, economic co-ordination and the financial aspects of agriculture policy.

With the introduction of the EU structural and cohesion funds, the department is concerned that these funds are fully committed, used effectively and drawn down over the programme period. Officials of the European Commission have served on steering committees with Irish civil servants to oversee the implementation of these programmes.

Ireland has participated in the European Monetary System since its inception in March 1979. Successive Irish governments promoted the policies necessary to qualify for membership of EMU at the outset and to ensure continued successful participation. Irish governments have insisted that development towards closer political integration must be based on the growing community of interest in the economic and social areas and, in particular, on the promotion of economic convergence between the more and less prosperous regions.

The Department of Finance took the lead role in preparing for Economic and Monetary Union and planning for the changeover to the Euro. The department put in place a number of initiatives in connection with the changeover.

- *The Single Currency Officers' Team* (SCOT) was set up in autumn 1995. It consists of a representative from every government department. Its remit is to co-ordinate preparations for the introduction of the Euro in the public sector.
- *The Euro Changeover Group* was set up in 1996. It includes representatives from the social partners, consumers and the financial services industry as well as from the Department of Finance and the Central Bank. Its function is to advise on technical issues and to co-ordinate changeover across the economy.
- *The National Information Programme* helps to prepare effectively for the Euro.
- *The National Changeover Plan* sets out the arrangements to facilitate the use of the Euro.

Department of Foreign Affairs

The primary function of the Department of Foreign Affairs is to advise the government on Ireland's external relations and to act as the channel of official communication with foreign governments and international organisations. The role of the Department of Foreign Affairs in relation to the EU is primarily one of co-ordination, and to an extent it can be regarded as a gatekeeper between Dublin and Brussels. It does not get involved in the details of domestic policy; rather it ensures that domestic departments adequately service meetings in Brussels and that policy developments in one sector do not impinge on general policy priorities. It integrates European business, maintains the priorities established between the various departments and ensures that policy remains coherent. It also acts as facilitator in disagreements between other departments over areas of competence.

The department plays a key role in Irish policy on European issues and in the domestic impact of European policies. The Minister for Foreign Affairs has the overall responsibility for the task of providing impetus and co-ordination to the development of Ireland's policy on the EU. Scott (1983: 84) noted that

> Foreign Affairs, hitherto a marginal department, made a successful quantum jump, enlarging its competences, mediating between other departments, and revolutionising its structure and staffing. However, it is important to recall that Finance kept the vital economic issues and major sources of funds to itself, leaving Foreign Affairs in sole charge of the political side, an area of absorbing interest to only a handful of officials, politicians, journalists and enthusiasts, and subject always to intervention by the Taoiseach.

There has been a significant expansion in the Irish foreign service since 1973, as shown in the following table.

Growth of Ireland's Foreign Service between 1973 and 1997

	1973	**1997**
Bilateral Embassies	18	40
Multilateral Missions	3	4
Career Consulates	5	5
Honorary Consuls*	13	64
Numbers of countries in which Ireland has honorary consuls	12	51

* Honorary consuls are non-career officers who are paid a modest annual honorarium for their services. They carry out consular and other work on Ireland's behalf in their countries of residence.

The explanation for this expansion has been Ireland's membership of the EU. While other factors such as development co-operation, globalisation and the establishment of friendly relations with many nations are relevant, the EU is the most significant factor. The 1996 White Paper on foreign policy stated:

> The single most important factor influencing Irish national development is our membership of the European Union. Fundamental national interests are engaged in both the internal development and external projection of the Union; it is imperative that our foreign service continues to maintain a coherent overview of the process (p. 321).

The priorities of Ireland's foreign service were outlined as follows: 'The over-riding objective of any diplomatic mission is to promote the interests and concerns of the country it represents. The interest which dominates for Ireland at this time is to contribute to the creation of jobs for Irish people by doing everything possible to increase foreign earnings' (Ambassador Hennessy 1995: 2).

Department of Agriculture and Food

This department operates and implements EU schemes and regulations for agriculture. The Common Agricultural Policy (CAP) continues to contribute to the development and modernisation of Irish agriculture, at both farm and processing level. It provides strong market support for those products on which Irish agriculture is particularly dependent, and it ensures vital outlets for agricultural exports through unlimited access to the EU market and by granting financial support in the form of export refunds so that Irish exports to countries outside the EU remain competitive.

Agriculture continues to be an important industry in Ireland, providing over 11 per cent of employment. Ireland is the largest net beef exporter in the northern hemisphere, exporting nine out of ten of its animals outside the EU.

While overall responsibility for the management of the CAP rests with the Commission, each member state plays an important role in its implementation. In Ireland the Department of Agriculture and Food is the relevant agency.

Nearly all of the staff in the department are involved in EU affairs in one way or another.

Community development. Ireland received substantial structural funds aid under various EU initiative programmes. This encouraged the process of community development and local initiative. Seven subregional review committees, which included representatives of the local authorities, social partners and government departments, participated in the preparation of the National Development Plan 1994–9. Cross-border initiatives were encouraged through the joint Ireland/Northern Ireland INTERREG programme, for example. The LEADER programme resulted in sixteen rural development groups being set up throughout the country. The main implementing bodies for the National Development Plan 1994–9 are set out at Appendix 23.

The Presidency System

Under the current system the presidency of the Council of Ministers is held by a different member state every six months, according to an agreed rotation. This schedule is set out at Appendix 24. Although the presidency is not a formal institution of the EU, the office has grown in political importance throughout the integration process and is highly prized by the member states for the prestige it confers on the holder. The presidency is an important role which carries fundamental responsibilities for the conduct of the Union's affairs. It fosters a sense of belonging and the urge to excel on the part of those holding office. The office has evolved from passively presiding over Council meetings to providing proactive leadership in shaping the internal work programme and managing external relations. The growing sophistication of the decision-making process has raised the profile of the presidency.

The Maastricht Treaty charged the European Council with giving political leadership to the Union as a whole, thereby again increasing the prestige of the presidency. Under the co-decision procedure the role of the presidency has been further strengthened in trying to resolve differences between the Council of Ministers and the European Parliament.

The successful organisation of an EU presidency is a formidable challenge for any member state. It represents an even greater challenge in small countries. The government set out its objectives for the EU presidency at an early stage. In the 1996 White Paper on foreign policy it stated:

> The main obligation for any Presidency is to ensure that the EU's business is discharged in an efficient, effective and impartial manner. During the six-month period of the presidency, Irish ministers will chair approximately forty Council of Ministers meetings and will supervise the work of approximately 200 working groups chaired by Irish personnel at official level. In carrying out their presidency duties ministers will endeavour to ensure that the political, economic and social agenda is advanced in a manner that will benefit the European Union (pp. 60–61).

During the presidency no fewer than 126 meetings, conferences and seminars were held in Ireland and hosted by ministers and officials. A total of 244 formal committees and working groups met and nearly 100 press releases were issued. This was in addition to the 40 council meetings and 2,000 working group meetings which took place in Brussels between July and December 1996. Scott (1994: 25) noted that 'the Irish "style" seems to be appreciated as emollient and sensitive, and if it is perhaps most obvious at the time of a Presidency, it is no surprise that Irish Presidencies are popular and well-regarded'.

The fifth Irish presidency of the EU, in the latter half of 1996, is regarded as having been the latest in a series of successful Irish presidencies over the past two decades. For a smaller member state like Ireland, the presidency provides a valuable opportunity to play a major international role not only with/on behalf of the EU and other member states but on the wider world stage.

The role of the Taoiseach during the presidency is of paramount importance. In the period October 1995 to January 1997, a total of eighty presidency-related meetings were held by the Taoiseach with foreign VIPs. The Taoiseach also participated in a number of international summits on the EU's behalf with the United States, Japan, Canada, the Organization for Security and

Co-operation in Europe, and World Food. This was in addition to meetings with the heads of state or government in other member states and with the accession states. The Minister for Foreign Affairs plays a key role in this process also. The Department of Foreign Affairs was supplemented by approximately 100 additional temporary staff for the presidency.

From February 1996 a full cabinet-level group, the Ministers' and Secretaries' Group (MSG), co-ordinated the EU presidency at the higher political level. The MSG met thirteen times during 1996 and was chaired by the Taoiseach, with the Tánaiste and Minister for Foreign Affairs, the Minister of State for European Affairs and the Ministers of Agriculture, Enterprise and Employment, Finance, Justice and Social Welfare also members. Other ministers attended as and when required. The secretaries general (and other officials as necessary) of these departments also participated in the MSG. A group of senior officials assisted in the preparation of the agenda for these meetings and dealt with all the administrative aspects. Presidency Co-ordinators were nominated in all the relevant departments.

An Interdepartmental Planning Group was concerned with the operational and logistical aspects of the presidency. The Centre for Management and Organisation Development in the Department of Finance had begun training needs analysis in the summer of 1994 and arranged a series of specialist seminars on the EU in early 1996.

The role of the Minister for Foreign Affairs and the part played by the Department of Foreign Affairs is of crucial importance to a successful EU presidency.

'It is irresponsible for a foreign minister to be asked to do so much,' according to a Dutch official quoted in *The Irish Times* on 12 December 1996 in advance of his country's accession to the EU presidency. 'Managing the EU's external relations is now an incredible burden. Our minister will pack his bags on January 1st and unpack them in July.'

> The legacy of the four previous Irish presidencies (1975, 1979, 1984 and 1990) is one to which Irish ministers and officials point with some pride. The first Rome Convention, the 'Dublin Formula' which facilitated the start of the Euro-Arab dialogue, the 1984 Dooge Committee which led to the Single European Act and the positive way the Community responded to German unification all owe something to Irish energy, ideas and skill (Tonra, 1996).

During the 1996 term the Irish presidency presented an outline for a draft revision of the EU's founding treaties. This was undoubtedly the most important Irish contribution yet made to the constitutional foundation of European integration. The text was widely praised for its clarity and for the delicate balance between the ambitious and the sceptical member states.

John Bruton, then Taoiseach, coined the following slogan for the Irish presidency, which was used to communicate effectively the EU's political objectives to concerned citizens: 'A peaceful Europe, secure jobs, sound money and safe streets.'

Progress towards monetary union was seen as one of the overriding achievements of the Irish EU presidency. This involved: the Stability and Growth Pact, a framework to link participating and non-participating countries and agreement on the legal status of the Euro.

The critical factors contributing to the success of the fifth Irish presidency include the objectivity and impartiality with which Ireland prepared for and carried out the presidency; the proactive establishment of good internal and external relationships with the key players; a consistent commitment to good strategic planning and management, as well as effective cross-departmental working and high levels of motivation: 'Bravo, Irish presidency!' enthused France's President Chirac. The achievement of a successful presidency was of major national importance and of lasting benefit to Ireland's future standing in the European Union and beyond.

Subsidiarity

'Subsidiarity' is an inelegant and confusing term with several meanings but no one has yet found a better expression. It is a word which is much used but little understood. It means that decisions are made as close to the people as possible. It is a practical principle for determining whether the EU should act in particular circumstances. Montesquieu wrote: 'When it is not necessary to make a law it is necessary not to make a law.'

Article 3b of the Maastricht Treaty lays down the principle of subsidiarity in the following terms: 'In areas which do not fall within its exclusive competence, the Community may take action only if and in so far as the objectives of the proposed action cannot be sufficiently achieved by the member states and can therefore, by reason of the scale or effects of the proposed action, be better achieved by the Community.' It also lays down the principle of proportionality: 'Any action of the Community shall not go beyond that which is necessary to achieve the objectives of this Treaty.'

The principle of subsidiarity was enshrined in Pope Pius XI's encyclical letter of 1931, *Quadragesimo Anno*:

> Just as it is wrong to withdraw from the individual and commit to a group what private enterprise and industry can accomplish, so too it is an injustice, a grave evil and a disturbance of right order, for a larger association to arrogate to itself functions that can be performed efficiently by smaller and lower societies.

On 2 June 1992 the Danish people narrowly voted – by 50.7 per cent to 49.3 per cent – not to approve ratification of the Treaty on European Union. This was the first occasion in the history of the EU that an agreement between governments of the member states to change the EU's 'Constitution' had failed to be ratified at national level. It resulted in a much greater emphasis on the principle of subsidiarity.

Subsidiarity is open to a number of alternative definitions and competing interpretations of those definitions.

The Treaty on European Union defines the principle of subsidiarity and gave it a new legal significance by setting it out as a general principle of EU law; by establishing subsidiarity as a basic principle of the European Union; and by reflecting subsidiarity in the drafting of several new Treaty articles (Articles 118a, 126–9, 129a, 129b, 130 and 130g). While the principle of subsidiarity has no direct effect, the European Court of Justice has the right to interpret and review compliance with it by EU institutions within areas falling under the EU Treaty. The institutions are obliged, when examining an EU measure, to see whether the provisions of the Treaty on subsidiarity have been observed. The Commission has a particular role to play in this respect given its right of initiative and its overall responsibility for monitoring observance of these Treaty provisions.

The virtue of subsidiarity is that it provides a guide for rebalancing the functions and powers of different tiers of government in response to the continued process of integration, while ensuring that the European Union features adequate democratic guarantees.

The creation of a 'Europe of the Regions' is not an inevitable development, but pressures for a stronger role for subnational government in EU policy-making are growing. Rhodes (1992: 280) concludes that 'Each line of argument involves a more prominent role for the regions. The European future may be uncertain but one point is clear: in one form or another it will involve a greater role for local and regional authorities and, as a result, conflict with national governments.'

In 1991 the EU Council of Ministers adopted by consensus the following resolution on the meaning of subsidiarity for the future of local government in Europe:

> Political and administrative decentralisation should be increased as a source of freedom, a means of involving citizens actively in public life and a way of adapting policies to local situations . . . responsibilities should formally be given to those authorities which are closest to the citizen and not to higher level authorities.

Communicating Europe

The 1995 Report of the Communicating Europe Task Force, chaired by the Minister of State for European Affairs, drew on empirical data to show that there exists in Ireland a low level of awareness of European issues and a desire for additional knowledge of these issues. The firm view of the government, backed by a general political consensus, is that membership of the EU and the fullest participation in the Union is fundamental to Ireland's economic and political interests. The report identified the need to improve public awareness of the major issues that go to the heart of assessing the balance of Ireland's interests in the Union. It stated that it was necessary to inform the public in a user-friendly manner as to what the Union's policies and programmes meant in practical terms, for each one of them. The Task Force produced a comprehensive report including twenty-seven recommendations aimed at facilitating improvement in focusing the government and political sector and also laying the foundation of European awareness through education and youth.

The introduction of a civics programme as part of the Junior Certificate curriculum in September 1997 has helped to raise European awareness at second level.

The Commission has tried in recent years to improve access to EU information. This is seen as a means of bringing the public closer to the EU's institutions and a way of stimulating a more informed and involved debate on EU policy. Interest groups, in particular, have always had close ties with the Commission. The proliferation of lobbyists has resulted in the drafting of a self-regulatory code of conduct by interest groups.

Additional steps have been taken to improve the following: access to data bases; the relay network of information on the EU (such as the strengthening of the CELEX automated documentation system on all EU law set up in 1970 for the institutions and made available to the public in 1981); the listing of documents on general topics in the official journal each week; the publication of work schedules and legislative programmes.

Early warning of Commission thinking has always been one of the criteria for successfully influencing subsequent decisions, whether on the content of legislation or on the acquisition of funds and contracts. The Commission has introduced a greater degree of transparency relating to the accessibility and intelligibility of draft legislation. The encroachment of EU legislation on domestic affairs is so vast that national governments cannot act as gatekeepers between national and supranational politics.

The syndrome of democratic deficit in the EU has a number of features, including: poor public identification with Europe; lack of popular participation in decision-making; limited understanding of the institutions and policies of the EU; inadequate dissemination of information; the absence of a truly European political system. The Maastricht ratification process shifted the terms of the debate on the democratic deficit. With a move towards intergovernmental decision-making (seen in the three-pillared architecture of the EU), the question of democratic control was made more acute.

The Commission offices in the member states are at the sharp end of information and communication. They provide information and documentation to the general public about developments in the EU. They also provide feedback to the Commission to enable it to produce material to an individual state's needs and circumstances. The opening of the European Public Information Centre as a one-stop shop for all kinds of information on Europe, the opening of Info Points about Europe around the country and the operation of a mobile information unit have brought a broad range of European information to a much wider audience.

Transnational Interest Groups

Many new alliances have been forged through cross-border co-operation between business partners and interest groups. The Irish social partners are affiliated to European agencies which represent similar bodies in other member states. The Confederation of Irish Industry (CII) and the Federation of Irish Employers (FIE) are members of the Union of Industries of the European Community (UNICE). The Confederation of the Food and Drink Industries of the EU (CIAA) represents the interests of its members at Union level. There is also a European trade union representative body, the European Trade Union Confederation, to which the Irish Congress of Trade Unions is affiliated; this European body is closely linked to national sectoral bodies. COPA (Comité des Organisations Professionelles Agricoles) is the umbrella body of farmers' organisations from all the member states and includes the Irish Farmers' Association as the Irish representative. COGECA (Comité Général de la Coopération Agricole de la CEE) is the representative body for agricultural co-operatives at Union level, and the Irish Co-operative Organisation Society Ltd is its Irish member.

The widening scope of EU policy-making has resulted in more domestic ministries becoming involved in the implementation of EU policies. A growing number of national agencies have begun to see the EU as a natural frame of reference and more public and private sector agencies have sought solutions at an international rather than a national level. In predicting that around 80 per cent of legislation implemented in the member states would have a supranational origin, then Commission President Jacques Delors had not exaggerated the impact integration would have on policy-makers at national and subnational level.

There has been a tenfold increase in ten years in the number of interest groups represented in Brussels. In 1985 there were no regions represented in Brussels; now there are over sixty regional offices located there, including Ireland West. There are now European federations representing organisations with a diverse range of interests such as outdoor advertising, the homeless, the heads of second-level schools, youth groups and family associations.

Enlargement

Ireland has a vital interest in how the EU is going to deal with the entry of central and eastern European states and in avoiding the danger that enlargement might lead to the fragmentation of the EU. Ireland is committed to the process of further enlargement, which is in the interests of the EU as a whole, and is seeking to ensure that the consequences of enlargement apply in a balanced way to existing member states.

The Copenhagen European Council of June 1993 set out the following criteria for accession:

- stable democratic institutions;
- the rule of law; human rights; protection of minorities;
- a functioning market economy;
- capacity to cope with competitive pressure and market forces;
- adherence to the aims of political, economic and monetary union.

Each enlargement reduces the influence of existing member states and increases the complexity of decision-making.

The Irish White Paper on foreign policy is quite clear in its support for enlargement, but on condition that 'the need for Union solidarity with the less developed regions of the existing Union, through the policy of cohesion, remains undiminished'. Ireland could become a net contributor to the EU in coming years if current trends continue. The White Paper recognises that after 1999 'there could well be reluctance on the part of the wealthier member-states to increase substantially contributions to the EU budget and corresponding pressures to divert funds towards support for the continued reconstruction and development of central and Eastern Europe in the perspective of enlargement'.

The Agenda 2000 programme unveiled by the Commission in July 1997 outlined plans for enlargement and radical reform of EU structural and farm spending. Poland, Hungary, the Czech Republic, Slovenia and Estonia are in the first group of states eligible for accession talks. Cyprus already has a place at the talks. It signals a fundamental realignment between East and West in the new Europe. Appendix 25 shows the applicant states.

Agenda 2000 confirms that Ireland is entering a most challenging period of its membership of the European Union. Its generous share of structural and cohesion funding is set to decline sharply as it becomes a victim of its own economic success. The next phase of CAP reform compounds the problem.

The EU itself faces the more fundamental task of smoothing the path for enlargement by streamlining its process of decision-making and by extending its capacity to act more coherently on the world stage. The EU's constitution was designed for just six countries and is unwieldy for the present membership of fifteen. Six more members will only exacerbate these problems. The 1997 Amsterdam summit failed to agree on new voting rules and other changes. Another round of constitutional reform is inevitable if the EU is to operate effectively as a union of up to twenty-one states.

Neutrality

Since joining the EU in 1973, Ireland has pursued a consistent strategy of supporting successive moves towards deeper integration. This was the case on EMS membership (1979), the Milan Council leading to the SEA (1985), the Dooge Committee (1984), the SEA (1986–7), the Maastricht Treaty (1992) and Economic and Monetary Union. A common defence policy is a possible development in the integration of security policy. This could pose difficulties for Ireland in view of its neutrality.

The Maastricht Treaty states that the Common Foreign and Security Policy 'shall include all questions related to the security of the Union, including the eventual framing of a common defence policy, which might in time lead to a common defence' (J.4.1).

Irish neutrality concerns were allayed in the Amsterdam Treaty of 1997. The text refers only to closer links between the EU and the WEU 'with a view to the possibility of the later integration of the WEU into the Union should the European Council so decide'. Launching the government's White Paper on the Amsterdam Treaty in January 1998, the Minister for Foreign Affairs, David Andrews, insisted that 'Ireland's policy of military neutrality remains unaffected by the provisions of the Amsterdam Treaty. If the issue of an EU common defence, which would involve a mutual defence commitment by Ireland, were to arise for decision in the future, it would be put to the Irish people for their decision in a referendum.'

Ireland's stance of military neutrality has been significant for the Irish public and is deeply embedded in national political culture. Neutrality is seen as a symbol of national identity, and as an expression of anti-militarism.

Ireland has been fairly treated in terms of representation within the institutions and the benefits from common policies, such as the CAP and cohesion. Its security concerns have been accommodated with sensitivity on the part of the other member states. The changing security environment has pushed back the case for the EU developing a traditional defence capacity. Appendix 26 sets out the relevant international organisations.

Conclusion

In 1946 Winston Churchill said: 'We must build a kind of United States of Europe. If at first all states of Europe are not willing to join the union, we must nevertheless proceed to assemble and combine those who will and those who can.' Ireland has accepted the invitation to move further along the path to union.

The range of areas included in the competence of the EU is increasing all the time. At the June 1990 summit meeting of EU leaders in Dublin the idea of an 'energy community' was put forward by the Dutch Prime Minister. Exploratory talks between the Soviet Union and the EU were held with a view to diversifying Western Europe's supply by strengthening its gas pipeline system with the Soviet Union. The two intergovernmental conferences held in December 1990 on political reform of the EU's institutions, and economic and monetary union have demonstrated the flexibility and evolutionary nature of the EU in broadening its competence in areas not mentioned in the original Treaty of Rome or in the Single European Act. The agreement between the EC and the seven countries of the European Free Trade Association on the creation of a European Economic Area is further evidence of this. At the same time the number of countries expressing an interest in membership of the EU is increasing. In October 1991 the European Commission President, Jacques Delors, argued that immediately the Maastricht summit was over, the EU needed to fix a new political and institutional rendezvous to prepare a structure for twenty-four to thirty members. Turkey applied for membership in 1987; Austria in 1989; Malta and Cyprus in 1990 and Sweden in 1991. Switzerland, Hungary, the Czech Republic, Finland and Poland have made it clear that they too might be interested in joining. Predicting where the eastern limits of an enlarged community might eventually lie has become impossible in the wake of the disintegration of the Soviet Union.

The political consequences of European integration are as important as the economic, if not more so. There will be more pooling of sovereignty and a strengthening of EU institutions and powers, as well as intensified inter-governmental and inter-agency co-operation. More and more functions are becoming subject to centralised direction.

The trends of internationalisation, globalisation, competition, liberalisation and harmonisation will continue to require constant reappraisal and review of the role, the functions and the procedures of public sector organisations.

Ireland has now been a full participant in the process of European integration for a generation. It has benefited enormously from membership of the European Union, and has at the same time contributed constructively to the Union's development. The benefits of membership in terms of financial transfers alone have been considerable. Ireland is by far the largest net beneficiary per head of EU funding. By the end of 1995, total net transfers to Ireland since accession amounted to IR£18.45 billion. However, Ireland's membership of the Union has always been about more than free trade and financial transfers, important as they may be. The period of our membership of the Union has coincided with an increase in national self-confidence, a strengthening of our identity and an increase in our international profile.

In Ireland the positive lessons of EU membership were rapidly absorbed, along with the experience of higher agricultural prices, a growing volume of transfers and the diversification of trade and diplomacy away from Britain. In recent years EU membership has come to be seen as part of an emancipating process for the Irish state and Irish society. Alongside this maturing goes an awareness that it will bear a growing responsibility for solidarity within the wider European polity.

With the prospect of major developments in the fields of political, social, economic and monetary union in the context of an enlarged EU, it is clear that the performance of the political system, the civil service and public service in general in managing the potential and challenges of a truly integrated Europe will shape the process of economic and social development in Ireland in the early years of the new millennium.

REFERENCES

Baker, T., J. FitzGerald and P. Honohan, *Economic Implications for Ireland of EMU*, ESRI Policy Research Series, Paper No. 28 (Dublin: Economic and Social Research Institute, July 1996)

Department of Foreign Affairs, *Challenges and Opportunities Abroad: White Paper on Foreign Policy Development*, Pn. 2133 (Dublin: Stationery Office, 1996)

FitzGerald, Garret, address to the Royal Irish Academy (10 November 1975)

Government of Ireland, *Report of the Constitution Review Group*, Pn. 2632 (Dublin: Stationery Office, 1996)

Hennessy, Ambassador Margaret, 'The Irish Foreign Service', speech at White Paper Foreign Policy Seminar, Trinity College, Dublin, 1995

Keatinge, Patrick, *Political Union*, Studies in European Union No. 1 (Dublin: Institute of European Affairs, 1991)

Keatinge, Patrick, *Towards a Safer Europe: Small State Security Policies and the European Union: Implications for Ireland* (Dublin: Institute of European Affairs, 1975)

Rhodes, R.A.W., 'The Europeanisation of Sub-Central Government: The Case of the UK', *Staatswissenschaften und Staatspraxis*, vol. 2, no. 2, Jahrgang (1992), pp. 272–86

Scott, Dermot, 'Adapting the Machinery of Central Government' in David Coombes (ed.), *Ireland and the European Communities: Ten Years of Membership* (Dublin: Gill & Macmillan, 1983), pp. 68–88

Scott, Dermot, *Ireland's Contribution to the European Union* (Dublin: Institute of European Affairs, 1994)

Tonra, B., 'The Irish Presidency of the European Union', *Integration* 3/96 (Bonn 1996)

BIBLIOGRAPHY

Barrington, A., 'The Netherlands Presidency of the European Union', 15–16 November 1996, Clingendael/ISEI/TEPSA Conference, The Hague

Department of the Taoiseach, *Communicating Europe: Report of the Communicating Europe Task Force* (February 1995)

Government of Ireland, *National Development Plan 1994–1999*, Pn. 0222 (Dublin: Stationery Office, 1994)

Humphreys, P.C., *The Fifth Irish Presidency of the European Union: Some Management Lessons*, Committee for Public Management Research, Discussion Paper (Dublin: Institute of Public Administration, 1997)

APPENDIX 21

Joint Committee on European Affairs

Extract from the Orders of Reference

Order of Dáil of 9 March 1995

(1) That a Select Committee of Dáil Éireann, consisting of 11 members of Dáil Éireann, excluding the *ex officio* members of the Committee referred to in paragraph (6), be appointed to be joined with a Select Committee of Seanad Éireann to form the Joint Committee on European Affairs.

(2) That the Joint Committee shall have power to appoint sub-Committees and to delegate any matter comprehended by paragraphs (3), (7), (8) and (9) to a sub-Committee.

(3) That a Bill initiated by the Minister for Foreign Affairs or a Minister of State at the Department of Foreign Affairs having passed its Second Stage may on motion made in Dáil Éireann by a member of the Government or a Minister of State be referred, with the concurrence of Seanad Éireann, to the Joint Committee.

(4) That in the case of a Bill originating in Seanad Éireann, the motion of referral in Dáil Éireann shall constitute a Second Reading of the Bill and the debate thereon shall be confined to the general principle of the Bill and where the Third Stage has been dealt with in the Joint Committee, the Bill shall on its receipt in Dáil Éireann after being passed by Seanad Éireann be set down for Report Stage, the First, Second and Third Stages being waived.

(5) That the report of the Joint Committee upon every Bill originating in Dáil Éireann which is referred to it shall be set down for Report Stage in Dáil Éireann.

(6) That the Minister for Foreign Affairs shall be an *ex officio* member of a Committee or sub-Committee which is considering a Bill referred to it and may nominate a Minister or Minister of State to be such *ex officio* member in his or her stead.

(7) That the Joint Committee shall consider such matters arising from Ireland's membership of the European Communities and its adherence to the Treaty on European Union as the Joint Committee may select and report thereon to both Houses of the Oireachtas.

(8) That the Joint Committee shall, in particular, consider:

   (i) such programmes and guidelines prepared by the Commission of the European Communities as a basis for possible legislative action and such drafts of regulations, directives, decisions, recommendations and opinions of the Council of Ministers proposed by the Commission,

   (ii) such acts of the institutions of those Communities,

   (iii) such regulations under the European Communities Acts, 1972 to 1994, and

   (iv) such other instruments made under statute and necessitated by the obligations of membership of those Communities,

as the Committee may select and shall report thereon to both Houses of the Oireachtas.

Joint Committee on Foreign Affairs

Extract from the Orders of Reference

Order of the Dáil of 1 March 1995

(1) That the Orders of Reference of the Joint Committee on Foreign Affairs are hereby rescinded and that a Select Committee of Dáil Éireann consisting of 21 members of Dáil Éireann, excluding *ex officio* members of the Committee referred to in paragraph (7), be appointed to be joined with a Select Committee of Seanad Éireann to form the Joint Committee on Foreign Affairs.

(2) That the Joint Committee shall have power to appoint sub-Committees and to delegate any matter comprehended by paragraphs (4), (8), (9) and (11) to a sub-Committee.

(3) That the Select Committee of Dáil Éireann shall consider the Estimates for Public Services submitted to Dáil Éireann in respect of Foreign Affairs and International Co-operation and report thereon to Dáil Éireann and the Select Committee shall have power to appoint a sub-Committee for this purpose.

(4) That a Bill initiated by the Minister for Foreign Affairs or a Minister of State at the Department of Foreign Affairs having passed its Second Stage may on motion made in Dáil Éireann by a member of the Government or a Minister of State be referred, with the concurrence of Seanad Éireann, to the Joint Committee.

(5) That in the case of a Bill originating in Seanad Éireann, the motion of referral in Dáil Éireann shall constitute a Second Reading of the Bill and the debate thereon shall be confined to the general principle of the Bill and where the Third Stage has been dealt with in the Joint Committee, the Bill shall on its receipt in Dáil Éireann after being passed by Seanad Éireann be set down for Report Stage, the First, Second and Third Stages being waived.

(6) That the report of the Joint Committee upon every Bill originating in Dáil Éireann which is referred to it shall be set down for Report Stage in Dáil Éireann.

(7) That the Minister for Foreign Affairs shall be an *ex officio* member of a Committee or sub-Committee which is considering –

(i) a Bill referred to it, or

(ii) Estimates for Public Services,

and may nominate a Minister or Minister of State to be such *ex officio* member in his or her stead.

(8) That the Joint Committee shall consider the impact on equality of policy and legislation in respect of the Department of Foreign Affairs and report thereon to both Houses of the Oireachtas.

(9) That the Joint Committee shall consider such aspects of Ireland's international relations as the Joint Committee may select and report thereon to both Houses of the Oireachtas.

(10) That any consideration by the Select Committee, the Joint Committee or a sub-Committee of security issues relating to Northern Ireland shall be in private session.

(11) That Dáil Éireann may refer reports relevant to the Department of Foreign Affairs to the Joint Committee for discussion, observations and recommendations, and the Joint Committee shall report thereon to both Houses of the Oireachtas.

(12) That the Joint Committee shall make an annual report to both Houses of the Oireachtas which shall detail:

  (i) the work carried out by the Committee,
  (ii) the work in progress by the Committee,
  (iii) the attendance and voting records at meetings of the Committee,
  (iv) its future work programme, and
  (v) such other matters as the Committee deems appropriate.

APPENDIX 22

QUALIFIED MAJORITY VOTING

	Qualified majority votes	**Number of members of the European Parliament**	**Commissioners**	**Population (millions)**
Austria	4	21	1	8.1
Belgium	5	25	1	10.1
Denmark	3	16	1	5.2
Finland	3	16	1	5.2
France	10	87	2	58.0
Germany	10	99	2	81.6
Greece	5	25	1	10.4
Ireland	3	15	1	3.6
Italy	10	87	2	57.1
Luxembourg	2	6	1	0.4
Netherlands	5	31	1	15.4
Portugal	5	25	1	9.4
Spain	8	64	2	39.2
Sweden	4	22	1	8.8
United Kingdom	10	87	2	58.2
	87	**626**	**20**	**370.7**

APPENDIX 23

Main Implementing Bodies, National Development Plan 1994–9

Programme	**Main government departments(s)**	**Other bodies**
Overall policy and co-ordination	Finance	
Industry	Enterprise and Employment*, Tourism and Trade, Agriculture, Food and Forestry, Arts, Culture and the Gaeltacht	Forfás, Forbairt, Industrial Development Agency (IDA Ireland), Shannon Free Airport Development Company (SFADCo), Údarás na Gaeltachta, An Bord Tráchtála, An Bord Bia, Teagasc, Irish Productivity Centre, Business Innovation Centres, Film Board and third-level educational institutes.
Human resources	Enterprise and Employment*, Education, Health, Justice	FÁS, CERT, second- and third-level educational institutes, National Rehabilitation Board, Aer Lingus.
Tourism	Tourism and Trade*, Arts, Culture and the Gaeltacht, Marine, Office of Public Works	Bord Fáilte, SFADCo, Central and Regional Fisheries Boards, Arts Council, CERT.
Agriculture, rural development and forestry	Agriculture, Food and Forestry*	Teagasc, Coillte Teo., Údarás na Gaeltachta.
Fisheries	Marine*, Arts, Culture and the Gaeltacht	Bord Iascaigh Mhara.
Transport	Environment*, Transport, Energy & Communications, Marine	Local authorities, National Roads Authority, Córas Iompair Éireann, Aer Rianta, harbour authorities.
Environmental services	Environment*, Marine	Local authorities, Environmental Protection Agency.

→

Programme	Main government departments(s)	Other bodies
Economic infrastructure (telecommunications, postal services, energy)	Transport, Energy & Communications*	Telecom Éireann, An Post, Electricity Supply Board, Bord Gáis Éireann, Bord na Móna.
Local development	Taoiseach, Tánaiste, Enterprise and Employment, Education, Environment, Agriculture, Food and Forestry	County Enterprise Boards, Area Development Management Ltd (ADM), area-based partnership companies, local authorities, educational institutions.
Tallaght Hospital	Health*	

* Lead Department for Programme (i.e. the department with primary responsibility)
Source: Ireland: National Development Plan 1994–1999.

APPENDIX 24

Presidency of the Council

	First semester	Second semester
1995	France	Spain
1996	Italy	Ireland
1997	The Netherlands	Luxembourg
1998	United Kingdom	Austria
1999	Germany	Finland
2000	Portugal	France
2001	Sweden	Belgium
2002	Spain	Denmark
2003	Greece	Not yet decided

APPENDIX 25

EU MEMBER STATES AND APPLICANT STATES

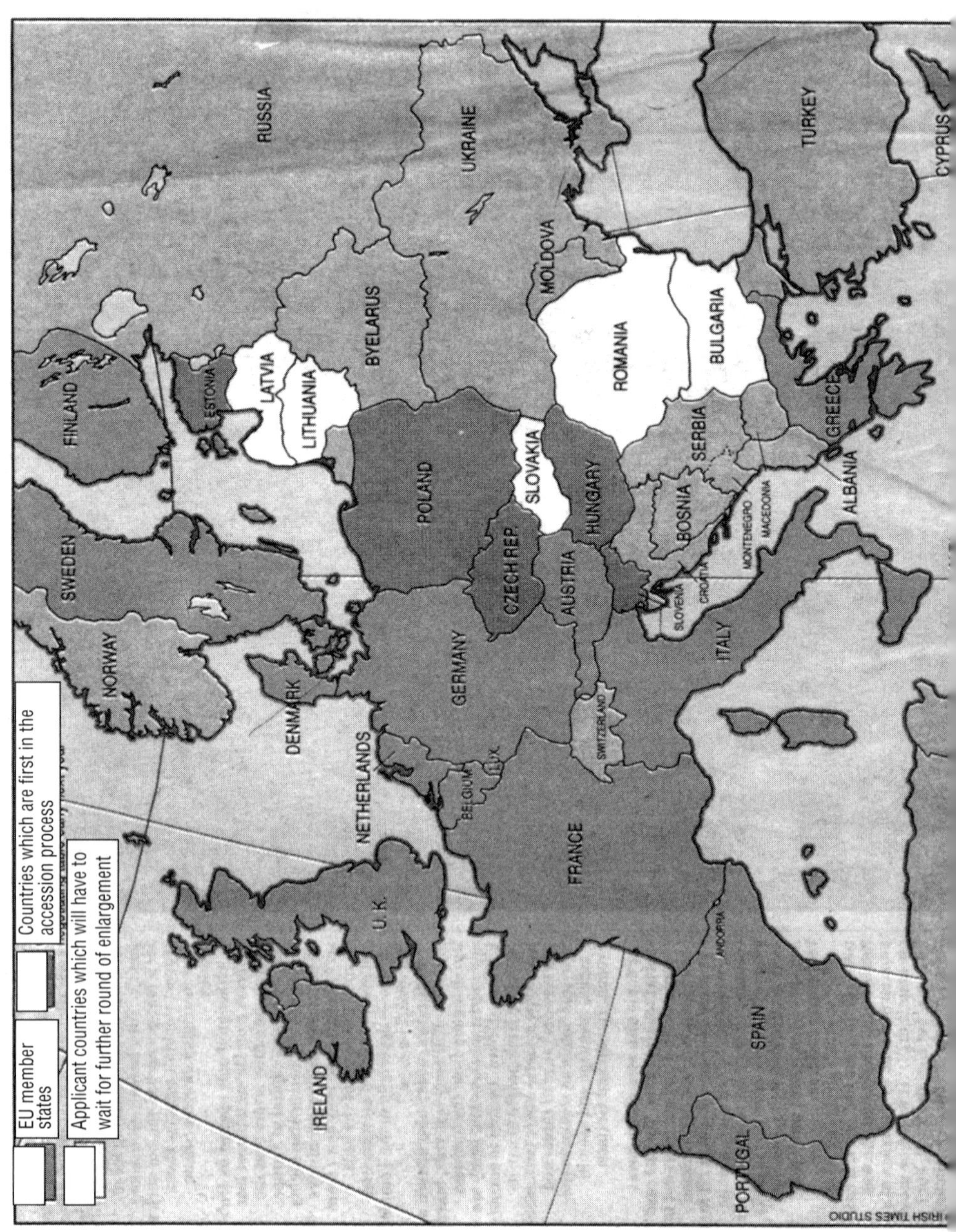

APPENDIX 26

Common Foreign and Security Policy

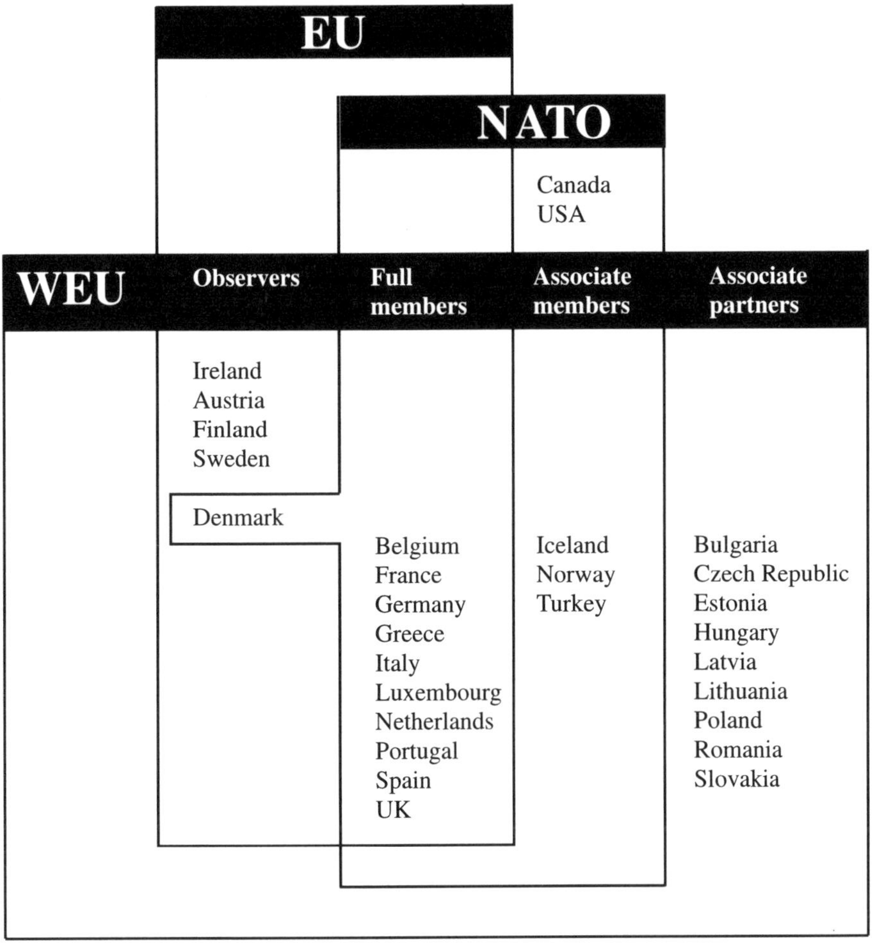

EU

NATO

Canada
USA

WEU

Observers	Full members	Associate members	Associate partners
Ireland Austria Finland Sweden Denmark	Belgium France Germany Greece Italy Luxembourg Netherlands Portugal Spain UK	Iceland Norway Turkey	Bulgaria Czech Republic Estonia Hungary Latvia Lithuania Poland Romania Slovakia

13

THE MANAGEMENT OF GOVERNMENT

Characteristics of Public Administration

In considering the efficiency and effectiveness with which the public sector tasks are carried out, it is necessary in the first instance to identify the unique aspects of public administration – those features distinguishing it markedly from management in the private sector:

(1) The prime purpose of public administration is to serve the public, i.e. to seek the common good.
(2) The public service is not judged on a profit basis.
(3) The activities of public servants are fixed by law.
(4) Public authorities have coercive powers; hence there is a need to provide for consultation, objection and appeal.
(5) The limited discretion and freedom of action of public administration.
(6) Public administration is carried on in a 'glass bowl' in that there is a high degree of transparency, with the taxpayers entitled to know how their money is being spent.
(7) Public administration has a social responsibility and has to balance achievement of the common good with the demands of vested interests. It also has to balance present necessities with future desirabilities.
(8) The much greater number of varying viewpoints which must be considered in the governmental process.
(9) There is a need for a high degree of consistency in the actions of public servants.
(10) Government departments work for, with and under the direction of politicians; hence public administration operates in a 'political milieu'. The way in which things are done often owes more to political factors than to bureaucratic rationality.
(11) Public administration must act to compress the various demands made upon it, e.g. education and health.
(12) Public administration deals with a great diversity of matters, many of which are purely governmental and which the government cannot opt out of, e.g. defence, prisons, social services, taxation.

(13) The scale, complexity, integrative and allocative functions of a society-wide base of public service operations, e.g. health and education.
(14) The difficulty of measuring much of the work of the public service.
(15) The concept of public accountability.
(16) In much of what the government does it is immune from competition. Public administration does not depend on clients or customers for financial support.
(17) The often simultaneous performance of competing functions in public administration, e.g. taxation and social welfare.
(18) An organisation culture determined by socio-political aims (in contrast to the market orientation of the private sector).

To this list might be added other aspects of the public service such as the fragmentation of authority and accountability, and the need for equity and for treating all citizens equally. Public sector management is largely concerned with a network of several different quasi-autonomous organisations which interact with each other. Indeed public service management has been described as 'getting things done through other organisations'.

Public Management

Private sector management models cannot be simply and directly transferred into the public sector. Private companies are essentially profit-making organisations, whereas public sector bodies aim to provide a high quality of 'service' (a much less measurable concept than 'profit'). Such differences, arising from fundamental institutional and political factors, account for the lack of success in past attempts to introduce business management practices directly into government.

Nevertheless, public administrators must ensure that the work is carried out with maximum efficiency and effectiveness. In order to achieve this, a new approach, termed 'public management', has developed which seeks to apply a business sector management approach to traditional public administration and to its concerns with democracy, accountability, equity, consistency and equality. It involves, for example, specialised methods of measuring outputs and outcome, always a problem in the public sector; hence the use of techniques such as performance indicators and cost-benefit analysis.

Action within the public service is subject to public accountability, enforced through the electoral system. The political process is not a limited one: all members of the public have the right of expression, and no issue, however small, can be assumed to be of no concern. In connection with the multifarious nature of the work undertaken in public management, Chase and Reveal (1983: 15–16) have commented:

> What makes public management so hard – and so interesting – is that all these players act simultaneously, with a few clear lines of authority, constantly changing public mandates, and frequent turnover of people. Getting the garbage picked up, a child treated for lead poisoning, a subway to the station on time, or an elderly person a social security cheque may not seem Herculean tasks. But when they are multiplied hundreds of times over, and their execution occurs in the context of the manager's environment, the real challenge of government becomes clear. The tasks can be done, and done well, by public managers who master their world; but such tasks can easily elude managers who are befuddled by the politics around them, disconcerted by the mixed signals they hear, and their own agenda and purpose.

The public service, particularly the civil service, operates under numerous constraints and controls which are not present in the private sector. Constraints include: social, economic, financial, legislative, political, international and accountability factors, such as the system of parliamentary questions, motions in the Dáil or Seanad, or the proximity of elections. An important constraint is the perplexity and vagueness of the objectives which the civil service organisations have, many of them of a social or redistributive nature, some of them conflicting. There are motivational constraints also in that the manager in the civil service is deprived of many of the motivational incentives and sanctions normally associated with such a post, e.g. there is little power to hire or fire, to award bonuses or to promote. Controls include these factors together with the Constitution, the cabinet, the judiciary and legal system, the Department of Finance, the Comptroller and Auditor General, the Public Accounts Committee, and public opinion and pressure groups.

The Change Challenge

People are long accustomed to hearing about the need for change in the public service. Over the past thirty years there have been frequent and increasingly persistent calls, from within and outside the public service, for public service reform. Those calls have grown in volume in more recent years, as the cost of maintaining public services has increased and as greater emphasis has been placed on value for money.

In Ireland there have been two major blueprints for the reform of the public service. The Devlin Report (1969) presented a comprehensive plan based on two underlying principles: greater emphasis on policy-making, and the need for greater integration of the public service. The recommendations can be summarised under the following headings: the establishment of a Department of the Public Service and of a Public Service Advisory Council; the introduction of a policy-making core to be called the Aireacht (the senior staff closest to the Aire – the minister); a unified staff structure in government departments; classifications of jobs; career development; improved personnel practices; administrative audits; and appellate procedures.

The White Paper *Serving the Country Better* (1985) was an important landmark in the development of the civil service and set out a blueprint for the future, together with a series of practical steps and initiatives to bring about the best possible, most cost-efficient and courteous service for the public. The focus in the White Paper was on the introduction in all departments of management systems based on corporate planning and emphasis on personal responsibility for results, costs and service. A change of emphasis from public administration towards public management was the central theme of the paper. The need for clear aims and objectives in all public services was underlined.

Both of these blueprints had one thing in common – a belief that some changes were needed. This was based on the belief that the delivery of services needed to be improved and that resources needed to be managed better.

Little progress was made in implementing the Devlin reform proposals due to concerns about the situation in Northern Ireland; entry to the European Community; the economic situation; changes of ministers and governments; and public apathy.

Ireland is not unique as far as change is concerned. Public administration all over the world is being subjected to radical change and modernisation reflecting the growing demands of society and the complexities of governing in today's global economy. Indeed in April 1996 the United Nations Assembly discussed, for the first time ever, reform of public administration. OECD member countries have all been undergoing major change and modernisation. Some examples, which are well known, are Australia, New Zealand, UK and Canada, all of which have the same model of administration, the Westminster model, as Ireland has.

In many respects public service reform reached a watershed in the late 1980s. The 1985 White Paper had not been widely welcomed. The debate surrounding it was overtaken by other, more immediate concerns in the 1986–7 period. The public financial situation resulted in budgetary cuts and constraints and staff retrenchment policies. However, these events placed the 1985 White Paper in a different light as they focused renewed attention on service delivery and the use and management of resources. In fact, the questions of how well the civil service was performing and being managed became central topics of a growing internal debate in the late 1980s and early 1990s. This, in turn, gave rise to a more critical self-analysis of management practices and the perceived constraints under which civil servants at all levels were operating.

It was in this debate, and the growing acceptance arising out of it that the civil service needed to manage better, that the Strategic Management Initiative (SMI) had its roots. (See Appendix 27.) Its main objective is delivering an excellent service for the customer, based on a high-performance organisation. The commencement of work on the extension of the SMI to the wider public service began in January 1997.

Strategic Management Initiative

It is useful to examine the concerns that led to the adoption of a strategic approach, how it developed, and progress to date.

Internal concerns. Following the 1987 retrenchments, management at various levels in the civil and public service increasingly voiced concerns, some of which were shared by staff at all levels. These internal concerns were:

- static/shrinking resources;
- demands for new and improved services;
- failure to identify and act on priorities;
- lack of context for key decisions;
- lack of corporate approach;
- focus on short term;
- need for better financial and personnel management.

External pressures. The concerns being raised internally were reinforced by views being aired publicly and by events that brought the workings of the public service to the notice of the media and the public. These external pressures were:

- public perception
  - poor performance
  - lack of accountability
  - poor value for money
- The Report of the Industrial Policy Review Group, 1991 (Culliton Report)
  - inattention to policy formation and analysis
  - concentration on regulation
- Beef Tribunal Report of July 1994
  - apparent lack of interdepartmental co-ordination
  - operational deficiencies
  - inadequate communications
- emerging 'Value for Money' role for Comptroller and Auditor General.

The internal concerns coupled with external pressures focused minds on developing an effective response – basically, an alternative, better way of managing and discharging the business of the civil service.

In 1988 and 1989 informal networks for assistant secretaries and principal officers were set up in response to calls for such fora to provide a means for discussing issues of concern to these officers. It was through these informal discussions that the debate gathered momentum and focused on finding a better way. In addition, the Secretaries' Conference endorsed a strategic approach and promoted pilot exercises. The key element of these discussions was a recognition that the civil service could do better, if the system:

- develops a framework within which direction and priorities are set;
- balances between the short and long term;
- makes more effective use of available resources;
- continually evaluates performance;
- provides a clearer sense of direction;
- provides greater clarity of role;
- promotes greater teamwork.

In essence, the civil service actively pursued a strategic approach based on the need for better planning and management in the future.

A Strategic Approach

The result was a belief that a strategic management process should be put in place in every department and office and that, over time, it should become an integral part of the approach to the day-to-day work of the civil service.

Strategic management is a process by which an organisation maintains a considered and coherent view of the likely development in its internal and external environment in the medium to long term. It develops plans designed to maximise its effectiveness and efficiency in the expected circumstances. It implements these plans and continually reviews progress and makes any necessary adjustments.

A strategic approach provides a better balance, more control and a framework for making key strategic decisions. It provides a more coherent view of what the civil service should be doing and how it might go about it. It is not a panacea to all the ills in the organisation, however.

The Strategic Management Initiative (SMI) was launched by the Taoiseach in 1994. It required each department to prepare a strategy statement and entailed the setting up of a co-ordinating group of secretaries to oversee its implementation. The parameters within which the SMI was set were that it was to address:

- government policy and objectives;
- three key issues
  - contribution to national development
  - provision of excellent services to the public
  - effective use of resources;
- linkage between departments and with agencies.

The SMI is action-oriented and results-oriented. Each department is required to produce an action-oriented statement of strategy setting out: its objectives; how it will meet its objectives; and how it will use its available resources to this end. The strategy statements must be results-oriented. The intended outputs are to be identified, together with effective methods of measuring output attainment.

The provision of a strategy statement amounted, in essence, to each department and office taking stock of what it was doing; determining what it should be doing in the context of its mandate, government objectives and client needs; and identifying what steps or strategies it should pursue to that end. In short, a searching self-analysis was called for and the putting in place of a management process to ensure ongoing improvements in efficiency and effectiveness. The SMI, therefore, is not a one-off exercise. It is an ever-continuing cycle of questioning and reviewing what the civil service is doing, assessing how well it is performing, asking what changes it should be making, setting and reviewing objectives and measuring their achievement. An important feature of the SMI process is that it is a matter for each department and office to devise and implement its own strategy. An extract from the Statement of Strategy of the Department of Finance is shown at Appendix 28.

The strength of the SMI process is the role of the co-ordinating group of nine secretaries. Its function is to: facilitate the process; evaluate strategy statements; recommend how interacting strategies can be co-ordinated; recommend changes to enable more efficient and effective management of the civil service; and report to government. The co-ordinating group reviewed the strategy statements and submitted a progress report to government.

The government decided in February 1995 to advance the process with a view to its deepening within departments and mandated the group to develop a modernisation programme. This decision was based on the perceived benefits of the SMI, which included more focus on: strategic issues and objectives; policy formation and evaluation; clients' needs and services; objectives and targets. It was noted that SMI led to better management cohesion and commitment (see Appendix 29).

Delivering Better Government

Delivering Better Government – A Programme of Change for the Irish Civil Service was published in May 1996. This was the second report of the Co-ordinating Group of Secretaries. It sets out the vision for the Irish civil service of the future and recognises clearly that quality services are the essence of an excellent civil service. It is a series of interdependent elements which collectively are aimed at improving service delivery and the management and performance of the civil (and public) service. Its overall purpose is to enable the civil service to meet the needs of government and the public more efficiently, effectively and economically. These elements are set out within an overall vision for the civil service – a vision that builds on the civil service's strengths and core values of integrity, impartiality and equity. In addition to setting the requirement for legislative change to clarify the allocation of authority, accountability and responsibility in the system (see Appendix 30), the report identified six specific areas which need to be addressed on a service-wide basis if the objectives of the SMI are to be achieved. These six areas are:

- quality customer service;
- human resources management;
- information technology;
- financial management;
- regulatory reform;
- openness and transparency.

In autumn 1996 the first meetings were held of the working groups set up to address these six key areas. These working groups involve senior civil servants and non-civil servants in developing further the key initiatives. In addition, there are three front-line groups on:

- customer service;
- training and development;
- information technology.

These front-line groups comprise administrative, executive and clerical staff at various levels in the civil service. They provide an important input to the relevant working groups in relation to issues affecting front-line staff in the areas in question.

The work of the various groups is overseen by an extended co-ordinating group made up of senior figures from the civil service, trade unions and private sector. This group is required to oversee the implementation of the change programme and to report regularly to government on the progress in developing the initiatives. This co-ordinating group held its first meeting in June 1996.

A cross-departmental team was established in November 1996 to support the development of the overall programme of change and its implementation in departments. This team is based in the Department of the Taoiseach and provides advice on issues of common concern. It provides support to the six working groups in developing programmes to implement the recommendations on delivering better government.

At the level of each department appropriate structures have been put in place to ensure consultation with and participation by all staff. Departments have nominated facilitators to provide liaison with the cross-departmental team. Some departments have engaged in extensive dialogue to ensure widespread participation. Others have set up in-house task forces representative of all grades. A newsletter has been issued to keep civil servants up to date on the development of the SMI process.

It is useful to consider these six areas in more detail.

Quality Customer Service

A key central aim of SMI and *Delivering Better Government* is to bring about a clearer focus on objectives, particularly in relation to meeting the needs of the consumer of public services. The culture of the civil service has not been conspicuously customer-oriented, leading to insufficient emphasis on service delivery. This is an area, however, where good progress has been made in recent years.

Delivering Better Government proposes an approach to quality service delivery based on the following principles:

- a specification of the quality of service to be provided by departments and offices to their customers;
- consultation with and participation by customers on a structured basis;
- the provision of quality information and advice to customers;
- reasonable choice for customers, in relation to the methods of delivery of services;
- the integration of public services at local, regional and national levels;
- a comprehensive system of measuring and assessing customer satisfaction;
- complaints and redress mechanisms, which operate close to the point of delivery.

It recommended the introduction of quality service initiatives based on these principles and under which each department would have a programme to improve the quality and delivery of services. The need for such improvements also stems from the fact that the public has the right to expect the same standard of service from the public service as from a private sector business. A quality service initiative for the civil service was launched in May 1997. This emphasises the importance of detailed customer service action plans and introduced the LO-Call 1-890 service on a phased basis. This allows people to contact government departments from anywhere in the country for the price of a local call.

Human Resources Management

The Co-ordinating Group of Secretaries stated that sufficient priority had not been given to the personnel function in the past. Before the advent of SMI, setting formal long-term objectives was not the norm. As a result, performance management systems did not evolve. It is now recognised that an improved system of accountability, as well as a more customer-oriented environment for service delivery, will require a corresponding improvement in staff management and greater attention to the needs of staff.

Every important aspect of human resources management is being looked at with a view to redirecting it towards a more strategic role while giving more authority to line management: recruitment; probation and promotion; the multiple grade structure; and the implementation of a performance appraisal and management system for the public service.

Significant progress is being made towards putting more resources into training and development (the target allocation is 3 per cent of payroll), based on the view that this is another area that all too often failed to be recognised as an investment in human capital. Increased flexibility in working and reporting arrangements has also been introduced as an integral part of restructuring. A results-driven civil service requires a highly flexible, responsive approach to the allocation of work and reporting arrangements. Without flexibility in the use of its principal resource – staff at all levels – the civil service cannot hope to respond effectively to changing needs and demands. The civil service is not immune from the turbulent and rapidly changing social and economic environment of contemporary society. To ignore it would render the civil service ineffective and lead to increasingly adverse effects on the contribution it can make to economic and social development.

Information Technology

Information technology, by virtue of its growing versatility and potential to enable radical improvements to be made in the way business is conducted, presents unparalleled opportunities to devise new approaches to existing tasks and new ways of working. In recent years there has been a very significant increase in the usage of information technology, with the result that it is now widely employed in practically all departments. Important gains have been made in efficiency, consequent on the computerisation of tasks that involve processing large volumes of data or transactions, such as tax demands or social welfare payments. In addition, many departments have made good use of the technology to support decision-making and service delivery. More recently, information technology has been applied extensively to support office activities and systems. Information technology, such as personal computers, is available to all as part of the job. There is increasing reliance on information systems for communicating within and between departments and with the EU institutions in Brussels.

Information technology has been increasingly integrated into departmental business planning. Staff development plans have been adapted to include IT training. There has been a greater allocation of budget control in respect of IT projects to user divisions. Consideration is being given to the implications of the emerging 'Information Society' for the civil and public service and the conduct of its business. Particular attention is being paid to the potential uses of the Internet by the civil and public service and to the development of 'Teledemocracy', electronic information services by public sector agencies.

Financial Management

The introduction of an effective accountability framework, involving greater delegation and increased emphasis on the measurement of results, necessitates the development of better financial management systems and the adoption of a more devolved approach to expenditure management generally.

A number of important initiatives are being pursued in this area. The system of multi-annual budgeting, announced by the Minister for Finance in his 1996 budget, is operating to a fixed annual cycle to produce a rolling three-year budgetary process. This is facilitating changing circumstances, both budgetary and economic, while accommodating existing and emerging priorities in public expenditure. Major programmes of expenditure are also being subject to a thorough review at least once every three years.

The budgets covering administrative costs were delegated in 1991 in most cases. In the 1990 budget the Minister for Finance explained the rationale for these budgets, which 'would involve a real reduction in funding each year because of greater efficiency but which would allow greater managerial flexibility within those budgets'. Departments have agreed three-year administrative budget contracts with the Department of Finance. The increased delegation of financial authority to departments is an integral part of this process. Enhanced financial management systems are being introduced. These include the incorporation of accrual accounting principles into departmental accounting procedures as necessary, as a first step in the development of financial management systems concerned with performance measurement and management.

Regulatory Reform

Regulatory simplification has been recognised internationally as an integral part of any strategy to foster growth, competitiveness and employment. There is a need for high-quality, easily understood and efficiently implemented regulations which are in the public interest. A proactive programme of managing and improving government regulations and the regulatory process has been introduced. The principles governing such improvements include:

- improving the quality, rather than quantity, of regulations;
- eliminating unnecessary and/or inefficient regulations (including legislation);
- simplifying necessary regulations and related procedures as much as possible;
- lowering the cost of regulatory compliance;
- making regulations more accessible to the public;

while in each case protecting the public interest. Each department is endeavouring to reduce red tape. It is intended that regulations be reviewed every five years on this basis. A good regulatory regime is essential to promoting a sound and socially responsible economic environment conducive to job creation and to fair competition.

Openness and Transparency

It is vital that there is a free flow of information between government and public administration, on the one hand, and those they serve on the other, the public. For civil servants, the introduction of freedom of information legislation and greater accountability to the Dáil through Oireachtas committees constitute major changes in terms of previous practices.

The Public Service Management Act 1997

The Public Service Management Act 1997, which came into effect on 1 September 1997, sets out a formal structure for assigning authority and accountability within the civil service in a clear and unambiguous manner. It clarifies the roles and duties of individual civil servants so that each person knows what is expected of him, either in an individual capacity or as part of a team, and is enabled to assume responsibility for the results of his work.

The reason for the introduction of this legislation is to improve the internal management of the civil service. These changes ensure greater efficiency and effectiveness on an ongoing basis in the way the civil service does its business and ensure it provides value for money. The pace and volume of business transacted by government departments have increased enormously in recent years. Prior to the passing of this legislation, 'It has long been recognised that the existing structures and reporting systems promote a risk-averse environment where taking personal responsibility is not encouraged and, equally, where innovative approaches to service delivery have not been developed' (*Delivering Better Government*, p. 22). The previous system had tended to concentrate too much responsibility in ministers for matters in which they may have had no direct or immediate involvement.

The Public Service Management Act provides a framework for formally assigning responsibility and accountability to heads of departments and in turn to other officers. The act signalled, as such, a clear change in the operation of the system of government. In accordance with the Constitution, ministers retain overall responsibility for their departments, which they exercise in accordance with the framework provided in the act. This is shown in Appendix 30.

The Public Service Management Act is a key element in advancing the strategic management process in the civil service. The key features are as follows:

> Each department publishes a statement of strategy every three years or within six months of the appointment of a new minister, which will be presented to the Oireachtas. These statements of strategy set out key objectives and the outputs to be achieved together with the resources to be used.
>
> In the light of the statements of strategy, each secretary general (the new title for secretary set out in the act) has responsibility for managing, implementing and monitoring government policies and delivering outputs as determined with the minister.
>
> In turn the secretary general is able to assign responsibility to civil servants at other levels, for specific matters such as:
>
> - achievement of specified outputs;
> - provision of policy advice;
> - operation of statutory schemes or programmes;
> - delivery of specified services;
> - ensuring that expenditures accord with the purpose for which the moneys have been allocated by the Oireachtas;
> - ensuring that value for money is achieved;

- exercising, on behalf of the secretary general, powers, duties and functions in respect of appointments, performance and discipline of personnel in the area of the assignment other than dismissals.

The Public Service Management Act 1997 contains a significant change in the terms of employment of civil servants. It provides the secretary general with the responsibility for appointment, performance, discipline and dismissals of staff below the grade of principal officer. Furthermore, these responsibilities, with the exception of dismissal, can be delegated to other officers within the department. The previous arrangements continue in respect of staff at principal and above. Prior to the passing of this act, established civil servants could be removed from office only by the government. The operation of these powers of appointment, discipline and dismissal now vested in the secretary general is contingent on the need to ensure that systems are in place to treat all civil servants fairly and equitably, on the basis of a transparent performance management system and in accordance with natural justice.

Performance Management System Initiative

The modern civil service, focused on the achievement of results, needs to be concerned with managing its performance. The development of a performance management system, geared to the specific needs of government departments, is an integral part of the reform process. The balanced score-card which aims to balance financial and operational measures is shown at Appendix 31.

Performance management is a process for establishing a shared understanding about what is to be achieved, how it is to be achieved and how progress is to be assessed. An effective performance management system creates a positive and motivating work environment by enabling everyone to be involved in setting and renewing their work objectives. In this way, each person knows what is expected of him, is given the necessary support and training to do the job, receives feedback on how he is doing and has a say in how work is carried out.

Achieving and maintaining the high standard of performance now required of the civil service requires systems to be in place to:

- identify and set clear work objectives at all levels;
- identify and follow up on training and development needs;
- provide feedback on how people are performing;
- provide a rational and transparent basis for decisions about rewards and sanctions; and
- convert high-level strategic objectives in the statements of strategy into individual and team objectives embedded in the day-to-day operational work programme of the organisation.

Performance management is central to the reform process. A prerequisite to providing quality service is better management of people through a focus on performance, flexibility in work arrangements and resource use, and the development of the skills and competences of people at all levels in the civil service. Efforts have been made to ensure ownership by staff. This sense of ownership has been, and continues to be, developed by involving all staff, right from the beginning, in the design of the performance management process. This was done in a number of ways, such as a staff survey of 5,000 people across the civil service, on the issues surrounding performance management. Every civil servant was written to letting them know what was happening at the different stages of the project. The unions in the civil service have also been involved in the process.

The development and use of performance indicators is an issue of growing concern in the public service. Hurley (1995) has noted that the development of an appropriate set of pragmatic and meaningful indicators of performance which will allow progress against objectives to be monitored, and performance to be actively managed at all levels, is a key aspect of the SMI that will require careful consideration. Twenty lessons from managerial use of performance indicators are set out in Appendix 32.

Freedom of Information

Purpose of the Act

The Freedom of Information Act 1997 came into effect on 21 April 1998. The purpose of the act is to provide a right of access to information held by public bodies. The long title of the Freedom of Information Act, which sets out its purpose, is included at Appendix 33. It states that it is to enable the public to obtain access to official information to the greatest extent possible consistent with the public interest and the right to privacy. The public bodies to which this act applies are set out at Appendix 34.

Freedom of information derives from the following broad principles:

- when government is more open to public scrutiny it becomes more accountable;
- if people are adequately informed and have access to information, there is likely to be greater appreciation of issues involved in policy decisions and stronger public ownership and acceptance of decisions made;
- groups and individuals who are affected by government decisions should know the criteria applied in making those decisions;
- every individual has a right:

  - to know what information is held in government records about him personally, subject to certain exemptions to protect key interests
  - to inspect files relating to him
  - to have inaccurate material on file corrected;
- citizens, as shareholders in public bodies, are entitled to examine and review the deliberation and processes of public bodies.

Principal Features of the Act

The Freedom of Information Act 1997 establishes three new statutory rights:

- a legal right for each person to access information held by public bodies;
- a legal right for each person to have official information relating to himself amended where it is incomplete, incorrect or misleading;
- a legal right to obtain reasons for decisions affecting oneself.

These rights are overseen by an independent Information Commissioner who reviews decisions made by public bodies under the act.

Obtaining Information

A person can exercise his right to obtain information by asking directly in writing for it from the public body concerned. The act imposes an obligation to assist the public when they make requests. Where a request is refused, reasons for the refusal and the grounds on which it is based must normally be given.

The act requires each public body to publish the rules, procedures, guidelines, interpretations and an index of precedents used by it for the purpose of procedures and recommendations. The reason for this is to help people to focus their requests for information.

Publication of Material by Public Bodies

Public bodies are expected to make information available to the public. Under Section 15 of the act, each public body is also required to prepare and publish a manual setting out what it does, what records it holds and how people can access these. This includes details of the services provided by the public body and how such services can be accessed by the public. This material should also include a general description of the classes of records it holds to facilitate public access to these records.

Procedures Governing Access

The right of access is exercised by a person asking directly for the information from the public body concerned in writing and referring to the act. Public bodies normally have up to twenty working days in which to respond to a request. Where a request is refused, reasons for the refusal and the grounds on which it is based must normally be given. The act allows the period within which the decision must be made on a request to be extended by up to twenty working days if the request or requests concern such a large number of records that compliance within the specified time-frame is impossible. The act also provides for internal review against an initial decision by the public body in respect of the following:

- refusal to grant a request;
- deferral of access to a document being prepared for the Houses of the Oireachtas;
- the provision of access in a form other than that requested;
- the granting of access to part only of the record;
- refusal to amend a record relating to personal information.

This review must be taken at a higher level than that at which the original decision was made and must be completed within three weeks.

Independent Review of Decisions

Where a request for access to information under this act is refused, deferred, delayed, only partly granted or where the information is edited, the person has a right of appeal to an independent Information Commissioner. The commissioner has the power to issue binding decisions. In addition, he has a mandate to report on the operation of the act generally, and on compliance by public bodies, or any particular public body, with its provisions. Decisions by the commissioner can be set aside only following a decision of the High Court. The commissioner reflects standard international practice in terms of:

- independence;
- powers to seek documents and compel witnesses;
- a mandate to operate informally;
- binding decisions, subject to review by the High Court;
- specific time limits;
- a mandate to review the operation of the act and compliance by public bodies;
- reporting directly to Parliament.

Protection of Sensitive Information

Certain exemptions are provided in the legislation so as to protect key sensitive information of government and of public bodies. These exemptions are based on standard practice in other countries with these types of law. Most of these exemptions are not absolute and many are subject to an overall test of whether disclosure is in the public interest. Exemptions provide for the protection of certain material relating to matters such as:

- meetings of the government;
- deliberations and functions of public bodies;
- law enforcement, defence, security and international relations;
- third party information (i.e. personal, commercially sensitive and confidential information);
- parliamentary and court matters;
- economic interests of the state.

However, for material to be protected under many of these exemptions, damage must be likely to be caused by the release of the information involved. Under two exemptions, those of law enforcement (Section 23) and defence, security and international relations (Section 24), a minister may, in the case of exempt information which is also of sufficient sensitivity or seriousness to justify his doing so, issue a certificate. Where such a certificate is issued, a review of the decision to refuse information is undertaken by members of the government, rather than the Information Commissioner. Information can be released in exceptional circumstances, notwithstanding possible damage, where the balance of public interest favours this course.

Comptroller and Auditor General

Article 33 of the Constitution stipulates that 'there should be a Comptroller and Auditor General (C & AG) to control on behalf of the state all disbursements and to audit all accounts of monies administered by or under the authority of the Oireachtas'. The Constitution requires the C & AG to report to the Dáil at stated periods as determined by law. As a constitutional officer the C & AG is appointed by the President on the nomination of the Dáil and holds office until the retiring age (sixty-five) prescribed by law. The C & AG may not be a member of the Oireachtas and may not hold any other office or paid position. The independence of the office is secured by the constitutional requirement that the C & AG cannot be removed from office except for stated misbehaviour or incapacity, and then only upon resolutions passed by both Houses of the Oireachtas. The main statutes are the Exchequer and Audit

Departments Act 1866 and the Comptroller and Auditor General (Amendment) Act 1993, which extended the range and scope of his remit.

The main statutory functions are: first, as Comptroller General of the Exchequer, to ensure that no money is issued from the Central Fund by the Minister for Finance except for purposes approved by the Oireachtas; second, as Auditor General, to audit government accounts for accuracy and regularity and to carry out such examinations as he considers appropriate in regard to economy and efficiency in the use of resources and the effectiveness of certain management systems.

The Comptroller and Auditor General (Amendment) Act 1993 consolidated and updated the statutory provisions in relation to the role of the C & AG. It gave the C & AG new statutory powers and, at the same time, extended his remit to a wide range of agencies. The provisions of the act related to the following broad changes:

- All non-commercial state bodies are now audited by the C & AG, as well as the health boards and Vocational Education Committees.
- In any year of account in which a body receives 50 per cent or more of its gross income directly or indirectly by way of grants from a department, it will be subject, at the C & AG's discretion, to examination by him of its books, records and accounts to establish that the public funds have been spent for the purpose for which they were provided.
- The most significant new provision relates to the value for money of public expenditure. The C & AG is empowered to carry out, at his discretion, examinations of the economy and efficiency with which departments use their resources and the measures used by departments for appraising the effectiveness of their own operations. The provisions extend the traditional non-statutory discretionary function of the C & AG of identifying and reporting in the Dáil on instances of loss, waste or uneconomic expenditure. These powers are now on a statutory basis.
- The duties of secretaries general, as accounting officers, in giving evidence before the Committee of Public Accounts are set out in statute for the first time. The act expressly prohibits an accounting officer from questioning or expressing an opinion on the merits of a governmental or ministerial policy.
- The act enables the C & AG, subject to the consent of the Minister for Finance, to charge fees in respect of any audit, examination or inspection.

Public bodies will be subject to Value for Money (VFM) reviews. The purpose of a value for money audit is to provide Dáil Éireann with independent assurance as to the economy, efficiency and effectiveness with which a body has used its resources in discharging its functions, that is:

- minimising the cost of goods, or services, having regard to appropriate quality (economy);
- maximising the output of goods, services or other results for the resources used to produce them (efficiency);
- the relationship between the intended results and the results of programmes and other activities (effectiveness).

Section 10 of the act reinforces the C & AG's right of access, as a constitutional officer of the state, to documents and information. Every effort is made at working level to meet the C & AG's office's requirements in this regard. However, if a document or a file which has been requested is deemed by the department to be of such a secret nature – for example, relating to the security of the state – as to preclude its release to the C & AG's staff, the document or file in question is shown in confidence to the C & AG personally.

This act has emphasised the importance of good management in the public service. Section 9 allows the C & AG to form opinions as to how well managed departments and the other bodies audited by him are. The C & AG is required to satisfy himself as to the adequacy of management effectiveness – the management system, procedures and practices for examining effectiveness. This involves examining:

- the organisation of the evaluation function;
- the system of reporting;
- the methodology used in effectiveness examinations; and
- the use made of effectiveness evaluation reports.

This allows the C & AG to make comparisons between different bodies and operations and to draw conclusions from these comparisons. The C & AG is enabled to cite examples of effective systems and good management which might repay study and emulation by management in other bodies. This has encouraged the development of performance management systems, including performance indicators, and mechanisms for the evaluation and review of public expenditure programmes. It is worth noting that the C & AG is precluded, under Section 11 (5), from questioning or expressing an opinion on the merits of policies or policy objectives in any of his reports.

In summary, the revised audit, inspection and VFM functions of the C & AG are having a major impact on the public sector. Public bodies are accountable to Dáil Éireann, through the Public Accounts Committee, for:

- the regularity of their transactions and the accuracy of their accounts;
- the evaluation of the effectiveness of their operations;
- the economical and efficient use of their resources in discharging their statutory functions.

Oireachtas Committees: Compellability and Privilege

The Committees of the Houses of the Oireachtas (Compellability, Privileges and Immunities of Witnesses) Act was enacted in 1997. The Minister for Finance in introducing the measure spoke of this important and radical legislation, 'which is a critical part of a family of legislation which I and my colleagues determined should represent a wider and long-term response to the problem I have mentioned – a dramatic improvement in the transparency of the process of governance and in the accountability of office-holders and public servants' (*Dáil Debates*, 21 November 1995, col. 1071).

There are two mechanisms which hold the government accountable to the Dáil: question time and the committee system. The Committees of the Houses of the Oireachtas (Compellability, Privileges and Immunities of Witnesses) Act 1997 strengthened the committee system.

The act confers on those Oireachtas committees whose terms of reference include provision for the calling of persons and papers, statutory powers to compel the attendance and co-operation of witnesses and the furnishing of documents. It confers High Court privilege and immunities, virtually identical with the absolute privilege of members of the Houses of the Oireachtas, on all witnesses giving evidence or, on direction, sending documents to such committees. Both elements of the act are, of necessity, intertwined. Clearly, it would be arbitrary to compel witnesses to answer questions without according to them the safeguards essential to protect them from what might otherwise be the legal consequences of full and frank responses to the questions put to them.

Under Article 15.13 of the Constitution, members of the Houses of the Oireachtas have absolute privilege in respect of utterances in either House. In 1976 this was extended by legislation to cover them at meetings of committees. On the other hand, witnesses appearing before such committees enjoyed only 'qualified privilege'. This did not prevent legal action being taken against a witness for anything he said before a committee but it did provide him with a defence against libel or slander unless it could be proved that he was actuated by a motive not connected with the privilege, for example ill will, spite or any other improper motive. The possibility of legal action with the attendant costs of representation, even where a good defence existed, constituted a serious hazard for any witness. In addition, however, the privilege which witnesses enjoyed did not extend to other legal actions such as for breaches of confidentiality and breach of duty of care, which could have resulted in their having to pay damages. One of the two major aims of the act was to correct this situation.

The other aim of this measure was in relation to compellability. Certain Oireachtas committees include in their terms of reference provision for the calling of persons and papers. While these requests to attend were in general honoured, there were well-publicised incidents which showed that committees had no statutory power to enforce such provisions. Under the terms of the act, virtually anyone a committee believes can provide information relevant to its mandate can be compelled to appear before it or provide evidence. This applies to individual members of the general public. The Taoiseach, the Tánaiste, ministers, ministers of state and their officials are all compellable. In the case of civil servants, only one restriction applies – they are debarred in giving evidence from expressing opinions in relation to the merits of policy. This does not preclude them from explaining particular policies. This restriction extends to the Garda Síochána and members of the Permanent Defence Forces. In keeping with convention, the President and members of the judiciary are exempt from the application of the legislation. The Attorney General and the Director of Public Prosecutions, because of their independent roles as defenders of the public interest, are exempted also. Compellability does not in any instance apply to:

- discussions at meetings of the government;
- discussions at meetings of committees appointed by the government;
- matters which are the subject of proceedings currently before the courts – sub judice;
- matters which would affect adversely the security of the state;
- matters related to law enforcement; and
- tax assessment information.

The act provides that non-attendance in response to an Oireachtas committee's direction shall be an offence, and also contains the provision that false evidence shall constitute perjury.

The power of compellability and the subsequent protection of witnesses' rights has assisted the operation of the committee system in Leinster House. It has enhanced the conditions for accountability and transparency in this regard. Committees are obliged to report to a plenary session of the Dáil on the work they have completed, the work on hand, attendance at meetings and their voting records. A full debate on that information takes place, thereby completing the cycle of transparency and accountability. The supreme principle of this act is that Parliament, through its elected representatives, must have the power to ensure that everybody in the public service is accountable to it. The act provides improved means for democratically elected public representatives to elicit information, and increases the accountability of office holders and public administration to Parliament.

Ethics in Public Office Act 1995

This measure is designed to protect the integrity of public decision-making by politicians and senior officials. It provides for the disclosure of registrable interests by persons holding public office or employment, deals with gifts to office holders and regulates personal appointments by office holders. It provides for select committees of each House of the Oireachtas to oversee key provisions. It amends the Prevention of Corruption Acts 1889 to 1916. The obligations imposed by the act are additional to the obligations which already applied generally to civil servants. Civil servants in the appropriate positions are required to observe provisions in official circulars which are more stringent than the equivalent statutory provisions. Annual written statements are required to be made by certain persons holding public office or employment in respect of their personal interests (and those interests of a spouse or child) which could materially influence them in the performance of their official duties.

Conclusion

The 1969 Report of the Public Services Organisation Review Group concluded that the civil service had worked reasonably efficiently, had served different governments loyally, had operated impartially and, within the framework of its organisation and resources, had done the best it could to promote the development of the nation. The report also found that the civil service had given its advice to ministers fairly and honestly and had implemented the final decisions of the government without reservations. Recruitment is based on merit and not favouritism. Sean Cromien, then secretary of the Department of Finance, wrote that the 'highest standards of individual propriety and personal commitment' have been the hallmark of the civil service (1985: 8). He went on to state:

> Senior civil servants – and indeed civil servants at all levels – nowadays have contact with their opposite numbers from other countries in international forums such as the EEC, OECD, United Nations and many other bodies. They have, I think, no sense of inferiority in comparing their performance with that of others and there seems to be no obvious reason why they should. They look on themselves, rightly or wrongly, as being as good as any in the world!

When Albert Reynolds launched the Strategic Management Initiative in February 1994 he had high praise for Irish public servants. Having commended their integrity and commitment, he continued: 'I am referring as well to ability, to creativity and to imagination. I am talking about capacity to develop policies and strategies, and see these carried through, on time, and within budget. I am talking about people operating to exacting standards of excellence.'

No organisation can afford to stand still or to rest on its laurels, however. The profound changes in society are a dominant feature of the late twentieth century. The depth and speed of change will be no less in the imminent twenty-first century. Central themes in the reshaping of organisational life are the necessity for flexible, responsive structures and systems based on knowledge as the most fundamental resource.

Internal concerns within the civil and public service in the late 1980s, coupled with external pressures, focused minds on developing an effective response – a better way of discharging the business of government. Civil service managers and trade unions have actively supported the strategic change process, which has brought the political and administrative systems together in providing a better-quality service to the people of Ireland.

Pressures relating to costs to the taxpayer, efficiency, the quality of management and effective deployment of people mean that virtually all public service organisations are re-examining the way they manage themselves, and are looking at what lessons can be drawn from other sectors, to give them more effective ways of working. The agenda for change in the public service across Europe is a strong one and one for which the impetus is gathering pace.

The aim of the change management process in the Irish public service has been to build upon the foundation of the good service that has been provided in the past. This is essential because of the importance of the services provided by the civil and public service to the well-being of the individual citizen and to the coherence of society as a whole. It is also essential for economic reasons because of the importance for national competitiveness of the work of the public service.

This work is vital in the realisation of the people's vision for Ireland in the twenty-first century. Accordingly, there have been significant changes in the public service in recent years. These have seen the development of a more open and flexible organisation operating to high standards of integrity, equity, impartiality and accountability. The Irish civil service has been working on a change management process, through the Strategic Management Initiative, for the last number of years. Its main objective is delivering an excellent service for the customer, based on a high-performance organisation.

The policy document *Delivering Better Government* sets out the vision for the Irish civil service of the future, and recognises clearly that quality services are the essence of an excellent civil service. It also addresses the conditions internal to the civil service which are necessary to achieve the changes envisaged. Key requirements are a new management structure, a new approach to human resources management and a new and fully integrated performance process. Other key elements are the reform of financial management systems and the effective use of information technology.

Central to this change management process is the devolution of authority and responsibility to line managers and staff. The person closest to the point of delivery is the person in the best position to make decisions, including resource allocation. The training and development of staff with the appropriate skills and expertise and the emphasis on performance measurement and evaluation are integral parts of this process.

New mechanisms have been created across the entire system of government to ensure a heightened degree of individual accountability for decisions and the use of public resources.

The change process has been successful in improving accountability and leading to better public administration.

There is no doubt that public management will continue to be equally, if not more, challenging in the years ahead.

REFERENCES

Blennerhassett, E., *Quality Improvement in the Irish Civil Service: Experience of a Pilot Programme* (Dublin: Institute of Public Administration, 1992)

Boyle, R., *Managing Public Sector Performance: A Comparative Study of Performance Monitoring Systems in the Public and Private Sectors* (Dublin: Institute of Public Administration, 1989)

Boyle, R., *Measuring Civil Service Performance* (Dublin: Institute of Public Administration, 1996)

Chase, Gordon and Elizabeth C. Reveal, *How to Manage in the Public Sector* (London: Addison-Wesley, 1983)

Cromien, Sean, 'As Good as Any: A Perspective from Inside the Civil Service', *Seirbhís Phoiblí*, vol. 6, no. 2 (April 1985)

Dence, R., 'Best Practices Benchmarking' in J. Holloway, J. Lewis and G. Mallory (eds.), *Performance Measurement and Evaluation* (London: Sage Publications, 1995), pp. 124–52

Government of Ireland, *Report of the Public Services Organisation Review Group, 1966–69* [Devlin Report] (Dublin: Stationery Office, 1969)

Government of Ireland, *Serving the Country Better: A White Paper on the Public Service* (Dublin: Stationery Office, 1985)

Government of Ireland, *Delivering Better Government: A Programme of Change for the Irish Civil Service, Second Report of the Co-ordinating Group of Secretaries* (Dublin: Stationery Office, 1996)

Hurley, J., 'SMI in the Public Sector in Ireland – Challenges and Imperatives for Top Managers', conference on Strategic Management – The Implementation Challenge, Dublin, 1995

Jackson, P., 'Public Service Performance Evaluation: A Strategic Perspective', *Public Money and Management* (October–December 1993), pp. 9–14

Jackson, P. and B. Palmer, *Developing Performance Monitoring in Public Sector Organisations: A Management Guide* (Leicester: The Management Centre, University of Leicester, 1992)

Kaplan, R.S. and D.P. Norton, 'The Balanced Scorecard – Measures that Drive Performance', *Harvard Business Review* (January–February 1992), pp. 71–9

Likierman, A., 'Performance Indicators: Twenty Early Lessons from Managerial Use', *Public Money and Management* (October–December 1993), pp. 15–22

National Economic and Social Forum, *Quality Delivery of Social Services*, Forum Report No. 6 (Dublin: National Economic and Social Forum, 1995)

APPENDIX 27

PUBLIC SERVICE REFORM 1969–97

The Devlin Report 1969	**Programme Budgeting Early 1970s**	**The White Paper 1985** *Serving the Country Better*
Separate policy work from execution. Reorganise departments into Aireachts (Cabinets) and executive units. Strengthen support systems in finance, planning, organisation and personnel.	Reform budgeting to meet major objectives. Clarify outputs in a five-year perspective. Improve planning mechanisms.	Introduce a 'modern, workable management system'. Emphasis on training and technology. Reward initiative. Clarify objectives, measure results.

Strategic Management Initiative 1995	***Delivering Better Government,* 1996**
Link management to government priorities for jobs, debt, pay. Departments to have statements of action linked to government's programme. Better co-ordination of strategy. Assess outcomes.	A programme of change for the Irish civil service. A number of key areas to be addressed in order to provide a more responsive and accountable service to customers: – delivering a quality customer service; – reducing red tape; – delegating authority and accountability; – introducing a new approach to human resources management; – ensuring value for money; – supporting change with information technology.

APPENDIX 28

STATEMENT OF STRATEGY OF THE DEPARTMENT OF FINANCE, 1997: EXTRACT

Our mission is:
To promote an economy which will maximise growth, sustainable employment and social progress.

Introduction

Following the introduction of the Strategic Management Initiative (SMI) in 1994, the Department carried out a comprehensive strategic analysis of its activities. We also completed a comprehensive organisational review of the Department during 1995 to ensure that it was structured in the best possible manner to support the achievement of its objectives.

A further strategic analysis, involving an extensive process of review and consultation within the Department, was recently undertaken. As a result, we have now identified the strategic priorities on which the Department should focus over the next three years. These take account of significant recent developments and future challenges, in particular the prospect of EMU – which it is assumed will come into effect from 1 January 1999 – and the future evolution of EU policies in general, the new national programme *Partnership 2000 for Inclusion, Employment and Competitiveness*, the public service change programme, and the implementation of a medium-term framework for budgetary management.

Mission

Our mission is:
To promote an economy which will maximise growth, sustainable employment and social progress.

Our mission involves:

- promoting policies which deliver international competitiveness and internal efficiency;
- managing the overall Government process of resource generation and allocation to secure optimum social and economic benefits;
- achieving ongoing improvements in efficiency and effectiveness across the public sector.

Strategic Priorities

The review of our strategy highlighted the need, in light of the challenges facing the Department over the coming years, to focus on four priorities:

Economic and fiscal policy covering:

- price stability;
- debt reduction;
- management of public expenditure;
- tax reform.

Incomes policy development in

- the economy generally
- the public service

with a view to competitiveness and a sound budgetary position.

The public service change programme which encompasses:

- enhanced accountability, flexibility and devolution of responsibility;
- improved human resources management;
- more efficient and cost-effective management of the public finances;
- improved delivery of quality services.

Our relationship with the EU, particularly in regard to:

- Economic and Monetary Union (EMU);
- Structural and Cohesion Funds;
- financial regulation.

Indicators of Success

We recognise the importance of performance measurement and the need to evaluate progress towards the achievement of our objectives. Accordingly, we have identified indicators of success in respect of each of our strategic priorities.

In setting our objectives, we make the assumption that there will be continuing national commitment to:

- debt reduction;
- tax reform;
- efficient and cost-effective management of the public finances;
- public service change;
- full participation in EU developments.

APPENDIX 29

SMI Benefits

- Focus on objectives
- Fully developed policy options
- Sound criteria for trade-offs between new and competing demands/initiatives
- Clear operational parameters for all
- More involvement by all
- More successful evaluation of outcomes
- Better use of resources (including IT)

Source: Hurley (1995).

APPENDIX 30

SMI – DELIVERING BETTER GOVERNMENT

	AUTHORITY FOR	ACCOUNTABLE TO
Ministers	• Policy • Specifying outcomes for Department and agreement with Secretary on outputs required to achieve those outcomes • Ensuring that the mechanisms are in place for the implementation and monitoring of policy and for the achievement of outputs • Overall resource allocation • Co-ordination of specific cross-Departmental policy issues as assigned by Government	• Electorate • Dáil • Oireachtas Committees for policy and implementation arrangements • Government • Taoiseach
Ministers of State	• Policy • Outcomes/Outputs • Mechanisms } in agreement with the Minister in respect of delegated functions • Resource allocation (as with Minister)	• Electorate • Dáil • Oireachtas Committees for policy and implementation arrangements →

	Authority for *(contd.)*	**Accountable to** *(contd.)*
	• Co-ordination of specific cross-Departmental policy issues as assigned by Government	• Government • Minister
Advisers/ Programme Managers	• Advice to Minister/Minister of State • Monitoring and facilitating the achievement of Government objectives as requested	• Minister/Minister of State
Secretaries/ Heads of Offices	• Managing the organisation to implement and monitor policy and to achieve agreed outputs • Policy advice • Ensuring that appropriate arrangements are in place to respond effectively to cross-Departmental issues • Mechanisms for ensuring that Departmental expenditure is in line with the limits set by Government, is in accordance with the purpose for which it was voted and that value for money is obtained • Appointments and discipline	• Government • Minister/Minister of State • Oireachtas Committees for action on implementation of policy and for ensuring value for money • Public (through Strategy Statements and regular reports on progress and through statements of customer services standards as appropriate)
Individual/ Teams of Civil Servants	• Specified outputs • Policy advice as part of a team/unit • Operation of statutory schemes • Provision of a quality service direct to the customer • Ensuring that Departmental expenditure is in accordance with the purpose for which it was voted and that value for money is obtained • Appointments and discipline	• Secretary • Line manager as relevant • Oireachtas Committees for action on implementation of policy and for ensuring value for money (at senior level)

Source: Delivering Better Government (1996), p. 25.

APPENDIX 31

Developing a Balanced Score-Card

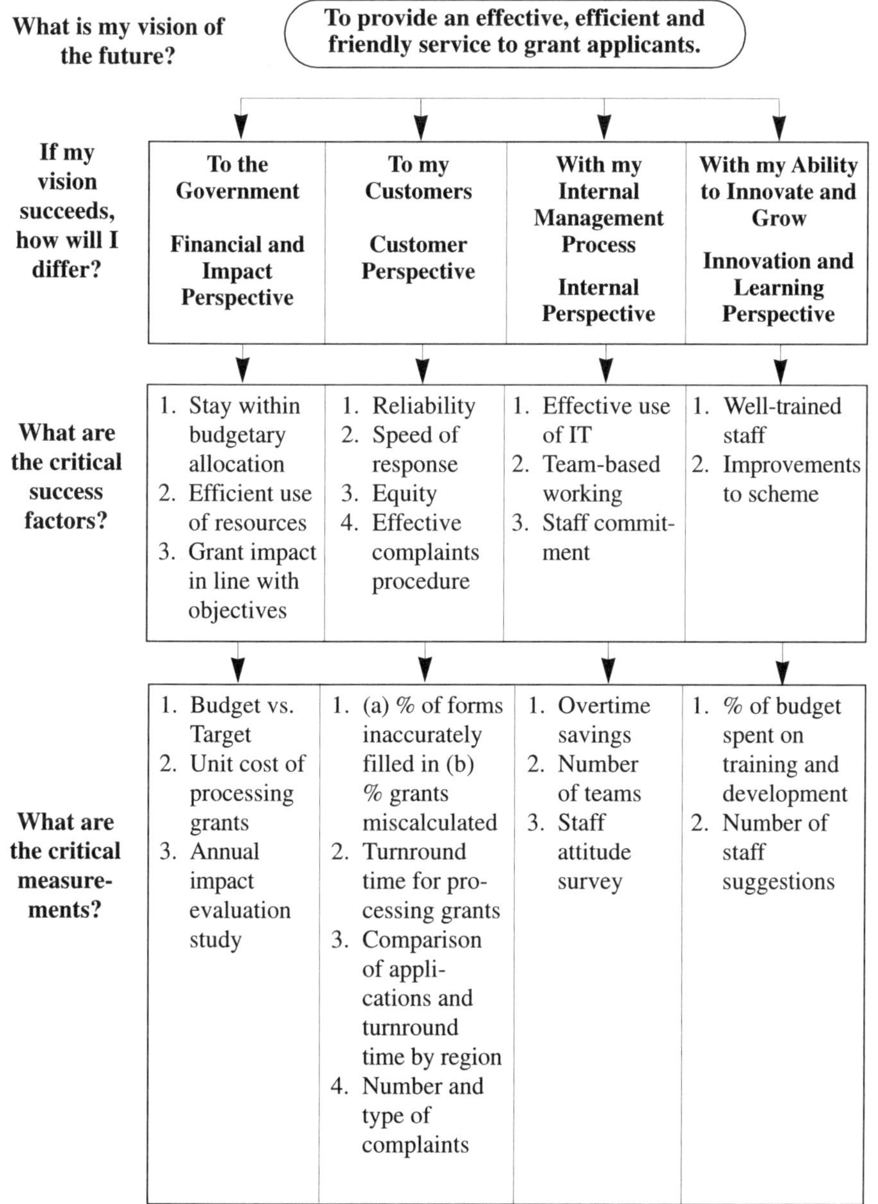

What is my vision of the future?
To provide an effective, efficient and friendly service to grant applicants.
If my vision succeeds, how will I differ?
To the Government
Financial and Impact Perspective
To my Customers
Customer Perspective
With my Internal Management Process
Internal Perspective
With my Ability to Innovate and Grow
Innovation and Learning Perspective
What are the critical success factors?
1. Stay within budgetary allocation
2. Efficient use of resources
3. Grant impact in line with objectives
1. Reliability
2. Speed of response
3. Equity
4. Effective complaints procedure
1. Effective use of IT
2. Team-based working
3. Staff commitment
1. Well-trained staff
2. Improvements to scheme
What are the critical measurements?
1. Budget vs. Target
2. Unit cost of processing grants
3. Annual impact evaluation study
1. (a) % of forms inaccurately filled in (b) % grants miscalculated
2. Turnround time for processing grants
3. Comparison of applications and turnround time by region
4. Number and type of complaints
1. Overtime savings
2. Number of teams
3. Staff attitude survey
1. % of budget spent on training and development
2. Number of staff suggestions

Source: R. Boyle (1996), p. 37, which is a framework adapted from Kaplan and Norton (1992).

APPENDIX 32

Twenty Lessons from Managerial Use of Performance Indicators

Concept

1. Include all elements integral to what is being measured.
2. Choose a number appropriate to the organisation and its diversity.
3. Provide adequate safeguards for 'soft' indicators, particularly quality.
4. Take account of accountability and politics.

Preparation

5. Devise them with people on the ground, who must feel ownership.
6. Build in counters to short-term focus.
7. Ensure that they fairly reflect the efforts of managers.
8. Find a means to cope with uncontrollable items and perceived injustices.
9. Use the experience of other organisations or other parts of the organisation.
10. Establish realistic levels of attainment before the first targets are set.

Implementation

11. Recognise that new indicators need time to develop and may need revision in the light of experience.
12. Link them to existing systems.
13. They must be easily understandable by those whose performance is being measured.
14. While proxies may be necessary, they must be chosen cautiously.
15. The period of introduction should be used to reassess internal and external relationships.

Use

16. The data on which the results are based must be trusted.
17. Use the results as guidance, not answers. Recognise that interpretation is the key to action.
18. Acknowledge the importance of feedback. Follow-up gives credibility; no feedback means atrophy; negative-only feedback encourages game-playing.
19. Trade-offs and complex interactions must be recognised; not all indicators should carry equal weight.
20. Results must be user-friendly and at appropriate levels of aggregation and response time.

Source: Likierman (1993).

APPENDIX 33

Freedom of Information Act 1997

Long Title of Act

- To enable members of the public to obtain access, to the greatest extent possible consistent with the public interest and the right to privacy, to information in the possession of public bodies;
- To enable persons to have personal information relating to them in the possession of such bodies corrected;
- To provide for a right of access to records held by such bodies, for necessary exceptions to that right and for assistance to persons to enable them to exercise it;
- To provide for the independent review both of decisions of such bodies relating to that right and of the operation of this Act generally (including the proceedings of such bodies pursuant to this Act);
- To provide for the establishment of the office of Information Commissioner and to define its functions;
- To provide for the publication by such bodies of certain information about them relevant to the purposes of this Act, to amend the Official Secrets Act, 1963, and to provide for related matters.

APPENDIX 34

Public Bodies to which Freedom of Information Act Applies

the Department of Agriculture, Food and Forestry
the Department of Arts, Culture and the Gaeltacht
the Department of Defence
the Department of Education
the Department of Enterprise and Employment
the Department of the Environment
the Department of Equality and Law Reform
the Department of Finance
the Department of Foreign Affairs
the Department of Health
the Department of Justice (including the Probation and Welfare Service)
the Department of the Marine
the Department of Social Welfare
the Department of the Taoiseach
the Department of Tourism and Trade
the Department of Transport, Energy and Communications
the Office of the Tánaiste
the Office of the Attorney General
the Army Pensions Board
the Blood Transfusion Service Board
the Board of the National Library of Ireland
the Board of the National Museum of Ireland
An Bord Pleanála
the Censorship of Publications Board
the Central Statistics Office
the Civil Service Commissioners
An Coimisiún Logainmneacha
An Comhairle na Nimheanna
An Comhairle na nOspidéal
the Commissioners of Charitable Donations and Bequests
the Companies Registration Office
the Competition Authority
the Commissioners of Public Works
the Defence Forces
the Employment Equality Agency
the Environmental Information Service
the Environmental Protection Agency
the Government Information Services
the Heritage Council

the Ireland–United States Commission for Educational Exchange
the Irish Manuscripts Commission
the Irish Medicines Board
the Irish Sports Council
the Land Registry
the Local Appointments Commissioners
the National Archives
the National Archives Advisory Council
the National Council for Curriculum and Assessment
the National Gallery of Ireland
the Office of the Appeal Commissioners for the purposes of the Tax Acts
the Office of the Chief Medical Officer for the Civil Service
the Office of the Commissioner
the Office of the Commissioner of Valuation and Boundary Surveyor for Ireland
the Office of the Comptroller and Auditor General
the Office of the Director of Consumer Affairs
the Office of the Director of Public Prosecutions
the Office of the Houses of the Oireachtas
the Office of the Official Censor of Films
the Office of the Ombudsman
the Office of the Registrar of Friendly Societies
the Patents Office
the Pensions Board
the Public Offices Commission
the Registry of Deeds
the Revenue Commissioners
the Social Welfare Appeals Office
the State Laboratory

and a range of other bodies in the public sector and including those in receipt of public moneys.

INDEX